INTERNATIONAL LAW

EIGHTH EDITION

By

REBECCA M.M. WALLACE, M.A., LL.B., Ph.D.

*Professor of International Human Rights and Justice,
Robert Gordon University, Aberdeen*

and

OLGA MARTIN-ORTEGA, Ph.D.

*Reader in Public International Law,
University of Greenwich, London*

with

FRASER JANECZKO, LL.B., LL.M.

Solicitor, Pinsent Masons, Edinburgh

and

KAREN WYLIE, M.A., M.Sc.

*Former Research Assistant, Robert Gordon University,
Aberdeen*

SWEET & MAXWELL      **THOMSON REUTERS**

First Edition 1986
Second Impression 1990
Second Edition 1992
Second Impression 1994
Third Impression 1995
Third Edition 1997
Second Impression 1998
Fourth Edition 2002
Fifth Edition 2005
Sixth Edition 2009
Seventh Edition 2013
Eighth Edition 2016

Published in 2016 by Sweet & Maxwell
part of Thomson Reuters (Professional) UK Limited
(Company No. 1679046).
Registered in England and Wales.
Registered office: 2nd Floor, 1 Mark Square, Leonard Street, London EC2A 4EG.

For further information on our products and services, visit
www.sweetandmaxwell.co.uk

Typeset by YHT Ltd, London
Printed in Great Britain by CPI Group (UK) Ltd, Croydon, CR0 4YY

No natural forests were destroyed to make this product;
only farmed timber was used and re-planted

A CIP catalogue record for this book is available from the British Library.
ISBN: 978-0-414-05551-3

Thomson Reuters and the Thomson Reuters logo are trademarks of
Thomson Reuters. Sweet & Maxwell ® is a registered trademark of
Thomson Reuters (Professional) UK Limited.

To John P. Grant, with gratitude for igniting my interest in international law and his continuing support.

To Ernesto Martin Aguilar, for his unconditional support.

FOREWORD

I am very happy, once again to write the Foreword for this, the eighth edition of Rebecca Wallace's and Olga Martin-Ortega's *International Law*. As the authors point out in their Preface, the book has more than one use: in their words it is a "narrative companion" to a casebook and a "general introductory test" and I would add that it is a useful first place for a practitioner to come to for a quick orientation. I especially commend the authors for keeping the text so very up to date.

Writing as a professor, I give it very high marks as a "narrative companion" to any public international law casebook, even one with ample notes and text. I have used prior editions in that way. Students want and need such a companion. It is compact and its coverage complete. For professors, it takes off the pressure, so that in class they can work out the problems they wish, emphasize with cases the legal method they want, even the Socratic, and avoid the didactic lecturing on topics, such as nature and sources of law, which will tend to leave many students cold.

I have also on occasion recommended the earlier editions to students who are not, *horribile dictu*, taking international law at all, but who wish a synoptic view of the field.

For the North American student or other reader, this book appears to have almost as much American material as British, citing U.S. cases, sources such as International Legal Materials and American (and Canadian) subjects. Thus, the discussion of such American doctrines as the Act of State and the functioning of executive agreements, including the recent Joint Comprehensive Plan of Action (known colloquially in the US as the "Iran Nuclear Deal"), in the American system is admirable.

The continued use of force on the one hand, and the attempts to cope with it and its consequences on the other, underline, if that is necessary, the abiding importance of law in the international system. The general reader may therefore find the book especially valuable and interesting. In the words of an earlier edition of the book, it is written "clearly and simply". The book also continues to serve the practitioner who wants an introduction, in a nutshell, to precise subjects of interest to him or her.

I welcome the eighth edition with enthusiasm.

17 March 2016

Don Wallace Jr., Chairman,
International Law Institute;
Professor, Georgetown Law,
Washington D.C.

PREFACE

This book is being published thirty years after the first edition appeared. These thirty years have witnessed considerable changes in the international legal landscape. The fact that the book is still being used underscores the need for a basic but comprehensive understanding of international legal principles, and an appreciation of the sources and the actors on the global stage. These thirty years have also witnessed our growth as scholars and individuals. Professor Wallace, a young academic when she had the determination and courage to add a new voice to international law teaching, has now inspired generations of law students globally with a passion for international law and set them enthusiastically in the pursuit of an international legal career.

Dr. Martin-Ortega, one of these privileged individuals to be touched by Professor Wallace's enthusiasm and energy, generosity and inspiration, was only starting her PhD when she came into contact with this text and with its author, who was to change her professional (and personal) path and guide her every step of the way to become the person and scholar she is today.

Dr Martin-Ortega is proud of continuing this work and hopes one day to be able to inspire and guide as much as her mentor.

As in the past thirty years, this book intends to give the reader the necessary tools for navigating the contemporary international legal framework and for the reader to become familiar with many of the ongoing debates in the field. Law and politics are inextricably linked and it is important to understand the power dynamics at play. As with previous editions, deliberate efforts have been made to keep the book concise, relevant and user-friendly, providing an introduction to the international legal system. This book should not only be accessible to law students, but also to those studying, or just interested in, politics, international relations and a range of related disciplines in the humanities and social sciences.

Every effort has been made to state the law as it is at 31 May 2016.

The authors acknowledge the support and assistance of Eva Shamouel and Nicola Thurlow of Thomson Reuters and especially to Nicola who has been instrumental in keeping this book alive, with her unstinting encouragement and enthusiasm over what are now numerous editions. We are indebted to her and look forward to working together with her and her team over many more years.

Dr Olga Martin-Ortega
London, June 2016.

Professor Rebecca M.M. Wallace
Aberdeen, June 2016.

CONTENTS

Foreword	vii
Preface	ix
Abbreviations	xv
Table of Cases	xix
Table of International Treaties and Conventions	xxxii
Table of Resolutions	xlvii
Table of National Legislation	l
Table of EC Secondary Legislation	lii
1. Introduction	**1**
Definition	2
Nature and Characteristics of International Law	2
The Development of International Law	5
2. Sources	**9**
Custom	11
Treaties	21
"General Principles of Law as Recognized by Civilized Nations"	25
Equity	26
Judicial Decisions	28
Decisions of National Courts	30
Writers	30
Other Possible Sources of International Law	31
Peremptory Norms of International Law	36
Conclusion	37
3. International Law and Municipal Law	**39**
Monistic School	40

Dualistic School 40
Municipal Law in International Law 41
International Law Before Municipal Courts 43
Conclusion 62

4. International Personality 63
States 64
Recognition of States and Governments 74
The Effect of Recognition in Municipal Law 81
Effect of Non-Recognition 84
Modes of According Recognition 87
International Organisations 88
Individuals 94
Other Non-State Actors 98
Conclusion 102

5. Territory 103
Occupation 104
Prescription 108
Conquest 109
Cession 111
Accretion and Avulsion 112
New States 112
Polar Regions 113
Airspace 116
Outer Space 120
Conclusion 122

6. Jurisdiction 125
Bases of Jurisdiction 126
International Criminal Jurisdiction 135
Extradition 140
Double Jeopardy 142
Immunity from Jurisdiction 142
Conclusion 158

7. The Law of the Sea 159
Territorial Sea 161
High Seas 173
Exclusive Economic Zone (EEZ) 184
Continental Shelf 188
Deep Seabed 196
International Tribunal for the Law of the Sea 197
Conclusion 200

8. State Responsibility **201**
Nature of Liability 203
Treatment of Aliens 212
State Responsibility for the Environment 229
Conclusion 239

9. Human Rights **241**
What are Human Rights? 242
United Nations 247
Other United Nations Conventions Guaranteeing
Particular Human Rights 260
Other Human Rights Protection Systems 263
Human Rights and International Criminal
Tribunals 263
Conclusion 269

10. The Law of Treaties **271**
Definition of a Treaty 272
Treaty-Making Competence 275
Observance and Application of Treaties 281
Treaty Interpretation 282
Third States 284
Amendment and Modification 285
Validity of Treaties 286
Termination of a Treaty 288
Consequences of Invalidity, Termination or
Suspension 292
State Succession 293
Conclusion 295

11. The Use of Force **297**
The Law Pre-1945 297
The Law Post-1945 298
Jus in Bello 322
Humanitarian Law 328
Conclusion 330

12. Arbitration and Judicial Settlement of International
Disputes **333**
Arbitration 336
The International Court of Justice 339
Conclusion 361

13. Conclusion   **363**

Bibliography   *367*
Using the Internet   *370*
Index   *373*

ABBREVIATIONS

AC	Appeal Cases (UK) 1891–
AD	Appellate Division, New York Supreme Court
AD 2d	Appellate Division Reports, New York Supreme Court, Second Series
AJLL	American Journal of International Law
All ER	All England Reports, 1935–
ASIL	American Society of International Law
AU	African Union. (Replacing the Organisation of African States, see below)
BFSP	British and Foreign State Papers, 1812–
Burr.	Burrow's Reports (King's Bench, U.K.), 1757–71
BYIL	British Yearbook of International Law
CAT	Convention Against Torture and Other Cruel, Inhuman or Degrading Treatment or Punishment
Cd., Cmnd., Cmnd.	UK Command Papers 1900–18, 1919–56, 1956–, respectively
CEDAW	Convention on the Elimination of All forms of Discrimination against Women
CETS	Council of Europe Treaty Series
CERD	Convention on the Elimination of All Forms of Racial Discrimination
Ch.	Chancery Reports (U.K.), 1891–
CMLR	Common Market Law Reports
Cranch.	United States Supreme Court Reports, 1801–15

CWILJ	Californian Western International Law Journal
DPP	Director of Public Prosecution
ECHR	European Convention for the Protection of Human Rights and Fundamental Freedoms
EctHR	European Court of Human Rights
ECJ	European Court of Justice
ECR	European Court Reports, 1954–
EEZ	Exclusive Economic Zone
EHRR	European Human Rights Reports
EJIL	European Journal of International Law
ER	English Reports
F (2d)	Federal Reporter, Second Series (US), 1924–
F (J)	Fraser, Justiciary Cases (Scotland), 1898–1906
F Supp	Federal Supplement (US), 1932–
GA	General Assembly (United Nations)
GAOR	General Assembly Official Records
Hague Recueil	Recueil des cours de l'Academie de droit international
Hudson	International Legislation
Hudson World Court Reports	(4 Vols, 1934–43)
ICC	International Criminal Court
ICCPR	International Covenant on Civil and Political Rights
ICESCR	International Covenant on Economic, Social and Cultural Rights
ICJ	International Court of Justice
ICJ Rep.	International Court of Justice Reports, 1947–
ICLQ	International and Comparative Law Quarterly
ICTR	International Criminal Tribunal for the Prosecution of Persons Responsible for Genocide and Other Serious Violations of International Humanitarian Law Committed in the Territory of Rwanda and Rwandan citizens responsible for genocide and other such violations committed in the territory of neighbouring States, between January 1, 1994 and December 31, 1994
ICTY	International Tribunal for the Prosecution of Persons Responsible for Serious Violations of Humanitarian Law

	Committed in the Territory of the Former Yugoslavia since 1991
IJRL	International Journal of Refugee Law
ILA	International Law Association
ILC	International Law Commission
ILM	International Legal Materials, 1962–
ILR	International Law Reports
ILO	International Labour Organisation
IMO	International Maritime Organisation
IMF	International Monetary Fund
ITLOS	International Tribunal for the Law of the Sea
JLSS	Journal of the Law Society of Scotland
KB	King's Bench (UK), 1901–52
LNOJ	League of Nations Official Journal
LNTS	League of Nations Treaty Series, 1920–45
LQ Rev.	Law Quarterly Review, 1885–
Moore Int. Arb.	International Arbitration, 5 Vols, 1898
NATO	North Atlantic Treaty Organisation
NE	North Eastern Reporter, 1885–1936
NYS	New York Supplement Reporter, 1888
NYS 2d	New York Supplement, Second Series, 1937–
OAS	Organisation of American States
OAU	Organisation of African States. (Now known as the African Union, see above)
OHCHR	Office of the High Commissioner for Human Rights
OJ	Official Journal of the European Communities
Oppenheim	L. Oppenheim, International Law, Vols 1 and 2
P	Court of Probate
PC	Privy Council
PCA	Permanent Court of Arbitration
PCIJ	Permanent Court of International Justice
PCIJ Rep., ser. A.	Permanent Court of International Justice, Judgments and Orders, 1922–30
PCIJ Rep., ser. A/B	Advisory Opinions, Judgments and Orders, 1931–40
PCIJ Rep., ser. B	Advisory Opinions, 1922–30
PD	Probate Division Reports (UK), 1875–90
Pet.	Peter's United States Supreme Court Reports, 1828–42
QB	Queen's Bench Reports (UK), 1891–1901, 1952–

QBD	Queen's Bench Division Reports (UK), 1875–80
RIAA	Reports of International Arbitral Awards, 1948–
SC	Security Council
SCOR	Security Council Official Records
SCR	Supreme Court Reports (Canada), 1876–
SLT	Scots Law Times
TIAS	Treaties and Other International Acts Series (US), 1950–30
TLR	Times Law Reports (UK), 1841–1952
UKTS	United Kingdom Treaty Series
UN	United Nations
UNCC	United Nations Compensation Committee
UNESCO	United Nations Educational, Social and Cultural Organisation
UNHCR	United Nations High Commission for Refugees
UNTS	United Nations Treaty Series, 1946–
US	United States Supreme Court Reports, 1875–
USC	United States Code
US Dept.	State Bull. United States Department of State Bulletin
UST	United States Treaties
UST.	United States Treaty Series
Ves.	Vesey Juniors Chancery Reports (UK), 1789–1816
Whiteman	Digest of International Law, 14 Vols, 1936–73
WHO	World Health Organisation
WLR	Weekly Law Reports (UK), 1953–
WTO	World Trade Organisation
YBILC	Yearbook of the International Law Commission

TABLE OF CASES

A v Secretary of State for the Home Department; sub nom. X v Secretary
of State for the Home Department [2004] UKHL 56; [2005] 2 A.C.
68; [2005] 2 W.L.R. 87 49

Accordance with International Law of the Unilateral Declaration
of Independence in respect of Kosovo I.C.J. Rep. 2010
p.403 359

Adams v Adams (Attorney General intervening) [1971] P. 188; [1970] 3
W.L.R. 934 PDA Div 85

Administrative Decision No.V (US v Germany) 7 R.I.A.A. 119
(1924) 213

Aegean Sea Continental Shelf, I.C.J. Rep. 1976 3 354

Aerial Incident (Israel v Bulgaria), I.C.J. Rep. 1959 127 351

Aerial Incident of July 27, 1955, I.C.J. Rep. 1960 146 348

Aerial Incident of July 3, 1988, 35 ILM 553 (1996) ICJ 338

Afghan Warlord case 155

Ahmadou Sadio Diallo (Guinea v Democratic Republic of Congo),
Judgment November 30, 2010 26

Ahmadou Sadio Diallo (Guinea v Democratic Republic of
Congo), Preliminary Objections, (2007) I.C.J. Rep. 2007
.... 23, 225, 227

Air Services Agreement case, 18 R.I.A.A. 416 301

Al Fin Corp's Patent [1970] Ch. 160; [1969] 2 W.L.R. 1405 Ch D 50, 87

Al-Adsani v United Kingdom (35763/97) (2002) 34 E.H.R.R. 11; 12
B.H.R.C. 88 .... 144, 155

Al-Jedda v United Kingdom (27021/08) (2011) 53 E.H.R.R. 23;
30 B.H.R.C. 637 282

Al-Skeine v Secretary of State for Defence. See R. (on the application of
Al-Skeini) v Secretary of State for Defence

Al-Skeini v United Kingdom (55721/07) (2011) 53 E.H.R.R. 18; 30
B.H.R.C. 561 282

Alabama Arbitration Awards Moore, I Int. Arb. 495 (1872) 28, 41

Alfred Dunhill v Republic of Cuba, 425 US 682 (1976) 61

AM Luther Co v James Sagor & Co; sub nom. Aksionairnoye Obschestvo

AM Luther Co v James Sagor & Co [1921] 3 K.B. 532; (1921) 7 Ll.
L. Rep. 218 CA... 82, 83
Ambatielos Arbitration (Greece v UK), 12 R.I.A.A. 83 (1956); 23 I.L.R. 306
(1956) 228
Amco Asia Corporation v The Republic of Indonesia, 24 ILM 1022 (1985) 221
Aminoil case. See Kuwait v American Independent Oil Co
Amoco International Finance Corp v Iran 15 Iran-USCTR 189; 82 A.J.I.L.
358 (1986) 218, 219, 220, 221
Anglo–Iranian Oil Co case, I.C.J. Rep. (Pleadings) 1951 81 220
Anglo–Iranian Oil Co case, I.C.J. Rep. 1952 3, 93 .... 284, 344
Anglo–Norwegian Fisheries case I.C.J. Rep. 1951 116 ....14, 15, 28, 107, 161,
163, 164, 165, 184
Antarctica cases, I.C.J. Rep. 1956 12.. 344
Applicability of Art.VI of the Convention on the Privileges and
Immunities of the UN (Advisory Opinion), I.C.J. Rep. 1989 177; 29
I.L.M. 98 (1990)... 91, 359
Applicability of the Obligation to Arbitrate under section 21 of the
United Nations Headquarters Agreement of 26th June 1947, I.C.J.
Rep. 1988, 12... 42, 99
Application for Review of Judgment No. 333 of the U.N. Administrative
Tribunal I.C.J. Rep. 1987 18.. 359
Application for Revision of the Judgment of 11th July 1996 Concerning
Application of the Genocide Convention (Preliminary Objections),
I.C.J. Rep., 2003, p.7 357
Application for Revision of the Judgment of 11th September 1992
Concerning the El Salvador/Honduras (Nicaragua Intervening)
case, I.C.J. Rep., 2003, p.392... 357
Application of the Convention on the Prevention and Punishment of the
Crime of Genocide (Bosnia and Herzegovina v Yugoslavia (Serbia
and Montenegro)) (Provisional Measures), Order of September
13, 1993, I.C.J. Rep. 1993 325..136, 342, 355
Application of the Convention on the Prevention and Punishment of
the Crime of Genocide (Bosnia and Herzegovina v Serbia and
Montenegro), February 26, 2007 ICJ 136
Application of the Convention on the Prevention and Punishment of
the Crime of Genocide; Bosnia and Herzegovina v Yugoslavia
(Preliminary Objections) I.C.J. Rep. 1996 595 .... 208, 295
Application of the Convention on the Prevention and Punishment of
the Crime of Genocide, (Bosnia and Herzegovina v Serbia and
Montenegro), Judgement of February 27, 2007 273
Application of the Interim Accord of September 13, 1995 (Former
Yugoslav Republic of Macedonia v Greece) I.C.J. Rep 2011, 644 ..... 283, 289
Application of the International Convention on the Elimination of All
Forms of Racial Discrimination (Georgia v Russian Federation)
October 15, 2008 General List No.140... 354
Arab Monetary Fund v Hashim (No.3) [1991] 2 A.C. 114; [1991] 2 W.L.R.
729; [1991] 1 All E.R. 871 HL 86
Arantzazu Mendi. See Spain v Owners of the Arantzazu MendiArbitration
Commission on Yugoslavia, (Opinion No.2) 92 I.L.R. (1993)........... 104
Armando Fernandez Larios, decision of 11th US Circuit Court of Appeals,
March 15, 2005... 155
Armed Activities on the Territory of the Congo (Democratic Republic of
the Congo v Uganda), Judgment of December 19 2005 146 305

Arrest Warrant of 11 April 2000 (Congo v Belgium), I.C.J. Rep. 2002 3 ....126, 133, 155, 352

Asakura v City of Seattle 265 US 332 at 341 (1924) 53

Asian Agricultural Products Ltd case, (1990) 30 ILM.................................. 214

Asylum case, I.C.J. Rep. 1950 266..13, 14, 343, 357

Attorney General for Canada v Attorney General for Ontario (Appeal No.100 of 1936) [1937] A.C. 326 58

Attorney-General of the Government of Israel v Eichmann, 36 I.L.R. 5 (1961)... 132

Avena and Other Mexican Nationals (Mexico v United States of America) Judgment of March 31, 2004...156, 354, 357

Baccus Srl v Servicio Nacional del Trigo [1957] 1 Q.B. 438; [1956] 3 W.L.R. 948.. 143

Baker v Canada (Minister of Citizenship and Immigration) 1999 2 S.C.R. 817.. 49

Baker v Carr, 369 US 186 (1962)... 62

Banco Nacional de Cuba v First National City Bank US Supreme Ct, 406 US 759 (1972); 92 S.L.T. 1808 60

Banco Nacional de Cuba v Sabbatino, 376 US 398 (1964) 59, 60

Bank of Bankoviⅹ v Belgium (52207/99) (2001) 11 B.H.R.C. 435 ECJ.......... 126

Barbados/Trinidad and Tobago Maritime Delimitation April 11, 2006, Arbitration Tribunal, Permanent Court of Arbitration 195

Barcelona Traction Light and Power Company case (Second Phase) I.C.J. Rep. 1970 3..15, 17, 26, 43, 208, 226, 227, 228

Beagle Channel Arbitration, 17 ILM 632 (1978)... 272

Belilos v Switzerland (A/132) (1988) 10 E.H.R.R. 466 277

Bensleys case... 207

Birdi v Secretary of State for Home Affairs Unreported, 1975 48

Bissau v Senegal case, I.C.J. Rep. 1990 64 355

Bloxém v Favre, 8 P.C. 101 (1883)... 41

Border and Transborder Armed Actions (Nicaragua v Honduras) case, May 11, 1992 356

Botswana/ Namibia, I.C.J. Rep. 1999 1045.. 283

Boumediene v Bush, 553 U.S. (2008) 129

BP case, 53 I.L.R. 297 (1974) 219, 220

Brazilian Loans case, P.C.I.J. Rep., ser.A, no.21, (1929) 43

Brcko International-Entity Boundary case 36 I.L.M. 1997, 396..................... 79

Brind v Secretary of State. See R. v Secretary of State for the Home Department Ex p. Brind

Buttes Gas & Oil Co v Hammer (No.3); Occidental Petroleum Corp v Buttes Gas & Oil Co (No.2) [1982] A.C. 888; [1981] 3 W.L.R. 787 HL 62

Buvot v Barbuit (1737) Cases, t. Talbot 281.. 43

Caire Claim, 5 R.I.A.A. 516 (1929).. 204, 206

Cameroon v Nigeria I.C.J. Rep. 2002 303 .... 284, 334

Canada v USSR, 18 I.L.M. 899 (1979) 122

Canevaro case (Italy v Peru), 11 R.I.A.A. 397; 6 A.J.I.L. 746 (1912) 225

Carl Zeiss Stiftung v Rayner & Keeler Ltd; Rayner & Keeler Ltd v Courts & Co [1967] 1 A.C. 853; [1966] 3 W.L.R. 125 HL 85

Caroline Incident, 29 B.F.S.P. 1137–1138: 30 B.F.S.P. 195–196........................ 303, 304

Case Concerning Application of the Convention on the Prevention

and Punishment of the Crime of Genocide (Croatia v Serbia),
Judgement, February 3, 2015.. 204
Case concerning the Arrest Warrant of 11 April 2000 (Democratic
Republic of Congo v Belgium) 2002 I.C.J. Rep. 3, para.76............... 211
Certain Criminal Proceedings in France (Republic of the Congo v France)
2003, ICJ decision.. 133
Certain Criminal Proceedings in France (Republic of the Congo v France)
Provisional Measures, Order June 17, 2003, I.C.J. Rep. 2003 102..... 345
Certain Expenses of the United Nations case, I.C.J. Rep. 1962 151........... 317, 359
Certain Questions of Mutual Assistance in Criminal Matters (Djibouti v
France), I.C.J. Rep. 2008 177 345
Chamizal Arbitration (1911) 5 A.J.I.L. 782 108
Cheung (Chung Chi) v King, The [1939] A.C. 160; [1938] 4 All E.R. 786;
(1938) 62 Ll. L. Rep. 151 PC (HK)... 44
Chorzow Factory (Indemnity) (Merits) P.C.I.J. ser.A, No.17 (1928).......204, 210, 211
Chorzow Factory (Jurisdiction) case P.C.I.J. ser.A, No. 9 (1927).................... 25, 210
City of Berne v Bank of England, 32 E.R. 636; (1804) 9 Ves. Jr. 347 Ch........ 82
Civil Air Transport Inc v Central Air Transport Corp [1953] A.C. 70;
[1952] 2 All E.R. 733 PC (HK)... 84
Civilian War Claimants' Association Ltd v The King [1932] A.C. 14, HL... 65, 212
Clipperton Island Arbitration (1932) 26 A.J.I.L. 390...................................... 106, 107
Commission v Kadi (C-584/10 P) [2014] 1 C.M.L.R. 24; [2014] All E.R.
(EC) 123; (2013) 163(7578) N.L.J. 20.. 361
Commissioners of Customs and Excise v Ministry of Industries and
Military Manufacturing, Republic of Iraq, 43 I.C.L.Q. 194 (1994)... 144
Compania Naviera Vascongada v The Cristina; Cristina, The [1938] A.C.
485; [1938] 1 All E.R. 719 HL 44, 143
Continental Shelf (Libyan Arab Jamahiriya v Malta) case I.C.J. Rep. 1985
13...17, 184, 192
Continental Shelf Case (Tunisia v Libya) I.C.J. Rep. 1982 18
....27, 184, 192, 193, 343, 344, 357
Continental Shelf Case. See Libya v Malta
Cooke v The United States 288 US 102 at 119–120 (1933)............................. 53
Corfu Channel (Assessment of Compensation) I.C.J. Rep. 1949 p.244 358
Corfu Channel (Merits) case I.C.J. Rep. 1949 4 ....173, 204, 231
Corfu Channel (Preliminary Objection) case I.C.J. Rep. 1948 15.................. 343, 344
Cristina, The. See Compania Naviera Vascongada v The Cristina

Danube Dam case. See Gabčikovo-Nagymaros Project (Hungary v Slovakia)
Danzig Railway Officials case P.C.I.J. Rep., ser.B, No.15 (1928) 4–47; 4
A.D. 587; Hudson, World Court Reports, Vol.II (1927–32) 237 94
Delimitation of Maritime Areas between Canada and France (St Pierre
and Miquelon) 1992 31 ILM 1145 ....166, 187, 337
Delimitation of the Maritime Boundary in the Atlantic Ocean (Ghana/
Côte d'Ivoire), Provisional Measures, Order of 25 April 2015,
ITLOS Reports 2015... 199
Delimitation of the Maritime Boundary in the Gulf of Maine Area. See
Gulf of Maine case
Democratic Republic of the Congo v Rwanda, I.C.J. Rep., 2006 632........... 281, 352
Denmark v Norway: Maritime Boundary in the Area between Greenland
and Jan Mayen Island I.C.J. Rep. 1993 38........................27, 166, 167, 187, 346
Dickson Car Wheel Company case (US v Mexico) (1931) 4 R.I.A.A. 669.... 226
Difference Relating to Immunity from Legal Process of a Special

Rapporteur of the Commission on Human Rights, I.C.J. Rep. 1999
62 359
Diggs v Schultz, 470 F (2d) 461 (1972) 53
Diplomatic and Consular Staff in Tehran, I.C.J. Rep. 1980 3 358
Dispute Concerning Delimitation of the Maritime Boundary between
Bangladesh and Myanmar in the Bay of Bengal (Bangladesh/
Myanmar) Judgment March 14, 2012 199
Diversion of Water from the Meuse case (1937) P.C.I.J. Rep., Series A/B,
No.70 26
Dralle v Republic of Czechoslovakia (1950) 17 I.L.R. 155 Austrian SC 143
Duff Development Co Ltd v Kelantan [1924] A.C. 797, HL 50

East Timor (Portugal v Australia) case, I.C.J. Rep. (1995) 90; 34 I.L.M. 1581
(1995) 208, 343
Eastern Carelia case P.C.I.J. Rep. ser.B, No.5 (1923) 360
Eastern Greenland case (1933) P.C.I.J. Rep., ser.A/B, No.53 .... 106, 273
Edye v Robertson, 112 US 580 53
Effect of Reservations Case, 22 ILM (1983) 274
Eichmann case. See Attorney-General of the Government of Israel v Eichmann
El Oro Mining and Railway Co case (Great Britain v Mexico) 5 R.I.A.A.
191 (1931) 229
Elettronica Sicula S.p.A. (ELSI) (US v Italy) I.C.J. Rep. 1989 15 341
Elliott, Ex p. See R. v Officer Commanding Depot Battalion RASC
Colchester Ex p. Elliott
Emin v Yeldag [2002] 1 F.L.R. 956; [2002] Fam. Law 419 Fam Div 86
Empire of Iran case (1963) 45 I.L.R. 57, Federal Constitution Court,
German Federal Republic 143
Empson v Smith [1966] 1 Q.B. 426; [1965] 3 W.L.R. 380 CA 153
English Channel Arbitration 18 ILM 397 (1979) 192, 280
Eritrea v Yemen (1998) 114 I.L.R. 1 107
Eritrea–Yemen Arbitration (first stage) October 9, 1998, 40 ILM 900 (2001)
PCA 338
Eritrea–Yemen Arbitration (second stage) December 17, 1999, 40 ILM 983
(2001) PCA 338
Exchange of Greek and Turkish Populations case P.C.I.J. Rep., ser.B.,
No.10 (1925) 42

Fabiani case (1896) 10 R.I.A.A. 83 25
Fagernes, The; sub nom. Coast Lines Ltd v Societa Nazionale di
Navigazione of Genoa (The Fagernes) [1927] P. 311; (1927) 28 Ll.
L. Rep. 261 CA 50
Fenton Textile Association v Krassin (1921) 9 Ll. L. Rep. 466; (1921) 38
T.L.R. 259 CA 83
Filartiga v Pena-Irala, 630 F. 2d, 786 (1980); 19 ILM 966. US Circuit of
Appeals 2nd Cir. 52, 134, 156, 247
Finnish Ships Arbitration, 3 R.I.A.A. 1479 (1934) 229
Fisheries Jurisdiction (Spain v Canada) I.C.J. Rep. 1998 432 347
Fisheries Jurisdiction (United Kingdom v Iceland) Merits (1974) I.C.J.
Rep. 1974 3 .... 16, 27, 185, 358
Fisheries Jurisdiction Case, I.C.J. Rep. 1973 3 .... 271, 287, 290, 291
Foster and Elam v Neilson 27 US (2 Pet.) 253 (1829) 54
France v Turkey (1927) P.C.I.J. Series A No.10 .... 19, 20, 28
Free Zones of Upper Savoy and Gex P.C.I.J. Rep., ser.A/B, No.46 (1932) .. 42, 203

Frontier Dispute (Burkina Faso v Mali) I.C.J. Rep. 1985 6................70, 104, 273, 341

Gabčíkovo-Nagyamaros Project (Hungary v Slovakia) 1997 I.C.J. Rep p.7,
    para.152...211, 231, 291, 344
Garcia-Mir v Meese, 688 F (2d) 1446 (1986)... 51
Gdynia Ameryka Linie Żeglugowe Spolka Akcyjna v Boguslawski; sub
    nom. Boguslawski v Gdynia Ameryka Linie Żeglugowe Spolka
    Akcyjna [1953] A.C. 11; [1952] 2 All E.R. 470 HL............................... 83, 84
Germany v US (La Grand case), 40 ILM 1069 (2001) 156
Government of Sudan and the Sudan People's Liberation Movement/
    Army Abyei (July 22, 2009), 48 ILM 1254 (2009). Arbitration
    Award... 338
Greenham Women against Cruise Missiles v Reagan, 591 F. Supp 1332
    (1984) 62
Guinea/Guinea-Bissau Maritime Delimitation case, 77 I.L.R. 636; 25
    I.L.M. 251 ....162, 167, 184, 193, 337
Gulf of Maine case, I.C.J. Rep. 1984 246...........................27, 184, 192, 193, 194
Gur Corp v Trust Bank of Africa Ltd [1987] Q.B. 599; [1986] 3 W.L.R. 583
    CA (Civ Div).. 86
Gut Dam Arbitration, 8 ILM 118 (1969) 230
Haile Selassie v Cable and Wireless Ltd (No.2) [1939] Ch.182 CA 83
Hamdan v Rumsfeld, 548 U.S. 557 (2006)... 129
Hartford Fire Insurance Co v California US Supreme Court, 113 S.Ct 2891
    (1993) 128
Hesperides Hotels v Muftizade; sub nom. Hesperides Hotels v Aegean
    Turkish Holidays [1978] Q.B. 205; [1977] 3 W.L.R. 656 CA (Civ
    Div)... 86
Home Missionary Society Claim, 6 R.I.A.A. 42 (1920) 204
I Congreso del Partido. See Owners of Cargo Lately Laden on Board the
    Playa Larga v Owners of the I Congreso del Partido Playa Larga,
    The (No.1)
I'm Alone case (Canada v United States), 3 R.I.A.A. 1607 (1933/35); 29
    A.J.I.L. 326 (1935). 181, 212
IMCO case, I.C.J. Rep. (1960) 150... 176
Interhandel case (Preliminary Objections), I.C.J. Rep. 1959 6.............229, 348, 349
International Status of South West Africa case, I.C.J. Rep. 1950 128........... 72
International Tribunal of the Law of the Sea, M/V Saiga (No.2) case 1999,
    120 I.L.R. 143.. 43
Intpro Properties (UK) v Sauvel [1983] Q.B. 1019; [1983] 2 W.L.R. 1; [1983]
    1 All E.R. 658 QBD.. 145
Iran–United States No.A/18 (1984) 5 Iran-U.S.C.T.R. 251............................ 225
Island of Palmas case, 2 R.I.A.A. 829 (1928)................28, 66, 103, 105, 107,
    108, 207, 337
Italy v Hambros Bank Ltd [1950] Ch. 314; [1950] 1 All E.R. 430.................. 47
Jan Mayen case. See Denmark v Norway: Maritime Boundary in the Area
    between Greenland and Jan Mayen Island
Janes Claim (US v Mexico), 4 R.I.A.A. 82 (1926)... 215
JH Rayner (Mincing Lane) Ltd v Department of Trade and Industry;
    Maclaine Watson & Co Ltd v Department of Trade and Industry;
    Maclaine Watson & Co Ltd v International Tin Council; TSB
    England and Wales v Department of Trade and Industry;
    Amalgamated Metal Trading Ltd v International Tin Council
    [1990] 2 A.C. 418; [1989] 3 W.L.R. 969 HL... 45, 47

Johnson v Browne 205 US 309 at 321 (1907)... 53
Jones v Saudi Arabia; Mitchell v Al-Dali; sub nom. Jones v Ministry of
the Interior Al-Mamlaka Al-Arabiya AS Saudiya [2006] UKHL 26;
[2007] 1 A.C. 270; [2006] 2 W.L.R. 1424 144
Joyce v DPP [1946] A.C. 347; [1946] 1 All E.R. 186 HL............................. 130
Juno Trader (Saint Vincent and the Grenadines v Guinea-Bissau),
December 18, 2004 197
Jurisdictional Immunities of the State (Germany v Italy), Judgement of
February 3, 2012 .... 145, 353
Kadi and Al Berakaat v Council of the EU and EC Commission,
Judgement of September 3, 2008 ECJ (Grand Chamber) 360, 361
Kasikili/Sedudu Island (Botswana/Namibia) (2000) 49 I.C.L.Q. 964 .... 109, 344
Kaur v Lord Advocate 1980 S.C. 319; 1981 S.L.T. 322 OH 48
Kiobel v Royal Dutch Petroleum Co 569 U.S. (2013) 156
Kisikili/Sedudu Island (Botswana v Namibia) case, I.C.J. Rep. 1999 1045   284
Krajina v Tass Agency [1949] 2 All E.R. 274; [1949] W.N. 309 143
Kuwait Airways Corp v Iraqi Airways Co (No.1) [1995] 1 W.L.R. 1147;
[1995] 3 All E.R. 694 144
Kuwait Airways Corporation v Iraqi Airways Company [2002] UKHL 19
.... 62
Kuwait v American Independent Oil Co, 21 ILM 976 (1982) 220
Lac Lanoux Arbitration, 24 I.L.R., 101–119 334
LaGrand (Germany v United States) June 27, 2001 (2001) 40 ILM 1069 ..... 205, 355
Land and Maritime Boundary between Cameroon and Nigeria
(Equitorial Guinea intervening) I.C.J. Rep. (2002) 303 195
Land and Maritime Boundary between Cameroon and Nigeria ICJ
October 10, 2002, General List No.94 175
Land, Island and Maritime Frontier Dispute (El Salvador v Honduras)
I.C.J. Rep. (1992) 351 ....104, 108, 165
Land, Island and Maritime Frontier Dispute (El Salvador v Honduras)
I.C.J. Rep. 1987 10 341
Land, Island and Maritime Frontier Dispute (El Salvador v Honduras)
(Nicaragua Intervention) I.C.J. Rep. 1990 92 353
Lauritzen v Larsen 345 US 571 (1953) 41
Legal Consequences for States of the Continued Presence of South
Africa in Namibia (South West Africa) Notwithstanding Security
Council Resolution 276 (1970) (Advisory Opinion) I.C.J. Rep. 1971
16 .... 313, 341
Legal Consequences of the Construction of a Wall in the Occupied
Palestine Territory (Advisory Opinion), I.C.J. Rep., 2004, 134. 110,
208, 306, 359
Legal Consequences for States of the Continued Presence of South
Africa in Namibia (South West Africa) Notwithstanding Security
Council Resolution 276 (1970) Advisory Opinion I.C.J. Rep. 1971,
16 72
Legality of the Threat or use of Nuclear Weapons case, Advisory Opinion
(1997) 35 ILM 809 ....28, 231, 328, 359
Legality of the Threat or use of Nuclear Weapons' I.C.J. Rep. (1996) 226...   208
Legality of the Use by a State of Nuclear Weapons in Armed Conflict
(Advisory Opinion) (1996) 35 I.L.M. 809; (1996) I.C.J. Rep. 226. 28,
93, 304, 323
Legality of the Use by a State of Nuclear Weapons in Armed Conflict
I.C.J. Rep. 1996 66 89

Legality of the Use of Force case (Yugoslavia v US) Provisional Measures, June 2, 1999, I.C.J. Rep. 1999, 916 320

Liamco case, 20 ILM 1 (1981) 219, 220

Liangsiriprasert v United States [1991] 1 A.C. 225; [1990] 3 W.L.R. 606 PC (HK) 128

Libya v Chad, Territorial Dispute 6 I.C.J. Rep. 1994. 22

Libya v Malta (1985) I.C.J. Rep. 13 17

Lockerbie case (Libya v United Kingdom), (1992) I.C.J. 3, 94 I.L.R. 478 ..... 129, 355

Loizidou v Turkey (Preliminary Objections) E.C.H.R. Series A Number 30 (1995) 277

Lord Advocate v Scotsman Publications Ltd [1990] 1 A.C. 812; [1989] 3 W.L.R. 358; 1989 S.L.T. 705 HL 49

Lotus case P.C.I.J. Rep., ser.A, No.10 (1927) 126, 135, 177

Lotus Case. See France v Turkey (1927)

Lovelace case, 1981 2 Selected Decisions H.R.C. 28. 256

Lusitania (United States v Germany) 7 R.I.A.A. 32 (1956) 212

Luther v Sagor. See AM Luther Co v James Sagor & Co;

M/V Saiga (No.2) 120 I.L.R. 143 .... 176, 181

M/V Saiga case (Saint Vincent and the Grenadines v Guinea) December 4, 1997 198

M/V Virginia G Case (Panama/Guinea-Bissau) ITLOS (2014) 175

Maclaine Watson v Dept of Trade and Industry. See JH Rayner (Mincing Lane) Ltd v Department of Trade and Industry

Made in the USA Foundation v United States, 56 F Supp (2d) 1226 (N.D. Ala. 1999) 57

Madzimbamuto (Stella) v Lardner Burke [1969] 1 A.C. 645; [1968] 3 W.L.R. 1229 PC Rhodesia. 85

Maret, The, 145 F.(d) 431 (1944) 87

Maritime Delimitation and Territorial Questions (Qatar v Bahrain) I.C.J. Rep. 1995 6 358

Maritime Delimitation in the Black Sea case (Romania v Ukraine) I.C.J. Rep. 2009 3 .... 188, 193

Maritime Delimitation on Territorial Questions between Qatar and Bahrain (Qatar v Bahrain) I.C.J. Rep. (2001) p.40 194

Maritime Delimitations and Territorial Questions case (Qatar v Bahrain) I.C.J. Rep. 1994 112 .... 272, 275, 283

Maritime Dispute (Peru v Chile) 27 January 2014 General List No.137, para.180 195

Martini (Italy v Venezuela) 2 R.I.A.A. 975, 1002 (1930), the Temple Case, I.C.J. Rep. 1962 p.6 211

Massey (US v Mexico), 4 R.I.A.A. 155 207

Mauritian Women case, 1981 1 Selected Decisions H.R.C. 67 256

Mavrommatis Palestine Concessions case, P.C.I.J. Rep., ser.A, No.2 (1924) 64, 213, 333

Mazibuko and the City of Johannesburg case April 30, 2008 43

McWhirter v Attorney General [1972] C.M.L.R. 882 CA (Civ Div) 47

Medellin v Texas, 552 U.S. (2008) SC (US) 54

Merge Claim, 22 I.L.R. 443 225

Mighell v Sultan of Johore [1894] 1 Q.B. 149 CA 143

Military and Paramilitary Activities In and Against Nicaragua (Nicaragua v The United States) (Merits) I.C.J. Rep. 1986 14 .... 15, 17, 18, 19, 24, 30, 37, 168, 205, 284, 299, 302, 303, 304, 305, 307, 329, 358

Military and Paramilitary Activities in and against Nicaragua, I.C.J. Rep.
1984 392 ....345, 347, 349, 350, 352, 360
Minister for Immigration and Ethnic Affairs Re Teoh, 1995 C.L.R. 273 49
Minquiers and Ecrehos case, I.C.J. Rep. 1953 47... 108, 343
Missouri v Holland, 252 US 416 (1920) 55, 57, 58
Monetary Gold case, I.C.J. Rep. 1954 32 343
Moore v Secretary of State for Scotland, 1985 S.L.T. 38 IH (Div 2) 48
Mortensen v Peters (1906) 8 F. (J.) 93; (1906) 14 S.L.T. 227 HCJ 41, 46
Mosul Boundary case, (1925) P.C.I.J. Rep., Series B, No. 12 25
Murray v Schooner Charming Betsy, 6 US (2 Cranch.) 64 (1804) 41
Naim Molvan, Owner of Motor Vessel Asya v Attorney General
of Palestine [1948] A.C. 351; (1947–48) 81 Ll. L. Rep. 277 PC
(Palestine) 176
Namibia (South West Africa) case, I.C.J. Rep. 1971 16 272
Nanni v Pace and the Sovereign Order of Malta, 8 A.D. 2 (1935–37) Italian
Ct of Cassation 100
Nationality Decrees in Tunis and Morocco case, P.C.I.J. Rep., ser.B, No.4
(1923) 69
Naulilaa case, 2 R.I.A.A. 1012 (1928) 300
Neer Claim, 4 R.I.A.A. 60 (1926) 215
Nercide, The, 9 Cr. 388 (US 1815) 51
Nicaragua (Merits) case. See Military and Paramilitary Activities In and
Against Nicaragua (Nicaragua v The United States) (Merits)
Nicaragua v Honduras, I.C.J. Rep. (2007) 1 163
North American Dredging Co. (U.S./Mexican), 4 R.I.A.A. 26 (1926) 65, 213, 223
North Sea Continental Shelf Cases, I.C.J. 1969 Rep. 3 ....12, 14, 19, 20, 22, 27, 35,
66, 191, 192, 284, 333
Northern Cameroons case I.C.J. Rep. 1963 15 360
Norwegian Loans case, I.C.J. Rep. 1957 9 .... 223, 348
Norwegian Shipowners Claim (Norway v US) 1 R.I.A.A. 307 (1922) 211
Nottebohm (Preliminary Objection), I.C.J. Rep. 1953 111 350
Nottebohm case (Second Phase), I.C.J. Rep. 1955 4 ....28, 69, 224, 225
Noyes Claim, 6 R.I.A.A. 308 311 .... 206, 215
Nuclear Test case (Australia v France), I.C.J. Rep. (1974) 253 .... 175, 273
Nuclear Test case (New Zealand v France), I.C.J. Rep. (1974) 457 .... 175, 273
Nuclear Test case I.C.J. Rep. 1974 477 358
Nuclear Tests cases I.C.J. Rep. 1973 99 237
Oil Platforms (Merits) case (Iran v United States), I.C.J. Rep. 2003 161 304
Owners of the Philippine Admiral v Wallem Shipping (Hong Kong) Ltd
(The Philippine Admiral) Telfair Shipping Corp v Owners of the
Ship Philippine Admiral Philippine Admiral, The [1977] A.C. 373;
[1976] 2 W.L.R. 214 PC (HK) 144
Pakistan v India (Ariel incident of August 10, 1999) 119
Paquete Habana, The, 175 US 677 (1900) 51
Paraguay v US I.C.J. 1998 248 156
Parlement Belge case (1879) 4 P.D. 129 143
Parlement Belge case (1880) 5 P.D. 197 47
Passage through the Great Belt (Finland v Denmark) (Provisional
Measures), I.C.J. Rep. 1991 12 354
Pedra Branca case, I.C.J. Rep. 2008 109
Peru v Chile. See Maritime Dispute (Peru v Chile)
Philippine Admiral, The. See Owners of the Philippine Admiral v Wallem
Shipping (Hong Kong) Ltd

Phosphate Lands in Nauru (Nauru v Australia, Preliminary Objections),
1993, 32 ILM 46 353
Polish Upper Silesia case, P.C.I.J. Rep., ser.A, No.7, (1929) 43, 219
Pope case, 8 Whiteman 709 215
Porto Alexandra, The [1920] P. 30. 143
Post Office v Estuary Radio Ltd [1968] 2 Q.B. 740, CA 41, 50
Prosecutor v Tadic, (1999) ILM, Vol.38, p.1518 .... 205, 329
Qatar and Bahrain (Qatar v Bahrain) Maritime Delimitation on Territorial
Questions I.C.J. Rep. 2001 4018, 163
Questions of Interpretation and Application of the 1971 Montreal
Convention arising from the Aerial Incident at Lockerbie (Libyan
ArabJamahiriya v United States) 31 ILM 662 (1992) 3 .... 119, 360
Questions Relating to the Obligation to Prosecute or Extradite (Belgium
v Senegal) July 20, 2012, I.C.J 113 ....42, 126, 140, 210, 267
Quintanilla Claim (Mexico v U.S.), 4 R.I.A.A. 101 (1926) 215
R v Markus. See Secretary of State for Trade v Markus
R v O [2008] EWCA Crim 2835; Times, October 2, 2008 CA (Crim
Div) 276
R. (on the application of Al-Skeini) v Secretary of State for Defence [2007]
UKHL 26; [2008] 1 A.C. 153; [2007] 3 W.L.R. 33 47
R. (on the application of Kibris Turk Hava Yollari) v Secretary of State for
Transport [2009] EWHC 1918 (Admin); [2010] 1 All E.R. (Comm)
253 QBD (Admin) 86
R. v Bartle and the Commissioner of Police for the Metropolis Ex p.
Pinochet (Respondent) (On Appeal from a Divisional Court of
the Queen's Bench Division); R. v Evans and the Commissioner
of Police for the Metropolis Ex p. Pinochet (Respondent) (On
Appeal from a Divisional Court of the Queen's Bench Division),
Judgment of November 25, 1998, 37 I.L.M. (1998) 1302 154
R. v Bow Street Metropolitan Stipendiary Magistrate Ex p. Pinochet
Ugarte (No.1); R. v Bartle Ex p. Pinochet Ugarte (No.1); sub nom.
R. v Evans Ex p. Pinochet Ugarte (No.1); Pinochet Ugarte (No.1),
Re [2000] 1 A.C. 61; [1998] 3 W.L.R. 1456 HL 43
R. v Bow Street Metropolitan Stipendiary Magistrate Ex p. Pinochet
Ugarte (No.2); sub nom. Pinochet Ugarte (No.2), Re; R. v Evans
Ex p. Pinochet Ugarte (No.2); R. v Bartle Ex p. Pinochet Ugarte
(No.2) [2000] 1 A.C. 119; [1999] 2 W.L.R. 27 154
R. v Bow Street Metropolitan Stipendiary Magistrate Ex p. Pinochet
Ugarte (No.3) [2000] 1 A.C. 147; [1999] 2 W.L.R. 827; [1999] 2 All
E.R. 97 .... 97, 154
R. v Chief Immigration Officer, Heathrow Airport Ex p. Bibi (Salamat)
[1976] 1 W.L.R. 979; [1976] 3 All E.R. 843 CA (Civ Div) 48
R. v Evans and the Commissioner of the Police for the Metropolis Ex p.
Pinochet. See R. v Bow Street Metropolitan Stipendiary Magistrate
Ex p. Pinochet Ugarte (No.3)
R. v Governor of Belmarsh Prison Ex p. Martin [1995] 1 W.L.R. 412; [1995]
2 All E.R. 548 128
R. v Horseferry Road Magistrates Court Ex p. Bennett (No.1); sub nom.
Bennett v Horseferry Road Magistrates Court [1994] 1 A.C. 42;
[1993] 3 W.L.R. 90; [1993] 3 All E.R. 138 HL 141
R. v Jones; Swain v DPP; Ayliffe v DPP; R. v Richards; R. v Pritchard; R.
v Olditch; R. v Milling [2006] UKHL 16; [2007] 1 A.C. 136; [2006] 2
W.L.R. 772 HL 45, 46

R. v Officer Commanding Depot Battalion RASC Colchester Ex p. Elliott
[1949] 1 All E.R. 373; [1949] W.N. 52 141
R. v Plymouth Justices Ex p. Driver [1986] Q.B. 95; [1985] 3 W.L.R. 689..... 141
R. v Sansom; R. v Williams; R. v Smith; R. v Wilkins (Joseph Herbert)
[1991] 2 Q.B. 130; [1991] 2 W.L.R. 366 128
R. v Secretary of State for Foreign and Commonwealth Affairs, Ex p.
Trawnik (1985) 82 L.S.G. 2739; Times, April 18, 1985 50
R. v Secretary of State for the Home Department Ex p. Ahmed
(Mohammed Hussain); R. v Secretary of State for the Home
Department Ex p. Patel (Idris Ibrahim) [1999] Imm. A.R. 22; [1998]
I.N.L.R. 570 49
R. v Secretary of State for the Home Department Ex p. Bhajan Singh
[1976] Q.B. 198; [1975] 3 W.L.R. 225CA (Civ Div) 48
R. v Secretary of State for the Home Department Ex p. Brind [1991] 1 A.C.
696; [1991] 2 W.L.R. 588; [1991] 1 All E.R. 720 HL............................. 48
R. v Secretary of State for the Home Department Ex p. Thakrar; sub
nom. R. v Immigration Officer at Heathrow Airport Ex p. Thakrar
[1974] Q.B. 684; [1974] 2 W.L.R. 593 45
Rainbow Warrior case, 26 ILM 1346 (1987) 207
Rann of Kutch Arbitration, 50 I.L.R. 2... 27
Rantsev v Cyprus (25965/04) (2010) 51 E.H.R.R. 1; 28 B.H.R.C. 313, Final
May 10, 2010 ECHR... 246
Rasul v Bus, 542 U.S. 466 (2004)... 129
Reel v Holder [1981] 1 W.L.R. 1226; [1981] 3 All E.R. 321 CA (Civ Div) 86
Reference by the Governor in Council Concerning Certain Questions
Relating to the Secession of Quebec from Canada, Re (1998) 161
D.L.R. (4th) 385.. 73
Reparation for Injuries Suffered in the Service of the United Nations,
Advisory Opinion, I.C.J. Rep. 1949 174 ....24, 28, 63, 64, 359
Request for an advisory opinion submitted by the Sub-Regional Fisheries
Commission (SRFC) Advisory Opinion April 2, 2015....................... 198
Request for Interpretation of the Judgment of 31 March 2004 in the case
concerning Avena and Other Mexican Nationals (Mexico v United
States of America), Judgment, I.C.J. Rep. 2009 3............................... 354
Reservations to the Convention on Genocide case, I.C.J. Rep. 1951 15....... 277
Responsibilities and Obligations of States Sponsoring Persons and
Entities with Respect to Activities in the Area, Case No.17,
Advisory Opinion (ITLOS Seabed Disputes Chamber, February 1,
2011), 59 ILM 458 (2011)... 199, 234
Restrictions to the Death Penalty case, 23 ILM 320 (1983) 278
Rights of Nationals of the United States in Morocco case, I.C.J.
Rep. 1952 176 69
Robert E. Brown case, 6 R.I.A.A. 120 (1923). 229
Roberts Claim, 4 R.I.A.A. 77 (1926) 214, 215
Rustomjee v R. (1876) 1 Q.B.D. 487.. 65
Sabbatino case. See Banco Nacional de Cuba v Sabbatino
Salem case (Egypt v US), 2 R.I.A.A. 1161 (1932)... 225
Salimoff v Standard Oil Co, 186 N.E. 679 (1993); (1993–1934) A.D. Case
No.8.. 87
Salomon v Customs and Excise Commissioners; sub nom. Solomon v
Customs and Excise Commissioners [1967] 2 Q.B. 116; [1966] 3
W.L.R. 1223 CA.. 41
Sambaggio (Italy v Venezuela), 10 R.I.A.A. 499.. 207

Schroeder v Bissell, 5 F (2d) 838 (1925) US Dist. Ct D.Conn. 52
Seaco v Iran 919920 28 Iran–USCTR 198 26
Secretary of State for Trade v Markus; sub nom. R. v Markus [1974] 3
W.L.R. 645; [1974] 3 All E.R. 705 127
Sei Fujii v California, 242 P. (2d) 617; (1952) 19 I.L.R. 312; (1952) SC (Cal)
.... 54, 55, 247
Selmouni v France, 25803/94 (2000) 29 E.H.R.R. 403; 7 B.H.R.C. 1 246
Serbia and Montenegro v United Kingdom, I.C.J. Rep., 2004, 1307 352
Short v Iran (1987) 16 Iran–USCTR 76 207
Sierra Leone Telecommunications Co Ltd v Barclays Bank Plc; sub nom.
Sierratel v Barclays Bank Plc [1998] 2 All E.R. 821; [1998] C.L.C.
501 76
Sokoloff v National City Bank, 145 N.E. 917 (1924); (1923–1924) 2 A.D.
Case No.19 87
Somalia v Woodhouse Drake & Carey (Suisse) SA (The Mary); Mary, The
[1993] Q.B. 54; [1992] 3 W.L.R. 744 .... 75, 84, 86
Sosa v Alvarez-Machain, 542 US (2004) (US SC) 141
South West Africa (Second Phase), I.C.J. Rep. 1966 6 .... 18, 26
Southern Pacific Properties (Middle East) Ltd v Arab Republic of Egypt,
32 ILM 933 (1993) 207, 220
Sovereignty over Pulau Ligitan and Pulau Sipadan (Indonesia v
Malaysia) (Philippines intervening), I.C.J. Rep. 2002 625 353
Sovereignty over Pulau Ligitan Pulau Sipadan, ICJ December 17, 2002
General List No.102 107
Spain v Owners of the Arantzazu Mendi [1939] A.C. 256; [1939] 1 All E.R.
719 HL 82
Starrett Housing Corp v Iran (Interlocutory Award) 4 Iran-USCTR 122;
23 ILM 1090 (1984) 218
Steiner and Gross v Polish State, 4 A.D. 291 (1928) 95
Sulaiman Al-Adsani v Government of Kuwait, 100 I.L.R. 465 144
T. Petitioner, 1966 S.C.L.R. 897 48
Tachiona v United States 386 F (3d) 205, 2004 US App. Lexus 20879 (2d
Cir. October 6 2004) (Tachiona II) 144
Temple case, I.C.J. Rep. 1961 17 Judgment on Preliminary Objections 351
Temple of Preah Vihear case, I.C.J. Rep. 1962 6 25
Teoh case. See Minister for Immigration and Ethnic Affairs Re Teoh
Territorial Dispute (Libya Arab Jamahiriya/Chad) (1994) 33 ILM 571;
I.C.J. Rep. (1994) 6 .... 104, 283, 345
Territory of Hawaii v Ho, 41 Hawaii 565 (1957); 26 I.L.R. 557 56
Texaco case, 53 I.L.R. 389 (1977); 17 ILM 1 (1978) 33, 220, 223
Thakrar v Home Secretary. See R. v Secretary of State for the Home
Department Ex p. Thakrar
Tin Council case. See Maclaine Watson v Dept of Trade and Industry
Trail Smelter Arbitration 3 R.I.A.A. 1905 (1938/41) 29, 230
Treacy v DPP; sub nom. R. v Treacy [1971] A.C. 537; [1971] 2 W.L.R. 112
HL 127
Treatment in Hungary of Aircraft of the USA, I.C.J. Rep. 1954 99 344
Trendtex Trading Corp v Central Bank of Nigeria [1977] Q.B. 529; [1977]
2 W.L.R. 356; [1977] 1 All E.R. 881 CA (Civ Div) 31, 45, 46, 144
Triquet v Bath (1764) 3 Burr. 1478 KB 43
Tyrer case (1978) 58 I.L.R. 339 59
Underhill v Hernandez, 168 US 250 at 252 (1897) 60
United States v Alvarez-Machain, 31 ILM 902 (1992) 141

United States v Belmont, 301 US 324 (1937).. 55

United States v Fawaz Yunis, 30 I.L.M. 403 (1991) (US CA (DC)).............. 51

United States v Guy W. Capps Inc., 204 F (2d) 655 (1953) (US CA, 4th
    Circuit)... 56

United States v Percheman, 32 US (7 Pet.) 51 (1833).................................... 54

United States v Pink, 315 US 203 (1942)... 55, 56

United States v Toscanino, 500 F. (2d) 207 (1974) (US CA)........................... 141

Upright v Mercury Business Machines, 13 A.D. (2d) 36; 213 (N.Y.S.) (2d)
    417 (1961) 87

US Diplomatic and Consular Staff in Tehran (Provisional Measures) I.C.J.
    Rep. 1979 7; (Judgment) I.C.J. Rep. 1980 3 ....146, 354, 360

US v Sisson 294 F. Supp 515 (D.Mass. 1968)...................................... 61

Van Gend en Loos v Nederlandse Tarief Commissie (26/62) [1963] E.C.R.
    1; C.M.L.R. 105 95

Velasquez Rodriguez v Honduras, Series C, Case No. 4 (1988)................. 206, 246

Voting Procedure on Questions Relating to Reports and Petitions
    Concerning the Territory of South West Africa (1955) I.C.J.
    Rep. 67 33

WS Kirkpatrick and Co v Environmental Tectonics Corp International
    493 US 400 (1990) 61

Walker v Baird [1892] A.C. 491... 47

Weinberger case, 1980 Selected Decisions H.R.C. 57 256

West Rand Central Gold Mining Co Ltd v King, The [1905] 2 K.B. 391
    KBD... 44

Western Sahara (Advisory Opinion) (1975) I.C.J. Rep. 12...........33, 70, 105, 108, 359

Westminster CC v Government of Iran [1986] 1 W.L.R. 979 Ch D.............. 148

WHO Nuclear Weapons case 360

Wimbledon case (1923) P.C.I.J. Rep., Series A, No. 1.................................... 23

Wood Pulp case [1988] 4 C.M.L.R. 901 128

Wulfsohn v R.S.F.S.R., 138 N.E. 24 (1923); (1923–1924) 2 A.D. Case No.16 ... 87

Yeager v Iran 17 Iran– USCTR 92.. 207

Yilmaz-Dogan v Netherlands, C.E.R.D. Report, G.A.O.R., 43rd Session,
    Supp.18, (1988)... 262

Youmans Claim 207

Zafiro case, 6 R.I.A.A. 160 (1925) 206, 215

TABLE OF INTERNATIONAL TREATIES AND CONVENTIONS

1714 Treaty of Utrecht............... 111
1794 Jay Treaty between the United States and Great Britain............... 336
1864 Geneva Convention for the Amelioration of the Condition of the Wounded and Sick of Armed Forces in the Field............................ 328
1856 League of Nations Convention between Russia, France and Great Britain............... 24
1871 Treaty of Washington between the United States and Great Britain.......................... 336
1876 Postal Convention Regulating Communications by Post (Belgium and Britain) 47
1881 Treaty between Argentina and Chile............. 272
1898 Treaty (Hong Kong/Britain)............................. 111
1899 Convention with Respect to the Laws and Customs of War on Land 323
1899 Hague Convention for the Pacific Settlement of International Disputes..................335, 336, 337
arts 9–14 335
1907 Convention on the establishment of an International Prize Court 324
1907 Hague Conventions I and II.........................323, 324
1907 Hague Conventions III, V, VII, VIII, IX...........323, 324
1907 Hague Convention for the Pacific Settlement of Disputes 335, 337
1916 Migratory Bird Treaty...... 57, 58
1919 Covenant of the League of Nations.................. 298
art.10..............................109, 298
art.22............................... 71
1919 Paris Convention on the Regulation of Aerial Navigation................ 116, 117
1919 Treaty of Versailles ...95, 111, 264
art.380............................. 23
1921 Statute of the International Hydrographic Organisation art.4..90
1922 Upper Silesian Convention.....95
1923 Convention for the Suppression of Traf-

fic of Women and Children...................... 247
Protocol (1947)............................. 247
1925 Protocol (Geneva) June 17, 1925...................... 324
1926 Brussels Convention for the Unification of Certain Rules relating to the Immunity of State Owned Vessels.......................144, 145
1926 Slavery Convention......... 247
1928 Kellogg-Briand Pact or the Pact of Paris: General Treaty for the Renunciation of War.............................109, 298
1928 General Act on the Pacific Settlement of International Disputes........................337, 345
1929 Nicaraguan Declaration Recognising the Jurisdiction of the Court as Compulsory, September 24, 1929............................. 351
1929 Nile Waters Agreement 294
1930 Hague Convention on Certain Questions Relations to the Conflict on Nationality Law.............................. 34
art.1................................ 224
1933 Montevideo Convention on the Rights and Duties of States.......... 65
art.1................................ 65
art.3................................ 68
art.9................................ 66
1935 Harvard Research Draft Convention on Jurisdiction with Respect to Crime....126, 135
art.13............................. 142
art.14............................. 142
1936 Treaty of Montreux in respect of the Straits of the Bosphorus and Dardanelles................ 172
1944 Chicago Convention on International Civil Aviation...................116, 117

art.1................................. 116
art.3(b)............................ 117
(c).................................. 117
art.3 bis.........................119, 120
art.4................................. 119
art.6................................. 118
art.12............................... 226
art.17............................... 118
art.18.............................118, 226
art.25............................... 119
art.84............................... 357
1944 Chicago International Air Services Transit Agreement ("Two Freedoms" Agreement).......................... 117
art.1(3)............................ 118
(4)................................. 118
(5)................................. 118
1944 Chicago International Air Transport Agreement ("Five Freedoms" Agreement)................ 117
1945 Charter of the United Nations... 37, 71, 90, 91, 110, 297
Preamble... 55
Ch.VI (arts 33–38)........................ 310
Ch.VII (arts 39–51)...94, 138, 139, 264, 310, 312, 320
art.1................................55, 299
(1)................................54, 300
(2).................................. 70
(3)................................. 247
art.2(3)..................297, 298, 333
(4)....................................24, 77, 78, 109, 287, 297, 298, 299, 300, 302, 303, 319, 320
(6)................................. 285
(7)..............311, 321, 322, 349
art.11.............................. 313
art.12.............................. 313
art.24.............................. 310
art.25.............................. 310
art.27.............................. 313
art.33.............................333, 334
art.34.............................. 342
art.36.............................. 343
art.39.............................. 310
art.40.............................. 311
art.41.............311, 312, 313, 322
art.42......................311, 313, 322
art.43.............................313, 316

art.51....120, 302, 303, 304, 305, 306, 307, 308
art.52.............................. 308
  (1)................................. 308
  (2)................................. 319
art.54.............................. 309
art.55.............55, 70, 247
art.56................................55, 247
art.77(1).......................... 72
art.92.............................. 339
art.94..........................342, 343
art.96.............................. 358
art.102............................ 274
art.104............................ 90
art.105............................ 90
1945 Charter of the Nurem-
    berg Military Tribunal
art.6.............................. 136
1945 Statute of the Interna-
    tional Court of Justice
    25
art.2............................... 340
art.26(1)......................... 342
art.34.............................. 341
  (1)................................. 64
art.35(2)......................... 342
art.36(1)......................... 343
  (2).......24, 346, 347, 349, 350, 351, 352, 360
  (3)................................. 346
  (5)..............................350, 351
  (6)................................. 349
art.37.............................. 345
art.38....9, 10, 11, 21, 26, 27, 30, 33, 37, 187, 193, 356
  (1).........................31, 356, 360
    (a)............................ 21, 22
    (a)–(c) 10
    (b)........................... 14
    (d) 10
  (2)............................. 10, 27
art.41....................353, 354, 355
art.59.....................28, 353, 356
art.60.............................. 357
art.61.............................. 357
art.62.............................. 352
art.63.............................. 352
art.65.............................. 358
art.66.............................. 358
art.69.............................. 356
art.71.............................. 100
1946 Convention on the
    Privileges and Immu-
nities of the United
    Nations.......................90, 158
art.VI 93
art.30.............................. 358
1946 United States Declara-
    tion Recognising the
    Jurisdiction of the
    Court as Compul-
    sory, August 26, 1926,
    ....347, 348, 349, 350
1947 Convention on the Privi-
    leges and Immuni-
    ties of the Specialised
    Agencies 90
1947 Headquarters Agreement
    between the United
    Nations and the
    United States...............90, 98
1947 Statute of the Interna-
    tional Law Commission
art.15.............................. 34
1948 Convention on the Pre-
    vention and Punish-
    ment of the Crime of
    Genocide......132, 136, 204, 260, 266, 295, 342, 345
art.4.............................. 97
1948 Universal Declaration of
    Human Rights.......32, 241, 247, 248, 249
art.2.............................. 248
art.14.............................. 216
arts 22–27 252
art.29(2)......................... 248
1949 Draft Declaration on
    Rights and Duties of States
art.9.............................. 109
art.11.............................. 109
art.13.............................. 42
1949 Geneva Red Cross Con-
    ventions 100, 133, 136, 137, 323, 329, 330
art.1(2)........................... 329
art.3................................264, 329
Additional Protocols (1977) .323, 329, 330
Protocol I 136, 329, 330
Protocol II 264, 329, 330
1949 Geneva Red Cross Con-
    vention I............323, 329, 330
art.46.............................. 290
1949 Geneva Red Cross Con-
    vention II 323, 329, 330

1949   Geneva Red Cross Convention III 323, 329, 330
1949   Geneva Red Cross Convention IV Relating to the Protection of Civilian Persons in Times of War 314, 329
1949   North Atlantic Treaty art.5................................... 308
1949   Revised 1928 General Act for the Pacific Settlement of International Disputes 33, 37
1950   European Convention on Human Rights and Fundamental Freedoms.....................48, 49, 263
       art.1................................. 282
       art.5................................. 49
       art.6................................. 144
       art.14............................... 49
       art.34............................... 95
       art.35............................... 95
Protocol No.4 (1964)...215
Protocol No.11 (November 1, 1998) 95
1951   Geneva Convention relating to the Status of Refugees................. 216
       art.1A(2).......................... 216
       art.32(1)........................... 217
       art.33............................216, 248
       (1)................................. 217
       (2)................................. 217
Protocol (1967) 216
1951   Treaty establishing the European Coal and Steel Community....... 288
1951   Treaty of Peace with Japan 111
1954   Convention for the Prevention of the Pollution of the Sea by Oil (OILPOL).................... 181
1954   Convention for the Protection of Cultural Property in the event of Armed Conflict...... 329
1955   Convention on Establishment art.3................................ 215
1956   Convention on the Abolition of Slavery, the Slave Trade and Insti-

tutions and Practices Similar to Slavery 247
1956   Treaty of Friendship, Commerce and Navigation 345
1957   European Convention for the Pacific Settlement of Disputes 345
1957   Treaty establishing the European Community (The EC Treaty) art.12.............................. 95
1958   Geneva Convention on Fishing and Conservation of Living Resources of the High Seas.................159, 181
       art.23.............................. 181
1958   Geneva Convention on the Continental Shelf   159
       art.1............................... 189
       art.2............................... 190
       art.3............................... 190
       art.5(1) 190
       (7)................................. 182
       art.6............................... 280
       (1)................................. 191
       (2)................................. 191
1958   Geneva Convention on the High Seas ...159, 176, 181
       art.1............................... 173
       art.2.............................174, 185
       art.5.............................175, 226
       (1)................................. 176
       (7)................................. 182
       art.6............................... 176
       art.10............................176, 177
       art.11 ....176, 177
       art.15............................131, 178
       art.19............................131, 177
       art.20............................. 178
       art.22............................. 178
       art.24............................176, 182
       art.25............................176, 182
1958   Geneva Convention on the Territorial Sea and Contiguous Zone.....159
       art.1............................... 161
       art.2............................... 161
       art.3............................162, 174
       art.4(1) 163
       (2)............................. 163
       (3)............................. 163

(4)............................... 164
(5)............................... 164
(6)............................... 164
art.5................................. 169
art.6................................. 163
art.7(2)............................ 164
(4)............................... 165
(5)...........................164, 165
art.8................................. 166
art.10............................... 166
art.11............................... 166
art.12............................... 167
art.14............................... 168
(4)............................... 169
(5)............................... 169
(6)............................... 169
art.15............................... 169
(2)............................... 169
art.16............................... 170
(2)............................... 170
(3)............................... 170
(4)............................... 171
art.17............................... 169
art.19............................... 171
art.20............................... 171
art.23............................... 171

1958 Geneva Conventions on
the Law of the Sea
...............................23, 36, 161

1959 Antarctic Treaty 115
art.1................................. 115

1959 Nile Waters Agreement ... 294

1961 Harvard Draft Convention on the Interna-
tional Responsibility
of States for Injuries
to Aliens
art.9................................. 215
art.10(3)(a) 218
(7)............................... 218
art.19............................... 229

1961 Vienna Convention on
Diplomatic Relations
..............36, 146, 151, 153, 157
Preamble........................ 147
art.1(e)............................ 151
art.3................................. 147
art.4................................. 147
art.9................................. 147
art.11 148
art.22............................... 148
(1)............................... 148
(2)............................... 148

art.23............................... 153
art.24............................... 148
art.25............................... 148
art.27(3)........................... 150
art.30............................... 148
(2)............................... 148
art.31(1)........................... 151
(a)–(c) 148
(2)............................... 152
art.32(1)........................... 152
(2)............................... 152
(3)............................... 152
(4)............................... 152
art.34............................... 153
art.37............................... 152
(2)............................... 153
(3)............................... 153
art.38............................... 152
art.39(2)........................... 153
art.41............................... 153
(3)............................... 149
art.47(b)........................... 153

1963 Limited Test Ban Treaty... 326

1963 Tokyo Convention on
Offences and Acts
Committed on Board
Aircraft......................... 118
art.4................................. 118
(b)............................... 135

1963 Treaty Banning Nuclear
Weapon Tests in
Outer Space and
Under Water.............175, 237
art.1(1)(b) 237

1963 Vienna Convention on
Consular Relations.... 157
art.36............................... 156
(1)............................... 156
art.41(1)........................... 157
(3)............................... 157
Optional Protocol......... 54

1964 Agreed Measures for the
Conservation of the
Antarctic Flora and
Fauna.......................... 115

1964 European Fisheries Convention 184

1965 Convention on the Settlement of Investment
Disputes between
States and Nationals
of Other States ...96, 222, 338

1965 Convention on Transit

Trade of Land-locked
States 174
1965 Declaration on the Inadmissibility of Inter-
vention in Domestic
Affairs of State 319
1966 Convention on the Elimination of All Forms
of Racial Discrimina-
tion....................... 260, 279
art.11 262
art.14................................95, 262
art.20.............................. 279
(4), (5) 279
art.22..............................262, 263
1966 International   Covenant
on Civil and Political
Rights ...32, 59, 70, 95,
248, 249, 251
art.1 255
art.2................................ 249
(1).......................248, 249, 256
art.3................................ 256
art.4(2)...........................245, 251
(6)................................ 251
art.5................................ 256
art.6...............................251, 253
art.7...............................251, 253
art.8(1) 251
(2)................................ 251
art.11 251
art.12(3) 251
art.14.............................. 95
art.15.............................. 251
art.16.............................. 251
art.17(1) 256
art.18.............................. 251
(3)................................ 252
art.19.............................. 253
art.21(a) 264
art.23(1) 256
art.25.............................. 264
art.26.............................. 256
art.27.............................. 256
art.40.............................. 253
(4)................................ 253
art.41..............................252, 255
art.42.............................. 255
(7)(c) 255
First Optional Protocol (1976)
.................................252, 255, 262
Second Optional Protocol
(1989)............................ 252

art.5................................. 255
1966 International   Covenant
on Economic, Social
and Cultural Rights
...............32, 248, 252, 254, 262
art.2(1)............................ 249
art.4................................. 252
art.16............................... 254
Optional Protocol
(2008)....................... 96, 257
1967 Treaty for the Prohibition
of Nuclear Weapons
in Latin America........ 327
Additional Protocol I... 327
Additional Protocol II.. 327
1967 Treaty on Principles Governing   the   Activi-
ties of States in the
Exploration   and
Use of Outer Space
including the Moon
and Other Celestial
Bodies.......................... 121
art.1............................... 121
art.2............................... 121
art.3............................... 121
art.4............................... 121
art.8............................... 121
art.9............................... 121
1968 Agreement on the Rescue
of Astronauts, the
Return of Astronauts
and the Return of
Objects   Launched
into Outer Space........ 122
1968 Convention   on   the
Non-applicability
of Statutory Limita-
tions to War Crimes
and Crimes Against
Humanity 136
1968 Treaty   on   the   Non-
Proliferation   of
Nuclear Weapons 326
1968 United   Kingdom–USSR
Agreement   on   the
Settlement of Mutual
Financial and Prop-
erty Claims 222
1969 American Convention on
Human Rights............96, 263
art.44................................ 96
art.75.............................. 278

1969 Convention   Guarantee-
      ing Immunities to
      Special Missions   157
      art.8...................................   157
      art.17.................................   158
1969 Convention   on   Civil
      Liability for Oil Pol-
      lution Damage   182
1969 Convention Relating to
      Intervention on the
      High Seas in Cases
      of   Oil   Pollution
      Casualties   182
      Protocol (1973)   182
      Amending Protocol
      (1976)............................   182
1969 Vienna Convention on
      the Law of Treaties
      ...36, 37, 271, 272, 274,
      278, 281, 295, 335
      art.2(1)(a)   272
      (c)   275
      (d)   276
      art.8...................................   275
      art.9...................................   275
      art.16.................................   281
      art.18.................................   276
      (a)................................   276
      art.19.................................   278
      (c)   278
      art.21(3)...........................   280
      art.26.................................   281
      art.27.................................   42
      art.30(4)(b)   282
      art.31.......................22, 282, 283
      (2)................................   283
      (3)................................   283
      art.32.................................   284
      art.34.................................   284
      art.35.................................   285
      art.36(1)...........................   285
      art.38.................................   284
      art.40.................................   285
      art.41.................................   286
      (1)(b)(ii).....................   286
      art.44.................................   292
      art.45.................................   292
      art.46..............................42, 275
      (2)................................   42
      art.48(1)...........................   286
      (2)................................   287
      art.49.................................   287
      art.50.................................   287

      art.51.................................   287
      art.52.................................   287
      art.53.......36, 209, 271, 288, 292
      art.56.................................   288
      art.58(1)...........................   288
      art.59(1)...........................   289
      art.60(3)...........................   289
      (5)................................   289
      art.61...............................290, 291
      art.63.................................   292
      art.64.......................36, 288, 293
      art.66.................................   293
      art.69(2)...........................   292
      (3)................................   292
      art.71(2)...........................   293
      art.79.................................   287
      art.84(1)...............................281
1970 Declaration on Principles
      Concerning the Sea
      Bed and the Ocean
      Floor and the Subsoil
      Thereof, Beyond the
      Limits of National
      Jurisdiction Decem-
      ber 17, 1970. 10 ILM
      230 (1970)....................   196
      art.1.................................   196
      art.3.................................   196
1970 Declaration on Principles
      of International Law
      Concerning Friendly
      Relations   and   Co-
      operation   among
      States in Accordance
      with the Charter of
      the United Nations
      ...33, 71, 300, 301, 302,
      303, 319, 329, 333
      para.X............................   109
1970 Hague Convention of
      the Suppression of
      Unlawful Seizure of
      Aircraft.....................118, 134
1971 Agreement   on   Meas-
      ures to Improve the
      Direct   Communica-
      tions Link (Hot-Line
      Upgrade Agreement)   327
1971 Agreement on Measures
      to Reduce the Risk of
      Outbreak of Nuclear
      War   (Accidents
      Agreement)   327

1971 Montreal Convention
for the Suppression
of Unlawful Acts
Against the Safety of
Civil Aviation...119, 134, 345
art.14(1)............................ 345
art.25................................ 119
1971 Protocol for the Sup-
pression of Unlaw-
ful Acts of Violence
at Airports Serving
International Civil
Aviation 119
1972 Convention for the Conservation of Antarctic
Seals.............................. 115
1972 Convention on International Liability for
Damages Caused by
Space Objects 122
art.II................................. 122
art.III................................ 122
art.IV 122
1972 Convention prohibiting
the development,
production and
stockpiling of Bacte-
riological (Biological)
and Toxin Weap-
ons and on their
Destruction................... 324
1972 European Convention on
State Immunity 145
1972 Extradition Treaty
between United
States and United
Kingdom...................... 140
1972 London Convention on
the Prevention of
Marine Pollution by
Dumping of Wastes
and Other Material.... 183
1972 Oslo Convention for the
Prevention of Marine
Pollution by Dump-
ing from Ships and
Aircraft......................... 183
1972 Stockholm Declaration of
the United Nations
Conference on the
Human Environment
Principle 21.................... 230
Principle 22.................... 231

Principle 24.................... 231
1972 Treaty on the Limitation
of Anti-Ballistic Mis-
sile Systems (ABM)... 327
1973 Convention for the
Prevention of Pol-
lution from Ships
(MARPOL) 182
Protocol (1978)............. 182
1973 Convention on the Prevention and Pun-
ishment of Crimes
against Interna-
tionally Protected
Persons including
Diplomatic Agents
............................134, 148, 215
1973 Convention on the Suppression and Punish-
ment of the Crime of
Apartheid 131, 260
art.1................................. 131
1974 Charter of Economic
Rights and Duties of
States 33
Preamble........................ 27
art. 2(c) 221
art.30............................... 230
1974 Convention Governing
the Specific Aspects
of Refugee Problems
in Africa 217
1974 Declaration on the Establishment of a New
International Eco-
nomic Order.............221, 303
1974 Paris Convention for the
Prevention of Marine
Pollution from Land-
based Sources............. 183
1975 Convention on the Registration of Objects
Launched into Outer
Space 122
1976 Barcelona Convention
for the Protection of
the Mediterranean
against Pollution........ 183
1976 Rules of the United
Nations Commis-
sion on International
Trade Law (UNICI-
TRAL)........................... 338

1977	Convention on the Prohibition of Military or Any Other Hostile Use of Environmental Modification Techniques	238
1977	European Convention on the Suppression of Terrorism	
	art.1	140
1978	Sovereign Immunity Act	45
1978	Vienna Convention on the Succession of States in Respect of Treaties	293, 294
1979	Agreement Concerning the Activities of States on the Moon and Other Celestial Bodies	121
1979	Convention on Long-range Transboundary Air Pollution	233
	art.5	231
	Protocol (1984)	232
	Protocol (1985)	233
	Protocol (1988)	233
	Protocol (1991)	233
	Protocol (1994)	233
	Protocol (1998)	232
	Protocol (1999)	233
1979	Convention on the Elimination of All Forms of Discrimination Against Women	260
	Optional Protocol (2000)	262
1979	International Convention against the Taking of Hostages	134
1979	Treaty on the Limitation of Strategic Offensive Arms	327
1980	Convention for the Conservation of Antarctic Marine Living Resources	115
1980	Convention, prohibiting and restricting the use of certain conventional weapons deemed to be 'Excessively Injurious' or to have Indiscriminate Effects	325
	Protocol	325
	Protocol II	325
1980	Conventional Weapons Treaty	
	Protocol 1	238
1981	Banjul Charter on Human and Peoples' Rights (African Union)	263
	art.24	230
1981	Declaration on Claims Settlement (Iran/United States)	222
1982	Convention on the Law of the Sea	27, 30, 160, 161, 176, 179, 183, 184, 281, 335, 345
	Pt IV (arts 46–54)	167
	Pt VIII	166
	Pt XI	160, 190, 196, 199, 200
	Pt XV s.2	197
	art.1	161
	art.2	161
	art.3	103, 162
	art.4	163
	art.5	162
	art.6	166
	art.7(1)	163
	(2)	164
	(3)	163
	(4)	163
	(5)	164
	(6)	164
	art.8	169
	art.10(2)	165
	(4)	165
	(5)	165
	art.11	166
	art.13	166
	art.14	167
	art.15	18, 167
	art.16	164
	art.17	197
	art.18	168
	art.19	169
	art.21	170
	art.22	170
	art.23	170
	art.24	169
	(2)	169
	art.25	170
	(2)	170

(3)................................ 170
art.27............................. 171
art.28............................. 171
art.30............................. 171
art.31............................. 171
art.33............................. 173
art.37............................. 172
art.38............................. 171
(2)................................ 172
art.39............................. 172
art.41............................. 172
art.44............................. 172
art.45(1)(b) 172
(2)................................ 172
art.46............................. 167
art.47............................. 168
art.48............................. 168
art.49............................. 168
art.52............................. 168
art.53............................. 168
art.55........................21, 184
art.56........................21, 185
(2)................................ 187
art.57............................. 184
art.58(1) 187
(3)................................ 187
art.59............................. 27
art.61(1) 186
(2)................................ 186
(3)................................ 186
art.62(2) 186
(4)................................ 186
(5)................................ 186
art.63(1) 186
(2)................................ 186
art.64............................. 186
art.69............................. 186
art.70............................. 186
art.73............................. 186
art.74........................27, 193
(1)...........................187, 195
art.76.......................114, 189
(6)................................ 190
(7)................................ 190
(8)................................ 195
art.77............................. 190
art.78............................. 190
art.81............................. 190
art.82............................. 190
art.83............................. 27
(1)...........................193, 195
art.86............................. 173
art.87............................. 174

(2)................................ 174
art.88............................. 175
art.91.........................175, 226
art.92............................. 176
art.94.................... 176, 177
art.97............................. 177
art.101.................... 131, 178
art.105.................... 131, 177
art.106............................ 178
art.108............................ 179
art.109(3) 180
(4)................................ 180
art.110............................ 178
art.111............................ 181
arts 116–120 181
art.121.........................166, 167
(3)................................ 166
art.124............................ 174
art.132............................ 174
art.153............................ 196
arts 156–188 196
art.192............................ 183
arts 192–238 183
art.211............................ 176
art.219............................ 176
art.246............................ 190
art.283............................ 197
art.284............................ 197
art.287............................ 197
art.288............................ 197
art.290............................ 198
art.292............................ 198
art.297(1) 198
art.298............................ 195
art.309............................ 160
Annex VI...................... 197
Statute of the International
Tribunal
art.15(2) 199
1982 Manila Declaration on
the Peaceful Settle-
ment of International
Disputes..................... 333
1983 Vienna Convention on
Succession of States
in Respect of Prop-
erty, Archives and
Debts 294
1984 Sino–British Joint Declaration the Question
of Hong Kong 111, 294
1984 Convention against Torture and other Cruel,

Inhuman or Degrad-
ing Treatment or
Punishment 134, 154,
251, 260
art.5(1)(c)........................   135
Optional Protocol (2002)
....   262
1985 Declaration on the
Human Rights of
Individuals who are
not Nationals of the
Country in Which
They Live....................   214
1985 Supplementary Extradition Treaty between
United States and
United Kingdom........   140
1985 Vienna Convention for
the Protection of the
Ozone Layer...............   234
1986 Convention on Assistance in the Case of a
Nuclear Accident or
Radiological Emer-
gency...........................   237
1986 Convention on the Law
of Treaties between
States and Interna-
tional Organisations..   272
1986 Definition of Refugee
Status (Cartagena
Declaration)...............   217
1986 UN Convention on Conditions for Registra-
tion of Ships   176
1986 Vienna Convention on
Early Notification of
a Nuclear Accident....   231
1987 Declaration on the
Enhancement of the
Effectiveness of the
Principle of Refrain-
ing from the Threat
or Use of Force in
International Rela-
tions............................   300
1987 Montreal Protocol on
Substances that
Deplete the Ozone
Layer   234
1988 Agreement on Arctic Co-
operation   113
art.4................................   113

1988 Agreement on Co-
operation on the
Detailed Design
Development Opera-
tion and Utilisation
of the Permanently
Manned Civil Space
Station   121
1988 Agreement relating to
the Delimitation of
the Territorial Sea in
the Straits of Dover
(Anglo-French) 167, 172
1988 Convention against Illicit
Traffic in Narcotic
Drugs.........................134, 179
1989 Basel Convention on the
Control of Trans-
boundary Movement
of Hazardous Waste
and their Disposal.....   235
1989 Convention on the Rights
of the Child.50, 243, 260, 262
art.20(3)   243
Optional Protocol
(2012)..............................   96
1989 Draft Articles on the
Status of the Diplo-
matic Courier and
the Diplomatic Bag
Not Accompanied
by the Diplomatic
Courier......................150, 151
art.28..............................   150
(2).................................   151
art.29..............................   151
1989 Hague Declaration on the
Environment   234
1989 Helsinki Declaration on
the Protection of the
Ozone Layer...............   234
1990 Charter of Paris for a
New Europe 32, 274
1990 Convention on the Protection of the Rights
of All Migrant Work-
ers and Members of
their Families   260
1990 Treaty on the Establishment of German Unity ...294
art.11...............................   294
art.12...............................   294
1991 Convention on Envi-

ronmental Impact
Assessment................. 233
art.2.1............................. 234
1991 Declaration on Yugosla-
via and Guidelines
on the Recognition
of New States in
Eastern Europe and
in the Soviet Union,
December 16, 1991..... 68
1991 Draft Convention on
Yugoslavia, Novem-
ber 4, 1991................... 68
1991 Madrid Protocol on Environmental Protec-
tion to the Antarctic
Treaty........................... 116
art.7............................... 116
art.19............................. 116
art.23.1.......................... 116
art.24............................. 116
Sch. 116
1992 Cairo Declaration 216
1992 Convention for the Suppression of Unlaw-
ful Acts against the
Safety of Maritime
Navigation................... 179
art.2............................... 179
art.3............................... 179
art.3.1(a) 179
art.5............................... 180
art.6.1............................. 180
art.6.2............................. 180
art.10............................. 180
1992 Convention on Biological
Diversity 235
art.2............................... 235
1992 Convention on Civil
Liability for Oil Pol-
lution Damage 182
Protocol.......................... 182
1992 Convention on the Establishment of an Inter-
national Fund of
Compensation for Oil
Pollution Damage
and Protocol 182
1992 Convention on the Protection and Use
of Transboundary
Watercourses and
Lakes 236

1992 Convention on the Transboundary Effects of
Industrial Accidents.. 235
art.1(a)............................ 236
(i), (ii).......................... 236
art.2............................... 236
1992 Framework Convention
on Climate Change ... 234
art.7..........................234, 235
1992 Protocol for the Suppression of Unlawful Acts
against the Safety
of Fixed Platforms
Located on the Con-
tinental Shelf 179
1992 Rio Declaration on the
Environment and
Development.............32, 230
Principle 2...................... 230
Principle 7...................... 229
Principle 15.................... 232
Principle 16.................... 232
Principle 17.................... 232
1992 Treaty on European Union
art.1(3)............................ 90
art.47............................. 90
1993 Convention on the Applicability of the Devel-
opment, Production,
Stockpiling and Use
of Chemical Weap-
ons and on their
Destruction................. 238
1993 Convention on the Prohibition of the Devel-
opment, Production,
Stockpiling and Use
of Chemical Weap-
ons and On Their
Destruction................. 324
1993 Declaration on the Elimination of Violence
against Women 261
1993 Nuuk Declaration on the
Environment and
Development of the
Arctic........................... 114
1993 Statute of the International Criminal Tri-
bunal for the Former
Yugoslavia 97, 206
art.3............................... 137
art.4............................... 137

art.5................................. 137
art.6................................97, 140
art.7................................. 97
art.15.............................. 265
art.20.............................. 207
1993 Vienna Declaration....217,
242, 250, 330
Pt I para.18 261
Principle 5.................241, 242,
244
1994 Arab Charter on Human
Rights 263
1994 Canadian   Declaration
Recognising   the
Jurisdiction of the
Court as Compul-
sory, May 10, 1994 348
para.2(d) 347
1994 Convention on Nuclear
Safety........................... 237
1994 Convention to Combat
Desertification   in
those   Countries
Experiencing   Seri-
ous Drought and/or
Desertification, par-
ticularly in Africa 233
1994 North   America   Free
Trade   Agreement
(NAFTA).................... 57
1994 Statute of the International Criminal Tri-
bunal for Rwanda......97, 206
art.2................................. 137
art.3................................. 137
art.15.............................. 265
art.20.............................. 207
1995 Dayton/Paris Agreement
for Peace in Bosnia
and Herzegovina....... 335
1995 Treaty on the South
East Asia Nuclear
Weapon Free Zone 175
1995 World Trade Organisation (WTO) 57
1996 African Nuclear Weapon
Free Treaty................. 175
1996 Comprehensive Nuclear
Test Ban Treaty........... 328
1996 Convention on Extradition between the
Member States of the
European Union 140

1996 Declaration   on   the
Establishment of the
Arctic Council: Joint
Communique of the
Governments of the
Arctic Countries on
the Establishment of
the Arctic Council...... 114
1996 Draft Code of Crimes
against Peace and
Security of Mankind . 136
art.8................................. 137
art.12.............................. 142
art.16.............................. 301
1996 Draft Articles on the
Responsibility   of
States for Interna-
tionally Wrongful Acts
art.19..............................204, 208
1997 Alta declaration on the
Arctic Environmental
Protection Strategy.... 114
1997 Convention on the Law
of Non-navigational
Uses of International
Watercourses.............. 236
1997 Convention on the Prohibition on the Use,
Stockpiling, Produc-
tion and Transfer of
Anti-Personnel (AP)
Mines and on their
Destruction   (the
Ottawa Convention)
.....................................238, 325
1997 Kyoto Protocol (1997) 234, 235
1998 Oslo Accords between
Israel and the PLO..... 98
1998 Statute of the International Criminal Court
(Rome Statute) 36, 97,
99, 136, 137, 206, 268,
276, 281, 301
Chs 4, 9......................... 207
art.1................................. 139
art.5(1) 137, 268
(a)................................. 139
(b)................................. 139
(c) 139
(d) 139
art.6................................. 268
art.7................................137, 268
art.8.....................137, 268, 330

	(2)xxii	330
	art.8 bis...........................	302
	art.12..............................	139
	art.13..............................	139
	art.14..............................	139
	art.15..............................	139
	art.25(4)..........................	269
	art.27..............................	155
	art.30..............................	207
1999	Basel Protocol on Liability and Compensation for Damage Resulting from Transboundary Movements of Hazardous Waste and Their Disposal............	235
1999	Optional Protocol to the Convention on the Elimination of Discrimination against Women........................	96
2000	European Charter of Fundamental Rights	216
2000	New Monetary Convention between the Holy See and Italy, December 29, 2000.....	99
2000	Optional Protocol to the Convention of the Rights of the Child on the Involvement of Children in Armed Conflict.......................	260
2000	Optional Protocol to the Convention on the Rights of the Child Concerning the Sale of Children, Child Prostitution and Child Pornography ...	260
2000	Protocol against the Smuggling of Migrants by Land, Sea and Air................	181
2000	UN Convention against Transnational Organised Crime	181
2000	United Nations Millennium Declaration.......	32
2001	Convention on Cybercrime (European Council)	134

2001	Draft Articles on the Prevention of Transboundary Harm from Hazardous Activities........................	238
art.1	239	
2001	Draft Articles on the Responsibility of States for Internationally Wrongful Acts.............................	36
	Ch.II...............................	205
	Ch.III	209
	art.1................................	202
	arts 1–32.........................	201
	art.2..............................202, 203	
	art.3................................	203
	art.4................................	205
	art.5................................	205
	art.6................................	205
	art.7......................205, 206, 207	
	art.8..............................205, 206	
	arts 8–11	205
	art.9................................	205
	art.10.............................205, 207	
	art.11.............................	205
	art.12.............................203, 204	
	art.13.............................203, 207	
	art.16..............................	203
	art.17.............................203, 207	
	arts 20–25.......................	203
	art.26..............................	203
	art.30..............................	208
	art.31.....................204, 208, 211	
	arts 33–35.......................	201
	art.34..............................	210
	art.35..............................	210
	art.36..............................	211
	(1)....................................	210
	art.37..............................	211
	art.39..............................	204
	art.40.............................208, 209	
	(2)....................................	209
	art.41..............................	208
	(1), (2)	208
	art.42..............................	209
	art.48..............................	210
	arts 49–52.......................	301
2001	Marrakech Accords and Declaration....................	234
2002	Agreement between Sierra Leone and United Nations	266

2002 Nuclear Arms Reduction
      Treaty (the Moscow
      Treaty).......................... 327
2004 Convention on Jurisdic-
      tional   Immunities
      of States and Their
      Property...................... 145
2004 Treaty   No.108–23
      between   United
      States   and   United
      Kingdom...................... 140
2005 Convention   on   Action
      against   Trafficking
      in   Human   Beings
      (Council of Europe).134, 276
2005 Convention on Jurisdic-
      tional Immunities of
      States and their Prop-
      erty............................ 145
2005 Regional   Co-operation
      Agreement on Com-
      bating Piracy and
      Armed   Robbery
      against Ships in Asia.   179
2006 Convention for the Pro-
      tection of all Persons
      from Enforced Disap-
      pearance.....................96, 281
      art.31.............................. 262
2006 Convention on the Rights
      of Persons with Dis-
      abilities......................... 260
      Optional Protocol.........96, 262
2006 Draft Articles on Diplo-
      matic Protection........... 36
      art.1................................ 213
      art.3................................ 223
      art.4................................ 224
      art.5................................ 225
      art.6................................225, 226
      art.7................................225, 226
      art.8................................ 226
      art.9................................ 227
      art.10.............................. 227
      art.11.............................. 227
      (a)................................ 227
      (b)................................ 227
      art.14.............................. 229

      art.15.............................. 229
      art.19.............................. 212
2007 Declaration   on   the
      Rights of Indigenous
      Peoples........................ 261
2007 Treaty of Lisbon............... 90
2008 Convention   on   Cluster
      Munitions................... 325
      art.1................................ 326
2008 Ilulissat   Declaration,
      May 2008..................... 114
2008 Treaty on the Functioning
      of the European Union 2008
      art.18.............................. 215
      arts 45–48...................... 215
      art.263(4)....................... 96
2010 Agreement between the
      United Nations and
      the   Government
      of Sierra Leone on
      August 11, 2010
2010 New START Treaty........... 327
2011 Aeronautical and Mari-
      time   Search   and
      Rescue   Agreement
      (SAR Agreement) 114
2011 Draft Articles on Respon-
      sibility   of   Interna-
      tional Organisations.. 36
2011 Kampala Declaration..... 268
2013 Agreement on Coopera-
      tion on Marine Oil
      Pollution   Prepared-
      ness and Response in
      the Arctic.................... 114
2013 Arms Trade Treaty............ 326
      art.22.............................. 326
2013 Yaoundé Declaration on
      the Gulf of Guinea
      Security   which
      addresses piracy and
      other illegal activities
      in West and Central
      Africa.......................... 179
2014 United Kingdom Dec-
      laration   deposited
      December 31, 2014..... 348
2015 Paris Agreement.............. 235

TABLE OF RESOLUTIONS

1950 General Assembly Resolution 377, November 3, 1950 314

1950 General Assembly Resolution 5/428 (Annex), December 1950 216

1960 General Assembly Resolution 1514 (XV), December 14, 1960 .... 32, 33 70, 71

1962 General Assembly Resolution 1803, December 14, 1962 .... 218, 220 para.4 219

1965 General Assembly Resolution 2131 (XX), December 21, 1965 319

1965 Security Council Resolution 216, November 12, 1965 69

1965 Security Council Resolution 217, November 20, 1965 69

1966 Security Council Resolution 221, April 9, 1966 322

1967 Security Council Resolution 242 (XXII), November 22, 1967 110

1970 ECOSOC Resolution 1503 (XLVII), May 27, 1970 259

1970 General Assembly Resolution 2625 (XXV), October 24, 1970 ...19, 33, 71, 78, 300, 319, 333 para.X 109

1970 General Assembly Resolution 2749 (XXV), December 17, 1970 ..... 196 art.1 .... 196 art.3 196

1971 General Assembly Resolution 2784 (XXVI), December 6, 1971 131

1973 General Assembly Resolution 3171 (XXVIII), December 17, 1973 221

1974 General Assembly Resolution 3201 (S-VI), May 1, 1974 221

1974 General Assembly Resolution 3314 (XXIX), December 14, 1974 .... 300, 301, 302 art.3 .... 301 art.5(2) 301

1975 General Assembly Resolution 3281 (XXIV), December 12, 1974 .... 27, 33, 221

1976 General Assembly Resolution, GAOR, 31st Session, Supp.39, p.10 69

1983 Security Council Resolu-

tion 541, November
18, 1983........................78, 110

1985 General Assembly Resolution 144 (XL)
December 11, 1985...214, 248

1987 General Assembly
Resolution 42/22,
November 1987.......... 300

1990 Security Council Resolution 660, August 2,
1990...........................110, 311

1990 Security Council Resolution 661, August 6,
1990...........................308, 312

1990 Security Council Resolution 662, August 9,
1990.............................. 110

1990 Security Council Resolution 664, August 18,
1990.............................. 149

1990 Security Council Resolution 665, August 25,
1990.............................. 312

1990 Security Council Resolution 666, September
13, 1990........................ 312

1990 Security Council Resolution 667, September
16, 1990........................ 149

1990 Security Council Resolution 670, September
25, 1990........................ 312

1991 Security Council Resolution 687, April 3, 1991
...........................312, 321, 339

1991 Security Council Resolution 688, April 5, 1991
.... 322

1991 Security Council Resolution 713, September
25, 1991........................ 312

1992 General Assembly
Resolution 47/191,
December 22, 1992..... 238

1992 Security Council Resolution 731, January 21,
1992.............................. 312

1992 Security Council Resolution 748, March 31,
1992...........................311, 312

1992 Security Council Resolution 777, December
19, 1992........................ 88

1993 General Assembly Resolution 48/7, October
19, 1993........................ 325

1993 General Assembly Resolution 48/75K,
November 1993.......... 325

1993 General Assembly
Resolution 48/141,
December 20, 1993..... 259

1993 General Assembly
Resolution 48/157,
December 20, 1993..... 325

1993 Security Council Resolution 827, May 25,
1993.....................97, 138, 264

1994 General Assembly Resolution 48/263, July
28, 1994........................ 160
art.1................................... 157
art.2................................... 157

1994 General Assembly Resolution 49/75 K,
December 15, 1994...328, 359

1994 Security Council Resolution 955, November
8, 1994.................97, 138, 264

1995 General Assembly Resolution 49/126, Janu-
ary 20, 1995................ 243

1995 General Assembly Resolution 50/46, Decem-
ber 11, 1995................. 268

1995 Security Council Resolution 986, April 14,
1995.............................. 312

1996 General Assembly
Resolution 51/204
December 17, 1996..... 198

1996 Security Council Resolution 1067, July 26,
1996.............................. 120

1997 General Assembly Resolution 51/229 May
21, 1997........................ 236

1998 Security Council Resolution 1199, September
23, 1998........................ 320

1999 Security Council Resolution 1244, June 10,
1999.............................. 94

1999 Security Council Resolution 1284, December
17, 1999........................ 312

2000 General Assembly Resolution 54/263, May 25, 2000...... 260

2000 Security Council Resolution 1308...... 311

2000 Security Council Resolution 1325, October 31, 2000...... 250

2001 General Assembly Resolution 56/83 December 1, 2001...... 201

2001 Security Council Resolution 1368, September 12, 2001......306, 307

2001 Security Council Resolution 1373, September 28, 2001......306, 307, 312

2002 Resolution of the Human Rights Commission Globalisation and its Consequences for the Effective Enjoyment of Human Rights 2002/28, April 22, 2002...... 245

2002 General Assembly Resolution 57/228B, May 13, 2002...... 266

2002 Security Council Resolution 1409, May 14, 2002...... 312

2002 Security Council Resolution 1422, July 12, 2002 ...318

2003 Security Council Resolution 1472, March 28, 2003...... 312

2003 Security Council Resolution 1483, May 22, 2003...... 312

2006 General Assembly Resolution 60/251, March 15, 2006...... 257

2006 General Assembly Resolution 61/36 December 18, 2006...... 239

2006 Security Council Resolution 1674, April 28, 2006 para.4...... 321

2006 Security Council Resolution 1706, August 31, 2006 Preamble, para.2...... 321

2007 Security Council Resolutions 1769 (2007)...... 317

2008 Security Council Resolutions 1816 (2008)...... 178

2008 Security Council Resolutions 1846 (2008)...... 178

2008 Security Council Resolution 1851 (2008)...... 178

2009 Resolution on the Law of Transboundary Aquifers, A/RES/63/124, December 11, 2009..... 236

2010 Security Council Resolution 1966 (2010), December 22, 2010, S/RES/1966(2010)..... 265

2011 Human Rights Council Resolution 16/21 and Decision 17/119, March 25, 2011 259

2011 Security Council Resolution 1973 (2011)...... 320

2011 Security Council Resolution 1976 (2008)...... 178

2011 Security Council Resolution 2015 (2008)...... 178

2011 Security Council Resolution 2020 (2008)...... 178

2011 Security Council Resolution 2125 (2008)...... 178

2013 Security Council Resolution 2100 (2013)...... 317

2013 Security Council Resolution 2118 (2013)...... 324

2014 UNGA Resolution 68/262 of 27 March 2014......79, 110, 111

2014 Security Council Resolution 2166 (2014), July 21, 2014...... 120

TABLE OF NATIONAL LEGISLATION

Australia
1994 Crimes (Child Sex Tourism Amendment) Act
Pt IIIA 128

Canada
Criminal Code
s.75 178
s.76 178
Canadian Declaration
para.2(d) 174
1982 State Immunity Act 145
1985 Coastal Fisheries Protection Act 174

Germany
Constitution
art.25 43

Iceland
1972 Resolution of the Althing, February 15, 1972 185
1972 Regulations July 14, 1972 185

Sierra Leone
2002 Special Court Agreement 2002, Ratification Act
2002 266

South Africa
Bill of Rights 43
1996 Constitution 43

United Kingdom
1964 Diplomatic Privileges Act
(c.81) 83, 153
1976 Fishery Limits Act (c.86).. 166
1978 State Immunity Act
(c.33) 45, 144
s.3(3)(a) 144
s.21 50
1980 Protection of Trading
Interests Act (c.11) 128
1987 Territorial Sea Act 1987
(Commencement)
Order (SI 1987/1270) 162
1988 Criminal Justice Act (c.33)
s.134 155
1989 Official Secrets Act (c.6)
s.15 130
1989 Extradition Act (c.33) 141
1993 Criminal Justice Act
(c.36) 127
1998 Scotland Act (c.46) 48
s.58(1) 59
1998 Human Rights Act (c.42) . 48
s.4 49
2002 European Union Extradition Regulations (SI
2002/419) 140
s.6 48
2001 Anti-Terrorism, Crime
and Security Act
(c.24) 140
s.23 49
2010 Constitutional Reform

and Governance Act
(c.25) 48
s.24 48

United States
Constitution
art.II(2) 52
art.VI 52, 56
Lieber Code 324
1789 Alien Tort Claims Act 155
1913 Act of Congress 57, 58
1918 Migratory Bird Treaty Act. 57
1965 Foreign Assistance Act
s.620(e)(2) 61
1972 Case Act (as amended
1977 and 1978) 56
1976 Foreign Sovereign Immunities Act 144

1978 Diplomatic Relations Act 153
1986 Omnibus   Diplomatic
Security and Anti-
Terrorism Act 135
1991 Torture Victim Prevention Act 156
1996 Helms-Burton Act 129
1996 Iran Sanctions Act 129
2001 Public Law 107–40 135
2010 Comprehensive   Iran
Sanctions   Account-
ability and Divest-
ment Act 129
2011 Executive Order 13590 129

Vatican City
1929. Fundamental Law of the
Vatican 99

TABLE OF EUROPEAN SECONDARY LEGISLATION

Directives
2004   Dir.2004/38 on the right
of citizens of the
Union and their
family members to
move and reside
freely within the
—territory of the
Member States 2004
OJ L158/77 216

1. INTRODUCTION

International law, specifically public international law,[1] is the focus of this text. Public international law is distinct from private international law or, to use the correct term, conflict of laws. It also should be distinguished from foreign relations law.[2] The term international law as used throughout the text refers therefore to public international law.

---

[1] The term was first coined by Jeremy Bentham in *Introduction to the Principles of Morals and Legislation* (1789).

[2] Private international law (conflict of laws) is a system of law, which is part of a state's domestic law and is utilised to determine the legal system applicable to a dispute and which jurisdiction should resolve it. Foreign relations law "consists of rules of public international law which are binding upon [a State], and such parts of [a State's] law as are concerned with the means by which effect is given to the rules of public international law or which involve matters of concern to [a State] in the conduct of its relation with foreign States and governments or their nationals." Restatement of the Law Third, The American Law Institute, Restatement of the Law, the Foreign Relations Law of the United States, Vol. 1, 1–488, 14 May 1986. Foreign relations law of the US, for example, encompasses both international law, which embodies the rules that determine the rights and obligations of states and international organisations, and that part of the domestic law of the US that involves matters of significant concern to the foreign relations of the US.

DEFINITION

Contemporary international law comprises those rules and norms that regulate the conduct of states and other entities which at any given time are recognised as possessing international personality,[3] for example, international organisations and individuals to the extent they are afforded it by states. This represents a working definition which acknowledges the "youthfulness" of the international legal system and recognises entities other than states as actors on the international stage. Although states remain the primary subjects of international law, they are no longer its only subjects. International law was initially concerned exclusively with regulating relations between independent states and then mainly in respect of diplomatic relations and the conduct of war.

The subjects of international law have increased and its content has expanded. Major problems of international concern demand collective state action. A consequence of collective action has been the proliferation in the number of international organisations particularly post-Second World War.

Modern technology has brought states and their peoples into closer and more frequent contact with each other and, accordingly, rules have had to evolve so that such contact is regulated. The subject matter of international law has also expanded, and the international legal system now encompasses within its ambit subject matter which traditionally was regarded as being exclusively within a state's domestic jurisdiction, e.g. treatment of a state's own nationals and a state's use of its territory. This in turn has had repercussions for individuals who are now recognised as possessing some, albeit at times limited, international personality. A further repercussion has been the eroding of state sovereignty in favour of greater recognition of human rights, which can lead to tension.

The traditional definition of international law, as a system that regulates state relations, is too rigid and outmoded. International law has had to be, and must continue to be, sufficiently flexible to accommodate developments in the international sphere. The international legal system must reflect, and help to shape, the contemporary international community.

NATURE AND CHARACTERISTICS OF INTERNATIONAL LAW

Is international law, law?

International law has had to confront this question since its origins. This is not the place to explore this question in detail, as

---

[3] International personality is dealt with in Ch.4.

it is more aptly suited for consideration within a jurisprudence class. The authors' approach in this textbook is premised on the assumption that international law is law. States acknowledge it as such, with some making explicit reference to international law in their constitutions. It is also evident that states generally like to be seen to be acting in accordance with international law and to this end legal advisers are employed to formulate, present and defend a state's position based on international law. Others recognise international law, but deny its effectiveness. However what many of those who are dismissive of international law fail to appreciate is that *their* expectations of international law may be unrealistic. Often, law cannot coerce states in matters which are highly political. International law cannot of itself, and by itself, dictate the policies and behaviour of states.

If force is used contrary to international law, international law is criticised for failing to maintain international peace, yet international law cannot prevent its own violation any more than a municipal criminal law can prevent crimes being committed, or contract law can prevent contracts from being broken. The violation of law does not in itself negate the legal hallmark of a system of law. Law is not a solution in itself, but is rather a means employed to handle a particular situation. The international legal system does not operate in a vacuum any more than any other legal system. International law is concerned with promoting international co-operation and achieving the co-existence of states, but depends on political willingness for its success.

It is undeniable that international law breaks down. However, when that happens, the fault lies not with international law itself, but those operating within the international legal system. Be that as it may, it is invariably international law that receives the bad press, especially when it fails to prevent a conflict or resolve a dispute because the issues involved are politically sensitive. What gets overlooked is that international law functions very effectively on a day-to-day level. Technology allows people to communicate globally, international travel is an everyday occurrence and the cross-boundary movement of goods is facilitated. Pressing the "on" switch of the television allows events to be viewed live regardless of time and location. All of this is taken for granted, yet it is only made possible through the efficient functioning of international law. Unfortunately such "low-key" successes of international law are not newsworthy and do not make the headlines.

What are the characteristics of international law?

The principal participants of the international legal system are states. States are equally sovereign.[4] International law is not imposed on states—there is no international legislature. The international legal system is decentralised. It is founded essentially on consensus and the consent of states to assume obligations that set parameters on, and thus perhaps limit, their behaviour. International law is made primarily by one of two ways: through the practice of states (customary international law) and through agreements entered into by states (treaties).[5] International rules, once established, have an imperative character and cannot be unilaterally modified at will by states. The absence of a strong enforcement machinery is highlighted by critics and sceptics as a weakness of international law. Admittedly there is no international police force, nor is there an international court with compulsory jurisdiction to which states are *required* to submit. However, the creation of a permanent International Criminal Court, as well as the creation of other judicial bodies and quasi-judicial bodies for the peaceful settlement of disputes, highlights an increasing commitment to the rule of law. This is further reflected in the increasing case load of the International Court of Justice (ICJ) to which states can refer their disputes for settlement. Such referral is, of course, not compulsory and states are not required to submit to the Court's jurisdiction: states must *consent* to submit to the jurisdiction of the Court.

International law is not however ineffective. International responsibility can be incurred if a breach of international law is established. Sanctions are permissible in certain circumstances and these may be adopted and influence an "offending" state's conduct. If international law is violated, there are a number of self-help measures that the "victim" state may adopt, e.g. a treaty may be suspended or terminated, or the assets of an "offending" state may be frozen. The United Nations Security Council may authorise diplomatic and economic sanctions, while the use of force may be authorised in specifically defined circumstances. Public opinion is also an effective sanction. States mostly want to be seen to be adhering to international law: why otherwise do they make considerable efforts to justify their particular position in international law? However, political pragmatism may dictate a route which adheres less closely to that which international law would dictate.

---

[4] This is a legal fiction, as obviously some states carry more weight politically than others in the international community.

[5] See Ch.2, "Sources".

The role of reciprocity in ensuring observance of international law should not be minimised. It is in a state's self-interest to respect, for example, the territorial sovereignty of another state premised on the expectation that such respect will be mutually reciprocated. The international legal system is intrinsically different from municipal law and to expect the international legal system to match the requirements of a domestic legal system is to invite disappointment.

THE DEVELOPMENT OF INTERNATIONAL LAW

International law as a legal system is of relatively recent origin.[6] Modern international law stems from the rise of the secular sovereign state in Western Europe. As in any community, law was required to regulate the relations of states with each other. The rules of war and those on diplomatic relations were the earliest expressions of international law. The Age of Discovery in the 16th and 17th centuries necessitated the evolution of rules governing the acquisition of territory. At the same time, the principle of the freedom of the seas was articulated allowing for the expansion of trade. International law grew out of necessity, namely, the need for states to co-exist.

International law sets the parameters of state action; these parameters established domestic competence within which states enjoyed freedom of action. International law continued to expand as international engagement increased and by the 19th century had become, geographically at least, a universal system. It remained, however, rooted in Western European traditions and values and its concept and content reflected this bias.

The 20th century witnessed major changes with commensurate repercussions for the international legal system. Two major wars underscored the need for international cooperation and out of this need the United Nations was created—a virtually universal institution designed to promote such cooperation. Matters once considered exclusively within domestic jurisdiction became the possible subjects of international review and regulation, and the use of force was limited except in strictly prescribed circumstances. New values occupied centre stage among the international community's priorities and individuals became a concern of international law. Following decolonisation, the mostly homogeneous international community became a diverse group of

---

[6] Although the embryo of international concepts was apparent within Greek City States, e.g. it was recognised that citizens of states in other territories had rights. There was, however, no concept of an international community as such.

states, with many of its foundational rules being challenged by the newly independent states.

The unparalleled expansion of international law during the 20th century continues to this day. International law in the 21st century is no longer the preserve of some 50 states, but rather encompasses 193 states.[7] The international legal system is no longer an exclusive "Western club" but is composed of a heterogeneous group of states, which differ politically, economically, culturally and ideologically, as well as many non-state actors.

International law is constantly evolving and developing to accommodate contemporary needs and demands. It is not simply lawyers' black letter law, and politics does play an influential role. It now operates within the changing context of globalisation. It has, for instance, to address the issue of non-state actors, their demands and responsibilities, e.g. transnational corporations and their liability for alleged violations of human rights and the role of non-governmental organisations in contemporary international society.

The existence of international law per se is generally not challenged, but the substantive content of its expression has been challenged and continues to be so. Human rights and the protection of the individual have assumed a high profile on the international agenda, as has sustainable development, with a particular emphasis on environmental issues such as climate change and bio-diversity. The European bias of international law has, arguably, been significantly reduced and other political ideologies are now heard within the international forum on a more equal basis. Modern technology has brought states into more frequent contact with each other, and in doing so has extended the remit of international law into new fields, e.g. outer space, the deep seabed and the internet. International law has had to meet, and continues to face, new challenges—challenges which demand an international response either at governmental level and/or by way of international regulation, as individual state action proves inadequate and deficient. These challenges today are multiple, many of which revolve around how to protect humans and their environments, from, inter alia, natural disasters and climate change, poverty, food and water scarcity, terrorism. A further concern is how to manage the mass migration of those fleeing for a better life, free from misery, war and hardship.

The expansion of international law has meant that the international legal system has become increasingly specialised and compartmentalised. Arguably this is accompanied by international law becoming more fragmented, and in turn the risk of people's

---

[7] This represents the number of Member States of the United Nations.

knowledge of it being similarly fragmented. The range of university courses on offer indicates this, e.g. international dispute resolution, international environment law, international trade law, international human rights law, international criminal law are but a few examples. "International" has become a much used prefix. The subject matter of this text is the contemporary international legal system, with an emphasis on its basic principles.

2. SOURCES

Rules and norms of any legal system derive authority from their source.[1] The sources articulate what the law is and where it can be found. In a developed municipal legal system, sources may be readily identifiable in the form, for example, of parliamentary legislation and judicial decisions. However, on the international plane there is neither an international legislature passing global legislation, nor is there an international court to whose jurisdiction all members of the international community are required to submit. Furthermore, the international legal system, unlike many municipal legal systems, does not possess a universally-applicable written constitution. There is no identification of the principal organs of government, investing them with authority, or defining the scope of their power and the procedures by which such power may be exercised.

In the absence of such "law-giving" sources, how is the lawfulness of alleged rules of international law assessed?

Article 38 of the Statute of the International Court of Justice (ICJ) provides an answer. This is a pragmatic response as art.38 does not mention "sources", but is rather a direction to the ICJ

---

[1] "Sources" may be interpreted in a variety of ways, e.g. the underlying reason why laws develop, but here its meaning is confined to that given in the text.

on how disputes which come before it should be approached. Article 38 of the ICJ Statute provides:

> "1) The Court, whose function is to decide in accordance with international law such disputes as are submitted to it, shall apply:
>
> (a) international conventions, whether general or particular, establishing rules expressly recognized by the contesting states;
>
> (b) international custom, as evidence of a general practice accepted as law;
>
> (c) the general principles of law recognized by civilized nations;
>
> (d) subject to the provisions of Article 59, judicial decisions and the teachings of the most highly qualified publicists of the various nations, as subsidiary means for the determination of rules of law."

Sources of international law have traditionally been characterised as formal or material. Formal sources constitute what the law is, whereas material sources identify where the law is to be found. Hence, art.38(1)(a)–(c) (treaties, custom and general principles) are formal sources, whereas art.38(1)(d) (judicial decisions and juristic teachings) are material sources.

Article 38(2) "recognizes the power of the Court to decide a case *ex aequo et bono*, if the parties agree thereto." Invoking this provision, states may request the Court to decide a case not just on the application of strict rules of law but by reference to such principles as fairness and equality. This provision has not as yet been used.

Article 38, although primarily a direction to the ICJ on how disputes coming before it should be tackled, is regarded as an authoritative statement on the sources of international law. Although art.38 does not profess to establish a hierarchy, in practice it does set out a hierarchy of procedure for the application of international law in the settlement of international disputes. Initially, existing relevant treaty provisions subsisting between the parties to the dispute must be applied. In the absence of a treaty provision, a custom, which is accepted as legally binding, is to be applied. If neither a treaty provision nor a custom can be identified then "general principles as recognized by civilized nations" may be invoked.

Judicial decisions and judicial writings may be utilised as a means of determining the rules of international law, but they are not themselves sources of law. The lack of a formal hierarchy of the sources of international law makes their interaction somewhat complex. This complexity is further compounded by the increasing specialisation and compartmentalisation of international law into discrete fields, what is described by the International Law Commission as "the fragmentation of international law".[2] Furthermore, art.38 does not reflect some of the non-traditional, more dynamic sources of law that contemporary international law relies on, such as the acts of international organisations and soft law.

The absence of a hierarchy between the sources of international law does not preclude some norms prevailing over others, as is illustrated at the end of this chapter.

Each source of law identified in art.38 is now considered. Custom is considered initially because, although cited second, historically it preceded treaties.

CUSTOM

In any society, rules of "acceptable" behaviour develop at an early stage and the international community was no exception. States initially, because of their limited relations with each other, often did, for whatever motives, what they wanted to do rather than what had been agreed. However, with increasing contact between states, certain norms of behaviour crystallised into rules of customary international law. Custom, through the absence of an international executive and legislature, has exercised an influential role in the formation of international law. As a legal system matures, the importance of custom recedes. In the context of international law custom, until at least recently, remained a dynamic source of law and its contribution is still reflected in many treaties, which mirror previously established rules of international customary law.

Definition of custom

What is meant by custom? Custom in international law is a practice followed by those concerned because they feel legally obliged to behave in such a way. Custom must be distinguished from mere usage, such as behaviour which may be done out of courtesy, friendship or convenience, rather than out of legal obligation or a feeling that non-compliance would produce legal consequences, for example sanctions imposed by other members of the international community.

---

[2] ILC, Fragmentation of International Law: Difficulties Arising from the Diversification and Expansion of International Law, UN Doc. A-CN.4-L.682, 13 April 2006.

How is custom differentiated from behaviour that is motivated by reasons other than legal obligation? A rule of customary
international law derives its law hallmark through the possession
of two elements: (i) a material element and (ii) a psychological
element.

The material element refers to the behaviour and practice
of states, whereas the psychological element (*opinio juris sive
necessitatis*) is the subjective conviction held by states that the
behaviour in question is compulsory and not discretionary.
Accordingly, any alleged rule of customary international law
must be assessed as to its two elements.

Material element—state practice

The material element refers to the behaviour of states. However
certain criteria have to be considered relating to the behaviour's
duration, frequency, consistency and universality. Also, for the
purposes of international law, what constitutes state practice?

Duration of practice

There is no set time limit and no requirement that the practice
should be engaged in since "time immemorial". The fact that a
practice has been engaged in only for a brief period of time will
not in itself be an impediment to the formation of a customary
rule, provided that the other requirements of custom are satisfied.
The relative unimportance of time, if other criteria are met, was
highlighted by the ICJ in the *North Sea Continental Shelf* cases,[3] in
which it stated:

> "Although the passage of only a short period of time is not
> necessarily, or of itself, a bar to the formation of a new rule
> of customary international law . . . an indispensable require-
> ment would be that within the period in question, short
> though it might be, State practice . . . should have been both
> extensive and virtually uniform in the sense of the provision
> invoked—and should moreover have occurred in such a way
> as to show a general recognition that a rule of law or legal
> obligation is involved."[4]

The length of time required to establish a rule of customary
international law will depend upon other factors pertinent to the
alleged rule. If, for example, the rule is dealing with subject matter
in which no previously established rules exist, then the duration

---

[3] I.C.J. Rep. 1969 at 3.
[4] I.C.J. Rep. 1969 at 43.

of the practice will require to be less than if there is an existing rule to be amended. Time has also become less important as international communication has improved. It is now much easier to assess a state's response to an alleged rule than it was previously. Time thus may be of little importance in assessing a state's behaviour, and its importance in any given case depends on other factors peculiar to the activity concerned. These are examined below.

Extent of state practice

The ICJ in the *Asylum* case[5] held that before state practice could be acknowledged as law, it had to be in accordance with a "constant and uniform usage" practised by the states in question.[6] Of course, although a particular pattern of behaviour may be engaged in frequently, it does not follow that the conduct is being practised out of any sense of legal obligation. Conversely, an activity engaged in, albeit infrequently, may be practised because of a feeling of a legal compulsion to act in such a way. The importance of frequency of practice will depend upon the circumstances surrounding each alleged rule. For instance, a state which is able to cite two examples of state practice to support its contention that the practice is law, will be in a better position than the state which can cite no such examples. However, a more significant factor than frequency is the consistency of practice, i.e. do those states engaging in the practice in question behave in a like manner, thus demonstrating conformity?

The Court's judgment in the *Asylum* case is again instructive on this point. In that case, the Court maintained that there was too much variance and discrepancy in both the state practice and the views expressed regarding diplomatic asylum for a rule of customary international law to have been established. Consequently, the Court concluded that it was impossible to find "any constant and uniform usage accepted as law".[7] The existence of diverging practice proved to be the stumbling block in that particular practice's evolution into law.

Inconsistency of practice per se, however, is not sufficient to negate the crystallisation of a rule into customary international law. Any inconsistency must be analysed and assessed in light of factors such as subject matter; the identity of the states practising the inconsistency; the number of states involved; and whether or not there are existing established rules with which the alleged rule conflicts. Inconsistency of practice is explored in greater

---

[5] I.C.J. Rep. 1950 at 266.
[6] I.C.J. Rep. 1950 at 277.
[7] I.C.J. Rep. 1950 at 266.

depth below, when the question of how customary international law may be amended or modified is discussed.

How many states must be involved in a particular activity before the practice is accepted as law? Universal practice is fortunately not necessary. Article 38(1)(b) speaks not of universal practice, but of a general practice. A practice can be general even if it is not universally followed by all states, nor is there any precise formula indicating how widespread a behaviour must be for it to cross the threshold into customary law.

What is more important than the number of states involved is the attitude of those states whose interests are actually affected. It is the stance of such affected states which is relevant and which has to be considered, as emphasised by the ICJ in the *North Sea Continental Shelf* cases

> "an indispensable requirement would be that within the period in question, . . . State practice, including that of States whose interests are specially affected, should have been both extensive and virtually uniform in the sense of the provision invoked "[8]

The number of states, therefore, is less consequential than is the identity of the states involved. Each alleged rule must therefore be examined and assessed in context. In every sphere certain states carry more weight than others—their interest is greater and their attitude to an alleged rule is of more importance. If an alleged rule is to attain legitimacy, a favourable response from "leading" states is a prerequisite. Hence, for example, Britain's greater contribution in the 19th century to the law of the sea, and the role of both the US and the then Soviet Union in developing the law of outer space.

Numbers are more important when the custom is a local, regional one, involving fewer states than general customary law. A regional custom is arguably more contractual in nature than a general one and therefore is required to be positively acknowledged and supported by all the states involved. Hence, the ICJ's emphasis in the *Asylum* case on a "constant and uniform usage".

Can a state choose not to be bound by a rule of customary international law? If a state opposes a rule of customary international law and expresses opposition to that rule from the time of the rule's inception, then the state will not be bound by the said rule. Opposition to the rule, however, must be demonstrated from the outset. Only then can the state concerned not incur liability. In the Anglo-Norwegian Fisheries case, the Court held that if the

[8] Above, fn.3 and 4.

particular rule in question was one of international law, it would be "inapplicable as against Norway inasmuch as she has always opposed any attempt to apply it to the Norwegian coast".[9]

Dissent which is expressed only after the rule has become established is too late to prevent the state from being bound, and likewise, early opposition by a state to a rule, if abandoned, loses its effectiveness. Dissent, of course, only prevents a rule from becoming binding on the dissenting state and does not affect the rule's application vis-à-vis other states.

Why is dissent important? Expression of dissent is vital as in reality attaining a state's consent is not practical. State consent is difficult to prove and consent has to be inferred. Silence, although it may stem from indifference, will be regarded as acquiescence and will serve to reinforce the particular practice as law.

A new state entering the international legal community after a practice has ripened into international customary law is bound by that rule, regardless of whether it agrees with the rule or not. Such a state may seek though to amend or modify the rule in question. How may this occur? Undoubtedly it is easier for custom to develop if there are no pre-existing conflicting rules. For example, in the exploration of outer space, rules of behaviour quickly evolved because not only were there no pre-existing norms regulating behaviour, there were only two states, the US and the then Soviet Union, actively engaged in exploration.

The position is different and more complicated if established rules of behaviour exist. In the situation where a "new" rule develops in an area where there is an existing rule, the "new" rule's future will depend on the number indulging in the behaviour contrary to the established rule relative to the number protesting against the creation of the new rule.

The practice of states in the application of the rules in question does not need to be perfect. That is in the sense that states should have refrained, with complete consistency, from behaviour contrary to the established rule. The ICJ does not maintain that state practice must be in absolute rigorous conformity with the rule for it to be considered as custom. In the Court's opinion it is sufficient that the conduct of states should, in general, be consistent with such rules, and that instances of state conduct inconsistent with a given rule should generally be treated as breaches of that rule, not as indications of the recognition of a new rule.[10]

---

[9] I.C.J. Rep. 1951 116 at 131. Arguably the opportunities for states to opt out of customary international law are fewer today than previously, given the increase in the use of treaties as a medium of international regulation.

[10] *Military and Paramilitary Activities In and Against Nicaragua (Nicaragua v The United States) (Merits)* I.C.J. Rep. 1986 14 at 98.

This raises the question as to how customary international law may be amended or modified if conflicting behaviour acts as a hindrance to the crystallisation of a practice into law. Contradictory behaviour has the effect of throwing uncertainty on the apparently established rule, which in turn produces ambiguity regarding the law of the subject matter. This was highlighted in the *Fisheries Jurisdiction (United Kingdom v Iceland) Merits*,[11] which came before the International Court of Justice in 1974, when in a Joint Separate Opinion, Judges Forster, Bengzon, Arechaga, Singh and Rudha expressed the view:

> "If the law relating to fisheries constituted a subject on which there were clear indications of what precisely is the rule of international law in existence, it may then have been possible to disregard altogether the legal significance of certain proposals which advocate changes or improvements in a system of law which is considered to be unjust or inadequate. But this is not the situation. There is at the moment great uncertainty as to the existing customary law on account of the conflicting and discordant practice of States. Once the uncertainty of such a practice is admitted, the impact of the aforesaid official pronouncements, declarations and proposals have an unsettling effect on the crystallisation of a still evolving customary law on the subject."[12]

It is also possible, as is reflected in the aforementioned Opinion, that while states may behave in contradiction to an established rule, the conflicting behaviour may itself be inconsistently expressed. In such circumstances, change, if it is to come about, will take longer than if the states demonstrate a consensus on the content of the emerging new law. If support is wide and consistent, then the practice's acceptance as law will be relatively smooth and rapid. Similarly, if there is substantial opposition to the "new" rule, the established accepted practice will remain as law. However, if the members of the international community are evenly divided in their support for the established law and the alleged new law, then a period of ambiguity will, as a consequence, follow. Indeed, there may be a time when two rules of customary law exist side by side. International customary law can accommodate change, but how quickly that change will occur is dependent upon the response of states to the proposed change of the law. There may well be a period in the change process when what is established and what is emerging exist simultaneously. In

---

[11] I.C.J. Rep. 1974 at 3.
[12] I.C.J. Rep. 1974 at 48.

such circumstances there is a fine line between the ending of the old law and the beginning of the new one.

This has the advantage, particularly if states are agreed upon the change they want, of providing flexibility, but the disadvantage of creating uncertainty as to what the law is at a particular time.

Evidence of state practice

Finally, what, for the purposes of establishing customary international law, constitutes evidence of state practice? Treaties, diplomatic correspondence, statements by national legal advisers in domestic and international fora are among the indicators of state practice. This was endorsed by Ammoun J in his Separate Opinion delivered in the *Barcelona Traction, Light and Power Company* case,[13] when he stated:

> "to return to State practice as manifested within international organisations and conferences, it cannot be denied, with regard to the resolutions which emerge therefrom, or better, with regard to the votes expressed therein in the name of States, that these amount to precedents contributing to the formation of custom."[14]

Notwithstanding these indicators, overt state practice continues to be important, as was emphasised by the ICJ in *Continental Shelf (Libya v Malta)*[15] when the Court stated:

> "It is of course axiomatic that the material of customary international law is to be looked for primarily in the actual practice and *opinio juris* of States even though multilateral conventions may have an important role to play in defining and recording rules, deriving from custom or indeed in developing them."[16]

The ICJ has also highlighted that, when considering the existence of a general custom, it is necessary to determine that from the practice of states as a whole: the fact the states party to the case have a common view of what the law is, is not sufficient.[17] However it

---

[13] (Second Phase) I.C.J. Rep. 1970 at 3.

[14] (Second Phase) I.C.J. Rep. 1970 at 303. As to the role of Resolutions in providing evidence of *opinio juris*, see statements in the *Nicaragua (Merits)* case, above, fn.10.

[15] I.C.J. Rep. 1985 at p.13.

[16] I.C.J. Rep. 1985 at 29–30. See, also the view of A. D'Amato, *The Concept of Custom in International Law* (Ithaca, NY: Cornell University Press, 1971), p.88.

[17] Above, fn.10, para.184.

should be noted that in the *Maritime Delimitation and Territorial Questions between Qatar and Bahrain* case[18] it was accepted that the parties to the case agreed that art.15 of the 1982 Law of the Sea Convention was part of customary law. The Court then proceeded to conclude art.15 was of a customary law character.

A state's response to a particular resolution adopted within an international organisation may be dictated by the occasion and circumstances pertaining at the time and this should be borne in mind when invoking resolutions and the like as evidence of the development of practice into law.[19]

This was acknowledged by the ICJ in the *Nicaragua* case[20] where documentary evidence before the Court included statements by "high-ranking official political figures, sometimes indeed of the highest rank" which could be "of particular probative value when they acknowledge facts or conduct unfavourable to the state represented by the person who made them".[21] Nevertheless, the Court stated it was natural that such statements should be treated with "caution".[22]

Practice in itself is not sufficient to establish custom. An alleged rule of customary international law has to manifest not only a material element, but also a psychological element, otherwise known as *opinio juris*.

Psychological element—Opinio juris sive necessitatis (Opinio juris)

States in their relations engage in behaviour other than that which is required of them legally. If certain rules are to evolve into law, it is necessary to distinguish rules which are regarded as legally obligatory from those which are discretionary. State behaviour on the international plane may be prompted by reasons of mere courtesy, convenience or tradition rather than by legal obligation. Similarly, humanitarian considerations are insufficient in themselves to generate legal rights and obligations and the ICJ as "a court of law" is competent to take account of moral principles only in so far as these are given a sufficient expression in legal form.[23]

Opinio juris was introduced as a legal formula in an attempt to distinguish legal rules from mere social usage, and refers to the subjective belief maintained by states that a particular practice is legally required of them. A practice which is generally followed

---

[18] I.C.J. Rep. 2001 at p.40.
[19] See, e.g. J. Brierly, *The Law of Nations* (Oxford: Clarendon Press, 1963), p.4.
[20] Above, fn.10, p.4.
[21] Above, at p.41.
[22] Above, fn.10, p.41.
[23] *South West Africa (Second Phase)* I.C.J. Rep. 1966 6 at 34.

but which states feel they are free to disregard at any time cannot be characterised as law. In the words of the International Court of Justice

> "not only must the acts concerned 'amount to a settled practice', but they must also be accompanied by the *opinio juris sive necessitatis*. Either the States taking such action or other States in a position to react to it must have behaved so that their conduct is evidence of a belief that this practice is rendered obligatory by the existence of a rule of law requiring it. The need for such a belief, i.e. the existence of a subjective element, is implicit in the very notion of the *opinio juris sive necessitatis*."[24]

The Court highlighted in the *Nicaragua* case that *opinio juris* may, albeit with due caution, be deduced from, inter alia, the attitude of the parties and states towards General Assembly Resolutions (and in the instant case particularly Resolution 2625 (XXV) entitled "Declaration on Principles of International Law concerning Friendly Relations and Co-operation among States in accordance with the Charter of the United Nations"). It was emphasised that the effect of consent to the text of such Resolutions cannot be understood as merely that of "reiteration or elucidation" of the treaty commitment undertaken in the Charter. On the contrary, it may be understood as an acceptance of the validity of the rule or set of rules declared by the Resolutions.[25]

The problem with *opinio juris* is one of proof. It is frequently difficult to determine when the transformation into law has taken place. How can a state's conviction be proved to exist? Essentially, what must be established is the state's acceptance, recognition or acquiescence as to the binding character of the rule in question. The onus of proof is on the state relying upon the custom. It is the party alleging the existence of custom which must demonstrate that the custom is so established that it is binding on the other party. Insufficient evidence of *opinio juris* is fatal to the formation of customary international law, as for example in the *Lotus* case[26] and the *North Sea Continental Shelf* cases.

---

[24] Above, fn.10 pp.108–109.
[25] Above, pp.99–100. The Court took US support of the 6th International Conference of American States Condemning Aggression; ratification of the Montevideo Convention on the Rights and Duties of States 1933; and the Declaration on the Principles Governing the Mutual Relations of States participating in the Conference on the Security and Co-operation in Europe as further evidence of an expression of *opinio juris*.
[26] P.C.I.J. Rep. ser.A, no.10 (1927).

In the *Lotus* case, although France identified previous instances where in practice the victim's flag state had refrained from criminal prosecution, in the Court's view France failed to demonstrate that states refrained from prosecuting because they had been conscious of a legal obligation requiring them to do so.

Similarly, in the *North Sea Continental Shelf* cases, the International Court of Justice maintained that, although the principle of equidistance was employed in the delimitation of the continental shelf between adjacent states, there was no evidence

> "that they so acted because they felt legally compelled to draw them in this way by reason of a rule of customary law obliging them to do so—especially considering that they might have been motivated by other factors".[27]

Opinio juris and state practice are complementary in the creation of customary international law.

How may customary international law accommodate change if *opinio juris* demands behaviour in accordance with the law? How may new rules evolve if activity contrary to the established rules is prohibited?

If too rigid a view were to be taken of *opinio juris* then obviously the law would become stunted and in time deficient. States, however, do act contrary to established rules and do so in the belief that the new behaviour, if not already law, will become law. What will determine the future of such behaviour—whether it becomes law or withers—is the response of other states. Their reaction determines whether or not the new practice gains the necessary *opinio juris*.

Finally, mention must be made of another category of custom known by the somewhat anomalous term of "instant custom". The term refers not to behaviour, which is constant, uniform and frequently engaged in, but rather to spontaneous activity practised by a great number of states responding to particular circumstances. Instant custom is relatively rare.

Two examples which illustrate instant custom are the doctrine of the continental shelf, precipitated by President Truman's Proclamation in 1945, and the unilateral seaward extension throughout the 1970s by coastal states (Exclusive Economic Zone). The doctrine of the continental shelf became established as customary international law on the basis of assertions (that is, claims of exclusive rights and the denial of access to others) and general acquiescence.

The Truman Proclamation, which was quickly followed by similar declarations from other states, was prompted by a need to

---

[27] Above, fn.3, pp.44–45.

fill a void in international law as to the rights and duties of states given advancing technology, namely the possibility of mining the continental shelf. Although mining of the continental shelf was a possibility, it was neither technologically nor economically feasible at the time. States' jurisdiction over the Exclusive Economic Zone became established customary international law in the 1970s. Coastal states particularly concerned with controlling the exploitation and conservation of fishery resources, rather than waiting for agreement in UNCLOS III,[28] increasingly took unilateral action and extended their sovereign rights beyond their territorial sea to a maximum limit of 200 miles.[29]

Instant custom may appear an unsatisfactory term, but the activity it describes, while not fitting into the mould of traditional custom, still falls under the umbrella of custom, rather than under any "new" source of law. Instant custom is a response to new situations which demand a speedy response by way of international regulation. However it is an exception to the norm.

As already said, customary international law demands the presence of two elements, the material and the psychological. Although art.38 of the Statute of the ICJ calls upon the Court to apply international custom, as evidence "of" a general practice "accepted as law" it is more accurate to define international custom as evidenced "by" general practice accepted as law. This is because custom is the source to be applied and that custom is evidenced by practice accompanied by the belief that the practice is accepted as law.[30] The role of custom as a source of international law has diminished not least because of the substantial increase in the number of states participating on the international plane; the extension of the subject matter of international law beyond the traditional realm of diplomatic relations and the rules of warfare; and the increased number and speed of interaction between international actors. These changes in the international community have meant that custom is no longer regarded as the most appropriate mechanism for the regulation of international discourse and behaviour. This, reinforced by the desire of states to be fully aware of any obligations undertaken, has led to the increasing use of treaties as the preferred means for the regulation of international relations.

TREATIES

Article 38(1)(a) does not mention the term "treaties", but refers to any "international conventions, whether general or particular,

---

[28] Third United Nations Conference on the Law of the Sea.
[29] See 1982 Convention on the Law of the Sea, arts 55 and 56.
[30] See R. Higgins, *Problems and Process: International law and how we use it* (Oxford: Clarendon Press, 1994), p.18.

establishing rules expressly recognised by the contesting states".
The effect of this direction to the Court is, if an existing treaty
provision pertains between the parties to the dispute before the
Court, then if relevant, the treaty provision must be applied.

A treaty, although it may be identified as comparable to a parliamentary statute in municipal law, differs from the latter, in that
it only applies to those states which have agreed to its terms, and
normally a treaty does not have universal application. States are
able to opt out, something which is not available to individuals
under national law.

Treaties are only examined in this chapter in so far as they
constitute a source of law.[31] Treaties, as art.38(1)(a) infers, may
be between two states (bipartite or bilateral) or between several
states (multipartite or multilateral).[32]

A distinction is sometimes drawn between "law-making
treaties" ("*traité-lois*") and "treaty contracts" ("*traité-contracts*").
The essence of that distinction is that "treaty contracts" are agreements between relatively few parties, and can only create particular law between the signatories, whereas law-making treaties, to
which there are many signatories, create law per se. However,
all treaties involve a contractual obligation for the parties concerned and, consequently, create law for all parties agreeing to
the terms of the treaty. In other words, a bilateral treaty does
not create a lesser law than the law created by a multilateral
treaty. Multilateral treaties may admittedly have a wider effect,
and as such, may be regarded as law-making, in that not only
do they have a greater number of signatories, but the provisions
of such a treaty may become customary international law, as the
Netherlands and Denmark attempted to argue, albeit unsuccessfully, in the *North Sea Continental Shelf* cases.[33] Multilateral treaties,
although they may never have the truly legislative effect of municipal legislation, have a quasi-legislative effect, which is at least
prima facie denied to bilateral treaties. The ICJ acknowledged in
Territorial Dispute (Libya v Chad)[34] that a principle first enunciated
in a treaty (art.31 of the 1969 Vienna Convention on the Law of
Treaties) had achieved the status of customary international law.
Conversely, a multilateral or bilateral treaty may merely spell out
what has been accepted as customary international law, and a
provision contained repeatedly in bilateral treaties may provide

---

[31] The technicalities of treaty law are examined in Ch.10.
[32] Participation in a treaty is not confined exclusively to states, but states are the
only entities which have locus standi before the ICJ in contentious cases. The
terms "bipartite" and "mulitpartite" are strictly correct, however the terms
"bilateral" and "multilateral" are more commonly used.
[33] Above, fn.3.
[34] 6 I.C.J. Rep. 1994.

evidence that a particular rule of customary international law exists. Alternatively, it may be argued that the insertion by states of a rule in a bilateral treaty is evidence that such a rule does not have the status of customary international law.[35]

Treaties represent the most tangible and most reliable method of identifying what has been agreed between states. Treaties regulate a diverse and extensive subject-matter including, inter alia, drug control; space exploration; the establishment of organisations; extradition; safety regulations in the air and at sea; the rights of the child; the elimination of discrimination against various groups, ranging from women to migrant workers; and the establishment of an International Criminal Court.

Customary law and law made by treaty have equal authority in international law, but, if a treaty and a customary rule exist simultaneously on the issue in dispute, then the treaty provisions take precedence, as is illustrated by the *Wimbledon* case.[36] In that case, the Permanent Court of International Justice, while recognising that customary international law prohibited the passage of armaments through the territory of a neutral state to the territory of a belligerent state, upheld art.380 of the 1919 Treaty of Versailles, which provided the Kiel Canal was to be "free and open to the vessels of commerce and of war of all nations at peace with Germany on terms of entire equality". In stopping a vessel flying the flag of a state with which she was at peace, Germany was, the Court maintained, in breach of her treaty obligations under the Treaty of Versailles.

Therefore, unless the parties have expressed otherwise, a rule established by agreement supersedes, for them, a previous conflicting rule of customary international law. Generally in the event of inconsistency the latter, be it custom or treaty, prevails as between the same parties. However, parties to a treaty may agree to adhere to the treaty obligations even in the light of subsequent general custom. Nevertheless, though modification of custom by treaty is common, there are few instances of customary law developing in conflict with earlier agreements. In such cases the principle, the latter in time prevails, will be applied on the presumption that the parties to the treaty have implied their consent.[37]

Where there exists customary international law comprising rules identical to those of treaty law "there are no grounds for holding ... that the latter supervenes the former, so that the

---

[35] See the ICJ's observations in *Ahmadou Sadio Diallo (Guinea v Democratic Republic of Congo)*, Preliminary Objections, Judgment of 24 May 2007, at paras 30–31.
[36] P.C.I.J. Rep. ser.A, No.1 (1923).
[37] One such example was the acceptance as law of the 200 mile EEZ in conflict with the 1958 Geneva Conventions on the Law of the Sea.

customary international law has no existence of its own".[38] Hence, the Court in the *Nicaragua* case conceded, although it was precluded from considering whether the US had infringed art.2(4) of the UN Charter's prohibition on the use of force,[39] it was still competent to consider whether the existing customary international law on the use of force had been violated.

A presumption exists against the replacement of customary rules by treaty and vice versa. Treaties are not intended to derogate from customary law, and a treaty which seemingly modifies or alters established custom should be construed so as to best conform to, rather than derogate from, accepted principles of international law. That is, unless the treaty in question is clearly intended to alter the existing rules of custom. A treaty will not however prevail over prior customary law if the latter is *jus cogens*.[40]

Whatever their legislative effect, treaties, unlike municipal legislation, do not generally have universal application. Nonetheless, this statement must be qualified. There are two types of treaties, which because of their purpose do produce consequences, which non-signatories cannot ignore. Namely, (i) those establishing a special international regime and (ii) those establishing an international organisation.

In 1920, a Committee of Jurists was appointed by the League of Nations to determine whether Finland, as successor state to Russia, was bound by the 1856 Convention under which Russia had agreed with France and UK to the non-fortification of the Åland Islands.[41] The Committee concluded the treaty extended beyond the three contracting parties. The islands enjoyed "a special international status", and until the 1856 Convention was replaced, every state interested had a right to insist upon it being complied with, while "any State in possession of the Islands must conform to the obligations binding upon it". Treaties of this type are, however, very unusual.

Constitutive treaties establishing international institutions, for example the United Nations, have created organisations which have subsequently been held to possess varying degrees of international personality.[42] This degree of personality has enabled such entities to operate on the international stage and has, in certain instances, been enforced against non-member states, e.g. in the *Reparations* case.[43]

---

[38] Above, fn.10, p.95.
[39] By virtue of the US reservation under art.36(2) of the ICJ Statute.
[40] See below, pp.36–37 and Ch.10.
[41] League of Nations Official Journal (1920), Sp.Supp.No.3, p.3.
[42] International personality is covered in Ch.4.
[43] *Reparation for Injuries Suffered in the Service of the United Nations, Advisory Opinion*, I.C.J. Rep. 1949 at 185.

"GENERAL PRINCIPLES OF LAW AS RECOGNIZED BY CIVILIZED NATIONS"

International law as a legal system would be undermined if the ICJ was unable to give decisions based on law because of an apparent absence of relevant legal rules (such situations are referred to as *non liquet*). In a municipal legal system, such situations would be tackled by deducing the relevant rules from those already existing, or from basic legal principles such as justice and equity. A *non liquet* situation is, or at least was, more likely to arise in international law[44] than in a developed, mature municipal legal system. Accordingly, "general principles of law" was inserted to "plug the gaps" and to avoid undermining international law, which would undoubtedly happen through an inability to render judgment through an insufficiency of law.[45]

General principles were those as understood by "civilized nations". The term "civilized nations" has, in post-colonial times, been dropped, for obvious reasons.

What then is understood by general principles? It is not clear whether general principles refers to those of the international legal system or those of municipal legal systems. Such ambiguity is advantageous, as it imposes no restraint on the principles which may be applied. In practice legal principles have been drawn from developed municipal legal systems. This does not mean judges have to have expertise in every legal system of the world. Legal systems can be divided into families, and consequently, common elements may be identified within each legal system. General principles are therefore those which are common to the major legal systems of the world, mainly the civilian legal system and the common law system.

Most of the parallels drawn from municipal law have related to procedural, administrative or jurisdictional situations. The principles applied by international tribunals and the ICJ and its predecessor, have been those of a state's responsibility for the acts of its agents[46]; the principle of *estoppel* (personal bar)[47]; no one must be a judge of his own case[48]; and the principle of reparation.[49] However not all general principle claims are recognised as such,

---

[44] It should always be borne in mind that the Statute of the ICJ is the direct successor of the Charter of the Permanent Court of International Justice, and that in the 1920s, international law was certainly a less developed system than it is today.

[45] See however the *Legality of the Threat or use of Nuclear Weapons case, Advisory Opinion* (1997) 35 I.L.M. 809 and 1343.

[46] *Fabiani* case 10 R.I.A.A. 83 (1986).

[47] *Temple* case I.C.J. Rep. 1962 at 6.

[48] *Mosul Boundary* case, P.C.I.J. Rep. ser.B, No.12 (1925) at 32.

[49] *Chorzow Factory (Indemnity) (Merits)*, P.C.I.J. Rep. ser.A, No.17 (1928) at 29.

e.g. *actio popularis*.[50] Analogies with municipal legal systems have also been in discrete areas of international law, e.g. commercial and administrative law, where international law was not particularly developed at the time. In the *Barcelona Traction* case,[51] the International Court of Justice emphasised:

> "If the Court were to decide the case in disregard of the relevant institutions of municipal law it would, without justification, invite serious legal difficulties. It would lose touch with reality, for there are no corresponding institutions of international law to which the Court could resort. . . . It is to rules generally accepted by municipal legal systems . . . and not to the municipal law of a particular State, that international law refers".[52]

A precise definition either to the extent or scope of general principles has not been universally agreed. The importance of general principles, however defined, is that recourse to them has prevented a case from being shelved on the grounds that international law as it exists lacks, or is inadequate for dealing with, the particular issue raised.[53] Whether a particular general principle is eligible for absorption by international law will depend upon the development of international law at any given time.

EQUITY[54]

> "The Court has not been expressly authorised by its Statute to apply equity as distinguished from law . . . Article 38 of the Statute expressly directs the application of general principles of law recognised by civilised nations, and in more than one nation principles of equity have an established place in the legal system . . . It must be concluded, therefore, that under Article 38 of the Statute, if not independently of that Article, the Court has some freedom to consider principles of equity as part of the international law which it must apply".[55]

---

[50] *South West Africa* case *(Second Phase)* I.C.J. Rep. 1966 p.6, see also *Seaco v Iran* 919920 28 Iran–USCTR 198 at 209.
[51] Above, fn.13. See also the ICJ's position in *Ahmadou Sadio Diallo (Guinea v Democratic Republic of Congo)*, Judgment 30 November 2010, para.47.
[52] Above, at 37.
[53] Possible general fundamental principles of international law are considered under *"jus cogens"* below, p.35.
[54] Equity is sometimes treated separately as a possible independent source of law.
[55] Separate opinion of Hudson J in *The Diversion of Water from the Meuse* case P.C.I.J. Rep. ser.A/B, no.70 (1937) at 76–77.

In the *Rann of Kutch Arbitration*,[56] equity was identified as constituting part of international law, while the ICJ in the *North Sea Continental Shelf* cases directed the parties involved to seek a solution by reference to "equitable principles".[57] Equitable principles are also referred to in multilateral treaties, e.g. the 1982 Convention on the Law of the Sea[58] and certain General Assembly Resolutions such as the preamble of the 1974 Charter of Economic Rights and Duties of States.[59]

Principles of equity in the sense of fairness, justice and reasonableness are akin to general principles, and it may be asked why they are not always considered under the umbrella of general principles. However, equity differs from those general principles most frequently applied in that while the latter has related mainly to procedural techniques, equity as a concept reflects values, which, though they may be hard to define, may profoundly affect the application of the law. Equity in itself cannot be a source of law in that it does not contribute to substantive law. It can, nevertheless, affect the way substantive law is administered and applied.

Equity therefore plays a subsidiary role in supplementing existing rules. Equity, as understood above, must be distinguished from the ICJ's power "to decide a case *ex aequo et bono*, if the parties agree thereto",[60] that is the Court may apply equity in precedence over all other rules. A judge can only exercise his or her power under art.38(2) if he or she has been expressly authorised so to do.[61]

In the event of the ICJ being unable to solve a dispute by reference to treaty law, custom or general principles, art.38 provides the subsidiary means of "judicial decisions and the teachings of the most highly qualified publicists of the various nations" may be employed. Judicial decisions and writings are subsidiary means of determining what the law is on a given issue and they constitute the material sources of international law, as distinct

---

[56] 50 I.L.R. 2.

[57] Above, fn.3, p.47; see also *Fisheries Jurisdiction (Merits)* I.C.J. Rep. 1974 3 at 33; *Continental Shelf (Tunisia v Libya)* case I.C.J. Rep. 1982 18 at 60; and *Gulf of Maine* case I.C.J. Rep. 1984 at 246, 314–315 and 325–330. A criticism levied against the utilisation of equity in maritime boundary cases is that it has introduced an "unduly subjective and uncertain element into international law". See also *Denmark v Norway: Maritime Boundary in the Area Between Greenland and Jan Mayen Island* (1993) I.C.J. 38, ad passim.

[58] Arts 59, 74 and 83.

[59] GA Resolution 3281 (XXIX) 14 I.L.M. 251 (1975) which highlights the "need to establish a just and equitable economic and social order".

[60] Art.38(2).

[61] Art.38(2) has never been invoked before the ICJ though some international arbitration awards have been decided *ex aequo et bono*.

from the formal sources. They are not the law as such, but rather are where the law may be found. However, the increasing growth of treaty law in particular has witnessed something of a decline in the employment of both judicial decisions and writings.

JUDICIAL DECISIONS

Judicial decisions may be applied "subject to the provisions of Article 59" of the ICJ Statute. Article 59 states "the decision of the Court has no binding force except between the parties and in respect of that particular case". However there is no rule of stare decisis (precedent) in international law whereby the Court is obliged to follow its previous decisions. Nevertheless, in spite of the absence of stare decisis, the ICJ and international tribunals do examine previous decisions and regularly take them into account when seeking the solution to a dispute. This promotes judicial consistency in which there is obvious value as it provides some degree of certainty for those participating in the legal system as to what the law is on a particular issue. Although, strictly speaking, the ICJ is only to apply the law and not to make law, it has delivered a number of judgments and Advisory Opinions, which have influenced and contributed to the development of international law. Among the most notable are the *Reparations* case[62] (legal personality of the United Nations), the *Nottebohm* case[63] (genuine link between individual and claimant state), the *Anglo-Norwegian Fisheries* case[64] (baselines from which the territorial sea may be drawn) and the *Legality of the Use by a State of Nuclear Weapons in Armed Conflict.*[65]

Similarly, arbitration decisions have contributed to the growth of international law, for example the *Alabama Arbitration Awards*[66] (duties of a neutral state) and the *Island of Palmas Arbitration*[67] (evidence of territorial sovereignty). Caution, however, should be exercised when assessing the contribution of a particular decision, for example the Court may be equally divided and the casting vote of the President may be necessary for a decision, as in the *Lotus* case.[68] Similarly, the importance of an arbitration decision will depend, for example, on the subject matter involved and the parties concerned.

Before assessing the contribution of any arbitration decision to the development of international law, reference should be made

---

[62] Above, fn.43.
[63] I.C.J. Rep. 1955 at 4.
[64] Above, fn.9.
[65] 35 I.L.M. 809 (1996), I.C.J. Rep. 1996 at 226.
[66] Moore, 1 Int.Arb.495 (1872).
[67] 2 R.I.A.A. 829 (1928).
[68] Above, fn.26.

to the contents of the *compromis*; namely the agreement concluded between the parties to the arbitration which may specify, for instance, the arbitration tribunal's jurisdiction and the law to be applied. If parties wish law, other than international law or in addition to international law, to be employed by an arbitration tribunal the intention must be stipulated in the *compromis*.[69] In the *Trail Smelter Arbitration*,[70] the Tribunal was instructed to "apply the law and practice followed in dealing with cognate questions in the United States of America, as well as international law and practice". It is therefore necessary to remember an arbitration tribunal, in settling a dispute between two states, may not necessarily be applying international law or at least may not be applying it exclusively.

A judicial decision by the ICJ may give the stamp of law to an alleged rule of custom. However, caution must be exercised. For instance, the ICJ in 1974 pronounced:

> "Two concepts have crystallised as customary law in recent years arising out of the general consensus revealed at that Conference [1960 Law of the Sea Conference]. The first is the concept of the fishery zone ... The second is the concept of preferential rights of fishing in adjacent waters in favour of the coastal State in a situation of special dependency on its coastal fisheries."[71]

The evidence produced by the Court in support of its contention was unconvincing. The Court took existing instances of preferential rights at face value and considered neither the reasons why preferential treatment was granted nor whether the parties concerned felt any legal obligation to provide preferential treatment for coastal states. The evidence produced in Court illustrated that relatively few states (21) put preferential rights into practice and that the practice was confined to a single geographical area (the North Atlantic). The Court did not attempt to demonstrate that states felt any legal obligation to act in the way they had done, nor has state practice since the Court's judgment supported the view that the Court was giving "judgment *sub specie legis ferendae*" and was anticipating "the law before the legislator had laid it down".[72]

---

[69] In the absence of any stipulation, international law will be applied.

[70] 3 R.I.A.A. 1905 (1938/41).

[71] Above, fn.11 at 23.

[72] That this is what the Court may have been seeking to do is borne out by Ignacio-Pinto J's declaration (at 37) that the Court gave him the impression it was "anxious to indicate the principles on the basis of which it would be desirable that a general international regulation of rights of fishing should be

The Court has also come in for criticism with respect to its assertion in the *Nicaragua (Merits)* case, that the necessary *opinio juris* could be deduced from the support of states for certain General Assembly Resolutions.

DECISIONS OF NATIONAL COURTS

Article 38 does not limit the judicial decisions that may be applied to those of international tribunals. If a national court's decision is relevant, it may be applied. The weight attached to a decision of a national court will depend upon the standing of the court concerned.

For example, in its decisions dealing with individual state boundaries, the United States Supreme Court has not only applied, but also played a role in developing, relevant principles of international law.

Similarly, decisions of the English Prize Courts have contributed to the growth of prize law—that is the law relating to vessels captured at sea during war.

A national court decision may also serve as evidence of a state's position on a particular issue. Nevertheless, it must always be borne in mind that, although a national court is apparently applying international law, it is more likely to be applying the rule in question because it is a rule of national law.

WRITERS

"Teachings of the most highly qualified publicists of various nations" may be referred to as a subsidiary means in an attempt to settle a dispute, as per art.38. Writers have played a considerable role in the development of international law. Their influence has been due, in part, to the absence of an executive and a legislative body and also to the "youthfulness" of the international legal system. During the formative period of international law, writers, because of insufficient state practice, were able to help determine, mould and articulate the scope, content and basic principles of international law. However, as substantive international law increased, for example, through the growth of customary international law, the role of writers declined. Nevertheless, international law is still a relatively young system and its boundaries are constantly being extended. Writers may still make a contribution by providing interpretations of the law, as well as in identifying and highlighting areas where international regulation should be encouraged, e.g. environmental pollution, climate change and the

adopted". However preferential fishing rights as articulated by the Court were not incorporated in the 1982 Convention on the Law of the Sea.

right to development. Writers may also prompt an assessment of the aims and values of international law. Writings, though they have receded in importance, are utilised not as a source of law in themselves but as a means of ascertaining what the law actually is on a given subject.[73] They are a subsidiary means of determining what the law is on a certain issue at a particular point in time and have a continuing role to play given the absence of stare decisis in international law. Writings do not necessarily carry less weight than judicial decisions. Clearly, however, which publicists are "the most highly qualified" cannot be conclusively stated.

The contemporary international community is very different from the one which existed when art.38(1) and its predecessor were initiated. It is relevant, therefore, after having examined all of the possible "sources" identified by reference to art.38(1), to ask whether these are the only sources. Article 38(1) does not profess to be exhaustive and it is, especially because of the developing character of international law, quite legitimate to look beyond art.38(1).

OTHER POSSIBLE SOURCES OF INTERNATIONAL LAW

Soft law

Soft law is the generic term used to describe non-legally binding international instruments but which contains norms, principles, commitments or standards expected to be complied with by states, and increasingly non-state actors. There is no accepted definition of soft law. It is a heterogeneous set of instruments which can be found in different forms, from treaties ("legal soft law") to voluntary resolutions, statements of intent and codes of conduct produced by international and regional organisations and statements by individuals, for example groups of eminent international lawyers purporting to articulate international principles ("non-legal soft law"). A requisite of soft law is that it must be in written form.

Soft law has become an important element of contemporary international law. The number of instruments which fall within the category of soft law has spawned during the last 60 years, particularly as the activity of international organisations and other non-state actors has increased. The subject matter of such instruments is becoming increasingly diverse and includes, inter alia,

---

[73] See, for instance, reference by Lord Stephenson in *Trendtex Trading Corporation v Central Bank of Nigeria* [1977] 1 All E.R. 881 at 902. Note also the International Court of Justice's statement on the cognisance to be given to documentary evidence produced in the form of extracts from books namely that "even if they seem to meet high standards of objectivity", above, fn.10 at 40.

economic measures, human rights provisions and environmental standards.

An advantage of soft law is that it may be employed to overcome deadlock in treaty negotiations when states do not agree about the scope of the obligations they are willing to assume. Alternatively, an alleged disadvantage is that it may discourage states from undertaking "hard law", that is legally binding obligations. On other occasions a non-binding soft law instrument is the first step in a lengthy process of concluding a treaty. This way soft law is intended to mould conduct on the international scene and may eventually become hard law. Subsequent state practice may be such to change the status of soft law to hard law through it becoming a custom or being included in a treaty with hard law obligations.

The 1948 Universal Declaration of Human Rights is an example of soft law. The Declaration was a statement of intent but led to the promulgation of the 1966 International Covenant on Civil and Political Rights,[74] and the 1966 International Covenant on Economic, Social and Cultural Rights.[75] Other examples of soft law are the Charter of Paris for a New Europe adopted in 1990 by the Conference on Security and Co-Operation in Europe,[76] where its members expressed their aspirations for a new era of democracy, peace and unity in Europe, and the 1992 Rio Declaration on the Environment and Development,[77] the 2000 Millennium Declaration or, arguably, the recent Sustainable Development Goals.

Acts of international organisations

The multiplication of international organisations is a phenomenon which started in the 20th century and continues today. The most notable of these, enjoying almost universal membership, is the United Nations. Each of the 193 Member States of the United Nations has one vote within the General Assembly. Voting on important questions requires a two-thirds majority, while on all other questions a simple majority will suffice. Only those resolutions adopted by the Assembly on procedure and budgetary issues are legally binding on members. All other resolutions are recommendations—statements on a given issue. However, certain General Assembly resolutions, namely "Declarations of Principle", although they carry no legal obligation, do have considerable moral force. Examples of these include Resolution 1514

[74] 999 U.N.T.S. 171.
[75] 993 U.N.T.S. 3.
[76] 30 I.L.M. 190 (1991).
[77] 31 I.L.M. 874 (1992).

(XV), "Declaration on the Granting of Independence to Colonial Countries and Peoples"[78] and General Assembly "Declaration on Principles of International Law Concerning Friendly Relations and Co-Operation Amongst States in Accordance with the Charter of the United Nations" 1970.[79] Although such resolutions may contribute to the development of international law, the status of customary international law was denied to General Assembly Resolution 3281 (XXIX) "Charter of Economic Rights and Duties of States" 1974[80] by the arbitrator in the *Texaco* case.[81]

Also in 1974 the General Assembly Sixth (Legal) Committee, in its review of the work of the ICJ, observed that General Assembly resolutions did not signify a source of international law additional to those set out in art.38 of the ICJ Statute. Nevertheless, there was acceptance that such resolutions could be evidence of custom.

That said, General Assembly resolutions cannot be dismissed out of hand as being of no significance, in the words of Lauterpacht J:

> "It would be wholly inconsistent with sound principles of interpretation as well as with highest international interest, which can never be legally irrelevant, to reduce the value of the Resolutions of the General Assembly—one of the principal instrumentalities of the formation of the collective will and judgment of the community of nations represented by the United Nations—and to treat them . . . as nominal, insignificant and having no claim to influence the conduct of the Members. International interest demands that no judicial support, however indirect, be given to any such conception of the Resolution of the General Assembly as being of no consequence."[82]

General Assembly resolutions however have no legal effect[83] and, before any law-making effect can be attributed to them, a consistent approach requires to be adopted towards them. This is in contrast to the current selective approach where their impact is dependent upon such factors as the subject matter of the resolution; how large a majority the resolution commands; and to what extent it receives

---

[78] GA Resolution 1514 (XV) 14 December 1960; see *Advisory Opinion—Western Sahara*, I.C.J. Rep. 1975 12 at 31 and following. For the effect of GA Resolutions in the evolution of the principle of self-determination.

[79] GA Resolution 2625 (XXV) 24 October 1970.

[80] 14 I.L.M. 251 (1975).

[81] 17 I.L.M. 1 (1978).

[82] Separate Opinion in *Voting Procedure on Questions Relating to Reports and Petitions Concerning the Territory of South West Africa*, I.C.J. Rep. 1955 67 at 122.

[83] Except, as outlined above, in relation to procedure and budgetary issues.

the support of the principally affected states in the given field. Nevertheless a vote in the General Assembly is cast by a state's representative and, as such, may reflect a particular state's position on a given issue and how a state votes may be the means of providing evidence of state practice. Thus, voting within an organisation may be a useful link in the international law-making process, that is, it may provide the evidence necessary for "law" to be attributed to usage. Therefore voting on General Assembly resolutions may provide an indication of what the law is, or possibly what the law should be, or indeed what it may become on a particular topic at a given time. As mentioned above, General Assembly resolutions are an example of what is known as "soft law".

There is an increasing number of regional organisations such as the Council of Europe, the European Union, the Organisation of American States, the African Union and the League of Arab States. These regional organisations can, via their internal measures, demonstrate what they, as representatives of a particular regional grouping of states, consider to be the law. Regional organisations enjoy varying degrees of legal personality and if this should extend to a treaty-making competence, the organisation in question may shape substantive international law by participating in treaties.

The International Law Commission

A criticism of custom is that it is diffuse and lacking in precision. In light of this, attempts have been made at codification—the Hague Conferences 1899 and 1907 compiled the existing customary law in the Conventions on the law of war and neutrality, and in 1930 the Hague Convention on Certain Questions Relating to the Conflict of Nationality Law was drawn up. Codification essentially involves a streamlining of all existing law on a particular subject and it is distinct from consolidation, which is simply a drawing together of all material on a particular subject.

In 1946, the International Law Commission (ILC) was established and charged with the task of furthering the progressive development and codification of international law. "Progressive development" is defined in art.15 of the ILC's Statute as

> "the preparation of draft conventions on subjects which have not yet been regulated by international law or in regard to which the law has not yet been sufficiently developed in the practice of States".

Codification however is defined as "the more precise formulation and systemisation of rules of international law in fields where there already has been extensive State practice, precedent and doctrine". Most codification has, since 1946, been effected via the ILC, and the Commission's work, even in instances where there is no treaty produced, is influential. It may result in a treaty subsequently. Nevertheless, the distinction between "progressive development" and "codification" is easier to maintain in theory than in practice. This was highlighted by ad hoc Sorenson J (Dissenting Opinion) in the *North Sea Continental Shelf* case, stating:

> "It has come to be generally recognised, however, that this distinction between codification and progressive development may be difficult to apply rigorously to the facts of international legal relations. Although theoretically clear and distinguishable the two notions tend in practice to overlap or to leave between them an intermediate area in which it is not possible to indicate precisely where codification ends and progressive development begins. The very act of formulating or restating an existing customary rule may have the effect of defining its contents more precisely and removing such doubts as may have existed as to its exact scope or the modalities of its application."[84]

The ILC has 34 members,[85] who sit as individuals rather than as state representatives.[86] It meets, as authorised by the General Assembly, for two sessions each year (amounting to two months in total). Initially the Commission met for 12 weeks in the year but this has been reduced since 2000 in an effort to make financial savings. The ILC may be invited by the General Assembly to look at a particular field of law. However, this is rare and the ILC as a rule normally initiates its own work programme. The ILC has been responsible for undertaking the preparatory work on particular subjects and this has culminated in a number of Conventions being opened for signature. The Commission works by way of reports produced by a Special Rapporteur who is appointed from among the Commission's members. A recent example is the appointment in 2012 of a Special Rapporteur on the topic of the Formation and evidence of customary international law (subsequently changed to the Identification of customary international law). Draft articles are prepared and subsequently submitted to Member States for their comments. A conference may then be convened, which will on the basis of the draft articles, produce a convention, which

---

[84] Above, fn.3 at 42–43.
[85] Increased from 15 members to 21 in 1956, to 25 in 1961 and to 34 in 1981.
[86] Elections are by the General Assembly from lists of national groups and are elected with regard, e.g. to equitable geographical distribution.

in due course will be opened for signature.[87] Topics covered by the ILC include the law of the sea (resulting in the 1958 Geneva Conventions on the Law of the Sea); the law on diplomatic relations (1961 Vienna Convention on Diplomatic Relations); the law of treaties (1969 Vienna Convention on the Law of Treaties); and the establishment of a permanent international criminal court (1998 Rome Statute of the International Criminal Court).

Instruments drafted by the ILC do not always become treaties. The ILC has been responsible for draft articles on a variety of topics including those on the Responsibility of States for Internationally Wrongful Acts 2001[88]; Draft Articles on Diplomatic Protection 2006[89]; and Draft Articles on Responsibility of International Organisations 2011.[90] In this preparatory work state practice can be identified and, as such, may assist the identification of customary international law. Again, the inter-relation of treaty law and customary international law and vice versa is illustrated.

Additional agencies other than the ILC are engaged in attempts to clarify existing law on given subjects, e.g. the United Nations Commission on International Trade Law, the International Labour Organisation and independent bodies such as the International Law Association.

PEREMPTORY NORMS OF INTERNATIONAL LAW

As this chapter has illustrated international law does not come in one single code or package. It is dependent on state consent to assume an obligation, through agreement by way of a treaty or practice via customary international law. This generates a highly fragmented legal system in which different subjects may have varying obligations, through the signing of different treaties and, even when a custom is a general norm, by objecting to it. However, there are certain norms which are peremptory. These are norms of general international law of which the content cannot be modified by agreement and from which no derogation may be made except by another norm of equal weight. Their technical term is *jus cogens*.[91] A treaty provision which conflicts with such a norm is void[92] and, should a new peremptory norm develop, any existing contrary treaty is rendered void and terminates.[93]

---

[87] Conferences may span a number of years.
[88] Report of the 53rd Sess., I.L.C. (2001), G.A.O.R. Suppl. 10, [XX] 56.
[89] Report of the 58th Sess. I.L.C. (2006) G.A.O.R. A/61/10, pp.22 and following.
[90] Report of the 66th Sess. I.L.C. (2011) G.A.O.R., Suppl. 10, Doc. A/66/10, 54 and following.
[91] The concept of *jus cogens* is examined more closely within the context of treaty law in Ch.10.
[92] Vienna Convention on the Law of Treaties, 1969, art.53.
[93] Vienna Convention on the Law of Treaties, 1969, art.64.

How does an international rule gain status as a peremptory norm? The only authoritative definition is that contained in the 1969 Vienna Convention on the Law of Treaties in which a peremptory norm of general international law is defined as one "accepted and recognised by the international community of states as a whole".[94] A peremptory norm may, it would appear, be derived from a custom or a treaty and not from any other source.

Jus cogens is the label for what is essentially the "public policy" of the international legal system. There remains, as might be anticipated, considerable uncertainty and indeed controversy as to the scope and extent of *jus cogens*. The prohibition on the use of force as expressed in the United Nations Charter was identified by the ILC as a "conspicuous example of a rule in international law having the character of *jus cogens*"[95] and subsequently endorsed as such by the ICJ in the *Nicaragua* case.[96] Other examples of norms warranting characterisation as *jus cogens* are the prohibitions on genocide, slavery, racial discrimination and torture,[97] and on the denial of peoples' realisation of self-determination within a colonial context.

CONCLUSION

The sources of international law cannot be definitively stated and continue to evolve in response to the growing number of actors and subject matters that may, from time to time, need to be accommodated in the international legal system. This has particularly been the case since the international community has experienced the growth of international organisations and the emergence of an increasing number of non-state actors which have acquired varying degrees of international personality and influence. Nevertheless, art.38 of the ICJ Statute provides the starting point for any consideration of the sources of contemporary international law.

---

[94] For the purposes of the Convention.

[95] Commentary of the Commission to art.50 of *Draft Articles on the Law of Treaties*, I.L.C. Yearbook, 1966, II, p.247.

[96] Above, fn.10 at 100.

[97] The absolute prohibition on torture obviously remains a contentious issue, particularly since 9/11 and the "war on terror" which has seen some states try to circumvent the prohibition on torture to justify using interrogation methods which arguably fall within the definition of torture.

3. INTERNATIONAL LAW AND MUNICIPAL LAW

Contemporary international law is not only confined to regulating the relations between states. The scope of international law continues to extend and is no longer exclusively concerned with the rules of warfare and diplomatic relations. Today, issues of social concern such as health, education, economics and the environment fall within the ambit of international regulation and the needs and rights of individuals are increasingly under the international spotlight.

Can individuals invoke international law before national courts? Can individuals obtain rights under international law which may be enforced within a municipal legal system?

The focus of this chapter is the extent to which national courts may give effect to rules of international law within the domestic system. The approach of a particular state's national courts to international law is determined by that state's attitude to, and reception of, international law. This attitude may, and does, differ according to the type of international law in question—treaty law or customary international law. Strictly speaking, the reception of international law by a state and its internal effect is a matter of municipal law. There is no universal, uniform practice stipulating how a state should incorporate international law into its domestic legal system. It is a state's perception of international law which determines the way in which international law becomes part of its municipal law and, consequently, states differ in the way their national courts are either required or allowed to give effect to international obligations.

Before looking at what happens in practice, brief mention must be made of the theories which have evolved on the relationship of national law to international law. The theorists traditionally have been divided between two principal schools of thought—(i) the monistic school; and (ii) the dualistic school.

MONISTIC SCHOOL

Monists have a unitary concept of law and see all law, and consequently international law and municipal law, as an integral part of the same system. In the event of a conflict between international law and municipal law, most monists would contend that international law should unquestionably prevail.

DUALISTIC SCHOOL

Dualists view national law and international law as independent of each other. Dualists maintain that the two systems regulate different subject matter. International law regulates the relations of sovereign states, while national law regulates affairs internal to the state, e.g. the relations of the executive vis-à-vis its citizens and the relations of individual citizens vis-à-vis each other. Accordingly, for dualists, the two systems are mutually exclusive; they can have no contact with, and no effect on, each other. If international law is applied within a state, it is only because it has been expressly incorporated into the state's municipal law. The question of primacy is not one to which dualists address themselves. Dualism, as formulated, does not admit a conflict can arise between the international legal system and a municipal legal system.

Sir Gerald Fitzmaurice stepped into the debate between monists and dualists in the mid-1950s, when he articulated what has become popularly known as the "Fitzmaurice compromise".[1] Fitzmaurice acknowledged that international law and municipal law have, for the most part, separate fields of operation and each is supreme in its own domain. Nevertheless, on occasion they have a common field of application and, should a conflict arise, what is involved, Fitzmaurice concluded, is not a conflict of legal systems but rather a conflict of obligations. If a state is, by its national law, unable to act in the manner required by international law,

---

[1] Fitzmaurice, "The General Principles of International Law Considered from the Standpoint of the Rule of Law" 92 Hague Recueil 5.

it is not its internal law (which the national courts will uphold) which is called into question, but rather the state's liability on the international plane for the non-fulfilment of its international obligations.[2]

In practice, the differences between international law and a particular national system is minimised and every effort is made to achieve harmonisation between the two systems.

For example, in the UK, there exists

> "a *prima facie* presumption that Parliament does not intend to act in breach of international law, including therein specific treaty obligations; and if one of the meanings which can reasonably be ascribed to the legislation is consonant with the treaty obligations and another or others are not, the meaning which is consonant is to be preferred".[3]

In the US, such a presumption is an established principle of interpretation, so "an act of congress ought never to be construed to violate the law of nations, if any other possible construction remains".[4]

What is meant by describing a country as monistic or dualistic in its approach to international law? A monistic state accepts international law automatically as part of its municipal law and does not require an express act of the legislature. In a dualistic state international law will only become part of its municipal law if it has been expressly adopted as such by way of a legislative act.

MUNICIPAL LAW IN INTERNATIONAL LAW

On the international scene, international law is unequivocally supreme, as is borne out by both arbitral and judicial decisions and international Conventions which reflect the accepted international legal position.

In the *Alabama Claims Arbitration*,[5] the arbitration tribunal concluded that neither municipal legislative provisions nor the absence of such provisions could be pleaded as a defence for non-compliance with international obligations, while the Permanent Court of International Justice in an advisory opinion expressed the view

---

[2] As illustrated in *Mortensen v Peters* (1906) 8 F. (J.) 93, see below, p.46.
[3] *Salomon v Commissioners of Customs and Excise* [1967] 2 Q.B. 116 CA—Lord Diplock at 143; also *Post Office v Estuary Radio Ltd* [1968] 2 Q.B. 740 CA.
[4] *Murray v Schooner Charming Betsy* 6 US (2 Cranch.) 64 at 118 (1804). Also *Lauritzen v Larsen* 345 US 571 at 578 (1953). For Canadian authority, see, e.g. *Bloxém v Favre* 8 P.C. 101 at 107 (1883, n.5).
[5] Moore, 1 Int.Arb. 495 (1872).

"a State which has contracted valid international obligations is bound to make in its legislation such modifications as may be necessary to ensure the fulfilment of the obligations undertaken."[6]

Article 13 of the 1949 Draft Declaration on Rights and Duties of States provides:

"Each State has the duty to carry out in good faith its obligations arising from treaties and other sources of international law, and it may not invoke provisions in its constitution or its laws as an excuse for failure to perform this duty."[7]

Article 27 of the 1969 Vienna Convention on the Law of Treaties[8] stipulates that "a party may not invoke the provisions of internal law as justification for its failure to perform a treaty",[9] nor may a state, pursuant to art.46 of the Vienna Convention

"invoke the fact that its consent to be bound by a treaty has been expressed in violation of a provision of its internal law regarding competence to conclude treaties as invalidating its consent unless that violation was manifest and concerned a rule of its internal law of fundamental importance."[10]

The overriding conclusion to be extracted from the foregoing is that a state should not seek to evade fulfilling an international obligation because of either the presence or absence of an internal legislative provision. This must be the standpoint at the international level if international law is to succeed and maintain credibility.

International tribunals may, of course, choose to look at national legislation, and that national legislation may be

---

[6] *Exchange of Greek and Turkish Populations* case P.C.I.J. Rep., ser.B., No.10 (1925) at 20. See also, *Free Zones of Upper Savoy and Gex* P.C.I.J. Rep., ser.A/B, No.46 (1932). Note, however, that Libya sought to justify its refusal to extradite the alleged perpetrators of the Lockerbie bombing on the grounds that, inter alia, the Libyan Constitution prohibits the extradition of nationals.

[7] This was prepared by the International Law Commission—Y.B.I.L.C., 1949, pp.286, 288. See also *Applicability of the Obligation to Arbitrate under section 21 of the United Nations Headquarters Agreement of 26th June 1947*, I.C.J. Rep., 1988, 12.

[8] 8 I.L.M. 679 (1969). See also Ch.10 below.

[9] See *Questions Relating to the Obligation to Prosecute or Extradite (Belgium v Senegal)* 20 July 2012, I.C.J., para.113. The Court held that Senegal could not justify a breach of its international obligations by invoking provisions of its internal law.

[10] A violation is manifest if it shall be objectively evident to any state conducting itself on the matter in accordance with normal practice and in good faith (art.46(2)).

employed as evidence of a state's compliance or non-compliance with international obligations.[11] Consideration of national law may help ascertain what a state's stance is on a particular issue at a given time[12] and an international tribunal may, in the absence of relevant international law, be required to refer to national law. This referral to national law was stressed by the International Court of Justice in the *Barcelona Traction, Light and Power Co* case.[13] The Court was confronted with issues pertaining to company law and held that "in this field international law is called upon to recognise institutions of municipal law that have an important and extensive role in the international field".[14]

Turning to the municipal scene, what is the position when municipal courts and tribunals are confronted with international law? How do they apply it and what happens in the event of a conflict between international law and municipal legislation?[15]

INTERNATIONAL LAW BEFORE MUNICIPAL COURTS

United Kingdom practice

There is no written constitution defining the internal status within the UK of international law.[16]

Customary international law

The UK essentially adopts a monistic approach to customary international law. Such a statement is, however, an over-simplification. Notwithstanding Lord Talbot's position in *Buvot v Barbuit*,[17] the

[11] For example the International Tribunal of the Law of the Sea, *M/V Saiga (No. 2)* case 1999, 120 I.L.R. 143.

[12] Highlighted by the Permanent Court of International Justice in *Polish Upper Silesia*, P.C.I.J. Rep., ser.A, no.7, (1926) at 22, *Brazilian Loans* case, P.C.I.J. Rep., ser.A, no.21, (1929), at 124–125.

[13] I.C.J. Rep. 1970 at 3.

[14] I.C.J. Rep. 1970 at 33.

[15] Of course international law may be invoked by national courts to interpret legislation, consistently, with international law. For instance the South African Constitution 1996 requires courts to consider international law when applying the South African Bill of Rights. See case *Mazibuko and the City of Johannesburg,* 30 April 2008.

[16] cf. art.25 German Constitution: "The general rules of public international law are an integral part of federal law. They shall take precedence over the laws and shall directly create rights and duties for the inhabitants of the federal territory."

[17] (1737) Cases t. Talbot 281, "That the law of nations, in its full extent was part of the law of England" and reaffirmed by Lord Mansfield in *Triquet v Bath* (1764) 3 Burr. 1478. Court of King's Bench. See also Lord Lloyd in *R v Bow Street Magistrates Ex p. Pinochet* (Number 1) [2001] 1 A.C. 61 at 90.

British standpoint was best presented by Lord Alverstone in the *West Rand Central Gold Mining Co* case[18]:

"It is quite true that whatever has received the common consent of civilised nations must have received the assent of our country, and that to which we have assented along with other nations in general may properly be called international law, and as such will be acknowledged and applied by our municipal tribunals when legitimate occasion arises for those tribunals to decide questions to which doctrines of international law may be relevant. But any doctrine so invoked must be one really accepted as binding between nations, and the international law sought to be applied must, like anything else, be proved by satisfactory evidence, which must shew either that the particular proposition put forward has been recognised and acted upon by our own country, or that it is of such a nature, and has been so widely and generally accepted, that it can hardly be supposed that any civilised State would repudiate it . . . that the law of nations forms part of the law of England, ought not to be construed so as to include as part of the law of England opinions of text-writers upon a question as to which there is no evidence that Great Britain has ever assented, and *a fortiori* if they are contrary to the principles of her laws as declared by her Courts."[19]

Lord Alverstone's emphasis was on assent and the need to demonstrate the existence and scope of any particular alleged rule of customary international law—an emphasis which has been reflected consistently in subsequent cases. In *The Cristina case*,[20] Lord Macmillan held that national courts, before acknowledging customary international law as part of domestic law, should initially be satisfied it (that is, custom) had the hallmark of consent.[21] In *Chung Chi Cheung v The King*,[22] Lord Atkin said:

"It must be always remembered that, so far, at any rate, as the courts of this Country are concerned, international law has no validity save in so far as its principles are accepted and adopted by our own domestic law. There is no external power that imposes its rule upon our own code of substantive law or procedure. The courts acknowledge the existence of a body of rules which nations accept amongst themselves. On any

---

[18] [1905] 2 K.B. at 391.
[19] [1905] 2 K.B. at 406–408.
[20] [1938] A.C. 485.
[21] [1938] A.C. at 490. See also Lord Wright at 502.
[22] [1939] A.C. 160.

judicial issue they seek to ascertain what the relevant rule is, and having found it, they will treat it as incorporated into the domestic law, so far as it is not inconsistent with rules enacted by Statutes or finally declared by their tribunals."[23]

Lord Denning in *Thakrar v Home Secretary*[24] said, "In my opinion, the rules of international law only become part of our law in so far as they are accepted and adopted by us."[25] However, three years later, in *Trendtex Trading Corporation v Central Bank of Nigeria*,[26] in considering the two schools, incorporation or transformation, Lord Denning concluded that the doctrine of incorporation was correct. Nevertheless, that case dealing with sovereign immunity predated the 1978 State Immunity Act and therefore was governed by judicial decisions. The real question was whether the rules of precedent applying to rules of English law incorporating customary international law meant that any change in international law could only be recognised by the English courts (in the absence of legislation) within the scope of the doctrine of stare decisis. Lord Denning concluded otherwise and held:

"International law knows no rule of *stare decisis*. If this court today is satisfied that the rule of international law on a subject has changed from what it was 50 or 60 years ago, it can give effect to that change—and apply the change in our English law—without waiting for the House of Lords to do it."[27]

The decision in *Trendtex* would appear to allow an exception from an application of the principle of stare decisis in cases where international law has changed since the earlier decision was delivered. In the light of the *Trendtex* case, it seems that if international law has changed then the "new" international law may be applied in spite of the earlier municipal decision. Lord Denning's submissions in favour of the doctrine of "incorporation" received judicial support in the *Tin Council* case.[28] In *R v Jones*[29] the reception of customary international law was further discussed. In that case the House of Lords accepted that aggression constituted a crime under customary international law. However the Law Lords qualified the automatic incorporation of customary international law

---

[23] [1939] A.C. at 167–168. Lord Atkin's statement is self-contradictory.
[24] [1974] Q.B. 684.
[25] [1974] Q.B. at 701.
[26] [1977] Q.B. 529.
[27] [1977] Q.B. at 554.
[28] *Maclaine Watson v Dept of Trade and Industry* [1988] 3 W.L.R. 1033; 80 I.L.R. 49; [1989] 3 All E.R. 523; 81 I.L.R. 671.
[29] [2006] UKHL 16.

as part of domestic law. For example Lord Bingham expressed the view that customary international law could only be assimilated into domestic criminal law where allowed by the constitutional process.[30]

Rules of customary international law inconsistent with municipal law

Any rule of customary international law which is inconsistent with a piece of UK legislation will not be enforced by UK courts. The domestic legislation will be upheld while the state will incur liability on the international scene, as in *Mortensen v Peters*.[31] In that case the High Court of Justiciary of Scotland quashed an appeal against a conviction made under a domestic legislative provision, which allegedly contravened customary international law. The Court, in dismissing the appeal, unanimously held, inter alia, that the relationship of municipal legislation and international law was one of construction and "of construction only" and it was not the function of the Court

> "to decide whether an Act of the Legislature is ultra vires as in contravention of generally acknowledged principles of international law. For us an Act of Parliament duly passed by Lords and Commons and assented to by the King, is supreme, and we are bound to give effect to its terms."[32]

The Court concluded that, while there was a presumption against Parliament violating international law

> "it is only a presumption, and as such it must always give way to the language used if it is clear, and also to all counter presumptions which may legitimately be held in view in determining, on ordinary principles, the true meaning and intent of the legislation. Express words will of course be conclusive, and so also will plain implication."[33]

Customary international law will be treated as part of UK law, provided there is no contrary judicial decision of a higher court, save possibly the exception admitted by the *Trendtex* case, or contrary statutory provision or now in the wake of *R v Jones* a constitutional impediment to incorporation.

---

[30] [2006] UKHL 16 wherein it was stated the offence of aggression could not be automatically incorporated into domestic criminal law without statutory provision.
[31] (1906) 8 F.(J.) 93.
[32] Above, at 100–101.
[33] Above, at 103.

Treaties

> "[A]s a matter of the constitutional law of the United Kingdom, the royal prerogative, whilst it embraces the making of treaties, does not extend to altering the law or conferring rights on individuals or depriving individuals of rights which they enjoy in domestic law without the intervention of Parliament. Treaties, as it is sometimes expressed, are not self-executing. Quite simply a treaty is not part of English law unless and until it has been incorporated into the law by legislation."[34]

A treaty does not become part of UK domestic law unless and until it is specifically incorporated as such by a legislative measure—an Enabling Act. The UK adopts, therefore, a dualistic approach to treaty law.

Why is an Enabling Act required? Treaty-making power is an executive function coming within the royal prerogative. The legislature does not participate and its consent is not required before the UK can undertake international obligations. An Enabling Act is a safeguard against the possible abuse of executive authority, as it prevents the executive from using its treaty-making competence to introduce domestic legislation without going through the required parliamentary procedures. Treaties regulating the conduct of war and the cession of territory do not demand an Enabling Act.[35]

The reason as to why an Enabling Act is required was spelt out by Sir Robert Phillimore in the *Parlement Belge* case[36] when he concluded that to recognise the immunity granted by a Convention[37] to a vessel other than a public warship as being enforceable in the national courts would be "a use of the treaty-making prerogative of the Crown which I believe to be without precedent, and in principle contrary to the laws of the constitution."[38]

In practice, the Enabling Act giving internal effect to a treaty will be passed before the treaty is ratified and the opportunity will then be taken to make national law compatible with international law. Historically there was also the practice known as the Ponsonby Rule whereby a treaty, following signature, was laid

---

[34] Lord Oliver in *Maclaine Watson v Department of Trade*, above, fn.28. See also Lord Bingham in *Al-Skeine v Secretary of State for Defence* [2007] UKHL 26.

[35] Treaties involving the cession of territory may be an exception to the principle that parliamentary consent is not required for a treaty.

[36] (1879) 4 P.D. 129. Probate, Divorce and Admiralty Division.

[37] Postal Convention Regulating Communications by Post (Belgium and Britain) 1876.

[38] Above, fn.36 at 154. See also *Walker v Baird* [1892] A.C. 491; *The Republic of Italy v Hambros Bank Ltd* [1950] Ch. 314; *McWhirter v Att.–Gen.* [1972] C.M.L.R. 882, also illustrate the need for an Enabling Act.

before both Houses of Parliament for 21 days prior to ratification and publication in the UK Treaty Series.[39] Although it was expedient to provide this opportunity for discussion, it was not legally required.[40]

The Constitutional Reform and Governance Act 2010 gives the UK Parliament a statutory role in the ratification of treaties and gives statutory force to aspects of the Ponsonby Rule. Under the 2010 Act, the government has a general statutory duty to publish a treaty that is subject to ratification or its equivalent, and lay it before Parliament for 21 sitting days.

In the event of a conflict between a national statute and a treaty, the national legislative measure will prevail. Such was the case with the European Convention for the Protection of Human Rights and Fundamental Freedoms (the European Convention), which was not part of UK domestic law until 1998, when the European Convention was incorporated by the Human Rights Act.[41] The position prior to 1998 continues to illustrate the stance taken vis-à-vis an international obligation which is not incorporated into UK domestic law.[42] In the event of an Act of Parliament containing provisions contrary to an international convention, that Act would prevail, although domestic legislation should always be construed as far as is possible to be in conformity with international obligations. There is a presumption in treaty interpretation that Parliament does not intend to violate the UK's international obligations.[43] The Human Rights Act also provides redress against public authorities which allegedly violate the European Convention.[44]

The incorporation of the European Convention coincided with a major constitutional change within the UK, namely devolution and the establishment of Governments and Assemblies in Scotland, Northern Ireland and Wales. Under the Scotland Act 1998, all acts of the Scottish Government and Scottish Parliament

---

[39] Hansard, HC Deb., Vol.171, cols 2003–2004 (1 April 1924).

[40] e.g. the Rule was not applied when the UK accepted the compulsory jurisdiction of the I.C.J. there being no requirement for ratification—Hansard, HC Deb., Vol.578, cols 1145–1146 (27 November 1957).

[41] The Act entered into force on 2 October 2000.

[42] *R. v Secretary of State for the Home Department and Another, Ex p. Bhajan Singh* [1976] Q.B. 198 at 207. See *R. v Chief Immigration Officer, Ex p. Bibi* [1976] 1 W.L.R. 979 at 984 CA; Lord Bridge in *Brind v Secretary of State* [1991] 1 All E.R. 722 at 722–723 HL. *Birdi v Secretary of State for Home Affairs*, unreported, 1975, but quoted in Singh at 207; *Kaur v Lord Advocate* 1981 S.L.T. 3222 at 322; *Moore v Secretary of State for Scotland* 1985 S.L.T. 38 ABD 41; obiter dicta of Lord Hope in T. Petitioner 1966 S.C.L.R. 897 at 910–911.

[43] With respect to the European Convention, all new legislation must include a "compatibility" clause.

[44] Human Rights Act s.6.

must be compatible with the European Convention.[45] Acts of the Westminster (UK) Parliament cannot be struck out on human-rights grounds but merely declared "incompatible".[46]

Notwithstanding the competence of Scottish courts mentioned above vis-à-vis the devolved Government and Parliament, UK courts are concerned with the application of national law and, if their provisions cannot be reconciled with international law, that is a matter solely for the consideration of the legislature and not the judiciary.[47]

An issue which has been raised is that of unincorporated treaties and whether they can create legitimate expectations for individuals. The acceptance of the principle of legitimate expectations was made by Lord Woolf in *R. v Secretary of State for the Home Department Ex p. Ahmed and Patel*[48] when he made reference to the Australian case of *Teoh*.[49] However the principle is of limited application and an individual can only anticipate that the executive will respect the relevant treaty provisions. Other interpretive practices which bring international law into the national legal order are used, in particular the use of international law as persuasive or influential authority. In the Canadian case of *Baker v Canada (Minister of Citizenship and Immigration)*,[50] the Supreme Court of Canada considered whether an immigration officer had unreasonably exercised his discretion in ordering the deportation of a Jamaican woman, thereby separating her from her four Canadian-born children. The Supreme Court held that the children's interests were important considerations which should have governed the immigration officer's exercise of discretion.[51]

---

[45] The Scottish Executive came into existence in May 1999, but is now referred to as the Scottish Government, and the impact of the Convention was reflected primarily in the administration of justice, giving Scotland hands-on experience of incorporation some 18 months ahead of the rest of the UK.

[46] Human Rights Act s.4. For an instance of incompatibility see the House of Lords' decision in *A v Secretary of State for the Home Department; X v Secretary of State for the Home Department* [2004] UKHL 56, in particular the judgment of Baroness Hale of Richmond, para.219–220, to the effect that s.23 of the Anti-terrorism, Crime and Security Act 2001 was incompatible with arts 5 and 14 of the European Convention of Human Rights. However, should the Scottish Parliament enact legislation incompatible with the Convention, that legislative measure may be deemed "ultra vires". The Scottish Parliament only has competence in certain areas, namely devolved matters such as tax and education. Reserved matters such as foreign affairs and defence are retained by Westminster.

[47] See e.g. Lord Templeman in *Lord Advocate v Scotsman Publishers Ltd* 1989 S.L.T. 705 at 710.

[48] [1999] Imm. AR 22.

[49] *Minister for Immigration and Ethnic Affairs Re Teoh*, 1995 C.L.R. 273.

[50] 1999 2 S.C.R. 817, para.69–71.

[51] para.67.

The Supreme Court used the 1989 UN Convention on the Rights of the Child which, at the time of the case, had not been incorporated into Canadian law, as "an aid in interpreting domestic law",[52] and found on that basis that the immigration officer had unreasonably exercised his discretion.[53]

Executive certificate

The executive certificate is a statement issued by the UK Foreign and Commonwealth Office relating to "certain categories of questions of fact in the field of international affairs. In such cases the statement is conclusive even in the face of contrary evidence".[54] A certificate may stipulate, for instance, whether a particular foreign state or government is recognised by the UK[55]; whether a particular person is entitled to diplomatic immunity; or the existence and scope of British jurisdiction in a foreign country. An executive certificate is accepted as conclusive by the courts, as was held in *The Fagernes*,[56] *Duff Development Co v Government of Kelantan*[57] and *Post Office v Estuary Radio Ltd*[58] and is only reviewable in certain defined circumstances, see *R. v Secretary of State for Foreign and Commonwealth Affairs, Ex p. Trawnik*.[59]

An executive certificate is not conclusive in the interpretation of statutes or the construction of documents: *Re Al-Fin Corporation's Patent*.[60] The courts still, however, determine what the effect is of such a factual situation, although they may not examine the basis on which the Foreign and Commonwealth Office made its decision.

United States practice

US law, with its roots in the English legal system, adopts a similar attitude to international law as that of the UK. Accordingly, with respect to customary international law, the US is monistic in its approach and, in respect of treaties, dualistic.

---

[52] para.70.
[53] para.76. On the use of persuasive and influential authority see further Knop, "Here and There: International Law in Domestic Courts", (2000), 32 *NYU J Int'l L & Pol* 501.
[54] L. Oppenheim, *International Law* (1967) Vol. I, para.357(a).
[55] s.21 of the 1978 State Immunity Act provides that the Secretary of State's certificate is conclusive evidence as to (i) whether a country is a state within the meaning of the Act; (ii) who is the head of state; and (iii) who is the government.
[56] [1927] P. 311 at 324.
[57] [1924] A.C. 797 HL.
[58] [1968] 2 Q.B. 740.
[59] *The Times*, 18 April 1985, p.4. In this case a certificate issued pursuant to the State Immunity Act 1978 s.21 was held only reviewable if a nullity.
[60] [1971] Ch. 160.

Customary international law

Judicial decisions confirm that customary international law is part of US law. Marshall CJ, in *The Nercide*,[61] declared, in the absence of an Act of Congress, that the Court was bound by the law of nations, which was part of the law of the land, while Gray J. in 1900 pronounced:

> "International law is part of our law, and must be ascertained and administered by the courts of justice of appropriate jurisdiction, as often as questions of right depending upon it are duly presented for their determination."[62]

This acceptance of customary international law was, however, qualified in that

> "this rule of international law is one which prize courts, administering the law of nations, are bound to take judicial notice of, and to give effect to, in the absence of any treaty or other public act of their own government in relation to the matter".[63]

This was also the case in *Garcia-Mir v Meese*,[64] whereby the decision of the Attorney-General detaining illegal Cuban immigrants was held to be a "controlling executive act", although the length of the detention was such as to constitute a violation of customary international law.

The position today remains the same as demonstrated in the case of *United States v Fawaz Yunis*,[65] in which it was stated "our duty is to enforce the Constitution, laws, and treaties of the US, not to conform the law of the land to norms of customary international law."

The Court proceeded to reiterate its previous judicial pronouncement by declaring:

> "Statutes inconsistent with principles of customary international law may well lead to international law violations. But within the domestic legal realm, that inconsistent statute simply modifies or supersedes customary international law to the extent of the inconsistency."[66]

---

[61] 9 Cr. 388 (US 1815).
[62] *The Paquete Habana* 175 US 677 at 700 (1900).
[63] Above, at 708.
[64] 688 F (2d) 1446 (1986).
[65] Heard by the US Court of Appeals (D.C.) 30 I.L.M. 403 (1991).
[66] Above.

Customary international law is accepted without any legislative measure as part of US law, provided there is neither a national judicial decision nor a national legislative measure to the contrary. In the event of a conflict between alleged international law and municipal legislation, the national Courts will uphold the municipal provisions:

> "International practice is law only in so far as we adopt it, and like our common law or statute law it bends to the will of Congress ... There is one ground only upon which a federal court may refuse to enforce an Act of Congress and that is when the Act is held to be unconstitutional. The act may contravene recognised principles of international law, but that affords no more basis for judicial disregard of it than it does for the executive disregard of it."[67]

However norms that have achieved *jus cogens* are part of US law. In *Filartiga v Pena-Irala*[68] the Court stated that torture perpetrated against an individual by a state official was contrary to the law of nations.

What is the internal status of customary international law? Customary international law is accepted as federal law and its determination by the federal courts is binding on the state courts.[69]

Treaty law

Under the US Constitution, the President has "Power by and with the advice and consent of the Senate, to make Treaties, provided two-thirds of the Senators present concur."[70]

Unlike the UK, the US legislature participates in the treaty-making process. The President, in the light of the US Constitution, has the power to make a treaty, but he may only ratify a treaty after the Senate has given its advice and approval. "All treaties made or which shall be made under the authority of the US shall be the supreme law of the land."[71]

What is the status of a treaty within US domestic law? "Supreme" only places treaties on an equal footing with federal

---

[67] *Schroeder v Bissell* 5 F (2d) 838 (1925) (US Dist. Ct D.Conn.).
[68] 2nd Circ. 1980, 630 F.2d, 876. For further discussion of this case see Chs 2 and 9.
[69] Restatement of Foreign Relations Law (Third) of the US (Revised) § III Reporters' No.3. This is the prevailing view. It has not always been so. State and federal courts decided international issues for themselves and consequently issues of international law were determined differently by courts in different states and the federal courts.
[70] art.II(2).
[71] art.VI of the US Constitution.

statutes.[72] In the event of a conflict between a treaty and a subsequent statute, the latter prevails. This was made unequivocally clear by the Supreme Court in *Edye v Robertson*,[73] when it refuted the contention that an Act of Congress, which conflicted with an earlier US treaty, should be declared invalid. The Court unanimously held that a treaty is a law of the land, as is an Act of Congress, that there was nothing which made a treaty "irrepealable or unchangeable" and the Constitution gave "it no superiority over an Act of Congress in this respect, which may be repealed or modified by an Act of a later date". Congress, of course, does not enjoy the competence to act on the treaty itself and thus Congress cannot repeal a treaty. What Congress may do, however, is to enact legislation which will subsequently be determined as being inconsistent with the law as previously represented.

A treaty provision cannot "be rendered negatory in any part of the United States by municipal ordinances or state laws."[74] However, a later treaty provision will not be regarded as having repealed by implication an earlier statute unless "the two are absolutely incompatible and the Statute cannot be enforced without antagonising the treaty."[75] A treaty is not repealed or modified by a subsequent federal statute unless that is the clearly expressed intention of Congress.[76]

The presumption exists when interpreting domestic legislation that Congress does not intend to infringe international law, and Acts of Congress should be construed as conforming to international law. Courts strive to interpret Acts of Congress so that they do not conflict with earlier treaty provisions. Nevertheless, in *Diggs v Schultz*,[77] although recognising that the Byrd Amendment allowing imports contrary to the UN Security Council embargo on (as was then) Rhodesian products was in blatant disregard of US treaty obligations, the Court concluded under the American constitutional scheme that Congress could denounce treaties if it saw fit to do so and there was nothing other branches of government could do.

In the US, a distinction is made between "self-executing treaties" and "non-self-executing treaties". "Self-executing treaties" are automatically part of US domestic law, i.e. no implementing legislation is required—whereas "non-self-executing treaties" are not incorporated into domestic law until the necessary enabling legislation has been passed. Some provisions of an international

---

[72] *Edye v Robertson* 112 US 580 at 599 (1884).
[73] Above.
[74] *Asakura v City of Seattle* 265 US 332 at 341 (1924).
[75] *Johnson v Browne* 205 US 309 at 321 (1907).
[76] *Cooke v The United States* 288 US 102 at 119–120 (1933).
[77] 470 F (2d) 461 (1972).

agreement may be self-executing, while other provisions in the same agreement may be non-self-executing. The distinction was initially made in *Foster and Elam v Neilson*,[78] when Marshall CJ submitted:

> "A treaty is in its nature a contract between two nations, not a legislative act. It does not generally effect of itself, the object to be accomplished, especially so far as its operation is intraterritorial but is carried into execution by the sovereign power of the respective parties to the instrument. In the US a different principle is established. Our Constitution declares a treaty to be the law of the land. It is, consequently, to be regarded in courts of justice as equivalent to an act of the legislature, whenever it operates of itself without the aid of any legislative provision. But when the terms of the stipulation import a contract, when either of the parties engages to perform a particular act, the treaty addresses itself to the political, not the judicial department; and the legislature must execute the contract before it can become a rule for the court."[79]

Similarly, in *Sei Fujii v California*,[80] it was observed that in order to determine whether a treaty is self-executing, courts must look to "the intent of the signatory parties as manifested by the language of the instrument, and, if the instrument is uncertain, recourse may be had to the circumstances surrounding its execution" and "for a treaty provision to be operative without further implementing legislation and have statutory effect and force, it must appear that the framers of the treaty intended to prescribe a rule that, standing alone, would be enforceable in the courts."

The determining factor as to whether a treaty provision will be self-executing within the US is the intention of the treaty framers. If the agreement is silent and the intention of the US is unclear, account must be taken of relevant circumstances surrounding its conclusion, such as any statement issued by the President or any views expressed by the Senate. A treaty provision, to be self-executing, must therefore be:

---

[78] 27 US (2 Pet.) 253 at 314 (1829).

[79] The treaty in *Foster v Neilson*, which Marshall CJ held was not to be self-executing, was later held by him to be self-executing, after the Spanish text was placed before the Court. *United States v Percheman* 32 US (7 Pet.) 51 (1833). In the case of *Medellin v Texas*, 552 U.S. (2008) the US Supreme Court held that the Optional Protocol to the 1963 Vienna Convention on Consular Relations, although binding as a matter of international law, was not of domestic binding effect because it was not self-executing and there was no incorporating legislative act.

[80] 242 P. (2d) 617 (1952); 19 I.L.R. 312 (1952) Supreme Ct of California.

(a) unambiguous,

(b) certain, and

(c) not forward-looking

(i.e. legally complete and not dependent on subsequent legislation for its implementation).[81]

Generally, agreements which can be readily given effect by executive or judicial bodies, federal or state, without further federal legislation are deemed self-executing, unless a contrary intention is manifest. Treaties covering issues on which Congress has regulated extensively are more likely to be interpreted as non-self-executing.

Self-executing treaties are advantageous in that they prevent delay in the execution of obligations and they obviate the need (i) to include the participation of the House of Representatives (excluded from the treaty-making process by the Constitution), and (ii) to further consult the Senate after having received its consent under the two-thirds majority rule.

Although there is no definitive rule as to what may and may not be the subject of a self-executing treaty, there nevertheless appears to be a generally assumed principle that "an international agreement cannot take effect as domestic law without implementation by Congress if the agreement would do what lies within the exclusive law-making power of Congress under the Constitution."[82]

Executive agreements[83]

Executive agreements are international agreements entered into by the President without the advice and consent of Senate. Executive agreements are nevertheless regarded as being of the same force as a treaty and thereby, under international law, can effectively bind the US. The validity of an executive agreement was upheld in *US v Belmont*[84] and in *US v Pink*.[85] In the latter case, it was

---

[81] Hence in *Sei Fujii*, above. The provisions of the Preamble and arts 1, 55 and 56 of the UN were held not to be self-executing, as they lacked "the mandatory quality and definitions which would indicate an intent to create justiciable rights in private persons immediately upon ratification", but rather were "framed as a promise of future action by member nations."

[82] Restatement of Foreign Relations Law (Third) of the US (Revised) § III, Comment i; cf. *Missouri v Holland* 252 US 416 (1920). See below.

[83] For definition of "executive agreement", see letter of 26 January 1973 from C. Browne, Acting Legal Adviser to Carl Marcy, Chief of Staff of the Committee on Foreign Relations of the US Senate, Digest of US Practice in International Law (1973) p.187.

[84] 301 US 324 (1937).

[85] 315 US 203 (1942).

held "A treaty is a Law of the Land under the supremacy clause (art.VI, cl.2) of the Constitution. Such international compacts and agreements as the Litvinoff Agreement have a similar dignity."[86] Executive agreements may be superseded by subsequent federal legislation, but whether an executive agreement can supersede a prior treaty or Act of Congress is unclear.[87] The argument against such an effect is based essentially on the view that it would be inconceivable that the act of a single person, the President, could repeal an Act of Congress. However, an executive agreement is federal law and there are not varying degrees of status for federal law. "All constitutional acts of power, whether in the executive or the judicial department, have as much legal validity and obligation as if they proceeded from the legislature."[88] If an executive agreement was held to supersede a statute, Congress could re-enact the statute and thereby supersede the intervening executive agreement as domestic law.[89]

Attempts have been made to subject executive agreements to greater congressional control, for example the abortive Bricker Amendment 1953–54, Department of State Circular 175, 1955 (as amended 1966)[90] and the Case Act 1972, as amended in 1977 and 1978. In the 1972 Case Act[91] it was required that "all international agreements other than treaties, hereafter entered into by the US, be transmitted to the Congress within 60 days after the execution thereof." The 1977 amendment required the procedure laid down in the Case Act to be applied to agreements made by any department or agency of the US Government and, in 1978, this was extended to cover oral as well as written agreements. In July 2015, Iran and a group of world powers known as the P5+1 signed the Joint Comprehensive Plan of Action (JCPOA). This agreement between Iran and the five Permanent Members of the United Nations Security Council (China, France, Russia, US and UK) and Germany will lift UN sanctions on Iran in return for it limiting its nuclear programme. The JCPOA is controversial in the US and clearly demonstrates a lack of agreement between Congress, which unsuccessfully attempted to prevent the agreement being adopted, and President Obama.

---

86 315 US 203 (1942) at 230.
87 See, e.g. *United States v Guy W. Capps Inc.* 204 F (2d) 655 (1953) (US CA, 4th Circuit).
88 The Federalist, No.64 (Jay) cited in *US v Pink*, above, fn.85.
89 Above, fn.81, § 115 Reporters' N. 5. An executive agreement has been held to prevail over a subsequent inconsistent state law—*Territory of Hawaii v Ho 41 Hawaii 565* (1957); 26 I.L.R. 557.
90 Foreign Affairs Manual, Vol. III.
91 P.L. 92–403, 86 Stat. 619; 1 US CA 112b.

Congressional executive agreements

A congressional executive agreement is an international agreement made by the President with the backing of a simple majority in both Houses of Congress. Such agreements have an advantage over the treaty as prescribed by the Constitution in that their use can simplify the legislative process. For example, a treaty goes to the Senate for consent and then subsequently often goes back to the Senate as well as to the House for implementation, whereas a congressional executive agreement can go to both Houses in the first instance, and thus "consent" and implementation are achieved simultaneously. The prevailing view is the Congressional executive agreement can be used as an alternative to the treaty method in every instance. Which procedure should be used is a political judgment, made in the first instance by the President, subject to the possibility that the Senate might refuse to consider a joint resolution of Congress to approve an agreement, insisting the President submit the agreement as a treaty.[92] Examples of Congressional Executive Agreements are those enacting US participation in the North America Free Trade Agreement (NAFTA) and the World Trade Organisation (WTO), which have led to objections that under the Constitution significant international obligations should be submitted to the Senate and the prescribed procedure.

However such a challenge against Congressional Executive Agreements has not been accepted by any court, see *Made in the USA Foundation v United States*.[93]

Problems peculiar to a federal state

In a unitary state, the authority to enter into international agreements and the competence (subject to legislative approval) to give internal effect to such legislation lies with the central government. This is not the case in a federal state, where legislative competence is divided between the federal government and the individual state governments. *Missouri v Holland*[94] illustrates how legislation may be introduced by the back door. A 1913 Act of Congress designed to protect migratory wild fowl was declared to be outside the legislative competence of the federal government, and within the residual power of the states' legislatures. In 1916, the US concluded the Migratory Bird Treaty with the UK (acting on behalf of Canada) and the Treaty was given internal effect within the US by the Migratory Bird Treaty Act 1918. Appeal was made

---

[92] Above, fn.88, § 303 Comment e.
[93] 56 F Supp (2d) 1226 (N.D. Ala. 1999).
[94] 252 US 416 (1920).

to the Supreme Court following a district Court's dismissal of a suit brought by the state of Missouri attempting to prevent Holland, a game warden, from enforcing the Migratory Bird Treaty Act. The Supreme Court held the Act of Congress being challenged was valid, as

> "the power of the Federal Government to make and enforce treaties is not a limitation on the reserved powers of States, but is the existence of a power not reserved to the States under the 10th Amendment being both expressly granted to the United States and prohibited to the States."[95]

In other words, there is no limitation on what could be the subject matter of a treaty, and the enforcement of a treaty, regardless of subject matter, falls within the exclusive competence of the federal government.

Missouri v Holland may be contrasted with *Attorney General for Canada v Attorney General for Ontario*.[96] Canada, like the US, is a federal state and in 1937, the Judicial Committee of the Privy Council was required to give its opinion on what was the position when the federal government did not have the competence to give internal effect to international obligations which it had undertaken.[97] The Committee advised:

> "There is no such thing as treaty legislation as such. The distribution is based on classes of subjects; and as a treaty deals with a particular class so will the legislative power of performing it be ascertained ... the Dominion cannot, merely by making promises to foreign countries, clothe itself with legislative authority inconsistent with the Constitution."

Further:

> "In a unitary State whose legislature possesses unlimited powers the problem is simple. Parliament will either fulfil or not treaty obligations imposed upon the State by its executive. The nature of the obligations does not affect the complete authority of the Legislature to make them law if it so chooses ..., in a federal State where legislative authority is limited ..., or is divided up between different Legislatures

---

[95] 252 US 416 (1920) at 431.
[96] [1937] A.C. 326.
[97] Legislation designed to give effect within Canada to draft conventions adopted by the International Labour Organisation and the League of Nations was claimed to be invalid, as the Dominion Parliament did not possess the competency to legislate on the subject matter concerned.

. . . the problem is complex . . . The question is not how is the obligation formed, that is the function of the executive; but how is the obligation to be performed".[98]

It may also happen in a federal state that the federal government will undertake an international obligation which is inconsistent with the law of a particular constituent part of the federation. As far as possible, the "offending" legislation will be interpreted as being consistent with international law, but the general principle regarding such a conflict is that it is the central government and not the constituent state which will have to answer to the international community.

A similar problem could potentially arise within the devolved UK. The UK remains responsible at the international level for (non) fulfilment of international obligations. However, the division in competence brought about by devolution might lead to a situation in which the Westminster (UK) Parliament finds itself without the internal competence to give effect to its international obligations, however, that would not absolve the UK of its international obligations.[99]

Suggestion

The State Department's Suggestion is the US counterpart of the UK executive certificate. However, the suggestion does not confine itself to merely giving the facts, but may include comments on the situation and indicate the executive's attitude. Although not regarded as conclusive, the suggestion will be treated as persuasive by the courts.

Act of state doctrine[100]

What if a measure of a foreign state is contrary to international law? The act of state doctrine precludes a court from inquiring into the validity of the public acts of a recognised foreign sovereign power within its own territory: "the Judicial Branch will not examine the validity of a taking of property within its own territory by a foreign sovereign government."[101]

---

[98] Above, fn.96 at 351, 352 and 347. The limited internal competence of the federal government was why Canada did not accede to the UN 1966 Covenants on Economic, Social and Cultural Rights and Civil and Political Rights until 1976.

[99] See, however, the Scotland Act s.58(1); see also the *Tyrer* case (1978) 58 I.L.R. 339.

[100] Act of state has a different connotation in British constitutional law—an alien who is injured abroad by an act authorised or subsequently approved by the Crown has no remedy in English Courts.

[101] *Banco Nacional de Cuba v Sabbatino* 376 US 398 at 428 (1964).

The essence of the act of state doctrine is that the act of one state's government cannot be successfully questioned by the courts of another: "Redress of grievances by reason of such acts must be obtained through the means open to be availed of by sovereign powers as between themselves."[102] In other words, the judiciary abstains from giving a decision in deference to the executive so as not to embarrass the conduct of the executive's foreign relations by questioning the acts of foreign states. The act of state doctrine is similar, but yet distinct from sovereign immunity[103] in that both are based on considerations of respect for the sovereign independence and equality of states, and on perceived limitations on the authority of domestic courts of one state to judge the activities of another state. However, whereas sovereign immunity relates to activities carried out and provides jurisdictional defence to suit, the act of state doctrine operates so as to preclude judicial scrutiny of the activities of foreign states in their own territories. Strict adherence to the act of state doctrine was maintained by the US Supreme Court in the *Sabbatino* case, even when the State Department had described the Cuban legislative measure as

> "manifestly in violation of those principles of international law which has long been accepted by the free countries of the West. It is in its essence discriminatory, arbitrary and confiscatory."[104]

The outcome of the *Sabbatino* case was that the Court gave effect to the Cuban decree, in spite of its having been contrary to international law.

The act of state doctrine as understood in the *Sabbatino* case has its basis in the separation of powers and the raison d'être of the *Sabbatino* position was the need to avoid conflict between the judiciary and the executive on decisions regarding the legal nature of foreign actions.

The *Sabbatino* decision prompted a response from Congress in the form of the "Hickenlooper Amendments" to the Foreign Assistance Act, whereby

> "no court in the United States shall decline on the ground of the . . . Act of State doctrine to make a determination on the merits giving effect to the principles of international law in a case in which a claim of title or other right to property is asserted by any party including a foreign State (or a party

---

[102] *Underhill v Hernandez* 168 US 250 at 252 (1897).
[103] Discussed below in Ch.6.
[104] Above, fn.101 at 403.

claiming through such State) based upon (or traced through) a confiscation or other taking ... by an act of that State in violation of the principles of international law."[105]

Accordingly, US Courts may review the acts of foreign governments which violate international law and which affect property owned by US citizens. The State Department can express in a "suggestion" that the act of state is to apply in a particular case.

Judicial determination of the legality of the foreign act of state will not necessarily interfere with the executive's conduct of foreign affairs.[106]

In *Alfred Dunhill v Republic of Cuba*,[107] the Legal Adviser to the State Department submitted a letter in which he stated that in the State Department's experience there was little support for the presumption "that adjudication of acts of foreign States in accordance with the relevant principles of international law would embarrass the conduct of foreign policy." Accordingly, he concluded it would not cause embarrassment to the conduct of US foreign policy if the Court demanded to follow the holding in the *Sabbatino* case.[108] In *W.S. Kirkpatrick and Co v Environmental Tectonics Corp International*,[109] the US Supreme Court declined to apply the act of state doctrine, stating:

> "The act of State doctrine does not establish an exception for cases and controversies that may embarrass foreign governments but merely requires that, in the process of deciding, the acts of foreign sovereigns taken within their own jurisdiction shall be deemed valid. That doctrine has no application to the present case because the validity of no foreign sovereign act is at issue".[110]

The act of state doctrine does not apply in respect of war crimes or offences over which there is universal jurisdiction. The act of state doctrine should be distinguished from the political question doctrine; namely, there are certain national issues so sensitive that they are non-justiciable.[111] Cases which raise the political question

---

[105] s.620(e)(2) of the Foreign Assistance Act of 1965, Pub.L.No.89–171; 301(d)(2), 79 Stat. 653, 659, as amended.

[106] See, *Banco Nacional de Cuba v First National City Bank* US Supreme Ct, 406 US 759 (1972); 92 S.L.T. 1808.

[107] 425 US 682 (1976).

[108] 425 US 682 (1976) letter of Monroe Leigh, Legal Adviser, Department of State—printed as App.706, 709, 710–711.

[109] 493 US 400 (1990).

[110] 29 I.L.M. 182 (1990), Scalia J at 189.

[111] *US v Sisson* 294 F. Supp 515 (D.Mass. 1968), in which the Court concluded that

doctrine are dismissed by the courts, unlike those involving the act of state doctrine, which are adjudicated.

The act of state doctrine is one of US municipal law. There is no rule of international law which requires the application of the act of state doctrine.

In English law the position is as expressed in the *Butts Gas and Oil Company v Hammer (No.3)*[112] namely that "there exists in English law a general principle that the courts will not adjudicate upon the transactions of foreign sovereign states".[113] However notwithstanding the general rule the House of Lords (the predecessor to the UK Supreme Court) refused to uphold an act of the Iraqi Government in *Kuwait Airways Corporation v Iraqi Airways Company*.[114] What was at issue in that case was a violation of international law by one state against another.

CONCLUSION

The relationship between domestic and international law is primarily a matter of domestic law. As has been seen, states differ in their approach to international law. What is important is that a state may not successfully employ either the existence of, or the omission of, a domestic law as a reason for non-compliance with international obligations. Arguably the majority of states generally comply with international law and bring domestic law into line with international norms. This is necessary for the functioning of international law which demands that states do not act unilaterally which would undermine the international legal framework.

---

a domestic tribunal was incapable of ascertaining facts pertaining during war and the defendant had submitted an issue of a political character not within the jurisdiction of the Court. The defendant had invoked as his defence to a charge of refusing to serve in the US armed forces that the US operations in Vietnam were contrary to international law. On non-justiciability of political questions, see also *Baker v Carr* 369 US 186 (1962) and *Greenham Women against Cruise Missiles v Reagan* 591 F. Supp 1332 (1984).

[112] [1982] A.C. 888.

[113] Above, at 931–932.

[114] [2002] UKHL 19.

4. INTERNATIONAL PERSONALITY

The possession of international personality means an entity is a subject of international law; is "capable of possessing international rights and duties, and has the capacity to maintain its rights by bringing international claims."[1]

A subject of international law has obligations and enjoys rights, the benefits of which may be claimed, and which, if denied, may be enforced to the extent recognised by the international legal system, via legal procedures. That is, the entity will have procedural capacity.

Which entities possess international legal personality? The concept of international legal personality is neither static nor uniform:

> "The subjects of law in any legal system are not necessarily identical in their nature or in the extent of their rights, and their nature depends upon the needs of the community. Throughout its history, the development of international life . . . and the progressive increase in the collective activities of States has already given rise to instances of action

---

[1] *Reparation for Injuries Suffered in the Service of the United Nations* I.C.J. Rep. 1949 at p.174.

upon the international plane by certain entities which are not States."[2]

As international law has developed and expanded in scope, new entities have been admitted as actors on the international scene. The personality enjoyed by such actors varies considerably.

Traditionally, states were considered the exclusive subjects of international law:

> "Since the law of nations is based on the common consent of individual States, and not of individual human beings, States solely and exclusively are the subjects of international law."[3]

However, although they remain the primary subjects, states are no longer the exclusive subjects of the contemporary international legal system. Throughout the 20th century the scope of international legal personality widened considerably to take account of, and accommodate, the proliferation of other actors in the international system, which are generally referred to as "non-state actors". States possess full international legal personality as an inherent attribute of statehood, however other entities possessing personality do so to the extent that states allow: that is, their international personality is derived via states.

The personality of states is original and that of other entities is derivative.

STATES

States are the principal "persons" of international law. International law is essentially the manifestation of relations between states, be it through practice contributing to the formation of customary international law or through international agreements (treaties). Only states may be parties to contentious cases before the International Court of Justice (ICJ).[4] States enjoy the exclusive discretion as to whether or not to espouse a claim on behalf of a national who has allegedly been aggrieved by another state; and once a state does take up a claim, the dispute is raised to the international level and becomes one between two states.[5] An individual cannot deny a state's right to espouse a claim on his or

---

[2] *Reparation for Injuries Suffered in the Service of the United Nations* I.C.J. Rep. 1949 at 178.

[3] L. Oppenheim, *International Law*, 2nd edn (1912).

[4] art.34(1), Statute of the International Court of Justice.

[5] See, e.g. *Mavrommatis Palestine Concessions* case P.C.I.J. Rep., ser.A, No.2 (1924). See also, Ch.8.

her behalf should it choose to do so[6] and a state does not act as the agent of its nationals when negotiating a treaty.[7]

What is a state?

A "state" in international law is an entity which has a defined territory; a permanent population; is under the control of a government; and engages in, or has the capacity to engage in, formal relations with other entities.[8]

This definition reflects the indices of statehood identified in the 1933 Montevideo Convention on the Rights and Duties of States (the Montevideo Convention).[9] The Montevideo Convention, regarded as representing in general terms the requirements of statehood demanded by customary international law, was adopted by the Seventh International Conference of American States (15 Latin American states and the US) and provides:

"The State as a person of international law should possess the following qualifications: (a) a permanent population, (b) a defined territory; (c) government; and (d) capacity to enter into relations with other states."[10]

In 1991, Opinion Number 1 of the Arbitration Commission of the European Conference of Yugoslavia—commonly known as the Badinter Arbitration Committee—stated, "the State is commonly defined as a community which consists of a territory and a population subject to an organized political authority" and "such a state is characterised by sovereignty".[11]

Permanent population

States are aggregates of individuals and, accordingly, a permanent population is a prerequisite of statehood. However, no minimum population is required, for example, China has over 1.4 billion people in it and states such as Nauru and Tuvalu have little more than 10,000. There is no requirement that the population be of homogeneous ethnicity or culture.

---

[6] *North American Dredging Company* case 4 R.I.A.A. 26 at 29 and following (1926).

[7] See, e.g. *Rustomjee v R.* (1876) 1 Q.B.D. 487 at 492; *Civilian War Claimants' Association Ltd v The King* [1932] A.C. 14 HL at 26.

[8] The American Law Institute, Restatement of the Law Third, The Foreign Relations Law of the United States, Vol.1, § 201.

[9] 164 L.N.T.S. 19; U.S.T.S. 881; 28 A.J.I.L., Supp., 75 (1934).

[10] art.1, Montevideo Convention.

[11] 92 I.L.R., pp.162, 165. The Badinter Arbitration Committee was set up in August 1991 by the Council of Ministers of the then European Economic Community (EEC). It was comprised of five members who were all presidents of constitutional courts of the EEC. The Committee's mandate was to express its views on certain matters in relation to the peace process following the breakup of Yugoslavia.

Defined territory

States are territorial units and

> "'territorial sovereignty' involves the exclusive right to dis-
> play the activities of a State. This right has a corollary, a duty:
> the obligation to protect within the territory the rights of other
> States, in particular their right to integrity and inviolability in
> peace and in war, together with the rights which each State
> may claim for its nationals in foreign territory. Without mani-
> festing its territorial sovereignty in a manner corresponding to
> circumstances, the State cannot fulfil this duty. Territorial sov-
> ereignty cannot limit itself to its negative side, i.e. to excluding
> the activities of other States, for it serves to divide between the
> nations the space upon which human activities are employed,
> in order to assure them at all points the minimum of protection
> of which international law is the guardian".[12]

Article 9 of the Montevideo Convention provides that:

> "The jurisdiction of States within the limits of national terri-
> tory applies to all the inhabitants. Nationals and foreigners
> are under the same protection of the law and the national
> authorities and the foreigners may not claim rights other or
> more extensive than those of the nationals."

However, while territory is necessary, there is no prescribed
minimum geographical size. Citing the same examples as above,
China is over 9.5 million km² and Nauru consists of 21 km². The
requirement of territory may be satisfied even if the entity's territorial boundaries are not precisely defined or are to some extent
in dispute, for example Israel, the borders of which have never
been agreed with its neighbours. Therefore, disputable borders
do not negate statehood. Another example is Somalia, the borders
of which are disputed both internally and externally. In respect of
the former, Somaliland broke away from Somalia after the government was overthrown in 1991, and continues to lobby to be recognised as a sovereign state. In the latter case Somalia has previous
and ongoing border disputes with Kenya and Ethiopia. This rule
that indefinite boundaries need not defeat a claim to statehood
was endorsed by the ICJ in the *North Sea Continental Shelf* cases:

> "The appurtenance of a given area, considered as an entity, in
> no way governs the precise determination of its boundaries,

---

[12] *Island of Palmas* case 2 R.I.A.A. 829, Huber J at 839 (1928).

any more than uncertainty as to boundaries can affect territorial rights. There is for instance no rule that the land frontiers of a State must be fully delimited and defined, and often in various places and for long periods they are not".[13]

However, one of the reasons advanced by the British for the non-recognition of Bophuthatswana as an independent state was the fragmentation of its territory within South Africa.[14]

A government

Statehood must be evidenced by the establishment of an effective government, that is one independent of any other authority and one which enjoys legislative and administrative competence.[15] Non-dependence was stressed by the International Committee of Jurists in 1920 in its Report on the Status of Finland. The Committee highlighted the difficulty of ascertaining the actual date when Finland became, in the legal sense, a sovereign state, but concluded it certainly was not one

> "until a stable political organisation had been created, and until the public authorities had become strong enough to assert themselves throughout the territories of the State without the assistance of foreign troops. It would appear that it was in May 1918, that the civil war ended and that the foreign troops began to leave the country, so that from that time onwards it was possible to re-establish order and normal political and social life, little by little."[16]

Statehood is not nullified if an established state is without an effective government for a period of time, for example during a civil war, e.g. Somalia. Somalia was ravaged by civil war from 1991 until 2004, but during that time continued to be recognised as a state and was a member of the United Nations. In 2012, the country emerged from an eight-year period of political transition and in August of that year Somalia's first formal parliament for over 20 years was sworn in. During the civil war Somalia was considered

---

[13] I.C.J. Rep. 1969 3 at 32.

[14] Other reasons are the pattern of population, the economic dependency on South Africa and primarily the fact "the existence of Bophuthatswana is a consequence of apartheid". See Hansard, HC, Vol.126, cols 760–761. (3 February 1988); U.K.M.I.L. 1986; 57 B.Y.I.L. 507 (1986).

[15] Again note the British position vis-à-vis Bophuthatswana and the latter's economic dependence on South Africa. Bophuthatswana was re-incorporated into South Africa on 27 April 1994 and ceased to exist as a separate political entity. The flag is no longer in use.

[16] L.N.O.J., Special Supp. No.3 (1920) 3.

a failed state in that despite possessing legal capacity it was unable to exercise it in the absence of an effective regime. Other such examples have included Afghanistan, Liberia, Sierra Leone and the Democratic Republic of Congo, thereby highlighting that the absence of an effective regime does not negate statehood.

In 1992, Croatia[17] and Bosnia-Herzegovina[18] were accorded recognition as independent states from the former Socialist Federal Republic of Yugoslavia by Member States of the European Community (now European Union), notwithstanding that large areas of their respective territories were controlled by non-governmental forces. Nor does military occupation terminate statehood, for example Germany's occupation of certain European states during the Second World War or the military occupation of Iraq following the overthrow of Saddam Hussein in 2003.

Capacity to enter into international relations

An important indicator of statehood is the response of other actors on the international stage. The first three criteria for statehood demands certain facts are fulfilled, but satisfying this criterion depends on recognition:

> "The political existence of the State is independent of recognition by the other States. Even before recognition the State has the right to defend its integrity and independence, to provide for its conservation and prosperity, and consequently to organise itself as it sees fit, to legislate upon its interests, administer its services, and to define the jurisdiction and competence of its Courts. The exercise of these rights has no other limitation than the exercise of the rights of other States according to international law."[19]

An entity may have the capacity to enter into foreign relations but, should other states decline to enter into relations with it, the entity in question is denied the opportunity to demonstrate this capacity in practice. For example, Southern Rhodesia (now Zimbabwe), a British self-governing territory until it declared unilateral independence from Britain in November 1965, had

---

[17] 15 January 1992, however, note Croatia was deemed not to have met the requirements laid down in the Draft Convention on Yugoslavia on 4 November 1991 and in the Declaration on Yugoslavia and Guidelines on the Recognition of New States in Eastern Europe and in the Soviet Union, of 16 December 1991 (92 I.L.R., p.178).

[18] 6 April 1992. For reservations with respect to the independence of Bosnia and Herzegovina prior to holding a referendum, see Opinion Number 4 (92 I.L.R., p.173).

[19] art.3, Montevideo Convention, above, fn.9.

a population, territory, a government and the capacity to enter into relations with other states. However, no other state was willing to enter into relations with it. Southern Rhodesia was therefore refused recognition as a state by the rest of the international community.[20] Similarly, governments consistently refused to enter into relations with the Transkei. The Transkei territory was declared by South Africa in 1976 to be a "sovereign and independent state", but the United Nations General Assembly subsequently adopted a resolution rejecting the "independence" as "invalid".[21] Similarly, the recognition of Bophuthatswana, Venda and Ciskei was denied by all members of the international community other than South Africa. The independence of Ciskei was refuted by the UN Security Council, which issued a statement calling upon "all Governments to deny any form of recognition to the so-called 'independent' Bantustans."[22]

An entity which possesses the ability to conduct foreign relations does not terminate its statehood if it voluntarily hands over all or part of the conduct of its foreign relations to another state, for example San Marino to Italy[23] and Monaco to France. Another "mini" European state is Liechtenstein, which operates within the Swiss economic system and has delegated a number of sovereign powers to Switzerland but, nevertheless, is still recognised as a sovereign state.[24] Similarly, the personality of a protected state which existed before the conclusion of the agreement establishing its dependent status, is not extinguished. See, for example, *Nationality Decrees in Tunis and Morocco* case[25] and *Rights of Nationals of the United States in Morocco* case.[26] Such relationships were characteristic of the British and French Empires, and most

---

[20] See Security Council Resolution of 12 November 1965, Resolution 216 (1965) S.C.O.R., 20th year, Resolutions and Decisions, p.8 and Security Council Resolution of 20 November 1965, Resolution 217 (1965) S.C.O.R., 20th Year, Resolutions and Decisions, p.8 in which the Smith regime was characterised as illegal, the declaration of independence as of "no legal validity" and UN Members were called upon to refrain from assisting the "illegal racist minority regime". cf. the United Nations' response to PAIGC Declaration of Guinea-Bissau's independence in September 1973.

[21] GA Resolution, G.A.O.R., 31st Session, Supp.39, p.10.

[22] S.C.O.R., 36th Year, Resolutions and Decisions, p.1. The legislation relating to the homelands was repealed in 1993, and the four homelands have since been reabsorbed into South Africa.

[23] San Marino was admitted to the UN in March 1992.

[24] Although denied admission to the League of Nations on the grounds that she could not discharge all the international obligations which would be imposed upon her by the Covenant, Liechtenstein has been a party to a case before the I.C.J. (the *Nottebohm* case, ICJ Rep. (1955), p.4). Liechtenstein became a member of the UN on 18 September 1990.

[25] P.C.I.J. Rep., ser.B, No.4 (1923).

[26] I.C.J. Rep. 1952, 176.

were terminated during the decolonisation movement following the Second World War.

Membership of a regional organisation does not negate the statehood of individual members, for example the European Union, although admittedly, sovereignty in certain areas of competence may be restricted.

Self-determination

Political self-determination, that is the principle whereby the political future of a colony or similar non-independent territory is determined in accordance with the wishes of its inhabitants, is closely linked to issues of statehood. The origin of the principle of self-determination dates back to the French Revolution, however, it has been since the end of the Second World War and, most importantly, since the decolonisation processes of the 1960s, that it has developed. Thus the principle, which some 40 years ago was articulated as "a formative principle of great potency",[27] has now evolved into a rule of international law.[28] One of the purposes of the United Nations, as established in the Charter (arts 1.2 and 55), is to "develop friendly relations among nations based on respect for the principle of equal rights and self-determination of peoples". The principle developed through a series of UN General Assembly Declarations and ICJ decisions. In 1966 the International Covenants on Civil and Political Rights and Economic, Social and Cultural Rights included the right to self-determination as a collective right of peoples.

The 1960 Declaration on the Granting of Independence to Colonial Territories and Peoples (GA Resolution 1514) reads (para.2):

> "All peoples have a right to self-determination; by virtue of that right they freely determine their political status and freely pursue their economic, social and cultural development."[29]

The aim of para.2 was identified in the *Western Sahara* case.[30] It was acknowledged therein "that the application of the right of

---

[27] G. Schwarzenberger, *Manual of International Law* (6th edn, 1976), p.59.

[28] See decision of the Chamber of the International Court of Justice in the Frontier Dispute (Burkino Faso/Mali) I.C.J. Rep. 1986 554 at 566–567 in which the Chamber was required to consider the relationship between self-determination and *uti possidetis*. It has also been suggested that it constitutes a rule of *jus cogens*; see Espiell in *UN Law/Fundamental Rights: Two Topics in International Law* (Cassese edn, 1979) p.167.

[29] GA Resolution 1514 (XV), 14 December 1960, G.A.O.R., 15th Session, Supp.16, p.66, para.2.

[30] Advisory Opinion I.C.J. Rep. 1975 12.

self-determination requires a free and genuine expression of the will of the peoples concerned."[31] Dillard J, in a separate Opinion (though concurring in the Court's Opinion), stated:

> "It seemed hardly necessary to make more explicit the cardinal restraint which the legal right of self-determination imposes. The restraint may be captured in a single sentence. It is for the people to determine the destiny of the territory and not the territory the destiny of the people".[32]

However, GA Resolution 1514 did not negate a title to colonial and similar non-independent territory which does not reflect the wishes of its people, but rather emphasises that "immediate steps" should be taken to ensure independence is attained in accordance with self-determination. The emergence of self-determination, as a cardinal principle in shaping the political future of a colonial or similar non-independent territory, means that such territories can no longer be considered as mere adjuncts of the administering state. They have, according to the 1970 Declaration on Principles of International Law Concerning Friendly Relations and Co-operation among States in Accordance with the Charter of the United Nations

> "a status separate and distinct from the territory of the State administering it; and such separate and distinct status under the [UN] Charter shall exist until the people of the colony or non-self-governing territory have exercised their right of self-determination in accordance with the Charter, and particularly its purposes and principles."[33]

This separate identity of an administered people is further reflected in several legal statements relating to the status of South West Africa (now Namibia).[34]

South West Africa was placed under a "C" Mandate by the League of Nations at the conclusion of the First World War. Mandates were introduced as a novel type of administration for those territories taken from defeated powers and "inhabited by peoples not yet able to stand by themselves under the strenuous conditions of the modern world."[35] After the conclusion of the

[31] Above, p.32.
[32] Above, p.122.
[33] Above, G.A. Res.2625 (XXV), "Declaration on Principles of International Law Concerning Friendly Relations and Co-operation among States in Accordance with the Charter of the United Nations" G.A.O.R., 25th Session, Supp.28 (A/2028) 121 (1970), 65 A.J.I.L. 243 (1970).
[34] South West Africa became the independent state of Namibia in November 1990.
[35] Covenant of the League of Nations art.22.

Second World War, the mandate system was replaced by that of trusteeship.[36] South Africa, however, refused to place South West Africa under that trusteeship system and this precipitated much political and legal argument on the status of South West Africa.[37] In the 1950 Opinion of the ICJ, Judge McNair pronounced the system involved a

> "new institution—a new relationship between territory and its inhabitants on the one hand and the government which represents them internationally on the other—a new species of international government, which does not fit into the old conception of sovereignty and which is alien to it."[38]

The sovereignty, Judge McNair maintained, was held to be in abeyance until the inhabitants of the territory obtained recognition as an independent state. The issues before the ICJ concerned the responsibilities and duties of South Africa, but against the backcloth of the self-determination movement there was a move away from the traditional view that a mandated/trusteeship territory only achieved international recognition on attaining independence, to one according such an entity at least a degree of international status. This view was articulated by Judge Ammoun when he concluded:

> "Namibia, even at the periods when it had been reduced to the status of a German colony or was subject to the South African Mandate, possessed a legal personality which was denied to it only by the law now obsolete . . . It nevertheless constituted a subject of law . . . possessing national sovereignty but lacking the exercise thereof . . . Sovereignty, . . . did not cease to belong to the people subject to mandate. It had simply, for a time, been rendered inarticulate and deprived of freedom of expression."[39]

Judge Ammoun's view illustrates what was then the emerging change in international attitude, namely, non-self-governing territories could no longer be dismissed as adjuncts of the

---

[36] The system applied only to 11 territories—10 former mandates and Somalia taken from Italy. No other territories were brought into the system as was envisaged by art.77(1) of the UN Charter.

[37] *International Status of South West Africa* case I.C.J. Rep. 1950, 128; *Legal Consequences for States of the Continued Presence of South Africa in Namibia (South West Africa) Notwithstanding Security Council Resolution 276 (1970)*. Advisory Opinion I.C.J. Rep. 1971, 16.

[38] Above, p.150.

[39] Above, fn.37, I.C.J. Rep. 1971 at p.68.

administering state, but rather enjoyed some status, be it one that fell short of full sovereignty.[40]

Self-determination is an issue which has generated considerable controversy. Contemporary international law does acknowledge self-determination as a legal right in the colonial context. However, a claim for self-determination outside the colonial context is one which still gives rise to considerable debate.

The issue of self-determination beyond the traditional context of colonialism has highlighted that self-determination may have an internal aspect as well as an external aspect. In the Canadian Supreme Court decision in *Re Reference by the Governor in Council Concerning Certain Questions Relating to the Secession of Quebec from Canada*,[41] the Court dealt with whether the province of Quebec enjoyed the right to secede unilaterally from Canada.[42] The Court concluded in the negative, holding that any right of self-determination could only arise in strictly limited circumstances and international law does not support the "right" of entities within an existing state to secede unilaterally. The Court accordingly upheld the principle of territorial integrity of existing states. It was also noted that no right of external self-determination would be recognised when full participation in civil and political life is available, namely internal self-determination, which may be interpreted as the right of a minority people to pursue political, economic, social, and cultural development, within the framework of an existing state.[43]

The Badinter Committee on Yugoslavia stated: "That whatever the circumstances, the right to self-determination must not involve changes to existing frontiers at the time of independence (*uti possidetis juris*) except where the State concerned agreed otherwise".[44]

Self-determination may be expressed legitimately without

---

[40] e.g. Hong Kong, could not satisfy the criteria for statehood because it was subject to the legal authority of the UK. The Hong Kong Special Administrative Region (HKSAR) was established on 1 July 1997, under the legal authority of China. The HKSAR has limited treaty-making competence and is able to conclude agreements independently of China in certain fields, e.g. shipping, trade, communications, financial and monetary. Foreign and Commonwealth Office, Paper, London, Application after 30 June 1997 of Multilateral and Bilateral International Agreements, Hong Kong Department, April 1996.

[41] (1998) 161 D.L.R. (4th) 385.

[42] The Court was asked whether such a right existed under the Canadian Constitution or by way of existing international law.

[43] See Final Report and Recommendations of an International meeting of Experts on the Further Study of the Concept of the Right of People for UNESCO, 22 February 1990, SNS–89/CONF.602/7.

[44] See Opinion No.2, 3 E.J.I.L. (1992) 183–184. The Committee's opinion was sought on whether "The Serbian population in Croatia and Bosnia-Herzegovina, as one of the constituent peoples of Yugoslavia, have the right to self-determination."

violating established international provisions protecting territorial integrity. However, the right of self-determination nevertheless has to be tempered otherwise: "if every ethnic, religious or linguistic group claimed Statehood, there would be no limit to fragmentation, and peace, security, and economic well-being for all would be much more difficult to achieve."[45]

Much of this controversy stems from an assumption that self-determination and its expression is premised on a granting of independence and thus the break-up of territorial units. The right to self-determination is not equivalent to a right of secession. In 2010, the ICJ reopened the debate on the necessary balance between the principle of self-determination of people and territorial integrity. In its Advisory Opinion on 22 July 2010, it considered the compliance of Kosovo's unilateral declaration from Serbia in 2008 with international law and reached the conclusion that such a declaration was not in violation of general international law.[46]

Self-determination remains current to the international scene. One example of internal self-determination was the referendum on Scottish independence held in 2014, the terms of which were agreed between the UK Government and devolved Scottish Government.[47] Also in 2014, the Crimean Peninsula declared itself independent from Ukraine and, after a referendum, was annexed by Russia.

RECOGNITION OF STATES AND GOVERNMENTS

The international community is not static. New states are born while existing states may become extinct. The post-conflict dissolution of the Socialist Federal Republic of Yugoslavia in 1991/92, for example, led to the creation of Bosnia-Herzegovina, Slovenia, Croatia and Macedonia as independent states, with Montenegro declaring independence from Serbia in 2006, followed by Kosovo in 2008. In 2008 South Ossetia declared independence from Georgia, though very few states have recognised it as an independent state. In July 2011 South Sudan attained independence from Sudan, becoming the youngest state in the international community. Governments come to power and are removed from power. Recognition essentially denotes a willingness on the part

---

[45] UN Secretary-General Boutros Boutros-Ghali, Agenda for Peace, reproduced in A. Roberts and B. Kingsbury, *United Nations, Divided World: The UN's Roles in International Relations*, 2nd edn, Oxford: Clarendon Press, 1993.

[46] *Accordance with international law of the unilateral declaration of independence in respect of Kosovo*, Advisory Opinion of 22 July 2010.

[47] The result of the referendum was 55% in favour of Scotland remaining as part of the UK against 45% in favour of Scotland becoming a separate state.

of the recognising entity to enter into relations with the entity being recognised.

The recognition of a state is of importance as it is concerned with status, that is the status of the entity in question: (i) on the international scene; and (ii) within the domestic legal system of the recognising state.

Recognition is a complex issue. Factors other than legal considerations influence decisions to recognise any given entity. A state is accorded recognition in the majority of cases by the executive. It is a matter of policy in which the recognising state has discretion: an entity seeking recognition cannot however demand recognition as of right. An apt description of recognition is that it is a political act which produces legal consequences.

Recognition of states and governments distinguished

Recognition as a state is the formal acknowledgment by another state that the entity being recognised possesses the attributes of statehood.

Recognition of a government is the formal acknowledgment by the recognising state that the regime in question is the effective government and, accordingly, signifies a willingness to treat that regime as such.

Recognition of a state is normally a one-off act—that is, once an entity has been recognised as a state, that recognition will not usually be retracted if the requirements of statehood continue to be fulfilled. If these requirements cease to be fulfilled, the state may no longer exist but de-recognition will not be necessary. Two states, for example, may be consolidated into a single state, as in 1990, when the Yemen Arab Republic (North Yemen) and the People's Democratic Republic of Yemen (South Yemen) united to form the Republic of Yemen. However, the governmental regime of a state may not always be accorded recognition but this does not negate a state's statehood. In normal circumstances, governments will be accorded recognition. The question of recognition is only raised when the regime in question has come to power by unconstitutional methods, e.g. by *coup d'état*. For example, in *Somalia (A Republic) v Woodhouse Drake & Carey (Suisse) SA*,[48] the English Court held the plaintiff could not recover any money held by the Company as the plaintiff had not been recognised by the UK as the interim government in power at that time. The judge identified several criteria which should be considered by UK courts when determining whether a government is the sovereign government of a state, for example

---

[48] [1993] Queen's Bench 54.

"(a) whether the entity is the constitutional government of the State;

(b) the degree, nature and stability of administrative control, if any, which are exercised over the territory of the State;

(c) whether the British Government has any dealings with that government, and, if so, the nature of those dealings; and

(d) in marginal cases the extent of international recognition that has been accorded the government of that State."[49]

An entity may therefore be recognised as a state, but it is possible for its governmental regime not to be accorded recognition. It is evident from the foregoing case that the UK courts are able to make an objective decision concerning the international legal personality of a government based on factors other than the official position of the UK Government. The decision in *Sierra Leone Telecommunications v Barclays Bank Plc*,[50] further reinforces that the courts enjoy a more central role than previously.

Before considering what happens in practice, the two principal schools of thought on recognition of states must be mentioned, albeit briefly.

Theories

The two principal theories on recognition of states are the constitutive school of thought and the declaratory school of thought.

(i) The constitutive theory. Supporters of the constitutive theory emphasise the act of recognition itself and maintain that it is the act of recognition which establishes (is constitutive of) the international personality of the entity in question. This is a precondition of legal status, as it is the act of recognition which: (a) creates a state; and (b) determines the legal personality of a new governmental regime. The constituent theory immediately raises two questions: what is the position of unrecognised entities; are they free to behave as they choose on the international scene unfettered by obligations imposed by international law? What is the position of an entity recognised by some states and not by others?

(ii) Declaratory (or evidentiary) theory. Supporters of this theory minimise the importance of the act of recognition and regard

---

[49] Above, at 372.
[50] [1998] All E.R. 821, QB.

recognition as only a formal acknowledgement of already existing circumstances. Thus the act of recognition is not regarded as what creates the state. See the response of the Arbitration Commission (Badinter Committee) in reply to the question whether the dissolution of the Socialist Federal Republic of Yugoslavia was a new state calling for recognition. The Commission's view was that

> "while recognition is not a prerequisite for the foundations of a State and is purely declaratory in its impact, it is nonetheless a discretionary act that other States may perform when they choose and in a manner of their own choosing ".[51]

Although the declaratory theory is more in line with state practice, it nevertheless remains too simple in that it denies some of the complexities which underline recognition. Recognition, when granted, has retroactive effect—that is, recognition is backdated. For example, the UK accorded recognition to the post-revolution regime in the Soviet Union in 1921, but the effect of that was that the recognition was backdated to 1917.

Existing states do treat unrecognised entities as having obligations under international law. Such unrecognised entities are not free to behave as they choose on the international scene. For example, in 1949, the UK demanded compensation from the Israeli state in respect of British aircraft shot down by Israeli airmen over Egypt; in 1957, compensation was also demanded by the British from the unrecognised Taiwan Government for damage done by Taiwan forces to British vessels; and in 1968, the US asserted that North Korea, which it did not recognise, had violated international law by attacking a US Navy vessel, *The Pueblo*.

Is there a duty to recognise?

The most notable exponent of the proposition that if an entity satisfies the formal factual requirements of a state or a government, then recognition should be awarded, was the late Sir Hersch Lauterpacht.[52] He did, however, acknowledge recognition should be withheld if the entity had come to power through a violation of international law, for example by the use of force contrary to art.2(4) of the UN Charter. Although states do look at the factual criteria which are manifested by an entity, the act of recognition is essentially governed by political expediency. A state can choose not to enter into relations with another entity. If a state

---

[51] See also Opinion Number 1, above, fn.11.
[52] H. Lauterpacht, *Recognition in International Law* (New York: Ams Press Inc., 1947), Chs 3 and 11.

was required to do so and there was a legal duty to recognise, recognition would not be discretionary but mandatory. In the case of Kosovo the international community has not responded uniformly: at the time of writing 56% of the UN's Member States recognise Kosovo (108 of 193 states).

Criteria for recognition of states

The criteria of statehood have already been considered and if the governmental regime in question appears effective and stable, then recognition will be accorded. "Effective" refers to the physical control of the territory in question. Does the regime enjoy control over most of the territory, and is that control likely to continue? An affirmative answer will characterise the control as effective. "Stable", on the other hand, refers to the regime's likelihood of continuing in power (see below, especially the distinction between recognition de facto and recognition de jure). The imposition of additional conditions upon Croatia, Slovenia and Bosnia-Herzegovina by the European Community in 1992 was clearly a political act[53] and is indicative of the application of the constitutive theory. Despite this, the decisions of the Badinter Committee favoured the application of the declaratory theory to the dissolution of Yugoslavia.[54] If all the criteria are fulfilled, the timing of recognition is a matter for the recognising state—and usually the timing is with regard to the recognising state's own national interests, e.g. commercial interests.

Existing states may refuse "statehood" to an entity, which has attained a characteristic of statehood in violation of international law, for example through the acquisition of territory by the use of force contrary to art.2(4) of the United Nations Charter, or to the principle of non-intervention.[55] However, in most instances,

---

[53] States applying for recognition were required to respect the rule of law, democracy and human rights, to reaffirm the inviolability of frontiers, to protect minorities and to adopt constitutional and political guarantees ensuring that the state has no territorial claim towards a neighbouring community state. See the EC Guidelines on Recognition of New States in Eastern Europe and the Soviet Union and a Declaration on Yugoslavia, 1991 *B.Y.I.L.* 62, 559 at 560, particularly, and A.V. Lowe and Colin Warbrick, "Recognition of States Part 2" 42 I.C.L.Q. 433.

[54] See (1993) 92 I.L.R. 162.

[55] See G.A. Res.2625 (XXV), "Declaration on Principles of International Law Concerning Friendly Relations and Co-operation among States in Accordance with the Charter of the United Nations" G.A.O.R., 25th Session, Supp.28 (A/2028) 121 (1970), 65 A.J.I.L. 243 (1970); the Alma-Ata Declaration which states "The Community and its Member States will not recognise entities which are the result of aggression", the Guidelines on the Recognition of New States in Eastern Europe and in the Soviet Union (1992) 31 I.L.M. 1486; Security Council Resolution (S.C. Res. 541, 18 November 1983) whereby all states were called

whether or not there has been an unlawful threat or use of force will be disputed, and generally it is not an issue which will be authoritatively resolved. For example, Indian intervention in Bangladesh was deemed by many governments to be illegal, while others argued to the contrary, justifying India's action as supporting the principle of self-determination. Territory acquired by the legitimate use of force, for example in self-defence, and then annexed from the aggressor may be an exception to the non-recognition-of-conquest rule.

An additional consideration which has been introduced to state recognition has been that of compliance with human rights, and upholding the rights of minorities. The Declaration on the Guidelines on the Recognition of New States in Eastern Europe and the Soviet Union[56] (The Alma-Ata Declaration) issued by the Foreign Ministers of the European Economic Council in December 1991, demanded, inter alia, "respect for the UN Charter, the Helsinki Final Act, and the Charter of Paris, 'especially with regard to the rule of law, democracy and human rights', . . . guarantees for the rights of ethnic and national groups and minorities."[57]

Recognition of governments

The question of whether to recognise a government does not arise when the government comes to power by constitutional procedures. The question only arises when the new governmental regime has assumed power by unconstitutional means.

British practice in the past has been not to look so much at how a government came to power, but to consider whether it displayed the criteria for recognition, namely effectiveness and stability. Recognition did not imply approval of the new regime. The British adopted an "acknowledgment of the facts" stance. The US, on the other hand, regarded recognition as a political weapon, not as something to be granted as a matter of international obligation. The US' granting or refusal was discretionary and could be withheld to further national policy. However, the UK and the US now adopt a similar stance in respect of the recognition of governments. Both states have placed less emphasis on recognition and do not formally recognise new regimes:

upon not to recognise the Turkish Republic of Northern Cyprus; and the *Brčko International-Entity Boundary* case 36 I.L.M. 1997, 396. See also UNGA Resolution 68/262 of 27 March 2014 which called upon states not to recognise any alteration in the status of Crimea and the city of Sevastopol as part of Ukraine following its annexation by Russia.

[56] Alma-Ata Declaration, above, fn.55, p.62.

[57] E.J.I.L. 16 December 1991, p.50. Similar conditions were demanded in respect of those entities claiming recognition as states following the breakup of the former Yugoslavia.

"In recent years, U.S. practice has been to de-emphasise and avoid the use of recognition in cases of changes of governments and to concern ourselves with the question of whether we wish to have diplomatic relations with the new governments."[58]

In 1980, the British Foreign Secretary announced that the Government had concluded

"there are practical advantages in following the policy of many other countries in not according recognition to governments. Like them, we shall continue to decide the nature of the dealings with regimes which came to power unconstitutionally in the light of our assessment of whether they are able of themselves to exercise effective control of the territory of the State concerned, and seem likely to continue to do so" (the 1980 Statement on Recognition).[59]

Although there is no formal acknowledgment of recognition, the same tests of effectiveness and likelihood of permanence still apply.[60] The general rule is that a new governmental regime will be recognised if it has effective control over the territory it claims to represent and is likely to maintain its control.

However, although minimising the act of recognition, the UK, in July 2011, did recognise the Libyan National Transitional Council as the sole governmental authority after the ousting of Colonel Gaddafi's regime. France and the US had made similar declarations of recognition the previous day. The UK Foreign Secretary emphasised this was not a change in UK practice, but rather a response to a unique set of circumstances.

De facto and de jure recognition

The practice of differentiating the recognition accorded to either a state or a government evolved in the 19th century. The practice was initiated by the UK but was also employed by other countries such as Canada. The US has generally accorded only de jure recognition. Such a distinction is of less significance given the decrease in importance of a formal act of recognition.

In reality, recognition is neither de facto nor de jure and what is referred to, by the use of these terms is rather the entity which is being recognised. If a government was recognised as the de facto government it implied that the government had effective control,

[58] Digest of U.S. Practice in International Law (1977) 19–21.
[59] *Hansard*, HL Deb., Vol.408, cols 1121–1122 (28 April 1980); Harris, p.156.
[60] The statement only refers to British practice in recognising governments which came to authority by unconstitutional means.

the control appeared to be permanent and there was every likelihood the regime would be a permanent one. A government that was recognised as de jure was one which had effective control and was firmly established. An entity recognised as de facto was one which manifested most of the attributes of sovereignty, whereas a de jure entity displayed all the characteristics of sovereignty. De facto recognition was not a substitute for de jure recognition, nor was it a lesser alternative. De facto recognition in essence meant the recognising state had certain reservations regarding the entity concerned.

The distinction was one generally applied in respect of governments rather than states. Israel, however, is an example of a state which was initially recognised de facto by some other states, e.g. Canada, while with respect to the Baltic States (Estonia, Latvia and Lithuania) the UK maintained de facto recognition in spite of the 1940 occupation of these territories by the USSR.

The benefit of the distinction was that it allowed the recognising entity to hold back and observe how a particular situation was going to develop. In particular, it prevented a state from according premature recognition. To afford recognition to insurgents while the existing government is still attempting to quell the situation is an unquestionable breach of international law. The advantage of the distinction being that it enabled cognisance to be taken of factual circumstances while still acknowledging the de jure government—even if that government was not in physical control of every part of the state's territory,[61] or was in exile abroad.[62] In the event of competing authority within a territory, the general rule has been to recognise that the de facto regime is competent within the area in which it has physical control, whereas the de jure authority remains competent for matters arising outside that territory.

THE EFFECT OF RECOGNITION IN MUNICIPAL LAW

In practice the distinction between de facto and de jure is minimal, as is reflected in the consequences that recognition has within the UK domestic legal system.

United Kingdom practice

A recognised state or government, de facto and de jure:

[61] The UK, during the Spanish Civil War (1936–39), recognised de facto General Franco's forces as they extended their control throughout the country, but still recognised the Republican government as the de jure regime.
[62] e.g. the Polish government in exile in London during the Second World War was recognised as the de jure government, though it had no control over Polish territory.

(a) enjoys locus standi in the UK courts and it can accordingly raise an action in the UK courts[63];

(b) enjoys immunity from suit[64] in the UK Courts and cannot be sued without its consent. In the *Arantzazu Mendi* case,[65] the House of Lords held that the UK Government recognised Franco's Nationalist government, "a Government which at present exercises de facto administrative control over the larger portion of Spain",[66] and the Nationalist government enjoyed immunity. This case also illustrates the unfortunate consequences that may arise from recognising a de facto government and a de jure government in respect of the same territory simultaneously. The Republican government's action seeking repossession of the vessel *Arantzazu Mendi*, which had been requisitioned under a decree by the Nationalist government, accordingly failed.[67] The case was initiated in the English courts, as the *Arantzazu Mendi* was in London at the time the Republican government issued its writ of possession;

(c) its legislative and administrative acts will be given effect to within the UK. In *Luther v Sagor*,[68] the Court of First Instance refused to give effect to a Soviet confiscation decree, as the Soviet regime had not been recognised by the British Government. However, by the time the case was heard on appeal, the UK Government had accorded de facto recognition to the Soviet regime:

> "The Government of this country ... recognised the Soviet Government as the Government in possession of the powers of sovereignty in Russia, the acts of that Government must be treated by the Courts of this country with all the respect due to the acts of a duly recognised foreign sovereign state."[69]

(d) recognition once granted is retroactive. It is backdated to the establishment of the entity in question. It does not relate

---

[63] *The City of Berne v Bank of England*, 9 Ves.347 (1804); 32 E.R. 636 (Ch.).
[64] *Luther v Sagor* [1921] 3 K.B. 532 CA.
[65] [1939] A.C. 256 HL.
[66] [1939] A.C. 256 HL at 258.
[67] Franco's Nationalist forces were in control of the Basque region of the country. The Republican government issued a requisition decree in respect of all vessels registered in the Port of Bilbao. Some nine months later, the Nationalist government also issued a decree taking control of Bilbao vessels. The owners of the *Arantzazu Mendi* accepted the latter decree, but opposed that of the Republican government.
[68] Above, fn.64.
[69] Above, at 543.

to the time recognition is accorded and in *Luther v Sagor*, Bankes J concluded the Soviet Government assumed the position of a sovereign government as of December 1917. British recognition of the Soviet Government was therefore backdated to 1917 and all legislative and administrative acts of the Soviet Government after that date had to be recognised as valid. *Luther v Sagor* therefore demonstrates that a government, be it a de facto or a de jure government, is entitled to immunity before British courts, that effect will be given to the legislative and administrative acts of a de facto and de jure regime, that recognition is retroactive and that generally the effects of de facto and de jure recognition are essentially the same.

There are, however, two major differences between de facto and de jure recognition. De jure recognition alone implies full diplomatic relations and immunities and privileges for representatives.[70] Only a de jure government can recover a public debt or state asset. It was recognised in *Haile Selassie v Cable and Wireless Ltd (No.2)*[71] that only the ousted, but still de jure recognised, government of a state whose new government was only recognised de facto, was entitled to sue for a debt recoverable in England. However, when the de facto regime, in this case the Italian Government, was recognised de jure, because recognition is retroactive, it assumed the right as the de jure regime to pursue the claim, whereas the former de jure regime of Haile Selassie was divested of any such right.

The retroactivity of recognition can create problems. This can arise if two governments are simultaneously recognised as the de jure regime of the same state. In reality, this does not happen. One de jure government will be superseded by another de jure government. The effect, however, of backdating recognition of a new regime can be to place a state in the position of recognising measures of two de jure regimes simultaneously. The question of retroactivity and its raison d'être was considered in the *Gdynia Ameryka Linie Żeglugowe Spolka Akcyjna v Boguslawski* case.[72] Here, a new provisional government established itself as the de facto government of Poland on 28 June 1945 and, at midnight on 5–6 July, the British Government accorded it de jure recognition. Prior to this, the British Government had recognised the government in exile in London as the de jure government of Poland. The issue

---

[70] *Fenton Textiles Assoc. v Krassin* [1922] 38 T.L.R. 259; see the Diplomatic Privileges Act 1964.
[71] [1939] Ch.182.
[72] [1953] A.C. 11.

which confronted the House of Lords was the effect of the de jure recognition of the provisional government on the validity of acts done by the government in London on 3 July 1945 with regard to Polish merchant marine personnel. The House of Lords emphasised English courts were required to regard as valid not only acts done by the new government after recognition, but also acts done by it before its recognition in so far as those acts related to matters under its control at the time when the acts were performed. This did not, however, involve invalidating all measures of the old government prior to the withdrawal of recognition. It was, the court maintained: "not inconsistent to say that the recognition of the new government has certain retroactive effects, but that the recognition of the old government remains effective down to the date when it was in fact withdrawn."[73] What emerges from *Gdynia Ameryka Linie v Boguslawski* is that retroactivity relates specifically to matters within the effective control of the new government, and the raison d'être of the retroactivity of recognition is to give validity to the acts of a formerly unrecognised regime, but not to invalidate the acts of the formerly recognised de jure authority.[74]

EFFECT OF NON-RECOGNITION

International law

At the international level, as already stated, non-recognition does not give an entity *carte blanche* to behave as it chooses. An unrecognised entity has obligations, which the international community requires it to discharge.

Municipal law

United Kingdom practice

As far as the UK is concerned,[75] the effect of non-recognition is the converse of the consequences of recognition.

An unrecognised state or government does not have locus standi in the British courts; does not enjoy immunity from the jurisdiction of the British courts and its legislative and administrative measures will be denied effect by British courts, e.g. *Somalia (A Republic) v Woodhouse Drake & Carey (Suisse) SA*.[76]

The non-recognition of legislative and administrative measures, for example those of a private law nature, can produce

---

[73] Above, at 45.
[74] See also Civil *Air Transport Inc v Central Air Transport Corp* [1953] A.C. 70, Judicial Committee of the Privy Council.
[75] And also, for instance, Canada.
[76] Above, fn.48.

severe repercussions for "innocent" persons. The UK withheld recognition from the Smith regime of Southern Rhodesia, following the unilateral declaration of independence in 1965, and accordingly refused to recognise judicial decrees made by judges appointed by the Smith regime. For example, a divorce granted by a Southern Rhodesian court in 1970 was not recognised as valid under English law.[77] The Southern Rhodesian situation was, of course, a unique one for the British courts. They were confronted with a regime which was in rebellion to the British Crown—hence the strict enforcement of non-recognition.

The consequences of applying non-recognition to its logical conclusion were identified by Lord Reid in the House of Lords case of *Carl Zeiss Stiftung v Rayner and Keeler Ltd (No.2)*,[78] where non-recognition of the measures adopted by the German Democratic Republic would mean

> "the incorporation of every company in East Germany under any new law made by the Democratic Republic or by the official act of any official appointed by its Government would have to be regarded as a nullity, so that any such company could neither sue nor be sued in this country. And any civil marriage under any such new law, or owing its validity to the act of any such official, would also have to be treated as a nullity, so that we should have to regard the children as illegitimate. And the same would apply to divorces and all manner of judicial decisions, whether in family or commercial questions. And that would affect not only status of persons formerly domiciled in East Germany but property in this country the devolution of which depended on East German law."[79]

The House of Lords in this case employed a legal fiction and successfully sidestepped the problem of non-recognition. The respondents argued that, as the UK did not recognise the German Democratic Republic, all its enactments should be considered nullities before the British courts. The House of Lords, however, maintained that as the UK recognised the Soviet Government as the de jure authority in East Germany, the acts of the unrecognised East German regime could be recognised as those of a subordinate body acting under the authority of the Soviet Union.

---

[77] *Adams v Adams* [1971] P. 188. This decision prompted the introduction of an Order-in-Council to give effect to Rhodesian decrees which were concerned with personal status. See also the earlier *Madzimbamiuto* case [1969] 1 A.C. 645, PC.

[78] [1967] A.C. 853.

[79] [1967] A.C. 853, at 907.

Therefore the German Democratic Republic became irrelevant for the House of Lords. As far as the House of Lords was concerned the German Democratic Republic was merely a subordinate, dependent administrative body created by the de jure regime. The House of Lords adopted a pragmatic approach. This approach was endorsed by the Court of Appeal in *Gur Corporation v Trust Bank of Africa Ltd*,[80] when it was held the unrecognised Ciskei government was acting as a subordinate body of the South African Government and accordingly enjoyed locus standi in the English courts.[81]

Mitigation of the strict non-recognition rule was advanced by Lord Denning in the Court of Appeal case, *Hesperides Hotels v Aegean Holidays Ltd*,[82] when he said, obiter dicta, that effect should be given to laws of a body in effective control, even if not recognised by the UK Government, which "regulate the day to day affairs of the people, such as their marriages, their divorces, their leases, their occupations and so forth."[83]

As seen, the 1980 Statement on Recognition has brought the judiciary into the arena of determining the status of the entity in question. Prior to 1980 recognition was exclusively an act of the executive which was binding on the courts. Now, recognition of governments which assume power by unconstitutional means is to be inferred through the dealings which the UK Government may have with the new regime. If the courts are in doubt as to the status of a particular regime they will have to assess the evidence available to them and exercise their judgment in deciding whether the regime is unrecognised or recognised. UK courts are no longer bound only by the official position of the government. The High Court in the *Somalia (Republic)* case in 1993[84] did not depart from the official government position—the decision reflects the change in British practice regarding the recognition of governments. The courts may still obtain certificates from the Foreign & Commonwealth Office, and accordingly a certificate may include, inter alia, confirmation of the dealings which the UK Government has with the new regime, and, of course, an explicit statement of non-recognition. The courts, when interpreting the terms "state" or "government" in a statute or another document

[80] [1987] Q.B. 599.
[81] See also the HL finding in *Arab Monetary Fund v Hashim* (No.3) [1991] 1 All E.R. 871.
[82] [1978] Q.B. 205 CA.
[83] Above, 218. For an application of the rule see *Emin v Yeldag* [2002] 1 F.L.R. 956, but see for limitations on the application *R. (on the application of Kibris Turk Hava Yollari and CTA Holidays) v Secretary of State for Transport* [2009] EWHC 1918 (Admin).
[84] Above, fn.48.

(such as a commercial one) look, of course, to the intention of the drafters or those of the parties.[85]

United States practice

If the executive unequivocally denies recognition, the courts must accept this as binding.[86] An unrecognised state or government cannot sue in the US courts. An unrecognised government may be entitled to immunity from the jurisdiction of the US Courts, if the regime in question can be shown to exist.[87] The executive may deny recognition, but may nevertheless in its "suggestion" indicate to the courts that cognisance may be taken of the measures promulgated by the unrecognised regime. Thus, in *Salimoff v Standard Oil Co*,[88] although the US Government's non-recognition of the Soviet regime was confirmed in a State Department Certificate, it was nevertheless acknowledged that the Soviet regime was exercising control and power in the territory of the former Russian Empire, and such a fact could not be ignored. In the absence of either explicit or implied direction to the court, the US courts have shown a willingness to modify the legal consequences of non-recognition being carried to their logical conclusion. In other words, common sense and fairness may demand that legal cognisance be accorded.[89]

MODES OF ACCORDING RECOGNITION

Recognition may be expressed or implied. In the absence of an express formal declaration of recognition, the establishment of diplomatic relations between a state and the entity concerned will be taken to imply recognition. Similarly, the conclusion of a bilateral treaty on a general topic implies recognition. A bilateral treaty for a specific purpose does not imply recognition, nor does participation in a multilateral treaty such as the UN Charter. It is possible for parties to be signatories to a multilateral treaty, even though one party does not recognise the other party. Admission to the UN is an acknowledgment of statehood for the purposes of the organisation. It does not constitute collective recognition by the international community, or recognition of the entity by

---

[85] e.g. *Re Al-Fin Corporation's Patent* [1970] Ch.160; *Reel v Holder* [1981] 1 W.L.R. 1226 CA.

[86] e.g. as in *The Maret* 145 F.(d) 431 (1944).

[87] *Wulfsohn v R.S.F.S.R.* 138 N.E. 24 (1923); (1923–1924) 2 A.D. Case No.16.

[88] 186 N.E. 679 (1993); (1993–1934) A.D. Case No.8.

[89] See *Sokoloff v National City Bank* 145 N.E. 917 (1924); (1923–1924) 2 A.D. Case No.19; *Upright v Mercury Business Machines* 13 A.D. (2d) 36; 213 (N.Y.S.) (2d) 417 (1961).

individual Member States of the United Nations.[90] The most salient factor at all times remains intention—that is, the intention of the recognising state. In October 2011 UNESCO, a specialised body of the UN, admitted Palestine as its 145th member. Many states made clear that they did not consider this as a recognition of Palestinian statehood, and indeed, the Palestinian Authority's request to become a member of the UN was blocked at the UN Security Council later that year.[91]

As seen, the international community is not static and states can, and do, break up. This will have obvious repercussions for the resulting states' membership of regional and international organisations. The practice that has developed stems from the partition of India in 1947. In this instance Pakistan was admitted to the UN as a new member, whereas India continued to occupy the Indian seat in the General Assembly. Nearly three decades later when Bangladesh split from Pakistan, the former had to apply for new membership of the UN, whilst Pakistan's membership continued. Likewise Russia retained the USSR's seat following the break-up of the USSR in 1991, with the acquiescence of the other former Soviet Bloc states.

However this practice was not followed on the dissolution of the SFRY. The consequences of the break-up were such that each of the republics was required to apply to the UN as individual members. Initially all of the constituent republics had to apply for UN membership, which Serbia and Montenegro did together under the name of "the Federal Republic of Yugoslavia". Following the subsequent spilt between Serbia and Montenegro, Serbia retained the FRY's seat and Montenegro had to apply for new membership, thus reverting to traditional practice.

INTERNATIONAL ORGANISATIONS

States are the primary subjects of international law, but they are not the exclusive subjects. Non-state actors, namely, international organisations, transnational corporations and individuals, are afforded a degree of international legal personality.

International organisations proliferated in number during the 20th century. An international organisation, for the purposes

---

[90] Admission of members is effected by a two-thirds vote of the General Assembly. See, e.g. SC Res.777 (1992), 19 December 1992. Note also the UK regarded its affirmative vote on admission of Macedonia to the United Nations as constituting recognition that Macedonia was a state (223 H.C. Debs., Col. 241, Written Answer, 22 April 1993 and UKMIL, 64 B.Y.I.L., 1993, 601). South Sudan was the most recent state to be admitted as a member of the UN. The General Assembly adopted a resolution, by acclamation, to admit the recently founded African state.

[91] See below, pp.98–99, for the Palestinian Authority's current status at the UN.

of international law, is an entity established by agreement and which has states as its principal members.[92] Organisations vary considerably in their competencies, importance and membership. The United Nations, for example, is a global (or "open") organisation enjoying almost universal membership, while the Council of Europe is an example of a regional (or "closed") organisation, as is the Organization of American States.

Before an international organisation can make any impact on the international scene, it must be afforded some degree of international personality. The degree of international personality enjoyed by international organisations varies. An international organisation may enjoy certain rights but not others, and while all states enjoy the same degree of personality, this is not true of international organisations. As highlighted by the International Court of Justice

> "international organizations are subject to international law which do not, unlike states, possess a general competence. International organizations are governed by the 'principle of speciality', that is to say, they are invested by the States which create them with powers, the limits of which are a function of the common interests whose promotion those States entrust to them."[93]

Determination of personality

International organisations frequently resemble states regarding the personality they possess and their legal personality may, to some extent, parallel that of states. Organisations may have the capacity to own, acquire and transfer property and to enter into contractual agreements and international agreements with states and other international organisations. They may pursue legal remedies and may enjoy rights and duties under international law. International organisations are restricted though by their constituent charter, that is, the agreement establishing the organisation. Determination of an organisation's personality thus demands the constituent document be examined. The International Court of Justice has acknowledged that the object of constituent instruments "is to create new subjects of law endowed with a certain autonomy, to which the parties entrust the task of realizing common goals".[94]

---

[92] Inter-governmental organisations are distinct from non-governmental organisations established by individuals.

[93] *Legality of the Use by a State of Nuclear Weapons in Armed Conflict* I.C.J. Rep. 1996 p.66 at 78.

[94] Above, at 75.

The constituent document may expressly provide that an organisation is to have international legal personality,[95] for example, art.47 of the Treaty on European Union states "The [European] Union shall have legal personality."[96]

Alternatively, and more commonly, personality may only be implied from the constituent document and consolidated through the practice of the organisation.

The United Nations

The United Nations Charter is silent on the organisation's international legal personality. Only two articles of the UN Charter deal explicitly with legal status, and then only with the United Nations' status within the municipal systems of its Member States. Article 104 provides that the United Nations is to enjoy within Member States' territory "such legal capacity as may be necessary for the exercise of its functions and fulfilment of its purposes", while art.105 provides that the United Nations "shall enjoy in the territory of each of its Members such privileges and immunities as are necessary for the fulfilment of its purposes."

Articles 104 and 105 do not grant international legal personality to the United Nations. They have been supplemented by the Convention on the Privileges and Immunities of the United Nations drawn up by the General Assembly in 1946.[97] This agreement is in force between the United Nations and every member of the organisation and provides for functional privileges and immunities for the United Nations (see also the Convention on the Privileges and Immunities of the Specialised Agencies).[98] The United Nations has also entered into agreements with host states in which it operates, for example the UN/USA Headquarters Agreement.[99]

Headquarters agreements are necessary, as an organisation can only establish itself within a state's territory when it has that state's consent. Such agreements determine the status of an organisation's headquarters and its capacities, privileges and immunities.

The capacity of the United Nations to be a party to agreements with states helped the International Court of Justice to conclude

---

[95] Exceptionally, a constituent document may deny an organisation personality, e.g. art.4 of the Statute of the International Hydrographic Organisation.

[96] When the Treaty of Lisbon entered into force in December 2009, the European Union replaced and succeeded the European Community, see also art.1(3) of the Treaty on European Union.

[97] 1 U.N.T.S. 15; 43 A.J.I.L. Supp.I.

[98] 33 U.N.T.S. 261.

[99] 11 U.N.T.S. 11 (1947) Supplemented; 554 U.N.T.S. 308 (1966); 687 U.N.T.S. 408 (1969).

in a 1949 advisory opinion that the Organisation did enjoy international legal capacity. The Court opined that the United Nations

> "was intended to exercise and enjoy, and is in fact exercising and enjoying, functions and rights which can only be explained on the basis of the possession of a large measure of international personality and the capacity to operate on the international plane."[100]

The advisory opinion was the result of a request, by the United Nations General Assembly, as to whether the Organisation could bring a claim in respect of injury sustained by a United Nations official while in the service of the United Nations. The ICJ took the opportunity to discuss the Organisation's international personality. The Court initially identified the objectives of the United Nations as an organisation, namely the promotion of international peace and security, and concluded that such objectives could not be fulfilled if the United Nations did not possess international personality. It was noted by the Court

> "throughout its history, the development of international law has been influenced by the requirements of international life, and the progressive increase in the collective action of States has already given rise to instances of action upon the international plane by certain entities which are not States. This development culminated in the establishment in June 1945 of an international organization whose purposes and principles are specified in the Charter of the United Nations. But to achieve these ends the attribution of international personality is indispensable."[101]

The Court's opinion was to the effect that

> "the organization was intended to exercise and enjoy and is in fact exercising and enjoying functions and rights which can only be explained on the basis of the possession of a large measure of international personality and the capacity to operate on an international plane . . . and it could not carry out the intentions of its founders if it was devoid of international personality. It must be acknowledged that its members, by entrusting certain functions to it, with the attendant

---

[100] Above, fn.1 at 179. The ICJ reaffirmed the independent legal personality of the UN, see *Advisory Opinion on the Applicability of Art.VI of the Convention on the Privileges and Immunities of the UN 1989* I.C.J. Rep. 177, 29 I.L.M. 98 (1990).

[101] Above, p.174.

duties and responsibilities, have clothed it with the competence required to enable those functions to be effectively discharged."[102]

As to whether the Organisation could initiate an international claim, the ICJ arrived at an affirmative conclusion.

The Court initially confirmed that the United Nations could espouse a claim for the damage caused to the interests of the Organisation, that is its administrative machinery, its property and assets. Furthermore, it could initiate a claim for reparation in respect of damage caused to the UN official or agent, or to persons entitled through the UN official or agent. In reaching this conclusion, the Court again made reference to the purposes and functions of the United Nations and held that UN officials could only perform their duties satisfactorily if afforded adequate protection. Individual states could not be expected to and, indeed, were not able to offer such protection. The Court expressed the view that

> "the functions of the organisation, are of such a character that they could not be effectively discharged if they involve the concurrent action, on the international plane, of 58 or more foreign offices, and the Court concludes that the Members have endowed the organization with capacity to bring international claims when necessitated by the discharge of its functions."[103]

The Court maintained in order

> "to ensure the independence of the agent, and consequently, the independent action of the organisation itself, it is essential that in performing his duties he need not have to rely on any other protection than that of the organisation . . . In particular, he should not have to rely on the protection of his own State. If he had to rely on that State his independence might well be compromised . . . and lastly, it is essential that . . . he should know that in the performance of his duties he is under the protection of the organisation."[104]

The Court endorsed the United Nations right of initiative against a non-member state (in this case, Israel) because the Court maintained the United Nations possessed objective personality as opposed to subjective personality. Objective personality being such that it may be enforced vis-à-vis all members of the

---

[102] Above, p.174.
[103] Above, p.174.
[104] Above, p.174.

international community because of the stated purposes of the Organisation and its almost universal membership.

The Court's opinion was a landmark one for not only the United Nations, but for international organisations generally. The Court emphasised that the rights and duties of an organisation (that is, any organisation) depend upon the purposes and functions of it as specified or implied in its constituent document and developed in practice. Both the General Assembly and the Economic and Social Council possess the legal competence to request an advisory opinion from the ICJ.[105] However, in respect of the World Health Organisation (WHO), the International Court of Justice, in the *Nuclear Weapons* case,[106] highlighted

> "international organisations do not, unlike States, possess a general competence, but are governed by the 'principle of speciality', that is to say, they are invested by the States which create them with powers, the limits of which are a function of the common interests whose promotion those States entrust to them. Besides, the World Health Organisation is an international organisation of a particular kind—a 'specialised agency' forming part of a system based in the Charter of the United Nations, which is designed to organise international co-operation in a coherent fashion by bringing the United Nations, invested with powers of general scope, into relationship with various autonomous and complementary organisations, invested with sectorial powers".

The Court therefore concluded

> "the responsibilities of the WHO are necessarily restricted to the sphere of public 'health' and cannot encroach on the responsibilities of other parts of the United Nations system. And that there is no doubt that questions concerning the use of force, the regulation of armaments and disarmament are within the competence of the United Nations and lie outside that of the special agencies."

The Court in that instance concluded it did not have jurisdiction to give an opinion.

The administration of territories by the United Nations under the trusteeship system and the competence of the Organisation

---

[105] The General Assembly, for instance, asked the ICJ for an *Advisory Opinion concerning the Legality of the Use of Nuclear Weapons*, 35 I.L.M. 809, The Economic and Social Council asked for an Opinion concerning the Applicability of art.VI of the Convention on the Privileges and Immunities of the UN.

[106] Above, fn.93.

to intervene for the maintenance and restoration of international peace and security have also served to reinforce the United Nations' international personality. The United Nations has in recent years been responsible for the interim administration of geographical areas within existing states, e.g. Cambodia (UNTAC),[107] East Timor (UNTAET),[108] and Kosovo, (UNMIK).[109]

A note of caution: while a treaty-making power is evidence of international personality, a general treaty-making power should not be deduced from the possession of some degree of personality. In other words, entities having a treaty-making capacity possess some international personality, but not all international entities necessarily possess a general treaty-making capacity.

The overriding conclusion is that no generalisation should be made regarding the international personality of international organisations. Each organisation should be examined and its international legal status assessed in the light of its constituent document and the organisation's own practice. The plethora of institutions on the international scene has resulted in the growth of law pertaining specifically to them.[110] The law of international institutions is now a specialised subdivision of international law and can be treated as an autonomous subject.[111]

INDIVIDUALS

Individuals have limited international legal personality, although contemporary international law increasingly recognises that an individual may possess both international rights and duties. The increasing focus on human rights over the last 70 years has prompted the conclusion of international and regional instruments guaranteeing the protection of human rights for individuals.[112]

Procedural capacity of individuals

The Permanent Court of International Justice in the *Danzig Railway Officials* case[113] recognised, exceptionally, that treaties

---

[107] UN Transitional Authority in Cambodia 1991.
[108] UN Transitional Authority in East Timor 2000.
[109] Set up in 1999 under the UN Charter Ch.VII, S.C. Res. 1244 (1999). During 2008, the European Union's Rule of Law Mission in Kosovo (EULEX) assumed most of UNMIK's functions, although the latter continues in limited fields of operation.
[110] A good general text on international institutions is P. Sands and P. Klein, *Bowett: Law of International Institutions*, 6th edn (London: Sweet & Maxwell, 2009).
[111] In a number of educational institutions, the law of international institutions is a separate course, independent of international law.
[112] See Ch.9.
[113] P.C.I.J. Rep., ser.B, No.15 (1928) 4–47; 4 A.D. 587; Hudson, World Court Reports, Vol.II (1927–32) 237.

could create rights for individuals, and in certain circumstances
these rights could be enforced in the domestic courts

> "the very object of an international agreement, according to
> the intention of the Contracting Parties, may be the adoption
> by the Parties of some definite rules creating individual rights
> and obligations and enforceable by the national Courts."[114]

The Central American Court of Justice, established in 1908, was
novel as it envisaged disputes between states and private individuals coming within the Court's jurisdiction. The Court's competence was to hear disputes between private individuals, nationals
of any one of the five Contracting Parties and any of the other contracting governments. The Court's importance was the potential
procedural capacity envisaged for individuals. The Court, however, ceased to function in 1918 after hearing only five cases—of
which four were declared inadmissible and the fifth failed on the
merits.

The Treaty of Versailles[115] provided for the espousal of claims
by individuals against governments and nationals of the defeated
states. However, as part and parcel of the peacekeeping treaty,
this did not represent a major enhancement of the individual's
position under general international law.

The tribunal established under the 1922 Upper Silesian
Convention, was notable for its competence to hear cases brought
by nationals of a state against their own state.[116]

Contemporary international law affords individuals a greater
measure of procedural capacity. Under arts 34 and 35 of the
European Convention on Human Rights, individuals can initiate claims alleging breaches of the Convention by their national
state.[117] The right of individual petition is similarly provided for
in art.14 of the 1966 International Convention on the Elimination
of All Forms of Racial Discrimination, while under the (First)
Optional Protocol to the International Covenant[118] on Civil and
Political Rights (1966) the Human Rights Committee is competent

---

[114] P.C.I.J. Rep., ser.B, No.15, (1928) 17; Hudson, p.247; cf. the concept of direct
effect employed by European Community law, e.g. Case 26/62 *Van Gend en
Loos v Nederlandse Tarief Commissie* [1963] E.C.R. 1; C.M.L.R. 105, with respect
to art.12 of the EC Treaty.

[115] 13 A.J.I.L. Supp.151; 16 A.J.I.L. Supp.207.

[116] See *Steiner and Gross v Polish State* 4 A.D. 291 (1928).

[117] Provided, that is, such a right has been recognised by the individual's state of
nationality. The European Convention, as modified by Protocol No.11, which
entered into force on 1 November 1998. N.B. the original Convention entered
into force on 3 September 1953.

[118] 6 I.L.M. 383 (1967).

to receive and consider "communications from individuals claiming to be victims of violations of any of the rights set forth in the Covenant." Other instruments providing for individual petition include the Optional Protocol to the Convention on the Elimination of Discrimination against Women (1999), the Optional Protocol to the International Covenant on Economic, Social and Cultural Rights (2008) and the Optional Protocol to the Convention on the Rights of Person with Disabilities (2006). The International Convention for the Protection for all Persons from Enforced Disappearance (2006) includes an optional complaints system for individuals to appeal to the Committee on Enforced Disappearance for assistance in locating disappeared persons. In December 2011, the UN General Assembly approved an Optional Protocol to the 1989 UN Convention on the Rights of the Child which provides for an individual complaints procedure.[119]

The American Convention on Human Rights provides for the initiation of a petition alleging a violation of the Convention by "any person or group of persons or non-governmental entity legally recognised in one or more Member States."[120]

In addition to the foregoing, individuals enjoy limited procedural capacity before the Court of Justice of the European Union.[121] Similarly, the Convention on the Settlement of Investment Disputes between States and Nationals of Other States 1965 provides a mechanism for the settlement of disputes between contracting parties and companies of the nationality of a contracting party on the consent of both sides.[122] Individuals do not, however, enjoy locus standi before the ICJ.

However, it has been increasingly recognised that individuals may be held responsible for certain conduct and the development of individual international criminal responsibility is now a notable feature of international law. Traditionally international law did not recognise individual responsibility except in the very limited case of piracy which under customary international law has long been recognised as an international crime. It is no longer believed that states are exclusively the perpetrators of conduct which breaches international law. The legal fiction that individuals do not participate on the international scene, and consequently may not be held responsible for their acts, was perceptibly dented in the latter half of the 20th century. See, for example, the Statutes of the International Tribunals for the former Yugoslavia (the

---

[119] This opened for signature in 2012 and entered into force on 14 April 2014, upon ratification by ten Member States.

[120] art.44.

[121] art.263(4) of the Treaty on the Functioning of the European Union.

[122] 4 I.L.M. 532 (1965).

ICTY)[123] and Rwanda (ICTR)[124] and the Statute establishing the International Criminal Court (ICC) also referred to as the Rome Statute.[125] Issues of individual international criminal responsibility are also increasingly being dealt with in national courts, through the application of the universal jurisdiction principle such as the *Pinochet* case.[126]

Individual responsibility derives from international law and is independent of the law of any state. At Nuremberg the International Tribunal held:

> "Crimes against international law are committed by men, not by abstract entities, and only by punishing individuals who commit such crimes can the provisions of international law be enforced."

Similarly, art.4 of the Convention on the Prevention and Punishment of the Crime of Genocide[127] provides that genocide is punishable as a crime irrespective of whether those committing it "are constitutionally responsible rulers, public officials or private individuals". The corollary of this acknowledgment that individuals may incur international responsibility is that they are under an obligation to refrain from such conduct.[128] Individuals, therefore, have limited rights and duties on the international scene. Other acts, which are now recognised as giving rise to individual responsibility at an international level, include, inter alia, hijacking, sabotage, terrorism, drug trafficking and acts against diplomats.[129] A major handicap to individuals exercising international personality has been a lack of procedural capacity, denied

---

[123] The International Tribunal for the Prosecution of Persons Responsible for Serious Violations of International Humanitarian Law Committed in the Territory of the Former Yugoslavia since 1991 (1993) established by Security Council Resolution 827 (1993).

[124] The International Criminal Tribunal for the Prosecution of Persons Responsible for Genocide and Other Serious Violations of International Humanitarian Law Committed in the Territory of Rwanda and Rwandan citizens responsible for genocide and other such violations committed in the territory of neighbouring states, between 1 January 1994 and 31 December 1994. Established under Security Council Resolution 955 (1994).

[125] Rome Statute, 2187 U.N.T.S. 90.

[126] *R. v Bartle & The Commissioner of Police for the Metropolis, Ex p. Pinochet* 24 March 1999, [1991] 2 All E.R. 97. Universal Jurisdiction is dealt with in Ch.6.

[127] Paris, 9 December 1948; T.S. 58 (1970) Cmnd.4421.

[128] The Statute of the ICTY affirms the principle of *ratione personae*, i.e. a person is not relieved of individual criminal responsibility for a crime because it was committed under superior orders (arts 6 and 7). This would only be considered as mitigating circumstances when passing sentence. See Ch.9 on human rights generally.

[129] See Chs 6 and 9.

to them because of the reluctance of states to grant them such capacity.

OTHER NON-STATE ACTORS

Non-state actors do not possess international legal personality as a right, however, they may enjoy certain rights, defined capacities and locus standi. Some of these non-state actors participate in international life actively and they influence the creation and development of international law.

Insurgents and rebel groups

Rebel groups are relevant to international law to the extent that they may have de facto control over certain territory. In such cases they may enter into international agreements which could be considered valid under international law. In the course of civil conflicts, rebel groups are also bound by international humanitarian law with regards to the conduction of hostilities. They do not, however, have locus standi in international law and therefore they could not be considered responsible as a group for its violations, notwithstanding the individual responsibility for international crimes that its members could bear. Similarly this could be said about terrorist groups such as Al-Qaeda. The self-proclaimed Islamic State of Iraq and the Levant, which at the time of writing controls a large part of Syria and Iraq, is another example of a non-state entity whose international personality is unsettled.

National liberation movements

The most notable national liberation movement is arguably the Palestine Liberation Organisation (PLO).[130] The Palestinian National Authority (established pursuant to the 1993 Oslo Accords between Israel and the PLO) enjoys non-member observer state status at the United Nations—such recognition, however, does not impute recognition by the Member States of the Organisation. Nevertheless, note the advisory opinion of the International Court of Justice in 1988, concluding that the US—as a party to the Agreement between the United Nations and the United States of America, regarding the Headquarters of the United Nations of 26 June 1947—was under "an obligation in accordance with section 21 of that Agreement, to enter into arbitration for the settlement

---

[130] The Palestinian Authority replaced the PLO in January 1996 and has been recognised by the Israeli Government. Another instance was the African National Congress (ANC), which is now the Majority Government of South Africa.

of the dispute between itself and the United Nations."[131] The case arose from a US law declaring illegal the establishment and maintenance of a PLO office in the US. An obligation was held to be incumbent on the US towards the PLO, in spite of the former's non-recognition of the Organisation.

In 2011 Mahmoud Abbas, the President of the Palestinian Authority and Chairman of the PLO, sought full member-state status at the UN. The bid was unsuccessful due to the Palestinians failing to garner the approval of 9 of the 15 members of the Security Council as required. Mahmoud Abbas returned to the UN in November 2012 with a lesser request that Palestine be admitted as a non-member observer state. The General Assembly voted overwhelmingly to accord this status which now allows the Palestinians to take part in General Assembly debates and eases the way for them to join other UN agencies.

On 1 January 2015, Palestine lodged a declaration with the ICC's Registrar declaring Palestine's acceptance of the jurisdiction of the ICC since 13 June 2014.[132] It became the 123rd member of the ICC three months later on 1 April 2015. On 6 January 2015, after Palestine acceded to the Rome Statute the Prosecutor, Fatou Bensouda, opened an initial examination over alleged crimes committed in the occupied Palestinian territory, including East Jerusalem, since 13 June 2014.[133] The Palestinians have also stated their intention to lodge a case at the ICC relating to Israel's continuing construction of settlements, which are illegal under international law.

The Holy See

The Holy See is another notable example of an entity possessing limited international personality. The Holy See, of which the Pope is the head, has a population which is neither permanent nor indigenous, and its function is exclusively religious. However, it is a party to international treaties on such diverse subjects as arbitration, non-proliferation and monetary matters. The New Monetary Convention between the Holy See and Italy, signed on 29 December 2000, authorised the Euro as official currency within the Vatican City. The Holy See also replaced the Fundamental Law of the State of the Vatican (7 June 1929) with one which

---

[131] See *Applicability of Obligation in Arbitrate Under section 21 of the United Nations Headquarters Agreement of June 26, 1947* I.C.J. Rep. 1988.
[132] ICC Press Release, *Palestine declares acceptance of ICC jurisdiction since 13 June 2014*, ICC-CPI-20150105-PR1080, 5 January 2015.
[133] ICC Press Release, *The Prosecutor of the International Criminal Court, Fatou Bensouda, opens a preliminary examination of the situation in Palestine*, ICC-OTP-20150116-PR1083, 16 January 2015.

entered into force on 22 February 2001. The latter draws a greater distinction between the legislative, executive and judicial powers and provides for a closer tie between the Governorate and the Secretary of State, for the maintenance of international relations.

The Holy See has permanent observer status at the United Nations and a presence at other international organisations, such as the Organization of American States and the specialised agencies of the UN, e.g. the World Health Organisation and the International Labour Organisation. Over 170 states have diplomatic relations with the Holy See.

The Holy See is an anomaly on the international scene, enjoying and exercising international personality because other international actors are willing to enter into international relations with it. The same is true of the Sovereign Order of Malta, which performs functions of a charitable nature from its headquarters in Rome.[134]

Non-Governmental Organisations (NGOs)

The proliferation of NGOs and the active role of civil society in international life has been one of the main features of the international scenario since the last decade of the 20th century. These organisations have diverse aims, from the protection of specific human rights and humanitarian needs, the environment, animal rights, religious interests, etc. However one common characteristic is their non-profit driven nature. They are entities of municipal law, created under the law of a particular state, but many of them act in a global way, extending their activities trans-nationally, and considerably influencing public opinion. However, such social influence has not translated into international legal capacity. Some NGOs, though, enjoy consultative status before international organisations, in particular, pursuant to art.71 of the United Nations Charter, nearly 3,000 organisations are accredited with such status before the Economic and Social Council. The International Committee of the Red Cross has a particular hybrid nature, because while it is constituted under Swiss law, it has the capacity to conclude agreements with states and has been given specific competences granted by the 1949 Geneva Conventions.

Transnational Corporations

Transnational corporations wield considerable power. These corporations negotiate with governments, some control economic resources which may exceed that of states, and the scope of their

---

[134] *Nanni v Pace and the Sovereign Order of Malta* 8 A.D. 2 (1935–37) Italian Ct of Cassation.

activities transcends national boundaries. The realisation of the increasing power and potential impact of such multi-national corporations led to calls for corporate accountability and an expectation that this be realised by way of the international legal system.

The first real attempt to address the issue of human rights and transnational corporations was undertaken by the UN Sub-Commission on the Promotion and Protection of Human Rights[135] which proposed Norms on the Responsibilities of Transnational Corporations and Other Business Enterprises with Regard to Human Rights. The Norms stipulated that:

> "Within their respective spheres of activity and influence, transnational corporations and other business enterprises have the obligation to promote, secure the fulfilment of, respect, ensure respect of and protect human rights recognized in international as well as national law, including the rights and interests of indigenous peoples and other vulnerable groups."[136]

However the Norms were wide-ranging and, by suggesting business had obligations regarding human rights, were generally considered to go too far. Consequently the Norms were rejected by states and corporations.

In 2005, Professor John Ruggie was appointed as Special Representative to the Secretary-General on the issue of human rights and transnational corporations and other business enterprises. Ruggie's work culminated in the UN Guiding Principles on Business and Human Rights.[137] The Guiding Principles envisage a three-pillar framework of "Respect, Protect, Remedy", and reflect a standard with which it is expected corporations will comply. The Guiding Principles are:

---

[135] The United Nations Sub-Commission on the Promotion and Protection of Human Rights was the main subsidiary body of the former Commission on Human Rights. In 2006 the Human Rights Council was established and assumed the responsibilities and mandates of the Human Rights Commission. At this time the Sub-Commission also ceased to exist and was replaced by the Human Rights Council Advisory Committee.

[136] U.N. Doc. E/CN.4/Sub.2/2003/12/Rev.2 (2003) at Section A.1, p.4.

[137] J. Ruggie, *Report of the Special Representative of the Secretary-General on the issue of human rights and transnational corporations and other business enterprises, John Ruggie, Guiding Principles on Business and Human Rights: Implementing the United Nations "Protect, Respect and Remedy" Framework*, A/HRC/17/31, 21 March 2011. The Report was presented to, and endorsed by, the Human Rights Council at its 17th Session.

"Grounded in recognition of:
(a) States' existing obligations to respect, protect and fulfil human rights and fundamental freedoms;
(b) The role of business enterprises as specialized organs of society performing specialized functions, required to comply with all applicable laws and to respect human rights;
(c) The need for rights and obligations to be matched to appropriate and effective remedies when breached."[138]

The Guiding Principles depart from the proposed Norms in that only states retain the obligation to protect human rights, whereas corporations have a responsibility to respect human rights. The UN Guiding Principles are not legally binding, rather they provide a normative framework which, when implemented, allow business enterprises to operate ethically. However despite their current voluntary nature it is possible that in the future the Guiding Principles could evolve from soft law into something more mandatory. In fact, a draft treaty on transnational corporations and other business enterprises with regard to human rights was proposed in 2014 to the Human Rights Council and it is being discussed.

CONCLUSION

There is no prototype international personality. States remain the primary subjects of international law and as such enjoy international personality as an inherent attribute of statehood and possess "the totality of international rights and duties recognised by international law."[139] However, given the development of international law, states are no longer the exclusive subjects of the international legal system. Non-state actors have been accommodated and attributed with at least a measure of international personality and acknowledged as actors on the international legal stage.

---

[138] Above, p.6.
[139] Above, fn.1 at 180.

5. TERRITORY

"State territory is that defined portion of the surface of the globe which is subjected to the sovereignty of the State. A State without a territory is not possible, although the necessary territory may be very small. The importance of State territory lies in the fact that it is the space within which the State exercises its supreme authority."[1]

Territory is a tangible attribute of statehood within which a state enjoys and exercises sovereignty. Territorial sovereignty may be defined as the "right to exercise therein, to the exclusion of any other State, the functions of a State".[2] A state's territorial sovereignty extends over the designated landmass, subsoil, the water enclosed therein, the land under that water, the seacoast to a certain limit[3] and the airspace over the landmass and territorial sea. The means whereby title to territory is established may appear to be only of academic interest—until, that is, a dispute arises and

---

[1] L. F. L. Oppenheim, *International Law*, "Peace" 8th edn, (1955), Vol.1, pp.451–452.
[2] Arbitrator Max Huber in the *Island of Palmas* case, Permanent Court of Arbitration, 2 R.I.A.A. 829 at 838 (1928). For further discussion, see "State Jurisdiction", Ch.8, below.
[3] Twelve nautical miles is the maximum allowed under the 1982 UN Convention on the Law of the Sea, art.3.

competing claims have to be assessed. Then the mode by which the parties claim to have established sovereignty over the territory will gain new relevance, e.g. in the *Case Concerning Land, Island and Maritime Frontier Dispute (El Salvador v Honduras)*, Nicaragua intervening,[4] both parties agreed to refer the dispute—concerning the boundaries between their respective territories—to the ICJ for resolution by reference to the principle *uti possidetis*.[5] The Court's decision had the effect of converting former colonial boundaries into accepted international frontiers.[6] It is also important to note the special status attributed to treaties establishing international boundaries. The boundary will continue to subsist even if the treaty falls.[7]

Historically, the need to demonstrate the existence of a valid title became necessary during the "Age of Discovery" when the European powers set sail in quest of new lands. Claims as to title to territory have been, and remain, a cause of conflict, e.g. the Falkland/Malvinas Islands, the situation in the Middle East, Kashmir, Gibraltar, the dispute between China and Japan over the Diaoyu/Senkaku Islands and the annexation of Crimea by Russia. How is a valid title to territory established? Discovery in itself is not sufficient to establish good title. Occupation is also necessary.

OCCUPATION

Occupation gives a state original title to territory. It is the means of establishing title to territory which is *terra nullius*, that is, claimed by no one and therefore susceptible to acquisition. Regarding occupation by the indigenous population this was of

---

[4] I.C.J. Rep. (1992) 351.
[5] The principle whereby the territorial boundaries of former colonies remain the same on the granting of independence. The practice evolved in the early 19th century when various former Spanish/American colonies attained independence. The practice continued throughout the granting of independence to colonies in the African continent throughout the 1950s and 60s. For further discussion of this principle see the case *Concerning the Frontier Dispute (Burkina Faso/Republic of Mali)* I.C.J. Rep. (1986) 554 at 565–567.
[6] See Opinion No.2 *Arbitration Commission on Yugoslavia* 92 I.L.R. (1993) that, except where otherwise agreed, "whatever the circumstances, the right to self determination must not involve changes to existing frontiers at the time of independence (*uti possidetis juris*)". See also Opinion No.3 in which the Arbitration Commission, in dealing with the internal boundaries between Serbia and Croatia and Serbia and Bosnia Herzegovina, highlighted that unless otherwise agreed the previous boundaries were frontiers protected by international law. It was again maintained that this arose from the principle of *uti possidetis*.
[7] See case *Concerning the Territorial Dispute between Libya Arab Jamahiriya/Chad* where the ICJ held "a boundary established by treaty thus achieves a permanence which the treaty itself does not necessarily enjoy." (1994) 33 I.L.M. 571 at 589; I.C.J. Rep. (1994) 6 at 37.

no consequence, provided the indigenous community was not administratively so well organised that it could be said to have a recognisable government. In the *Western Sahara* case, state practice of the late 19th century was such to indicate

> "that territories inhabited by tribes or peoples having a social and political organisation were not regarded as *terrae nullius*. It shows that in the case of such territories the acquisition of sovereignty was not generally considered as effected unilaterally through 'occupation' of *terra nullius* by original title but through agreements concluded with local rulers. Such agreements with local rulers, whether or not considered as an actual 'cession' of the territory, were regarded as derivative roots of title, and not original titles obtained by occupation of *terrae nullius*."[8]

Occupation is preceded by discovery. Discovery, per se, does not establish a good title, giving only an inchoate rather than a definite title of sovereignty. An inchoate title must be completed within a reasonable period by the effective occupation of the territory in question.[9] Publication of discovery can of course intimate to the international community a discovering state's prior interest, and such a discovery is good against any subsequent title founded on alleged discovery. An inchoate title does not prevail over the continuous and peaceful display of authority by another state.

Effective occupation

Effective occupation applies to the actual exercise of sovereignty. What will be regarded as sufficient to establish a good title will vary in each particular instance:

> "Manifestations of territorial sovereignty assume . . ., different forms, according to conditions of time and place. Although continuous in principle, sovereignty cannot be exercised in fact at every moment on every point of a territory. The intermittence and discontinuity compatible with the maintenance of the right necessarily differ according as inhabited or uninhabited regions are involved, or regions enclosed within territories in which sovereignty is incontestably displayed or again regions accessible from, for instance, the high seas."[10]

---

[8] *Western Sahara* case I.C.J. Rep. (1975) 12 at 39.
[9] *Island of Palmas* case, above, fn.2 at 846.
[10] Above, at 840.

Max Huber was the sole arbitrator in a sovereignty dispute over the Island of Palmas between the US and the Netherlands. The Island of Palmas, the US alleged, was included in the cession of the Philippines to the US by the Spanish at the conclusion of the Spanish–American War in 1898. The Dutch claimed the island on the basis of the exercise of sovereignty over a considerable length of time.

The display of sovereignty required to establish title by occupation, for example over territory inhospitable to habitation, may therefore be minimal and in certain circumstances may be little more than symbolic. Assessing the respective claims of Norway and Denmark to East Greenland, the Permanent Court of International Justice[11] highlighted the relative test to be utilised in establishing occupation and observed:

> "It is impossible to read the records of the decisions in cases as to territorial sovereignty without observing that in many cases the tribunal has been satisfied with very little in the way of the actual exercise of sovereign rights, provided that the other State could not make out a superior claim. This is particularly true in the case of claims to sovereignty over areas in thinly populated or unsettled countries."[12]

Minimal overt action may be sufficient to establish effective occupation over small, uninhabited territory.

An important and necessary condition of occupation is "the actual, and not the nominal, taking of possession".[13] The form of the actual taking is dependent on factors such as the geographical and geological terrain of the particular territory. In the *Clipperton Island Arbitration*,[14] a declaration of sovereignty was made on behalf of France communicated to the French Consulate in Honolulu and transmitted to the Government of Hawaii along with publication (in English) of the French claim in the Honolulu journal, *The Polynesian*. This was sufficient to establish a good title to the island for France.

Discovery must be reinforced by an intention (*animus*) or will to act as sovereign. How that intention will be inferred depends on the facts in any particular case. Normally, the exercise of exclusive authority is evidenced when the state establishes an organisation with legal and administrative competence. However, in respect of

---

[11] *Eastern Greenland* case (1933) P.C.I.J. Rep., ser.A/B, No.53, pp.22–147; Hudson, World Court Reports, Vol. III (1932–35), p.151.

[12] *Eastern Greenland* case, p.46; Hudson, p.171.

[13] *Clipperton Island Arbitration* (1932) 26 A.J.I.L. 390 at 393.

[14] The Arbitrator established that the Island at the date relevant to the dispute was "*territorium nullius* and, therefore, susceptible of occupation."

Clipperton Island, it was held that France's actions had been sufficient and had made it apparent in a precise and clear manner that the island was considered French territory. France had never had the *animus* of abandoning the island, and the fact France had not exercised authority in a positive manner did not imply the forfeiture of an acquisition already definitively perfected. The French title was further substantiated by the absence of any French intention to abandon the territory.

Characteristics of effective occupation

Max Huber's articulation of effective occupation is still regarded as the leading statement on the subject.

In the *Island of Palmas* case it was established that effective occupation must be open and public and involve the continuous, peaceful display of state authority for an extensive period. An inchoate title based on such a display of state authority would be regarded as superior to any other claim to title, irrespective of its basis.

Max Huber went to great lengths to attribute the acts of the Dutch East India Company to the Netherlands, thereby emphasising that occupation, if it is to be effective, must be exercised on behalf of a state. In *Eritrea v Yemen*[15] it was stated:

> "The modern international law of the acquisition (or attribution) of territory generally requires that there be: an intentional display of power and authority over the territory, by the exercise of jurisdiction and State functions, on a continuous and peaceful basis. The latter two criteria are tempered to suit the nature of the territory and the size of its population, if any."[16]

Private individuals cannot legitimately purport to act on behalf of the state of which they are a national without that state's authorisation.[17] In international law

> "the independent activity of private individuals is of little value unless it can be shown that they have acted in pursuance of a licence or some other authority received from their Governments or that in some other way their Governments have asserted jurisdiction through them."[18]

[15] (1998) 114 I.L.R. p.1.
[16] (1998) 114 I.L.R. p.69.
[17] See further "State Responsibility", Ch.8; see also *Sovereignty over Pulau Ligitan Pulau Sipadan,* ICJ 17 December 2002 General List No.102.
[18] *Anglo-Norwegian Fisheries* case I.C.J. Rep. (1951) 116—Lord McNair at 184.

The exercise of state functions was similarly emphasised in the *Miniquiers and Ecrehos* case.[19]

The UK's claim to sovereignty over the Falkland Islands is "derived from early settlement, reinforced by formal claims in the name of the Crown and completed by open, continuous, effective and peaceful possession, occupation and administration of the Islands since 1833".[20]

Critical date

The critical date in a territorial claim is the date on which the attribution of territorial sovereignty is decisive, as the state which can demonstrate an effective title in the period immediately preceding the critical date has the superior claim. For example the critical date in the *Island of Palmas* case was 1898, in the *Western Sahara* case, 1884 and in the *El Salvador v Honduras* case, 1821.[21] Determining the critical date lies with the body adjudicating the territorial dispute. There is no general rule governing the selection of the critical date. The selection is made in the context of the relevant circumstances peculiar to each case. The consequences of establishing a critical date are that actions undertaken subsequent to that date have no legal effect.

PRESCRIPTION

Claimants to title of territory based initially on discovery and occupation may invoke the principle of prescription to consolidate a claim.

Prescription is the acquisition of title by a public, peaceful and continuous control of territory. Prescription involves a de facto exercise of sovereignty. It is distinct from occupation in that the latter can only arise in respect of virgin territory (*terra nullius*), while prescription can work to establish a title over any territory. Prescription can validate an initially doubtful title, provided the display of state authority is public. It must be public, as a title acquired via prescription implies the acquiescence of any other interested claimant. Protest from such a claimant or a dispossessed sovereign[22] can bar the establishment of title by

---

[19] I.C.J. Rep. (1953) at 47.
[20] British Government response to Report on the Falklands, Fifth Report of the Foreign Affairs Committee of the House of Commons, Session 1983–84, HC, Papers 268–1, Vol.1, pp.xiv–xvii; Misc.1 Cmnd.9447 (1985). The Report for its part concluded that the historical and legal evidence available demonstrated "such areas of uncertainty" that it was "unable to reach a categorical conclusion on the legal validity of the historical claims of either country." para.22.
[21] Above, fns 2, 8 and 4 respectively.
[22] *Chamizal Arbitration* (1911) 5 A.J.I.L. 782.

prescription. What form must such protest take? Previously, force could legitimately be used. Today, diplomatic protests would have to be expressed and normally formally registered in the appropriate international fora.

As to the length of time required before prescription will give good title, there is no accepted prescribed period and much will depend on the circumstances of each particular case, such as the geographical nature of the territory and the existence or absence of any competing claims. There has to date been no decision of an international tribunal conclusively acknowledging title founded on prescription. The difficulty in establishing good title based on prescription is illustrated in the *Kasikili/Sedudu Island* case.[23] In this instance, Namibia was precluded from utilising prescription to establish title.

CONQUEST

Conquest is a mode of acquisition peculiar to the international community. It has no counterpart in municipal law. Conquest is taking possession of enemy territory by military force in time of war. To be effected there had to be not only the actual taking over (*factum*) but also an intention to take over (*animus*), i.e. the conqueror only acquired the territory if intending to do so. Frequently the vanquished power would cede territory to the conqueror under treaty. In the absence of a treaty the territory could only be annexed if hostilities between the belligerent parties had ceased.

Conquest is no longer recognised as a valid means of acquiring territory under international law. Although historically there were no rules restricting a state's use of force, this is no longer true. The 20th century witnessed the outlawing of war, e.g. art.10 of the Covenant of the League of Nations, the 1928 Kellogg Briand Pact and art.11 of the 1949 Draft Declaration on Rights and Duties of States, which imposes a duty on every state "to refrain from recognising any territorial acquisition by another State in violation of Article 9".[24]

The 1970 Declaration of Principles of International Law concerning Friendly Relations and Co-operation among States in accordance with the Charter of the United Nations, para.X, provides that:

---

[23] *Kasikili/Sedudu Island (Botswana v Namibia)* (2000) 49 I.C.L.Q. 964. See also the case of *Pedra Branca* I.C.J. Rep. 2008 for further articulation by the Court on prescription.

[24] i.e. prohibition on the use of war as an instrument of national policy and the use of force contrary to art.2(4) of the UN Charter. Ch.11 deals with the use of force in international law.

"The territory of a State shall not be the object of acquisition by another State resulting from the threat or use of force. No territorial acquisition resulting from the threat or use of force shall be recognised as legal."

This has been interpreted as meaning that territory cannot be acquired lawfully through the use of force, even if the use of that force is in accordance with the UN Charter (self-defence). The Security Council's denunciation of Israel's retention of territory taken during the 1967 War as unlawful is founded on the principle that force cannot give a good title[25]; accordingly, talks have centred on pre-1967 borders ever since.[26] Another example is the international condemnation[27] precipitated by the Iraqi invasion of Kuwait and subsequent annexation of that territory in August 1990 culminating in UN Security Council Resolution 660,[28] calling for the immediate and unconditional withdrawal of all Iraqi forces from the territory of Kuwait, declaring the Iraqi annexation as "null and void" having no legal validity "under any form and whatever pretext".[29] In respect of Russia's annexation of Crimea from Ukraine in March 2014, the UN General Assembly passed a resolution in which, inter alia, it called upon states to desist and refrain from taking action—whether by use of force or otherwise—aimed at disrupting the territorial integrity of Ukraine and not to recognise any alteration in the status of Crimea and the city of Sevastopol.[30]

Nevertheless, it must be acknowledged that de jure recognition by other states may validate titles based on conquest, for example Indian control over Goa, Danao and Diu (Portuguese territories on the Indian subcontinent invaded and taken by India in December 1961). The US consistently refused to recognise the 1940 occupation of Estonia, Latvia and Lithuania by the Soviet

---

[25] e.g. Security Council Resolution on the Middle East, 22 November 1967— Security Council Resolution 242 (XXII), S.C.O.R., 22nd Yr., Resolutions and Decisions 1967, p.8.

[26] See the International Court of Justice's Advisory Opinion in the *Legal Consequences of the Construction of a Wall in the Occupied Palestine Territory*, I.C.J. Rep., 2004, 134. Where the International Court expressed the view the construction of the wall was contrary to international law.

[27] Note also the UN Security Council response to the Turkish Republic of Northern Cyrpus (S.C. Res. 541 (1983)); the only state which has recognised the TRNC is Turkey. The matter as yet remains unresolved following the rejection of the Greek Cypriots in 2004 of a proposed single federal state.

[28] Adopted by 14–0, the Yemen abstaining.

[29] For text of Resolution see 29 I.L.M. 1323 (1990) and Resolution 662 of 9 August 1990, adopted by 15–0; for text, see 29 I.L.M. 1327.

[30] UNGA Resolution 68/262 of 27 March 2014, adopted by 100–11, with 58 abstentions. A draft Security Council resolution regarding the same situation failed after it was vetoed by Russia (with China abstaining).

Union. The UK accorded only de facto recognition.[31] In 2014, Russia annexed the Crimean peninsula, formerly part of Ukraine, following a referendum in Crimea. Prior to the annexation, the UN General Assembly called states not to recognise any change in the status of Crimea or the Black Sea port of Sevastopol.[32] A draft Security Council Resolution urging Member States not to recognise the results of the referendum or any alteration in the region's status was vetoed by the Russian Federation.[33]

What of territories acquired by conquest when the use of force was accepted under international law? In accordance with the doctrine of intertemporal law, the law applicable when title was claimed to have been established will be applied. The essence of this doctrine is "a juridical fact should be appreciated in the light of the law contemporary with it, and not of the law in force at the time when the dispute in regard to it arises or falls to be settled."[34] To do otherwise and afford retroactive effect to new doctrines would be "highly disruptive" as "every State would constantly be under the necessity of examining its title to each portion of its territory in order to determine whether a change in the law had necessitated, as it were, a reacquisition."[35]

CESSION

This, the transfer of territory by one sovereign to another, is the most usual form of acquiring derivative title to territory. Cession is always effected by treaty—most frequently in a peace treaty at the conclusion of a war, as in the Treaty of Versailles, 1919; the Treaty of Peace with Japan, 1951[36]; the 1841 cession of Hong Kong by China to Great Britain after the Opium War[37]; and that of Gibraltar to Great Britain pursuant to the Treaty of Utrecht 1714. To some extent the cession may be forced on the defeated power, in which case the latter's consent to the transfer of sovereignty

---

[31] See Ch.4, above, "Recognition". The three states now enjoy independent status and have been admitted to the UN.
[32] G.A. Res. 68/262, 27 March 2014. The resolution was adopted by 100 votes to 11, with 58 abstentions.
[33] S.C. 7138th Meeting, 15 March 2014.
[34] *Parry and Grant, Encyclopaedic Directory of International Law*, edited by J.P. Grant and J.C. Barker, 2nd edn (New York: Oceana, 2003).
[35] P.C. Jessup, "The Palmas Island Arbitration" (1928) 22 A.J.I.L. 735 at 740.
[36] 112 B.F.S.P. 1; 136 U.N.T.S. 45.
[37] Hong Kong and the new Territories were leased to Britain under Treaty in 1898. Hong Kong was restored to China at a handover ceremony at midnight on 30 June 1997. The ceremony marked the return of Hong Kong to Chinese sovereignty and the establishment of a Hong Kong Special Administrative Region (HKSAR) as provided for by the Sino–British Joint Declaration on the Question of Hong Kong 1984. Under the terms of that Declaration, the British agreed to return the entire territory to China.

will be recorded in the cession treaty. Cession requires that one party assumes sovereignty and another relinquishes it; one sovereign state is replaced by another. The acquiring sovereign cannot possess greater rights than those possessed by its predecessor. Should a third state have acknowledged rights in the territory, that is a right of passage, these must be respected. In the past, land has been ceded under an exchange agreement (for example in 1890 Great Britain and Germany exchanged Zanzibar and Heligoland) or purchased (as in the cases of Louisiana from France in 1803, and Alaska from the Soviet Union in 1867). The emergence of the principle of self-determination has made the cession of territory between states less likely.

Recognition of title to territory by an entity which comes to "statehood" by unconstitutional means, e.g. by revolt, will depend on recognition by the other members of the international community and title may finally only be established when there is an "acknowledgement of the facts".[38]

ACCRETION AND AVULSION

Both accretion and avulsion refer to geographical processes; these are relatively rare occurrences.

Accretion involves the gradual increase in territory through the operation of nature, for example the gradual shifting of a river's course leading to additional territory through the formation of alluvial deposits.

Avulsion refers to a violent change, such as a sudden alteration in a river's course, or the emergence by volcanic action of an island in territorial waters, i.e. the Island of Scutsey, which appeared in Icelandic territorial waters in 1963, and the emergence of an island in the Red Sea's Zubair archipelago as a result of volcanic activity at the end of 2011.

If accretion occurs on a boundary river (that is, between two states) then the international boundary changes, whereas with cases of avulsion the international boundary will remain where it was originally established. If the river is navigable the boundary will follow the *thalweg*, namely the centre of the navigable channel. If the river is not navigable the middle of the river stream will constitute the boundary.

NEW STATES

The attainment of independence, in accordance with the principle of self-determination (which may also be invoked to substantiate a claim of title to territory, e.g. with regard to the British claim

---

[38] See, further, Ch.4 generally.

over the Falkland Islands,[39] or the constitutional granting of independence to former colonial possessions) involves the replacement of one sovereign by another and thus gives a derivative title to territory.

POLAR REGIONS

The Arctic

The Arctic consists largely of ice rather than land. It is incapable of occupation in the accepted sense of the term. However, navigation by submarines is possible below the frozen masses, and to a greater extent, due to increasing ice melt, sea navigation is also possible. Sovereignty over such land, e.g. Eastern Greenland, can be established by minimum overt acts. Greenland belongs to Denmark while Norway exercises sovereign rights over Spitzbergen. The Russian Federation and Canada, both determined to eliminate any potential foreign, and possibly hostile, settlement, have also asserted sovereignty over extensive areas in the Arctic region. Both countries have utilised a modification of the contiguity principle (the principle whereby the occupying state may claim territory which is geographically pertinent to its area of lodgment) namely the sector principle. By this principle, all land falling within the triangle between the east–west extremities of a state contiguous to the Pole and the Pole itself should be the territory of that state, unless another state has a previously recognised established title.

In September 1985 Canada declared its intention to establish straight baselines round the Arctic archipelago from latitude 60°E to the Beaufort Sea in the west and thereby all waters, including Hudson Bay and several routes of the North West Passage, within the baselines. These were designated Canadian as of 1 January 1986. Although the Canadian action did not meet with US approval, an agreement on Arctic Co-operation[40] was concluded between the two countries in 1988 and provides that Canadian permission will be sought before American icebreakers and other vessels navigate the North West Passage.[41] The US and the other Arctic states have not utilised the sector principle. The major argument against claims in the Arctic is that what lies beneath the frozen wastes are high seas and not land and are not, therefore, capable of national appropriation. In August 2007 Russian

---

[39] See statement of the Foreign Secretary, "Our case rests on the facts, on prescription and on the principle of self-determination." (1983) 54 B.Y.I.L. 461.

[40] 28 I.L.M. 141 (1989); A.J.I.L. (1989) at 63–64. Canada continues to conduct annual military exercises in the Arctic region.

[41] Above, art.4.

explorers planted a Russian flag on the seabed, some 14,000 feet below the North Pole.[42] The other Arctic states dismissed the Russian action as having no legal consequence.

In December 2014, Denmark submitted to the UN Commission on the Limits of the Continental Shelf a claim in which it argued an area surrounding the North Pole is connected to the continental shelf of Greenland, a Danish autonomous territory. Arctic states have agreed to abide by the decision reached by the UN Commission, however it could prove to be a protracted process, especially given the opposition of Russia.

The environmental protection of the Arctic region is one of paramount importance for the survival of the planet. A series of Declarations reaffirmed this commitment and stressed the need for additional cooperation to deal with Arctic pollution, e.g. the 1993 Nuuk Declaration on the Environment and Development in the Arctic and the 1997 Alta Declaration on the Arctic Environmental Protection Strategy (AEPS). In 1996 the Arctic Council was formed and has continued to develop the work begun by the AEPS. The Council's purpose is set out in its founding document, the Ottawa Declaration, as being to

> "provide a means for promoting cooperation, coordination and interaction among the Arctic States, with the involvement of the Arctic indigenous communities and other Arctic inhabitants on common Arctic issues, in particular issues of sustainable development and environmental protection in the Arctic."[43]

The Arctic Council has provided a forum for the adoption of two major agreements: the Aeronautical and Maritime Search and Rescue (SAR) agreement signed in 2011, which entered into force in 2013, and the Agreement on Cooperation on Marine Oil Pollution Preparedness and Response in the Arctic, signed in 2013.

Climate change is now one of the major threats to the Arctic region. The Ilulissat Declaration, signed in June 2008 by the five Arctic Ocean states (Canada, Denmark, Norway, Russia and the US) acknowledged

> "climate change and the melting of ice have a potential impact on vulnerable ecosystems, the livelihoods of local inhabitants

---

[42] Russia, pursuant to art.76 of the 1982 United Nations Convention on the Law of the Sea, has extended its continental shelf beyond 200 nautical miles. See further "Law of the Sea", Ch.7.

[43] Declaration on the Establishment of the Arctic Council: Joint Communique of the Governments of the Arctic Countries on the Establishment of the Arctic Council, 19 September 1996, para.1(a).

and indigenous communities, and the potential exploitation of natural resources."[44]

The Arctic is estimated to hold the world's largest reserves of gas and oil, which makes it very attractive to energy companies for exploration and exploitation. The majority of these reserves are offshore, in the Arctic's shallow and biologically-productive shelf seas. Exploration and exploitation of these reserves, experts allege, could have a devastating effect on the delicate environment of the Arctic and great implications for climate change at the global level. In 2015, the US blocked new initiatives to drill for oil and gas in the region, delaying, for now, further destruction of the Arctic.

Antarctica

All of Antarctica has been the subject of territorial claims, though that made by Admiral Byrd on behalf of the US has never been officially adopted. The US favours an internationalisation of the area and has not recognised any of the claims made by other states (Argentina, Australia, Chile, France, New Zealand, Norway and the UK). The sectors claimed by Argentina, Chile and the UK overlap to some extent.[45] The other states involved appear to have recognised each other's respective claims. However, in an attempt to avoid a "scramble for Antarctica", the Antarctic Treaty was drawn up in Washington in 1959,[46] and entered into force in 1961. The Treaty designates Antarctica exclusively for peaceful purposes and prohibits any measures of a "military nature".[47] The Treaty also provided for the regular meetings of the Consultative Parties[48] and these parties have been responsible for the adoption of some initiatives designed to afford comprehensive protection of the Antarctic environment, such as Agreed Measures for the Conservation of the Antarctic Flora and Fauna 1964[49]; the 1972 Convention for the Conservation of Antarctic Seals[50]; and the 1980 Convention for the Conservation of Antarctic Marine Living Resources.[51] The raison d'être of the last, for example, is to curtail

---

[44] The Ilulissat Declaration, 28 May 2008 p.1.
[45] The UK in 1955 initiated proceedings seeking a declaration from the ICJ, but the latter struck the case from its list in 1956, as it had not received any response from either Argentina or Chile.
[46] Antarctic Treaty 1959, 402 U.N.T.S. 71; (1960) A.J.I.L. 477. The Treaty suspends all territorial claims for the lifetime of the Treaty and does not provide for its own termination.
[47] Above, art.1.
[48] Of which there are 29.
[49] 17 U.S.T. 996.
[50] 1080 U.N.T.S. 176; 11 I.L.M. 251 (1978).
[51] 19 I.L.M. 841.

the use of resources by certain restrictive measures such as open and closed seasons.[52]

The most extensive agreement with respect to the Antarctic environment is the 1991 Madrid Protocol on Environmental Protection to the Antarctic Treaty and the four annexes, which form an integral part of the Protocol.[53] The key article is art.7, which prohibits "any activity relating to mineral resources other than scientific research". This prohibition will remain in force with no possibility of review until 50 years have lapsed following the entry into force of the Protocol. The Protocol entered into force 30 days after ratification by all states who were Antarctic Treaty Consultative States on the date when the Protocol was adopted.[54] Reservations are not permitted.[55] Article 19 provides a choice of dispute settlement, either by reference to the International Court of Justice or the Arbitral Tribunal, as established in accordance with the Schedule to the Protocol.

AIRSPACE

Every state enjoys exclusive sovereignty over the airspace above its territory to a height once thought to be indeterminable. In the wake of outer-space programmes it is now recognised there is an upward limit to airspace, although it has yet to be established. State sovereignty over airspace quickly became customary international law in the early 20th century, and was crystallised in the 1919 Paris Convention on the Regulation of Aerial Navigation,[56] and art.1 of the 1944 Chicago Convention on International Civil Aviation.[57] International law does not give a right of innocent passage through airspace and entry into a state's airspace requires the permission of the host state. The Chicago Convention initiated the establishment of the International Civil Aviation Organisation (ICAO). The ICAO is a specialised agency of the United Nations and is based in Montreal. Its functions are primarily to supervise the application of air law, report any breaches of the Chicago Convention and conduct research into matters of air transport and navigation which are of international importance.

The Chicago Convention, which entered into force in 1947,

---

[52] For a synopsis of all measures recommended by Antarctic Treaty Consultative meeting and approved by Antarctic Treaty Consultative Parties, see 35 I.L.M. 1165 (1996).

[53] See 30 I.L.M. 1460 (1991). The annexes are: Environmental Impact Assessment; Conservation of Antarctic Fauna and Flora; Waste Disposal and Waste Management; Prevention of Marine Pollution.

[54] art.23.1. The Protocol entered into force on 14 January 1998.

[55] art.24.

[56] 11 L.N.T.S. 173.

[57] 15 U.N.T.S. 295.

replaced the 1919 Paris Convention rules on aerial navigation. The Chicago Convention recognises the exclusive sovereignty of all states over their airspace that is regardless of whether or not they are Contracting Parties to the Convention. The Chicago Convention applies only to civil aircraft and not state aircraft, which, for the purposes of the Convention, are defined as "aircraft used in military, customs and police services".[58] Such aircraft require authorisation by special agreement.[59] The primary stipulation of the Chicago Convention is contained in art.6, namely that the scheduled international aircraft of a contracting state must, before flying into or over the territory of another contracting state, have that state's permission and comply with any conditions of the said authorisation. Thus, the regulation of airspace is effected via interstate agreement.

The failure of the Chicago Conference to reach agreement on the granting of reciprocal rights of overflight or of transportation of passengers and cargo led to the adoption of two supplementary agreements: (i) the International Air Services Transit Agreement (the "Two Freedoms" Agreement),[60] and (ii) the International Air Transport Agreement (the "Five Freedoms" Agreement).[61] The "Two Freedoms" Agreement refers only to transit rights, namely each contracting state must grant to all other contracting states:

(a) the privilege of flying across its territory without landing; and

(b) the privilege of landing for non-traffic purposes (for example, refuelling or maintenance).

The "Two Freedoms" Agreement does not provide for commercial rights in the territory of the grantor state.

The "Five Freedoms" Agreement embraces the aforementioned freedoms plus three additional freedoms, which are traffic rights. These are:

(c) the privilege of putting down passengers, mail and cargo taken on in the territory of the state whose nationality the aircraft possesses;

(d) the privilege of taking on passengers, mail and cargo destined for the territory of the state whose nationality the aircraft possesses; and

---

[58] Chicago Convention, above, art.3(b).
[59] Above, art.3(c).
[60] 84 U.N.T.S. 389.
[61] 171 U.N.T.S. 387; 149 B.F.S.P. 1.

(e) the privilege of taking on passengers, mail and cargo des-
     tined for the territory of any other contracting state and
     the privilege to put down passengers, mail and cargo
     coming from any such territory.

The practice has been for the third and fourth freedoms to be
granted in conjunction, while the fifth freedom, being more
extensive, has not been so readily granted. However the Five
Freedoms Agreement has not been widely adopted and the 1944
Chicago Convention, art.6 excludes scheduled flights and as
such this has prompted the regulation of international scheduled flights through a network of bi-lateral and multi-lateral
agreements.

   A state granting the freedoms may require (i) transit flights to
follow designated routes,[62] (ii) airlines of states granted the freedoms to provide reasonable services at the airports they use,[63] and
(iii) payment for the use of airports.[64] A "host" state may revoke
permission granted "to an air transport enterprise of another State
in any case when it is not satisfied that substantial ownership and
effective control is vested in nationals of a Contracting State."
Permission may also be revoked when an air enterprise fails to
comply with the laws of the territorial state, or when it fails to
perform its obligations under the agreement.[65]

Aircraft in distress

Aircraft possess the nationality of the state in which they are
registered[66] and may only be validly registered in one state.[67] The
1963 Tokyo Convention endorses that, for jurisdiction purposes,
it is the state of registration which is competent to exercise jurisdiction over offences and acts committed on board.[68] Contracting
states to the Tokyo Convention, other than the state of registration, may exercise criminal jurisdiction in respect of, for instance,
offences which have effect on their territory or have been committed by or against one of their nationals or permanent residents.[69]
The increase in hijacking and terrorist activities in the 1960s and
1970s relating to aircraft prompted the adoption of the Hague
Convention for the Suppression of Unlawful Seizure of Aircraft

---

[62] Two Freedoms Agreement, art.1(4).
[63] Above, art.1(3).
[64] Above, art.1(4).
[65] Above, art.1(5).
[66] Chicago Convention, art.17.
[67] Above, art.18.
[68] Tokyo Convention on Offences and Acts Committed on Board Aircraft 1963,
     U.K.T.S. 126 (1969) Cmnd.4230.
[69] Above, art.4.

1970,[70] the ICAO Montreal Convention for the Suppression of Unlawful Acts Against the Safety of Civil Aviation,[71] and the Protocol[72] whereby attacks against individuals in airports are brought within the ambit of the Convention. These Conventions (and the Protocol), which are all in force, require contracting parties to exercise jurisdiction[73] or to extradite the alleged offender. Following the 1988 Lockerbie aerial incident, Libya maintained that all obligations under the Montreal Convention had been fulfilled.[74]

Contracting parties are required by art.25 of the Chicago Convention to render assistance to civil aircraft (of other contracting parties) that find themselves "in distress" in their airspace.

There are no established rules of international law as to what response a "host" state should make on the appearance of an unauthorised civil aircraft in its airspace. Although arguably such an aircraft, not being "in distress", does not come within the ambit of art.25 it would be untenable to allege the "host" state enjoys discretion as to its response. If the host state is not a party to the Chicago Convention, there is still, on humanitarian grounds, no reason for a distinction to be made between its position and that of a party to the Convention. The international community will not accept death and injury to innocent air passengers. Unfortunately, the violation of air sovereignty has precipitated some states to shoot first and ask questions later, for example the 1953 Aerial Incident in which an Israeli aircraft was shot down in Bulgarian airspace; the 1973 shooting down of a Libyan aircraft by Israel; the shooting down in 1983 of a South Korean aircraft by the Soviet Union; and the destruction by Indian Air Force planes of a Pakistani aircraft.[75] Such a response, in particular from a contracting party of the Chicago Convention is especially regrettable when, under art.4, contracting states undertake that civil aviation is not to be used for any purpose inconsistent with the aims of the Convention. Owing to the regularity of such incidents and, in particular, the 1983 incident involving the South Korean aircraft, the Assembly of the ICAO adopted unanimously art.3 *bis* of

---

[70] 10 I.L.M. 133 (1971).

[71] 10 I.L.M. 1551 (1971).

[72] Protocol for the Suppression of Unlawful Acts of Violence at Airports Serving International Civil Aviation (1971).

[73] The Hague Convention requires the imposition of "severe penalties".

[74] See *Case Concerning Questions of Interpretation and Application of the 1971 Montreal Convention arising from the Aerial Incident at Lockerbie (Libyan Arab Jamahiriya v United States)* 31 I.L.M. 662 (1992).

[75] *Ariel Incident of August 10, 1999 (Pakistan v India)*. Note the ICJ held it lacked jurisdiction to judge the case, although it held that India and Pakistan were obliged to resolve the dispute by peaceful means.

the 1944 Convention.[76] Under this provision, the use of weapons against civil aircraft in flight is prohibited, save for the derogation allowed under art.51 of the U.N. Charter.[77] Article 3 *bis* recognised what has become an established rule of customary international law. This was endorsed in Security Council Resolution 1067, which "condemns the use of weapons against civil aircraft in flight as being incompatible with elementary considerations of humanity, the rules of customary international law as codified in art.3 *bis* of the Chicago Convention and the standards and recommended practices set out in the annexes of the Convention".[78] This resolution was issued following the shooting down of two US civilian aircraft by Cuban military aircraft on 24 February 1996. Cuba claimed that it was acting in defence of its sovereign right to protect its borders and the US aircraft were suspected of forming part of a paramilitary terrorist organisation in a war against their country. The US claimed the fundamental question was whether it was acceptable to shoot down two unarmed civilian aircraft. In 2014, the Security Council again reaffirmed "the rules of international law that prohibit acts of violence that pose a threat to the safety of international civil aviation",[79] following the downing of Malaysian Airlines flight MH17 over Ukraine. In this instance, reports suggest that the plane was downed by a Russian surface to air missile operated by Russian-trained Ukrainian separatists.

The Chicago Convention does not identify any sanctions which are to be adopted against "offending" contracting parties, and states are left to take whatever measures they see fit in the circumstances. Thus, following the shooting down of the South Korean aircraft, a number of states refused, for a time, Soviet airlines landing rights and cancelled flights by their own aircraft to the then Soviet Union.

OUTER SPACE

The launching of the first artificial satellite round the Earth by the Soviet Union in 1957 heralded the beginning of outer space exploration and the evolution of a legal regime regulating activities in outer space. Contrary to the position in respect of airspace, states have accepted that satellites may pass above their territory and no state has contended that such activity constitutes a violation of airspace sovereignty. The exploration of outer space has modified inevitably the belief that airspace extends upwards indefinitely. It

---

[76] 23 I.L.M. 705 (1984).
[77] See Ch.11, "The Use of Force".
[78] Security Council Resolution 1067 (1996), 26 July 1996, para.6.
[79] Security Council Resolution 2166 (2014), 21 July 2014.

is now recognised that national sovereignty must cease at some point.

The United Nations Committee on the Peaceful Uses of Outer Space, established in 1958, has been responsible for the measures adopted regulating outer space activity and all such measures recognise outer space is (i) to be used for peaceful means; and (ii) that it is the common heritage of all mankind.

The 1967 Treaty on Principles Governing the Activities of States in the Exploration and Use of Outer Space including the Moon and Other Celestial Bodies (the Outer Space Treaty)[80] affirms

> "exploration and use of outer space including the Moon and other celestial bodies, shall be carried out for the benefit and in the interests of all countries, irrespective of their degree of economic or scientific development, and shall be the province of all mankind."[81]

No area of outer space is to be appropriated by any state[82] and the exploration is to be conducted "in accordance with international law, including the Charter of the United Nations".[83] Article 4 is particularly important in that it prohibits the installation of nuclear weapons or any other weapons of mass destruction in outer space. Jurisdiction over an object once launched into space remains with the state of registration.[84] Article 9 requires states to conduct exploration so as to avoid the harmful contamination of outer space and "also adverse changes in the environment of the Earth resulting from the introduction of extra terrestrial matter". Agreement was reached in 1988 between the representatives of the US, Canada, Japan and nine Member States of the European Space Agency on the establishment of a permanently manned civil space station.[85] The primary purpose of creating such a station is to promote collaborative efforts in the field of, e.g. biomedical studies.

The Outer Space Treaty has been revised and clarified by the 1979 Agreement Concerning the Activities of States on the Moon and Other Celestial Bodies (the Moon Agreement).[86] In particular, the Moon Agreement provides the natural resources of the moon and other celestial bodies should be exploited as the common

---

[80] 610 U.N.T.S. 205.
[81] 610 U.N.T.S. 205, art.1.
[82] Above, art.2.
[83] Above, art.3.
[84] Above, art.8.
[85] Agreement on Co-operation on the Detailed Design Development Operation and Utilisation of the Permanently Manned Civil Space Station.
[86] 18 I.L.M. 1434 (1979).

heritage of mankind in accordance with an international legal regime. This Treaty entered into force on 11 July 1984. The Outer Space Treaty has been supplemented by two further agreements:

(a) the 1968 Agreement on the Rescue of Astronauts, the Return of Astronauts and the Return of Objects Launched into Outer Space[87]; and

(b) the 1972 Convention on International Liability for Damages Caused by Space Objects.[88]

The 1968 Agreement is essentially concerned with securing co-operation between contracting parties for the rescue and return of astronauts, while the 1972 Convention establishes the strict liability of a launching state "for damage caused by its space object on the surface of the earth or to aircraft in flight",[89] and fault liability "in the event of damage being caused elsewhere other than on the surface of the earth to a space object of one launching state or to persons or property on board such a space object".[90]

Every launch and its intended purpose must be registered by the launching state on a public register maintained by the Secretary-General of the United Nations. This is required by the 1975 Convention on the Registration of Objects Launched into Outer Space,[91] introduced when the voluntary registration system initially envisaged proved unsatisfactory.[92]

An important by-product of space exploration has been the development of telecommunications networks. The operation, co-ordination and monitoring of these telecommunications networks and services falls within the remit of the International Telecommunications Union (ITU), a specialised agency of the United Nations, based in Geneva. One of the primary roles of the ITU is to promote the working together of government and private industry.

CONCLUSION

States enjoy territorial sovereignty; however that sovereignty is not unfettered. A state may, for instance, have to recognise

---

[87] 63 A.J.I.L. 382 (1969).

[88] 10 I.L.M. 965 (1971).

[89] Liability Convention art.II. Article VI establishes joint and several liability in the event of a joint launch.

[90] Liability Convention art.III. See also COSMOS 954 Claim (*Canada v USSR*) 18 I.L.M. 899 (1979).

[91] 14 I.L.M. 43 (1975).

[92] The Agreements on outer space are the product of the UN Committee on the Peaceful Uses of Outer Space established in 1958.

that its territory has to be used for the benefit of another state, e.g. have a right of passage or take water for irrigation purposes. Alternatively, a state may have to refrain from taking certain action on its territory, e.g. the stationing of forces. Such rights attached to territory have to be recognised by successor states. Benefits may also exist for the international community, e.g. rights of passage along international waterways such as the Suez Canal.

The increasing awareness and concern for environmental issues has in recent years led to further restrictions being imposed on a state's territorial sovereignty.[93] Developments in technology and the growth of internet activity have to an extent eroded state territoriality.

---

[93] Such restrictions are discussed more fully in Ch.8, "State Responsibility", below.

6. JURISDICTION

Jurisdiction is an attribute of state sovereignty. A state's jurisdiction refers to its competence to govern persons and property by its municipal law (criminal and civil). This competence
embraces jurisdiction to prescribe and proscribe, to adjudicate
and to enforce the law. Jurisdiction is primarily exercised on a
territorial basis, but there are exceptions. For example, there will
be persons within a state's territory who will be immune from
that state's jurisdiction. Likewise, there will be occasions when a
state may exercise jurisdiction beyond its territory. The exercise
or non-exercise of jurisdiction is governed by a state's municipal
law.

In international law, jurisdiction relating to the allocation of competence between states is an ill-defined concept.
International law confines itself to criminal rather than civil
jurisdiction. Civil law is the concern of private international law, more correctly described as the conflict of laws,
though civil jurisdiction may be reinforced by criminal law
sanctions.

International law does not prescribe rules *requiring* the
exercise of jurisdiction. This, however, has to be qualified in
light of international conventions which, for example, require

a contracting party to extradite or prosecute the alleged offender.[1]

International law concerns itself primarily with the propriety of the exercises of state jurisdiction. The exercise of jurisdiction remains, for the most part, within a state's discretion.

BASES OF JURISDICTION

The bases on which jurisdiction may be exercised by a state are:

    (a) the territorial principle;

    (b) the nationality principle;

    (c) the protective (or security) principle;

    (d) the universality principle; and

    (e) the passive personality principle.

The first four principles are those accepted by the Harvard Research Draft Convention of 1935. The Harvard Draft Convention, although not binding on any state and not in itself purporting to constitute state practice, remains of interest because of the extensive study of state practice which was undertaken at the time. The passive personality principle was not adopted by the Harvard Draft Convention.

The bases of jurisdiction are not listed in any hierarchy. No state can claim precedence simply on the principle on which it exercises jurisdiction. A state may legitimately possess jurisdiction concurrently with another state and other factors will determine which state will exercise jurisdiction, for example, the physical presence of the alleged offender.

What contemporary international law demands is that there be a tangible link between the alleged offender and/or the forum of the incident and the state exercising jurisdiction.[2]

---

[1] See, e.g. ICJ, *Questions Relating to the Obligation to Prosecute or Extradite (Belgium v Senegal)*, Merits, 20 July 2012.

[2] *Lotus* case P.C.I.J. Rep., ser.A, No.10 (1927) at 25, in which the Court emphasised the need for a prohibition to be evident under international law for a state's jurisdiction to be instituted. Otherwise, the state enjoyed a wide measure of discretion in the exercise of its jurisdiction. See also the decision of the European Court of Human Rights *Bank of Banković v Belgium* No.52207/99 (2001) 11 B.H.R.C. 435; and also Joint Separate Opinion of Judges Higgins, Kooijmans and Buergentahl *Case Concerning the Arrest Warrant of 11 April 2000* I.C.J. Rep. 2002 p.3. However note the ICJ's stance in *Belgium v Senegal*, above fn.1, and its conclusion that states party to the 1984 Convention against Torture enjoy "a common interest to ensure, that acts of torture are prevented and that, if they occur, their authors do not enjoy impunity", para.68. The Court went on

Territorial principle

This is the favoured basis for the exercise of state jurisdiction. Events occurring within a state's territorial boundaries and by persons within that territory, even if their presence is temporary, are, as a rule, subject to the application of that state's laws.

It is possible that an offence may not be committed entirely within the territory of one state. A crime may be initiated in one state and consummated in another. If a person stands near to the border between two countries and fires a gun and thereby injures a person on the other side, which state has jurisdiction? The answer is both. The state from which the gun was fired has jurisdiction under the subjective territorial principle, while the state where the injury was sustained has jurisdiction under the objective territorial principle.

The subjective territorial principle allows the exercise of jurisdiction by the state in which a crime is initiated.

The objective territorial principle gives jurisdiction to the state in which the crime has been completed and has effect—the forum of injury.

Both states may legitimately claim jurisdiction; from a practical perspective, jurisdiction is more likely to be exercised by the state which has custody of the alleged offender. There is no rule of international law which gives a state, in which a crime is completed, exclusive jurisdiction. The state in which the crime was initiated is, therefore, not restricted from exercising jurisdiction.

A state may bring preparatory criminal acts within the ambit of its criminal law. See for example, in the UK, the Criminal Justice Act 1993. There is:

> "No rule of comity to prevent [the UK] Parliament from prohibiting under pain of punishment persons who are present in the United Kingdom, and so owe local obedience to our law, from doing physical acts in England, notwithstanding that the consequences of those acts take effect outside the United Kingdom."[3]

Nor is there anything

to observe that the common interest was in compliance with the relevant obligations under the Convention against Torture (para.69).

[3] Lord Diplock in *Treacy v D.P.P.* [1971] A.C. 537 HL at 561. The case related to attempted blackmail by a letter mailed in England to a person in Germany. See also the case of *R v Markus* [1974] 3 All E.R. 705. Note, this Act generally extends to England and Wales only, with separate legislation covering Scotland and Northern Ireland.

"in precedent, comity or good sense that should inhibit the common law from regarding as justiciable in England inchoate crimes committed abroad which were intended to result in the commission of criminal offences in England; therefore conspiracies abroad to commit offences in England constituted offences in English law even though no overt acts pursuant thereto took place in England."[4]

A consequence of globalisation has been the increase in crimes which may be termed "transnational". Such crimes include, for example, human trafficking. Such crimes have demanded a modification of the territorial principle. For example, certain states, whose nationals are alleged principal offenders in child sexual exploitation, have initiated legislative measures to extend the territorial application of their relevant criminal legislation. Australia led the way with the Australian Crimes (Child Sex Tourism Amendment) Act.[5] Other countries which have followed the Australian lead include Sweden, Norway, France and Japan.

More controversial has been the exercise of jurisdiction based on the effects principle so as to regulate the affairs of foreign nationals abroad, because such activities have an economic impact in the regulating state. The most frequent application of this principle, which is essentially an extension of the objective territorial principle, has been by the US, e.g. anti-trust legislation, but certain European states have invoked the principle. The European Court of Justice affirmed what is relevant in the application of EU competition rules is the place where the agreement is implemented.[6] The response of those critical of the principle[7] has resulted in the US courts modifying their approach by introducing a "reasonableness" test and a balancing of the national interests when considering the potential application of its jurisdiction.[8] The US practice to restrict investment in countries such

---

[4] Somchai *Liangsiriprasert v The Government of the United States of America* Privy Council [1991] 1 A.C. 225, PC—reaffirmed in *R. v Sansom*, [1991] 2 Q.B. 130 CA. See, however, the CA's decision in *R. v Governor of Belmarsh Prison, Ex p. Martin* [1995] 2 All E.R. 548, where the Court declined to apply a UK Act of Parliament extraterritorially in respect of certain acts occurring outside the relevant territory. The Court declined to do so.

[5] 1994, Pt III A.

[6] See, e.g. *Wood Pulp* case [1988] 4 C.M.L.R. 901.

[7] See, e.g. the United Kingdom's Protection of Trading Interests Act 1980 c.11.

[8] See, however, *Hartford Fire Insurance Co v California* US Supreme Court 113 S. Ct 2891 (1993) in which the Supreme Court declined to carry out a balancing exercise between US and UK interests and found in favour of the US Court, apparently on the basis there was no conflict with UK legislation. This was despite the fact that the acts of the UK insurance company were deemed to be lawful in the UK.

as Libya and Cuba through imposing sanctions on foreign companies has been severely criticised as a "clear violation of the principle of extra-territoriality". For example, the Organization of American States (OAS) declared that the US Helms-Burton Act 1996 did not conform to the "applicable norms of international law in respect of the exercise of jurisdiction of States and its limits on such exercise."[9]

The blowing up of PanAm Flight 103 over Scottish territory in December 1988 led to the arrest of two suspects who were subsequently tried. The trial was a unique event in that it was the first occasion when a national court (the Scottish High Court of Justiciary) had sat outside its own territory. Although the High Court sat in the Netherlands (Camp Zeist), it was a Scottish court applying Scots law in respect of offences, which took place within Scottish jurisdiction. The High Court sat with a three judge bench, not with a jury. The venue of the High Court was moved to the Netherlands to counter the fears that the suspects would not receive a fair trial in Scotland.[10]

The issue of jurisdiction has arisen in the context of the suspected terrorist detention centre at Guantanamo Bay. The US Government denied foreign held detainees the right to challenge their detention before domestic US courts.[11] In *Boumediene v Bush*,[12] the US Supreme Court found a statutory prohibition on the US federal courts from exercising jurisdiction in respect of petitions by enemy combatants detained at Guantanamo Bay to be unconstitutional, opening the way for challenges before US courts.

Nationality principle

Jurisdiction exercised on this principle relates to the nationality of the offender. A state may exercise jurisdiction over any of its

---

[9] 35 I.L.M. 1322 (1996) Organisation of American States: Inter-American Juridical Committee Opinion Examining the US Helms-Burton Act of 27 August 1996. The EU has also expressed opposition to the Helms-Burton Act, namely its validity under international law, its extraterritorial reach and its impact on trade interests in the EU. See, 35 I.L.M. 397 (1996). Similarly the US signed Executive Order 13590 in November 2011 which increased sanctions on foreign firms doing business in Iran. This extended the sanctions included in the Iran Sanctions Act of 1996 and the Comprehensive Iran Sanctions Accountability and Divestment Act, 2010.

[10] *Lockerbie* case, (1992) I.C.J. 3, 94 I.L.R. 478. One suspect was acquitted whilst the other, Abdelbaset al-Megrahi, was given a life sentence and subsequently released on compassionate grounds in 2009 due to terminal illness. He had served eight and a half years.

[11] See cases *Rasul v Bush* 542 U.S. 466 (2004); *Hamdan v Rumsfeld* 548 U.S. 557 (2006); and *Boumediene v Bush* 553 U.S. (2008).

[12] Above.

nationals wherever they may be and in respect of offences committed abroad. Although universally acknowledged as a basis of jurisdiction, the nationality principle is utilised more extensively by civil law countries than those with a common law system. The latter restrict jurisdiction exercised on the nationality principle to more serious crimes, such as in the case of the UK, offences committed under the Official Secrets Act 1989 (s.15); some sexual offences; murder; manslaughter; football hooliganism; and bigamy.

The US has similarly restricted prosecutions on the grounds of nationality to such crimes as treason, drug trafficking and crimes by or against the armed forces.

The fact that jurisdiction may be claimed on the nationality principle does not preclude the state in which the offence was committed from exercising jurisdiction by way of the territorial principle.

Protective (security) principle

On the basis of this principle a state may exercise jurisdiction in respect of offences which, although occurring abroad and committed by non-nationals, are regarded as injurious to the state's security. Although acknowledged as a justification for the exercise of jurisdiction, it remains ill-defined. It is undoubtedly open to abuse if "security" or "vital interests" are given a broad interpretation. However, the justification lies in the need for a state to be protected from the prejudicial activities of a non-national when such activities are not, for instance, unlawful in the country in which they are being carried out.

A state may claim jurisdiction on this principle, for example, in respect to plans to overthrow its government or counterfeit its currency. The protective principle was invoked by Israel in conjunction with the universality principle in the case against Adolph Eichmann (see below), while in the English Courts it has been said "no principle of comity demands that a State should ignore the crime of treason committed against it outside its territory."[13] "Lord Haw Haw" (real name William Joyce) was found guilty of treason because of his pro-Nazi propaganda radio broadcasts from Germany to Britain during the Second World War. His duty of allegiance was founded on his having acquired a British passport, albeit fraudulently.

Universality principle

The exercise of jurisdiction on the universality principle is that there are particularly offensive acts which are contrary to

---

[13] *Joyce v D.P.P.* [1946] A.C. 347 HL at 372.

international law and prohibited by the international community. When states exercise universal jurisdiction they try the crimes of non-nationals committed outside of their territory. There are only a few crimes over which states may exercise universal jurisdiction and this practice is become increasingly restricted due to its controversial effects. States have exercised universal jurisdiction over piracy, slavery, international crimes—including genocide, crimes against humanity and war crimes (see below International Criminal Jurisdiction)—and other crimes such as drug-related offences.

Piracy was the first universal crime over which all states could exercise jurisdiction, regardless of the alleged offender's nationality or where the crime was committed. Under customary international law, the crime of piracy has long been recognised as one over which all states could exercise jurisdiction, provided that the alleged offender was apprehended either on the high seas or within the territory of the state exercising jurisdiction. In the case of piracy, the arresting state may also legitimately punish the alleged offenders. This rule of customary international law is reaffirmed in art.19 of the 1958 Geneva Convention on the High Seas and art.105 of the 1982 UN Convention on the Law of the Sea. Piracy in international law—piracy *jure gentium*—is strictly defined. This is in contrast to piracy in municipal law, where the term is used with less precision. Piracy, for the purposes of international law, is essentially any illegal act of violence or depredation which is committed for private ends on the high seas or without the territorial control of any state.[14] Only acts which satisfy this definition of piracy are susceptible to the exercise of jurisdiction on the universality principle. Attempts to commit acts of piracy, even though unsuccessful, will also constitute the offence of piracy. A 1971 UN Resolution (GA Resolution 2784 (XXVI)) characterised apartheid as a crime against humanity and two years later a Convention[15] was adopted, identifying apartheid as a crime subject to universal jurisdiction.[16] However the number of states which have signed and ratified this Convention remains low.

Universal jurisdiction over the international crimes of genocide, crimes against humanity and war crimes has been more controversial.

---

[14] art.15 of the 1958 Convention on the High Seas; art.101 of the 1982 Convention on the Law of the Sea; see pp.175 below.

[15] International Convention on the Suppression and Punishment of the Crime of Apartheid, 30 November 1973 and entered into force 18 July 1976.

[16] International Convention on the Suppression and Punishment of the Crime of Apartheid art.1; the Convention which entered into force in 1976 has been adopted by just over 100 states. The UK and the US are not parties.

In 1961 Israel claimed jurisdiction in the *Eichmann* case[17] on two cumulative grounds, namely

> "a universal source (pertaining to the whole of mankind), which vests the right to prosecute and punish crimes of this order in every state within the family of nations; and a specific or national source, which gives the victim nation the right to try any who assault its existence."[18]

Some states have exercised universal jurisdiction over international crimes by prosecuting foreign nationals for crimes committed outside their borders, however reliance on universal jurisdiction has been limited. For example, in 1999 Belgium amended its penal code to provide for universal jurisdiction in respect of genocide and crimes against humanity, without the need for a link between the suspect, victims or incident and Belgium. On 8 June 2001, four defendants were convicted of international crimes arising from the Rwandan genocide. However, in April 2003 the law was amended and Belgium's jurisdictional powers were restricted as tension grew between the US and Belgium following attempts to have former members of the US Administration investigated.

Equally, there were Spanish jurisdictional provisions allowing Spanish Courts to exercise universal jurisdiction over acts perpetrated by Spanish nationals or foreigners outside of Spanish national territory, including piracy, drug trafficking, genocide and terrorism. From the late 1990s through the next decade, the Spanish Courts were very active in the use of universal jurisdiction over international crimes and proceeded to indict a great number of foreign dictators, military commanders and government officials accused of committing grave atrocities against its own people. The highest profile case was that against General Augusto Pinochet, arrested in London in 1998 pursuant to a Spanish arrest warrant. Pinochet was not extradited to Spain by the UK and so did not stand trial there (see below, Immunity from Jurisdiction). However his arrest prompted an international movement for the accountability of the most serious crimes and this was fundamental in the development of international criminal jurisdiction, discussed below. In 2014, the Spanish government passed a law severely limiting the exercise of universal jurisdiction by Spanish courts, effectively ending the pending cases and the options for victims to use this jurisdictional forum to pursue justice for the worst crimes.

---

[17] *Attorney-General of the Government of Israel v Eichmann* 36 I.L.R. 5 (1961).
[18] For Genocide Convention, see 78 U.N.T.S. 277; 4 A.J.I.L. Supp.6 (1951).

The ICJ considered universal jurisdiction in the *Case Concerning the Arrest Warrant* of 11 April 2000 *(Congo v Belgium)*.[19] War crimes amounting to grave breaches of the 1949 Geneva Conventions and crimes against humanity were allegedly committed by a national of the Democratic Republic of Congo (DRC) who had made a speech in August 1998 inciting racial hatred, which led to violence. Belgium, through the law described above, issued an international arrest warrant in absentia. No Belgian national was a victim of the alleged offences, nor was the accused in Belgium when the warrant was issued. The issue of Belgian jurisdiction was dealt with in the joint Separate Opinion of Judges Higgins, Kooijmans and Buergenthal as the ICJ upheld the DRC's assertion that the individual in question enjoyed diplomatic immunity as Minister for Foreign Affairs. In their Separate Opinion the Judges concluded in the affirmative that a state may claim jurisdiction over an alleged offender who is not in their territory and who has no other link with it, as such jurisdiction is not prohibited by international law. An opposing stance was adopted by President Guillaume, President of the ICJ, in a Separate Opinion in which he observed:

"States primarily exercise a criminal jurisdiction on their own territory. In classic international law, they normally have jurisdiction in respect of an offence committed abroad only if the offender, or at least the victim, is of their nationality, or if the crime threatens their internal or external security. Additionally, they may exercise jurisdiction in cases of piracy and the situations of subsidiary universal jurisdiction provided for by various Conventions if the offender is present on their territory. But apart from these cases, international law does not accept universal jurisdiction; still less does it accept the universal jurisdiction in absentia."[20]

Quasi-universal jurisdiction

Only international crimes "proper" are susceptible to universal jurisdiction under customary international law, that is, irrespective of whether or not a state is party to any international

---

[19] I.C.J. Rep. 2002 p.3.
[20] Subsidiary universal jurisdiction was used by President Guillaume to cover the exercise of jurisdiction over alleged offenders arrested on national territory and not extradited. In the Joint Separate Opinion the term territorial jurisdiction was used. See also the ICJ's decision in *Certain Criminal Proceedings in France (Republic of the Congo v France)* 2003 and the UK case of the Afghan Warlord against whom proceedings for the commission of alleged torture were initiated in the UK courts. In this case the alleged offender is not a British national, the crimes alleged took place exclusively outwith UK territory and no British national was a victim of the alleged crimes.

agreement. However, there is nothing to preclude offences currently regulated by way of Convention from crystallising into customary international law.

A growing number of crimes which are of international concern have been tackled by way of Conventions. These Conventions provide a quasi-universal jurisdiction by way of an obligation on contracting parties to either extradite the alleged offender to a state which has a link with the offence, or to exercise jurisdiction over the alleged offender. The types of offences which have been dealt with in this way include drug trafficking, slavery, terrorist activities and torture. The Hague Convention on the Suppression of Unlawful Seizure of Aircraft 1970[21] and the Montreal Convention for the Suppression of Unlawful Acts against the Safety of Civil Aviation 1971[22] were the response of the international community to hijacking. Both Conventions have been adhered to by a large number of states and impose obligations on contracting states to punish offenders with "severe penalties" implemented by way of their domestic law or alternatively extradite the alleged offender to a state which has a link with the offence. Similar provisions are contained in the Convention on the Prevention and Punishment of Crimes against Internationally Protected Persons including Diplomatic Agents,[23] the 1979 International Convention against the Taking of Hostages,[24] the 1984 UN Convention Against Torture and Other Cruel, Inhuman or Degrading Treatment or Punishment,[25] the 1988 Convention against Illicit Traffic in Narcotic Drugs,[26] the Council of Europe Convention on Action Against Trafficking in Human Beings[27] and the European Council Convention on Cybercrime.[28] The latter is the international response to the tackling of crimes committed via the internet and other computer networks, particularly copyright, computer related fraud, child pornography and network-security violations.[29] Such agreements are effective only between contracting parties. States do not automatically possess competence under customary international law to apprehend and punish

---

[21] 860 U.N.T.S. 105; 10 I.L.M. 133 (1971).

[22] 10 I.L.M. 1151 (1971); see Ch.5, above.

[23] 13 I.L.M. 41 (1974).

[24] 18 I.L.M. 1456 (1979).

[25] 23 I.L.M. 1027 (1984) and 24 I.L.M. 535 (1985). In *Filartiga v Pena-Irala* 630 F. 2d 876 (1980), a US tribunal held torture was a recognised crime under international law and every country could exercise jurisdiction over the alleged offenders of such an offence.

[26] 28 I.L.M. 493 (1989).

[27] CETS 197, 16 May 2005.

[28] Convention on Cybercrime, (ETS no.185) 23 November 2001.

[29] Although concluded under the auspices of the European Council, Japan, US, Canada and South Africa have ratified the Convention.

alleged offenders. As highlighted, what the Conventions spell out are the particular situations in which states are required to exercise jurisdiction or alternatively initiate extradition proceedings.

Passive personality principle

The link between the state exercising jurisdiction and the offence is the nationality of the victim. In such instances a state may exercise jurisdiction over a non-national in respect of an act which has taken place outwith its boundaries. Historically it has not been widely accepted as a basis of jurisdiction—see Moore J's objection in the *Lotus* case[30]—but civilian legal systems recognise it more readily than common-law systems. The vigorous opposition of countries of the Anglo–American tradition was responsible for the principle not being adopted by the Harvard Draft Convention. Nevertheless, the passive personality principle is recognised in art.4(b) of the 1963 Tokyo Convention on Offences Aboard Aircraft[31] and art.5(1)(c) of the 1984 Convention Against Torture and Other Cruel, Inhuman or Degrading Treatment or Punishment.[32] Although the principle is not generally accepted by the US for ordinary torts or crimes, it is increasingly accepted as applied to terrorist and other organised attacks on a state's nationals by reason of their nationality, or to assassinations of a state's diplomatic representatives or other officials.[33]

INTERNATIONAL CRIMINAL JURISDICTION

The most serious crimes in international law committed by individuals are considered international crimes and they can be tried, albeit with important limitations, at the International Criminal Court (ICC). This permanent court and the definition of what crimes trigger the international criminal responsibility of individuals have been in the making since the end of the Second Wold War. Today, international crimes are considered to be: genocide, crimes against humanity, war crimes and the crime of aggression. The concept of international crimes, that is, crimes committed by individuals which initiate individual criminal responsibility in

---

[30] P.C.I.J.Rep., ser.A, No.10, (1927), pp.141–148.

[31] 704 U.N.T.S. 219.

[32] Above, fn.25.

[33] Third Restatement of the Law—The Foreign Relations Law of the United States—para.402g. The US passed the Public Law 107–40 authorising the use of united Armed Forces against those responsible for the attacks launched against the US (SJ 23 (18 September 2001)). This authorised the US to exercise its right to self-defence and to protect US citizens both at home and abroad. The US also has the Omnibus Diplomatic Security and Anti-Terrorism Act of 1986. See also above, fn.25 at para.47 and separate opinion above, para.16.

international law, developed with the cases brought against the Nazi leaders. The Charter of the Nuremberg Military Tribunal, and in particular art.6, referred to crimes against peace, violations of the laws and customs of war and crimes against humanity, for which there was to be individual responsibility. The judgments of the Tribunal are now accepted as international law.[34]

Since 1948, the International Law Commission (ILC) attempted to codify international crimes and to draft a statute for a permanent international criminal court. In 1954 the ILC produced the Draft Code of Offences Against Peace and Security of Mankind, which was updated and culminated in the final draft in 1996, which defines the most serious crimes. In 1998, the Rome Statute of the International Criminal Court (ICC)[35] codified the elements of the crimes and it is now used as the main reference for the definition of the offences.

International Crimes

Genocide has been unanimously condemned by the UN General Assembly and the 1948 Convention on the Prevention and Punishment of the Crime of Genocide (the Genocide Convention) was one of the first human rights instruments. The prohibition of genocide is now recognised as a *jus cogens* norm.[36] The Genocide Convention provides for trial by either the territorial state or by an international penal tribunal, but a state which encourages, practises or fails to punish genocide would be acting contrary to customary international law of a fundamental nature. The ILC's Draft Code declares certain crimes, including genocide, as ones for which there is individual responsibility and thereby calls for an exercise of the "broadest possible jurisdiction" under the principle of universal jurisdiction.[37]

The specific elements of international crimes have continued

---

[34] See Convention on the Non-applicability of Statutory Limitations to War Crimes and Crimes Against Humanity 1968. Note also the Geneva Red Cross Conventions 1949 contain provisions for universal jurisdiction in respect of grave breaches. Offences which fall within the characterisation of grave breaches include torture or inhuman treatment and the taking of hostages. The 1977 Protocol I to the 1949 Conventions extended grave breaches to include attacking civilian populations.

[35] Statute of the International Criminal Court, UN Doc. A/CONF.183/9; 37 I.L.M. 1002 (1998); 2187 UNTS 90.

[36] The *Case Concerning the Application of the Convention on the Prevention And Punishment of the Crime of Genocide (Bosnia And Herzegovina v Yugoslavia (Serbia And Montenegro))* (Provisional Measures), Order of 13 September 1993 and the *Case Concerning the Application of the Convention on the Prevention and Punishment of the Crime of Genocide (Bosnia and Herzegovina v Serbia and Montenegro*, ICJ 26 February 2007.

[37] The International Law Commission Draft Codes of Crimes Against the Peace

to develop through the practice of international courts. Both the Statutes of the International Criminal Tribunals for the Former Yugoslavia and Rwanda, explained below, distinguish war crimes, genocide and crimes against humanity respectively.[38] This distinction is retained in the Rome Statute of the ICC with the addition of the crime of aggression.[39] The Rome Statute definition of genocide mirrors that of the Genocide Convention. War crimes are defined in the Rome Statute as grave breaches of the Geneva Conventions of 12 August 1949, including wilful killing; torture or inhuman treatment, including biological experiments; wilfully causing great suffering, or serious injury to body or health; extensive destruction and appropriation of property, not justified by military necessity and carried out unlawfully and wantonly; compelling a prisoner of war or other protected person to serve in the forces of a hostile power; wilfully depriving a prisoner of war or other protected person of the rights of fair and regular trial; unlawful deportation or transfer or unlawful confinement; taking of hostages; as well as a long list of other serious violations of the laws and customs applicable in international armed conflict and non-international armed conflicts.[40] The definition of crimes against humanity includes similar acts committed as part of a widespread or systematic attack directed knowingly against any civilian population.[41] The majority of the states that have ratified the Rome Statute have incorporated the definition of international crimes into their criminal codes and laws and assumed some level of jurisdiction over them.

Initially the crime of aggression was left undefined by the Rome Statute as an agreement could not be reached. A definition was agreed at the ICC Review Conference held in Kampala, Uganda, in 2010, as "the planning, preparation, initiation or execution by a person in a leadership position of an act of aggression." It contains the threshold requirement that the act of aggression must constitute a manifest violation of the Charter of the United Nations. However, these new provisions will not come into force until 2017 at the earliest.

International and hybrid courts

The creation of a permanent international criminal court was one of the goals set after the Second World War but the political

---

and Security of Mankind 1996 art.8. Report (A/48/10). UN G.A.O.R., 49th Sess, Supp.No.10 UN Doc.A/49/10 (1997).

[38] Statute of ICTY arts 3, 4 and 5 and Statute of ICTR arts 2 (genocide) and 3 (crimes against humanity).

[39] Above fn.35, art.5(1).

[40] Above, art.8.

[41] Above, art.7.

tensions of the Cold War did not allow for progress on this front. Significant steps were taken by the international community in the 1990s to create accountability mechanisms to enforce jurisdiction over individuals for international crimes, but they fell short of establishing one permanent international court. These efforts were partly rekindled by the humanitarian crisis in the former Yugoslavia. In 1993, the International Criminal Tribunal for the former Yugoslavia (ICTY) was created by the UN Security Council acting under Ch.VII of the UN Charter for the purpose of

> "prosecuting persons responsible for serious violations of international humanitarian law committed in the territory of the former Yugoslavia between 1st January, 1991 and a date to be determined by the Security Council upon the restoration of peace."[42]

This was the first occasion the Security Council had created an international tribunal using Ch.VII powers and could therefore be said to be a truly international entity.[43]

Equally, the genocide in Rwanda which culminated in the death of some 800,000 Tutsis and moderate Hutus, prompted the establishment of the International Criminal Tribunal for Rwanda (ICTR), also under Ch.VII of the UN Charter, by UN Security Council Resolution 955, to try those who participated in breaches of international humanitarian law in Rwanda. This Statute is based on that of the ICTY and had a similar institutional framework. The ICTR is located in Arusha, Tanzania.

Both the ICTY and ICTR were designed to establish a judicial process aimed at preventing the continuation of crimes against humanity as well as contributing towards the restoration and maintenance of peace and security. They differed from their predecessor, the Nuremberg Military Tribunal, in that they could also hear cases of crimes perpetrated in the course of inter-state war and internal strife. Both tribunals have now been functioning for over 20 years and have produced a substantial body of jurisprudence which has made a significant contribution to international criminal law. The activities of both Tribunals are now coming to a close.[44]

The experience of both the ICTY and the ICTR heightened calls for the creation of a permanent court and gave the impetus

---

[42] S.C.Res 827, U.N. SCOR, 48th Year, 3217th mtg at 1, reprinted in 32 I.L.M. 1203 (1993).

[43] The Nuremberg Tribunal was established in very different circumstances, when there was no government in power.

[44] See Ch.9 for more detail.

necessary to reach an international agreement. The international efforts towards the creation of the ICC culminated in the Rome Statute[45] which opened for signature in July 1999 and entered into force on 1 July 2002. As mentioned above, the ICC has jurisdiction over "persons for the most serious crimes of international concern",[46] namely genocide (art.5(1)(a)), crimes against humanity (art.5(1)(b)), war crimes (art.5(1)(c)) and the crime of aggression (art.5(1)(d)).

The ICC's jurisdiction is complementary to national criminal jurisdictions (art.1). In other words, the ICC will only exercise its jurisdiction when a state is unable or unwilling to do so. The ICC is not designed to be a substitute for national courts, the primary responsibility to prosecute those responsible for international crimes remaining with states. The ICC may exercise its jurisdiction only if

> "one or more of the parties involved is a state party; the accused is a national of a state party; the crime is committed on the territory of a state party; or a state not party to the Statute may decide to accept the ICC's jurisdiction over a specific crime that has been committed within its territory, or by its national."[47]

The ICC will only have jurisdiction when: a situation has been referred to the Prosecutor by a state party (arts 13 and 14); the Security Council refers a situation to the Prosecutor; or the Prosecutor initiates an investigation on his or her own authority (arts 13 and 15).[48]

In addition to the foregoing institutions a number of hybrid (domestic-international) tribunals have been established to try international crimes in specific situations. These include tribunals with jurisdiction over crimes committed in Sierra Leone, Cambodia, East Timor and Lebanon, as well as the so called War Crimes Chambers of Bosnia and Herzegovina and the hybrid panels provided by UNMIK in Kosovo, on which international judges work alongside national judges and prosecutors.[49]

In 2013, the Extraordinary African Chambers were constituted within the Senegalese court system, and in agreement with the African Union, to prosecute former Chadian president

---

[45] Above, fn.35.
[46] Above, art.1.
[47] art.12. However, these conditions do not apply when the Security Council, acting under Ch.VII of the Charter, refers a situation to the Prosecutor.
[48] See Ch.9 for more details on the activities of the ICC.
[49] See Ch.9.

Hissène Habré for the crimes of genocide, crimes against humanity, war crimes and torture committed during his rule, between 7 June 1982, and 1 December 1990. The Extraordinary African Chambers were created following the ruling of the ICJ demanding that Senegal prosecutes or extradites Habré in the case *Questions relating to the obligation to prosecute or extradite (Belgium v Senegal)*, 20 July 2012.[50]

EXTRADITION

If an alleged offender is in a territory other than the state seeking to exercise jurisdiction, the lawful method of securing his or her return to stand trial is to request his or her extradition. Extradition is the handing over of an alleged offender (or convicted criminal who has escaped before completing his or her prison term) by one state to another.

Extradition as a rule is effected by bipartite treaty (also known as bilateral treaties).[51] There is no duty to extradite in the absence of a treaty.[52] Extradition treaties normally relate only to serious crimes and impose the same obligations on both the parties concerned, that is, the offence must be designated a crime under the domestic laws of the two states concerned. A state's own nationals may be protected from extradition, as may be persons who have committed offences of a "political" or "religious" character.[53] Many states do not allow their nationals to be extradited to another state.

At European level, a significant development is the European arrest warrant, which aims to simplify the procedures for surrendering individuals within the EU's territorial jurisdiction for the purposes of conducting a criminal prosecution; or executing a custodial sentence or spell in detention. A European arrest warrant may be issued by a state's judicial authority for offenses for which the maximum period of the penalty is at least one year in

---

[50] ICJ Report 2012, p.422. Habré was convicted of crimes against humanity, and torture and rape on 30 May 2016.

[51] See for example treaty of April 2004, between US and UK (Treaty No.108–23). The treaty replaces the 1972 Extradition Treaty and the 1985 Supplementary Treaty. See also Convention on Extradition between the Member States of the European Union 1996 and incorporated into UK law by the European Union Extradition Regulations 2002, pursuant to the Anti-Terrorism, Crime and Security Act 2001.

[52] The ILC's Draft Code of Crimes, above, fn.37 seeks to impose an obligation on a state to extradite an individual alleged to have committed crimes against humanity (art.6).

[53] See for example the European Convention on the Suppression of Terrorism 1977, art.1 listing those offences which may not be regarded as either political or inspired by political motives.

prison. In such cases, the requested member state is bound to surrender the individual subject to the warrant.

A domestic tribunal does not normally concern itself with the means by which the accused is brought before it. If the alleged offender has been procured by illegal means, e.g. kidnap or in violation of an extradition treaty, this will not preclude the domestic tribunal from exercising jurisdiction. Unlawful arrest does not affect its jurisdiction to hear a case. However, this established rule was modified to some extent in the *Toscanino* case,[54] in which it was stated a court was divested of jurisdiction when the accused had been brought before it through the illegal conduct of the law enforcement authorities. Forcible abduction, involving brutality and like behaviour by a state's representatives, could impair a state's exercise of jurisdiction. The norm, however, is that a state will, in the absence of protest from other states, try alleged offenders brought before the courts by irregular means as in the case of *Ex p. Elliott*[55] and *R. v Plymouth Magistrates Court, Ex p. Driver*.[56] In *R. v Horseferry Magistrates' Court, Ex p. Bennett*[57] the UK House of Lords held that where a defendant has been forcibly brought before a court by an abuse of process, the UK Courts should refuse to exercise jurisdiction. Bennett had been taken from South Africa to the UK in a manner which appeared to contravene the Extradition Act 1989, and which was contrary to international law.[58] The US Courts have taken a somewhat different stance, as is illustrated in the *US v Alvarez-Machain*[59] and the Supreme Court's judgment in *Sosa v Alvarez-Machain*.[60]

A state whose sovereignty has been violated may initiate an international claim against the offending state. Argentina lodged a complaint with the UN Security Council in protest at the abduction of Adolph Eichmann to Israel, and called for his "immediate return". The claim was dropped, and in August 1960 Argentina and Israel announced in a joint decision that any violation of international law which had occurred had been "cured". States will only refrain from exercising jurisdiction over persons ille-

---

[54] *US v Toscanino* 500 F. 2d. 207 (1974) (US Ct of Appeals, 2nd Circuit). cf. *United States v Alvarez-Machain* 31 I.L.M. 902 (1992) where a Mexican national was forcibly removed from his country and brought before a US court. The Supreme Court held the Federal Court could exercise jurisdiction, despite the flagrant breach of international law, as this was a matter to be considered only by the Executive.

[55] [1949] 1 All E.R. 373.

[56] [1986] Q.B. 95.

[57] [1993] 3 All E.R. 138.

[58] See in particular, opinions of Lords Griffiths and Bridge.

[59] (1992) 119 L.Ed. 2d 441.

[60] 542 US (2004).

gally brought before their courts from another state if the latter protests.

DOUBLE JEOPARDY

What of the person who is susceptible to the jurisdiction of more than one country? Does conviction or acquittal in one country constitute a bar to a subsequent prosecution elsewhere?

International law does not provide an unequivocal answer, although art.13 of the Harvard Draft Convention does provide that no state should prosecute or punish a non-national who "has been prosecuted in another State for a crime requiring proof of substantially the same acts or omissions and has been acquitted on the merits, or having been convicted, has been pardoned."

Article 13 refers only to non-nationals. Regarding the person who finds himself or herself required to do in one state something which is prohibited in another, art.14 of the Harvard Draft Convention provides "no State shall prosecute or punish an alien for an act which was required of that alien by the law of the place where the alien was at the time of the act or omission." Article 14 applies only to non-nationals. Article 12 of the International Law Commission's 1996 Draft Code of Crimes Against the Peace and Security of Mankind upholds the principle of *non bis in idem* in relation to two scenarios, the second being subject to exceptions. The first situation is where an individual is tried for crimes by an international criminal court and is convicted or acquitted. In such instances the principle of *non bis in idem* applies fully. The second situation is where an individual may not be tried for a crime under the code arising from the same act or omission, as was the subject of the national trial unless one of these exceptions applies:

(a) if the individual was tried by a national court for an ordinary crime and not a more serious one (e.g. murder, not genocide); and

(b) if the proceedings in the national court were not impartial or independent.

IMMUNITY FROM JURISDICTION

Sovereign immunity and diplomatic immunity are the two principal exceptions to the exercise of territorial jurisdiction. Sovereign immunity refers to immunities enjoyed by foreign heads of state. Today, the term "state immunity" is more commonly employed. Diplomatic immunity refers to the immunities enjoyed by their official representatives.

State immunity

"Par in parem non habat imperium"—one cannot exercise authority over an equal. All states are equal. No state may exercise jurisdiction over another state without its consent. Historically, a sovereign and his or her state were regarded as synonymous. The ruler of a foreign state enjoys complete immunity—the principle that this extends to acts done in a private capacity was confirmed in *Mighell v Sultan of Johore*[61] and still applies today. The principle of absolute immunity was established in the *Parlement Belge* case,[62] in which it was held the *Parlement Belge*, a mail packet vessel belonging to the Belgian King, was entitled to complete immunity. The principle was confirmed in subsequent cases, e.g. the *Porto Alexandra*,[63] the *Cristina*,[64] *Krajina v Tass Agency*[65] and *Baccus SRL v Servicio Nacional del Trigo*.[66]

Traditionally a state was likewise immune from the jurisdiction of the courts of another state. States in the 20th century, however, became increasingly involved in commercial activities to such an extent that a point was reached when state enterprises enjoyed an immunity not enjoyed by non-state counterparts. Such immunity placed state enterprises in a privileged position. Consequently, a number of states adopted a modified absolute-immunity policy. A distinction was drawn between the public acts of a state (government acts) *jure imperii* and private acts (trading and commercial acts) *jure gestionis*. Immunity was granted in respect of *jure imperii* acts, but not in respect of *jure gestionis*. Not all states abandoned the doctrine of absolute immunity, however, and as a result some states were affording complete immunity to the commercial activities of foreign states, whereas the same privileges were not being reciprocated.

Moves towards the modified state immunity approach

Concerned at the privileged position enjoyed by foreign governments, the courts of a number of European states handed down judicial decisions curtailing the scope of immunity to government acts only (*jure imperii*), e.g. *Dralle v Republic of Czechoslovakia*[67] and the *Empire of Iran* case.[68] The so-called "Tate-letter" issued by the US State Department in 1952 intimated a similar change

---

[61] [1894] 1 Q.B. 149.
[62] (1879) 4 P.D. 129.
[63] [1920] P. 30.
[64] [1938] A.C. 485.
[65] [1949] 2 All E.R. 274.
[66] [1957] 1 Q.B. 438.
[67] (1950) 17 I.L.R. 155, Austrian S.C.
[68] (1963) 45 I.L.R. 57, Federal Constitution Court, German Federal Republic.

in American policy, that is, "the immunity of the sovereign is recognised with regard to sovereign or public acts (*jus imperii*) of a state, but not with respect to private acts (*jus gestionis*)."[69] A state acting in a manner similar to a private individual was no longer to be placed in the advantageous position of receiving immunity, and was to be liable in the same way and to the same extent as a private individual under similar circumstances. The American Foreign Sovereign Immunities Act of 1976[70] confirms restrictive immunity as American policy. The Act spells out the type of acts which are commercial and those which are private. A notable change of policy is provided for in the Act—the decision as to whether or not Sovereign immunity is to be accorded is now the responsibility of the Courts rather than the US State Department.

An increasing number of states followed the US and adopted a restrictive immunity policy. The number of states acceding to the 1926 Brussels Convention for the Unification of Certain Rules relating to the Immunity of State Owned Vessels,[71] under which government-owned vessels engaged in commercial purposes are subjected to the same legal regime as private vessels, also increased.

The UK and Commonwealth countries, however, maintained a strict adherence to absolute immunity—at least until the 1970s, when for example Britain adopted a restricted immunity policy. The common law was shaped by decisions of the courts—*The Philippine Admiral*,[72] *Trendtex Trading Corp v Central Bank of Nigeria*,[73] and *I Congreso del Partido*.[74] In the UK the State Immunity Act was introduced in 1978 and entered into force on 22 November of that year. Sovereign immunity in Britain is now governed primarily by the statutory law which spells out the instances when, and in respect of what activities, a state will not be immune from proceedings in the British Courts.[75] Canada likewise adopted

---

[69] 6 Whiteman, 569–571.

[70] 90 Stat. 2891; P.L. 94–583 (1976); 15 I.L.M. 1388 (1976).

[71] U.K.T.S. 15 (1980) Cmnd.7800.

[72] [1977] A.C. 373, JC.

[73] [1977] Q.B. 529 CA.

[74] [1981] 3 W.L.R. 329 HL.

[75] See *Commissioners of Customs and Excise v Ministry of Industries and Military Manufacturing*, Republic of Iraq 43 I.C.L.Q. 194 (1994), where it was held a contract dealing with parts for an Iraqi super gun fell within s.3(3)(a) of the Act concerning commercial transactions and is therefore not immune from proceedings. cf. *Kuwait Airways Corp v Iraqi Airways Co* [1995] 1 W.L.R. 1147. See also *Sulaiman Al-Adsani v Government of Kuwait* 100 I.L.R. p.465 and the subsequent decision of the European Court of Human Rights (ECtHR) in *Al-Adsani v United Kingdom* (2001) 34 E.H.R.R. 273, concluding no violation of art.6 of the European Convention of Human Rights and Fundamental Freedoms (a right

the restrictive doctrine in the State Immunity Act 1982. The State Immunity Act enabled the UK to become a party to both the 1926 Brussels Convention and the 1972 European Convention on State Immunity.[76]

The 1972 Convention was initiated in an attempt to obtain among states a uniform approach to the issue of sovereign immunity. The Convention specifies the circumstances in which sovereign immunity may and may not be claimed before the courts of contracting states. Immunity may not be pleaded in proceedings in respect of contractual obligations to be carried out in the state exercising jurisdiction. States are also required, with certain exceptions, to give effect to judgments against them.

Today, most countries have adopted a restrictive immunity approach in respect of state trading enterprises.

At the international level, the International Law Commission has been addressing the issue of state immunity and a set of Draft Articles, following the model of the European Convention on State Immunity, was produced in 1986. These, after being referred to an ad-hoc committee, became the Draft UN Convention on Jurisdictional Immunities of States and Their Property 2004.[77]

The ICJ addressed the issue of state immunity from civil suit in *Jurisdictional Immunities of the State (Germany v Italy)* in 2012.[78] In this case, Germany claimed that Italy had breached its sovereign immunity by: (1) allowing civil claims to be made against Germany in Italian courts for war crimes committed by German armed forces during the Second World War,[79] (2) taking measures of constraint against a German property situated in Italy, and (3) declaring a Greek judgment concerning similar acts rendered against Germany enforceable. The ICJ found Italy in violation of Germany's sovereign immunity, finding, in respect of each of the three claims: (1) acts committed by German armed forces during the Second World War were clearly sovereign acts (*acta jure imperii*) and so attracted state immunity, (2) the constrained property in question (an Italian-German cultural exchange centre)

---

to fair trial) in which access to the English Courts had been denied by the defence of state immunity. See also *Jones v the Ministry of the Interior Al-Mamlaka Al-Arabiya as Saudiya (the Kingdom of Saudi Arabia) and Secretary of State for Constitutional Affairs* [2004] EWCA Civil 1394; and *Tachiona v United States* 386 F(3d) 205, 2004 US App. Lexus 20879 (2d Cir. 6 October 2004) (Tachiona II).

[76] 66 A.J.I.L. 923; 11 I.L.M. 470 (1972).

[77] The Convention on Jurisdictional Immunities of States and their Property opened for signature from 17 January 2005 but is not yet in force.

[78] ICJ, 3 February 2012.

[79] Note, the difference between the rules applicable to states and individuals who may not be entitled to rely upon immunity in respect of violations of international criminal law.

was used for sovereign purposes and immunity, having not been waived, existed in respect of it, and (3) the Italian court had erred in declaring the Greek judgment enforceable and should have afforded Germany state immunity.

Diplomatic immunity

"[T]he institution of diplomacy, with its concomitant privileges and immunities, has withstood the test of centuries and proved to be an instrument essential for effective cooperation in the international community, and for enabling States, irrespective of their differing constitutional and social systems, to achieve mutual understanding and to resolve their differences by peaceful means; ... [w]hile no State is under any obligation to maintain diplomatic or consular relations with another, yet it cannot fail to recognise the imperative obligations inherent therein now codified in the Vienna Conventions of 1961 and 1963 ... The rules of diplomatic law ... constitute a self-contained regime which, on the one hand, lays down the receiving State's obligations regarding the facilities, privileges and immunities to be accorded to diplomatic missions and, on the other, foresees their possible abuse by members of the mission and specifies the means at the disposal of the receiving State to counter any such abuse."[80]

The second principal exception to territorial jurisdiction is diplomatic immunity—representatives of a foreign state are immune from the application of the host state's municipal law. Diplomatic law was the earliest expression of international relations, for example diplomatic immunity was accorded to representatives from Greek city states. Generally, the privileges and immunities afforded by customary international law have not been controversial and have been adopted and respected by states. The customary law was codified in the 1961 Vienna Convention on Diplomatic Relations (the 1961 Convention).[81]

The 1961 Convention, which came into force in 1964, deals with the immunities of foreign missions and foreign personnel in receiving host states and has been adhered to by the majority of independent states.

Diplomatic relations exist only through the mutual consent of states. Although all independent states enjoy the capacity to establish diplomatic relations, there is no right to diplomatic

---

[80] *Case Concerning US Diplomatic and Consular Staff in Tehran* (Provisional Measures) I.C.J. Rep. 1979 7 at 19–20 and (Judgment) I.C.J. Rep. 1980 3 at 40.
[81] 500 U.N.T.S. 95; 55 A.J.I.L. 1064 (1961).

relations. The establishment of diplomatic relations indicates unequivocally the recognition of an entity as a state by the recognising state. The cessation of diplomatic relations may be used as an expression of disapproval (an instance of a retorsion, e.g. the severance of relations between the UK and Argentina following the Falkland Islands dispute in 1982)[82] but will not negate recognition already accorded.

Another example was the severing of diplomatic relations between the US and Cuba in 1961 following the Bay of Pigs invasion, whereafter both countries closed their embassies in Havana and Washington respectively. It was not until 2015 before relations improved to the point where they reopened their embassies, with the Cuban Embassy in Washington doing so in July of that year, and a month later the US Embassy reopening in Havana.

Diplomatic privileges and immunities have, as their raison d'être, a functional objective—the purpose of such privileges and immunities is not to benefit individuals, but to ensure the efficient performance of the functions of diplomatic missions as representing states.[83] The consent, *agrément*, of the host state must be obtained for the proposed head of the mission.[84] Reasons for refusal of *agrément* need not be provided. The receiving state may, at any time and without providing reasons, notify the sending state that the head of the mission or any member of the diplomatic staff of the mission is *persona non grata*, or that any other member of the staff of the mission is unacceptable to the receiving state. The sending state is required to either recall the person concerned or terminate his or her functions at the mission.

Should the sending state refuse or fail to do this within a reasonable period, the receiving state may refuse to recognise the person concerned as a member of the mission.[85]

Article 3 of the 1961 Convention spells out the functions of a diplomatic mission as consisting of, inter alia

"(a) representing the sending State in the receiving State;

(b) protecting in the receiving State the interests of the sending State and of its nationals within the limits permitted by international law;

(c) negotiating with the government of the receiving State;

(d) ascertaining by all lawful means conditions and develop-

---

[82] Relations were resumed in the summer of 1990.
[83] Preamble to the Vienna Convention.
[84] art.4 of the Vienna Convention.
[85] art.9.

ments in the receiving State, and reporting thereon to the government of the sending State;

(e) promoting friendly relations between the sending State and the receiving State, and developing their economic, cultural and scientific relations."

Article 11 provides that, in the absence of specific agreement, the receiving state may require that the size of the mission be kept within reasonable limits.

The premises of a diplomatic mission are inviolable,[86] that is premises which are currently being used for the purposes of a mission—see *Westminster CC v Government of Iran*.[87] Agents of the receiving state may not enter there without the consent of the head of the mission and the receiving state must "take all appropriate steps to protect the premises of the mission against any intrusion or damage and to prevent any disturbance of the peace of the mission or impairment of its dignity."[88] Article 22 further provides that the premises of the mission, their furnishings and other property and the means of transport of the mission are immune from search, requisition, attachment or execution. The archives and documents of the mission are inviolable "at any time and wherever they may be."[89] The private residence of a diplomatic agent enjoys the same inviolability and protection as the premises of the mission.[90] Inviolability also extends to an agent's papers, correspondence[91] and his or her property.[92] The receiving state is, accordingly, under a duty to afford a high level of protection (higher than that afforded to "ordinary" aliens) and must accord "full facilities for the performance of the functions of the mission."[93]

Respect for the inviolability of a foreign mission precluded the British police from entering the Libyan "People's Bureau" in April 1984. On 17 April 1984, a demonstration against the Gaddafi regime occurred outside the Libyan "People's Bureau" in St James's Square, London. Shots were fired from inside the Bureau

---

[86] art.22(1).
[87] [1986] 1 W.L.R. 979, Ch D.
[88] art.22(2).
[89] art.24.
[90] art.30. Premises of the mission include only the private residence of the head of the mission and not the private residence of a diplomatic agent. For English authority see *Intro Properties Ltd v Sauvel* [1983] Q.B. 1019 CA.
[91] Subject to the instances covered in art.31(1)(a)–(c).
[92] art.30(2).
[93] art.25. Note also the 1973 Convention on the Prevention and Punishment of Crimes Against Internationally Protected Persons, Including Diplomatic Agents, 13 I.L.M. 50 (1974).

and a police constable on duty outside the premises was hit and died from the injuries sustained. The "People's Bureau"'s inviolability was respected by the UK[94] and continued to be respected for a limited period after the diplomats had left for Libya, even though the mission premises had been used to endanger and harm the host state's nationals.[95] The diplomats left on 27 April, but the diplomatic status of the premises did not cease until midnight on 29 April, and at 6am on 30 April, the British police legally entered the "People's Bureau". The sanction invoked by the UK against Libya was a severance of diplomatic relations with Libya and expulsion of the members of the mission. Inviolability is an absolute principle under the Vienna Convention and entry to mission premises is prohibited in all circumstances, save with the consent or invitation of the head of the mission.[96]

The 1979 Iranian hostages incident is an illustration of a receiving state's failure to afford due protection to a foreign embassy. On 4 November 1979, during a demonstration, several hundred armed individuals overran the US Embassy Compound in Tehran. Mission archives and documents were seized and 52 American nationals were taken as hostages. Iranian security personnel failed to counter the attack and in the subsequent case before the ICJ, the lack of protection afforded to the mission was held to be directly attributable to the Iranian Government, even though the initial seizure was "executed by militants not having an official character."[97]

The 1990 Iraqi order demanding the closure of diplomatic missions in Kuwait and the withdrawal of all privileges and immunities brought a response from the UN in the Security Council Resolutions 664 and 667. The former[98] called for an immediate rescission of the Iraqi order, while the latter[99] condemned the acts perpetrated by Iraq against diplomatic premises and personnel in Kuwait. It called for the immediate protection and well-being thereof and for the cessation of any action hindering the diplomatic and consular mission in the performance of their functions.

Inviolability does not mean extra-territorial jurisdiction. The

---

[94] The exact legal nature/status of a People's Bureau nevertheless remains obscure.

[95] art.41(3) provides "the premises of the mission must not be used in any manner incompatible with the functions of the mission."

[96] This is not to deny that, although legally prohibited, there may be occasions where it could be argued entry might be justified because of, for example, a threat to the host state or the Embassy in question is being used to store armaments, e.g. Pakistani raid on the Iraqi Embassy in 1973.

[97] Above, fn.80 p.30. Note also the seizure of the Japanese Embassy by rebels in the Peruvian capital of Lima in 1996.

[98] Adopted 18 August 1990 by a vote of 15–0; 29 I.L.M. 1323 (1990).

[99] Adopted 16 September 1990 by a vote of 16–0; 29 I.L.M. 1323 (1990).

premises are not an extension of the sending state's territory. Acts committed on mission premises are within the territorial jurisdiction of the receiving state. Only in exceptional cases, possibly for humanitarian reasons of a severe nature, will a state grant asylum to an individual within an embassy. To do otherwise would be regarded as a grave violation of another state's sovereignty.

Since 2012 Julian Assange, the founder of the internet site WikiLeaks, has enjoyed diplomatic asylum in the Ecuadorean Embassy in London, avoiding extradition to Sweden to face charges of sexual assault. Assange alleges if extradited to Sweden he will be sent to the US to face charges related to the publication of WikiLeaks. At the time of writing Assange remains within the Embassy, unable to leave, as the UK has indicated he would be arrested if he were to leave the mission.

Diplomatic staff enjoy free movement and travel within the territory of the host state, subject to laws regulating entry into certain areas for reasons of national security. The receiving state must also allow and protect free communication by the mission for all official purposes and the diplomatic bag, which must be clearly marked as such, must be neither opened nor detained.[100] The absence of "visible external marks" from the crate used in the attempted abduction from the UK of Mr Dikko, an ex-government minister of Nigeria, legitimised the opening by UK customs officials of the container in question and kept their actions within the bounds of the Convention.[101] The right of challenge in respect of the diplomatic bag was accepted practice before 1961. In the event of a bag being challenged the sending state could either agree to the bag being opened and inspected or being returned unopened to its original source. The right of challenge is not included in the Convention. The degree of scrutiny to which the diplomatic bag may be subject has remained controversial. It is a sensitive issue, as the bag may be used to import illegally, inter alia, drugs and/or weapons.

In an attempt to address the issue the International Law Commission has been considering the status of the diplomatic bag and in 1989 adopted Draft Articles on the Status of the Diplomatic Courier and the Diplomatic Bag Not Accompanied by the Diplomatic Courier. The 1989 Draft Articles are designed to establish a comprehensive and essentially uniform regime applicable to all kinds of couriers and bags employed for official communications which are involved primarily in diplomatic and consular relations. The central provision is Draft Article 28 which

---

[100] art.27(3).
[101] Mr Dikko, a member of the overthrown Nigerian government, was kidnapped in London and drugged in the attempt to procure his return to Nigeria where he was wanted on criminal charges.

enunciates the basic principle of inviolability. However, the competent authorities of the receiving state or the transit state may request the opening of the bag in their presence by an authorised representative of the sending state, if they have serious reason to believe the consular bag contains something other than correspondence, documents or articles intended exclusively for official use. If this request is refused, the bag is to be returned to its place of origin.[102] The International Law Commission has proposed to the General Assembly that an international conference be convened with the purpose of establishing and international convention on the subject, using the 1989 Draft Articles as a basis.

The person of a diplomatic agent is inviolable and is not liable to any form of arrest or detention; the receiving state must treat such a person with due respect and must take all appropriate steps to prevent any attack on his or her person, freedom or dignity.[103] A "diplomatic agent" is, for the purposes of the 1961 Convention, the head of the mission or a member of the diplomatic staff of the mission.[104]

A diplomatic agent enjoys absolute immunity from the criminal jurisdiction of the receiving state. Nevertheless, in 1987, the US took the first steps towards an indictment of an Ambassador prior to the termination of official accreditation. Following a car accident involving two US nationals, one of whom was seriously injured, Ambassador Abisinito, Papua New Guinea's Extraordinary and Plenipotentiary to the US was charged by the District of Columbia police with "failing to pay full time and attention to driving". Ambassador Abisinito was recalled by Papua New Guinea on 17 February 1987 and his accreditation to the US ceased as of 24 February. However, it was not until January 1988 that the US Attorney's Office informed Mr. Abisinito's criminal lawyers that prosecution was not "currently being contemplated".[105]

The diplomatic agent is also immune from the receiving state's civil and administrative jurisdiction, except in the case of

> "(a) a real action relating to private immovable property situated in the territory of the receiving State, unless he holds it on behalf of the sending State for the purposes of the mission;
>
> (b) an action relating to succession in which the diplomatic

---

[102] Draft art.28(2). NB: "consular" bag and not "diplomatic" bag.
[103] art.29.
[104] art.1(e).
[105] Washington Post, 14–15 February 1987; Columbia Journal of Law, 1988; Legal Times, 4 May 1987; Diplomatic Note of the Embassy of Papua New Guinea, 24 February 1987. cf. Former Syrian Ambassador to the GDR 121 I.L.R. 595.

agent is involved as executor, administrator, heir or legatee as a private person and not on behalf of the sending State;

(c) an action relating to any professional or commercial activity exercised by the diplomatic agent in the receiving State outside his official functions."[106]

In such instances, immunity from jurisdiction is not available. A diplomatic agent is not obliged to give evidence as a witness.[107] The immunity enjoyed by a diplomatic agent is extended to the members of his family (normally spouse and children under the age of 18) if they are not nationals of the host state.[108] The immunity of a national of the receiving state is limited to official acts performed in the exercise of his or her functions.[109] Immunity is from jurisdiction and not from liability. The sending state may waive the right to immunity,[110] as did Thailand in the summer of 1991, when one of its London embassy staff was apprehended by customs officials at Heathrow Airport for allegedly possessing and attempting illegally to import heroin. In 1997, a diplomat from the Republic of Georgia was held responsible for the death of a 16-year-old American girl in a car accident. The President of Georgia waived the immunity of the diplomat and stated in the American press, "the moral principle of just punishment outweighs the antiquated Cold War-era practice of diplomatic immunity".[111] Waiver must be express.[112] If a diplomatic agent or other person enjoying immunity initiates proceedings, they are then precluded from claiming immunity from jurisdiction in respect of any counter claim which is connected with the principal claim.[113] Waiver of immunity from jurisdiction in respect of civil or administrative proceedings does not imply waiver of immunity with regard to the execution of the judgment. A separate waiver is necessary.[114] A host state always reserves the right to declare a member of the diplomatic mission a *persona non grata*.[115]

---

[106] art.31(1).
[107] art.31(2).
[108] art.37. Other persons may be treated as a diplomat's family in certain instances. It is British practice to treat certain persons, e.g. a person who fulfils the social duties of hostess to the diplomatic agent—sister or adult daughter of either an unmarried or widowed diplomat—as a member of the diplomat's family.
[109] art.38.
[110] art.32(1). Waiver however is unusual.
[111] See, ASIL Newsletter, January–February 1997, Letters, p.4.
[112] art.32(2).
[113] art.32(3).
[114] art.32(4).
[115] For example, in 1988 the Cuban Ambassador and his commercial attaché

Not all the staff of a foreign mission enjoy the same immunities. The Vienna Convention distinguishes between diplomatic agents, administrative and technical staff (e.g. archivists, clerical and secretarial staff), and service staff (e.g. kitchen staff). The administrative and technical staff, if non-nationals of the host state, enjoy complete immunity from criminal jurisdiction, but their immunity from civil and administrative jurisdiction extends only to acts performed in the fulfilment of their duties.[116] Non-national service staff likewise enjoy immunity only in respect of their official acts.[117] Distinguishing between mission staff and their respective immunities was an innovation in the 1961 Convention and represents a modification of the absolute immunity previously enjoyed under, e.g. English law—see *Empson v Smith*.[118]

A diplomat who is either recalled or who is declared by the sending state as *persona non grata* is allowed a period of grace during which his/her immunity continues. Thereafter, if the diplomat has not left the country the individual may be sued for private acts committed during his/her term of office. Immunity continues to subsist in respect of official acts.[119]

In addition to immunity from jurisdiction, diplomatic agents are, with certain exceptions such as purchase tax, exempt from taxes levied in the host state.[120] Mission premises are similarly exempt from local taxes except for those levied in respect of specific services rendered.[121] The right of immunity carries with it an obligation: it is the duty of all persons enjoying such privileges and immunities to respect the laws and the regulations of the receiving state. Such persons are also required not to interfere in the internal affairs of the receiving state,[122] e.g. in the political affairs of the host state.

The 1961 Convention was made part of UK law by the Diplomatic Privileges Act 1964 and part of US municipal law

---

were expelled from the UK following a shooting incident in London. The UK Government's decision to hold the Ambassador personally liable for the actions of one of his staff was unprecedented and earned the UK a reputation for taking tough action on abuses of diplomatic immunity.

[116] art.37(2).

[117] art.37(3).

[118] [1966] 1 Q.B. 426 CA.

[119] art.39(2).

[120] art.34. This can be a contentious topic however as demonstrated by the many diplomatic missions in London refusing to pay the congestion charge since its launch in 2003, arguing that it is a direct tax and thus prohibited from being imposed on diplomatic missions by the 1961 Vienna Convention on Diplomatic Relations. The UK Foreign Office insists the congestion charge is not a tax, but rather a charge for a service rendered for which there are no legal grounds to exempt diplomats.

[121] art.23.

[122] art.41.

by the Diplomatic Relations Act 1978. The American legislation
applies the 1961 Convention's provisions to all states and not just
to those who have become parties to the 1961 Convention. The
1961 Convention does not preclude states either through practice
or agreement, extending to each other more favourable treatment than that afforded by the 1961 Convention's provisions,
art.47(b).

Heads of state

The evolution of international criminal law has impacted upon
some of the jurisdictional rules of immunity in the case of international crimes. A number of questions were addressed in the
case involving General Pinochet, dictator and former president of
Chile.[123] These can be identified as being:

(a) Is the claim for immunity made by a serving or a former
head of state?

(b) Is the claim made in respect of the official government act
or a private act?

(c) Is the making of the claim consistent with international
law?

The various facets of the *Pinochet* case illustrate an increasing
tension between preserving the traditional absolute immunity
approach and an evolving human rights culture. One of the issues
in respect of Pinochet was the extent to which a former head of
state could enjoy immunity. The House of Lords, on 25 November
1998, held that a former head of state could only be immune for
acts which fell within his functions as a head of state, although it
remains unresolved as to which acts may be categorised as official
and those which may be deemed personal. It was also held that
an individual could not claim immunity, nor could a state, in
respect of acts which are prohibited by international convention
and to which the state concerned is a contracting party of the said
convention. The House of Lords therefore ruled that a former
head of state is not entitled to immunity for such acts as torture,
hostage-taking and crimes against humanity, committed while he

---

[123] *R. v Bow Street Metropolitan Stipendiary Magistrate Ex p. Pinochet Ugarte* (No.2)
[2001] 1 A.C. 119, *R. v Bow Street Stipendiary Magistrate Ex p. Pinochet Ugarte*
(No.3) [2000] 1 A.C. 147; [1999] 2 W.L.R. 272, *R. v Bartle and the Commissioner of
Police for the Metropolis Ex p. Pinochet*, 24 March 1999, [1991] 2 All E.R. 97, *R. v
Evans and the Commissioner of the Police for the Metropolis Ex p. Pinochet*, 24 March
1999, House of Lords.

was in his post.[124] Accordingly, Chile could not claim immunity of liability after having signed and ratified the 1984 Convention against Torture.[125] However, Pinochet was deemed by a number of medical professionals to be unfit to stand trial and accordingly the British Foreign Secretary declined to extradite him from the UK to Spain.

The legacy of the Pinochet jurisprudence has been to some extent to muddy the waters, at least as to the issue of immunity of heads of state particularly when acts of torture are alleged. The issue was raised in the *Al-Adsani* case, in which a more cautious position was adopted and the Kuwaiti government claim of state immunity was upheld, in civil proceedings initiated in the English Court for damages in respect of physical injuries and mental suffering, constituting torture, sustained in Kuwait. In the *Arrest Warrant* case the ICJ upheld the DRC immunity claim and recognised that the accused, a senior minister, had diplomatic immunity as a Minister for Foreign Affairs.[126]

Notably, Heads of State do not enjoy immunity before the International Criminal Court[127] or other international criminal tribunals.[128] Former head of states have faced trial, for example, the former President of Serbia Slobodan Milošević before the ICTY, and in 2015 the trial against the former president of Chad, Hissène Habré, started before the Extraordinary African Chambers of the African Union in Senegal. In 2004 the Special Court of Sierra Leone held that Charles Taylor, at the time

---

[124] House of Lords, *R. v Bartle and the Commissioner of Police for the Metropolis and Others (Appellants), Ex Parte Pinochet (Respondent) (On Appeal from a Divisional Court of the Queen's Bench Division); R. v Evans and Another and the Commissioner of Police for the Metropolis and Others (Appellants), Ex p. Pinochet (Respondent) (On Appeal from a Divisional Court of the Queen's Bench Division)*, Judgment of 25 November 1998, 37 I.L.M. (1998) 1302.

[125] The Convention Against Torture and Other Cruel, Inhuman or Degrading Treatment or Punishment 1987, above fn.25. Chile ratified the Convention on 30 September 1988.

[126] See above, fn.19. Also there is criminal jurisdiction over individuals in respect of torture committed in the UK or elsewhere by way of the Criminal Justice Act 1988 s.134. Note also the case *Against the Afghan Warlord*. See also the decision of the Spanish Court convicting Adolfo Scilingo (Argentina) for crimes against humanity whilst serving as a member of the Military Junta. The decision is noteworthy, as it is the first successful prosecution for the Spanish Court in what it claims is its right under international law to try in Spain anyone accused of atrocities committed abroad, *Time Magazine*, 2 May 2005, p.18. See also decision of 11th US Circuit Court of Appeals 15 March 2005 upholding a US jury's decision, 2003, that Armando Fernandez Larios was guilty of crimes against humanity in Chile while serving as General Pinochet's bodyguard.

[127] Article 27, Rome Statute of the ICC. Also consider the arrest warrants issued by the ICC in respect of Omar Al Bashir, president of Sudan.

[128] For example, consider the prosecution before the ICTY of former president of Serbia, Slobodan Milošević.

President of Liberia, could not invoke his Head of State immunity before the Court.

In the US, the Alien Tort Claims Act 1789 (ATCA)[129] has been utilised to seek redress for human rights violations which have occurred outside the US. The Act provides the District Courts with jurisdiction in any civil action raised "by an alien for a tort only, committed in violation of the law of nations or a treaty of the United States." The Act was virtually unused until employed as the basis of jurisdiction in the *Filartiga* case.[130] The Act was reinforced by the US 1991 Torture Victim Prevention Act, which extends to "any individual" defendant. The Act has been used in a number of cases and the extent of its use has become an issue, polarising human rights groups and corporate business organisations. Particularly significant have been the lawsuits instituted under ATCA against corporations for alleged violations of human rights committed abroad. One important case in this regard was *Kiobel v Shell*[131] in which Nigerian refugees in the US brought a case against Shell Oil, a Dutch/UK multinational, alleging the company had assisted the Nigerian military in the torture and killing of environmentalists who were protesting Shell's activities in the Ogoni region of the Niger Delta. However the US Supreme Court ruled in April 2013 that the ATCA did not apply to alleged abuses which occurred outside the US. Human rights organisations were disappointed at the unanimous ruling that the "mere presence" of a multinational organisation in the US was not enough of a connection to allow for extraterritorial jurisdiction. However the Justices offered a split opinion leaving open the possibility of the Act being used in cases where a stronger connection can be made between alleged human rights abuses by foreign individuals or companies and the US.

Consular relations

Consuls represent their state in another state, with the consent of the latter. Consuls are concerned not with political affairs, but rather with administrative issues, e.g. the issue of visas. They also give various forms of assistance to nationals of the sending state when they are in the territory of the receiving state. Consuls have the right to access and communicate with nationals who have been detained in another country.[132] Failure to do so has resulted

---

[129] 28 U.S.C. 1350 (1988).
[130] *Filartiga v Pena-Irala* 630 F (2d) 876; (1980) 19 I.L.M. 966. US Circuit of Appeals 2nd Circuit.
[131] *Kiobel v Royal Dutch Petroleum Co.* 569 U.S. (2013).
[132] The Vienna Convention on Consular Relations (1963), art.36.

in action being initiated before the ICJ.[133] Consuls are posted in provincial towns as well as in capital cities.

Consular relations, unlike diplomatic relations between states, have been largely governed by bipartite agreements. The Vienna Convention on Consular Relations (the 1963 Convention)[134] was adopted in 1963 to regulate, on a universal basis, the position and functions of consuls. The 1963 Convention entered into force in 1967. If two states have a bipartite agreement and both are parties to the 1963 Convention, the provisions which extend the greater immunities prevail. Consular immunities, unlike diplomatic immunities, may not be assumed, but must be shown to derive from either the 1963 Convention, or from a bipartite agreement. The immunities and privileges enjoyed by consuls and consular premises resemble those accorded to diplomatic agents and diplomatic missions; however, they are more limited in their scope.

The principal difference is that, in the absence of special agreement, consuls are immune from arrest, detention and the criminal process only in respect of acts and omissions in the performance of their official functions. A consular officer must appear if summoned before the courts and later plead and prove immunity by virtue of the act or omission in question being in the performance of his official functions. Some states have, by special agreement and on a reciprocal basis, extended full immunity from criminal jurisdiction to consular personnel, e.g. the American–Soviet Union Convention. A consular officer may only be arrested or detained in respect of a grave crime and pursuant to a decision by a competent judicial authority.[135] Proceedings against a consular officer should be conducted "with the respect due to him by reason of his official position" and save when charged with a grave crime, "in a manner which will hamper the exercise of consular functions as little as possible".[136] Members of a consul's family do not enjoy the same extensive jurisdictional immunities as the members of a diplomat's family, but they are exempt from such restrictions as immigration controls, customs duties and taxes, if they are not nationals of the receiving state.

---

[133] Germany and Paraguay both brought cases against the US. See *Paraguay v US* (1998) I.C.J. 248 and *Germany v US (La Grand case)* 40 I.L.M. 1069 (2001) where a judgment was passed on 27 June 2001. The ICJ in 2001 held that the US was in breach of its obligations under art.36(1) of the Convention in that the US had not informed the La Grand brothers of their rights under art.36(1) "without delay". See also *Avena (Mexico v United States)* Decision of the ICJ General List No.128 31 March 2004.

[134] 596 U.N.T.S. 261.

[135] art.41(1).

[136] art.41(3).

Special missions

Special ad hoc missions sent by a state to fulfil a specific purpose in another state are a recent innovation. There are no rules of customary international law on the subject. A Convention Guaranteeing Immunities to Special Missions was drawn up in 1969 (the 1969 Convention).[137] The 1969 Convention, which entered into force on 21 June 1985, is based essentially on the 1961 Vienna Convention on Diplomatic Relations. Under art.8 of the 1969 Convention, the sending state must inform the host state of both the size and composition of the mission, while art.17 provides that the location of the mission must be mutually agreed by the states concerned, or must be in the Foreign Ministry of the receiving state.

International organisations

International organisations enjoy those privileges and immunities from the jurisdiction of a member state as are necessary for the fulfilment of the organisation's purposes. Such immunities include immunity from legal process, financial controls, taxes and duties. The immunities and privileges to be enjoyed by the organisation and its personnel vis-à-vis member states are provided for in the constituent charter of the organisation and supplementary agreements adhered to by members of the organisation, e.g. the General Convention on the Privileges and Immunities of the United Nations 1946.[138] The General Convention gives immunity from the legal process to, inter alia, the property and the assets of the UN, unless such immunity is waived, as well as immunity from criminal jurisdiction for its representatives.

CONCLUSION

Jurisdiction is a multi-faceted topic, but essentially the exercise is an attribute of state sovereignty. Although there now exist some limitations on the exercise of that sovereignty these are subject to checks and balances, which at all times give cognisance to the primacy of states. However notwithstanding this, the developments in international criminal law highlight that states and their citizens can no longer act with impunity without potentially facing sanctions.

---

[137] 9 I.L.M. 127 (1970).
[138] 1 U.N.T.S. 15; 43 A.J.I.L. Supp.

7. THE LAW OF THE SEA

The law of the sea[1] regulates the relations of states, both coastal and landlocked, in respect of those areas subject to coastal state jurisdiction and in relation to those areas of the sea and the seabed beyond national jurisdiction. The rules governing the sea are drawn from both custom and treaty.

In the 1950s, the profusion of claims, the advance of technology and the need for a protection of conventional sea uses were responsible for the Geneva Conventions on the Law of the Sea. The Conventions were the outcome of the initial work undertaken by the International Law Commission. The four Conventions adopted by the 1958 Conference (the First UN Conference on the Law of the Sea) were the Convention on the Territorial Sea and Contiguous Zone,[2] the Convention on the High Seas,[3] the Convention on the Continental Shelf[4] and the Convention on Fishing and Conservation of Living Resources of the High Seas.[5]

---

[1] As distinct from Admiralty law or Maritime law, which is concerned principally with relations between private persons involved in the transport of passengers or goods.
[2] 516 U.N.T.S. 205.
[3] 45 U.N.T.S. 82.
[4] 499 U.N.T.S. 311.
[5] 599 U.N.T.S. 285.

The Conventions all entered into force, however by 1982, three-quarters of the states of the world were not a party to them. The Conventions, which codified certain existing state practices and also articulated rules of progressive development, proved inadequate, particularly with regard to the continental shelf and the ocean bed which, with advancing technology, came within the potential acquisition of certain states. In 1960 a Second UN Conference in Geneva attempted, albeit unsuccessfully, to address some of these issues and no treaty was adopted.

The need to preserve the seas as the "common heritage of all mankind" and the danger of a "scramble for the seas" precipitated the calling of the Third United Nations Conference on the Law of the Sea (UNCLOS III). The 1982 Convention on the Law of the Sea,[6] adopted on 30 April 1982, in Montego Bay, Jamaica, was the culmination of protracted negotiations over nine years. The Convention was opened for signature in December 1982 and was designed as a "complete package" with limited provision for reservation.[7] The 1982 Convention was the subject of considerable opposition, primarily from western states who were concerned about the provisions regarding the exploitation of the deep seabed contained in Pt XI.[8] Attempts to resolve disagreement over Pt XI were unsuccessful until 1994, when the UN General Assembly adopted a Resolution and Agreement Relating to the Implementation of Pt XI of the 1982 Convention.[9] The adoption of this Agreement was key to the implementation of the 1982 Convention and this is reflected in the preamble of the Resolution, which notes "the desire to achieve universal participation" in the 1982 Convention. The Agreement modifies the terms of Pt XI in relation to the deep sea.[10] A state cannot become a party to the Agreement independently of the 1982 Convention.

The Agreement sought to address the concerns of western states regarding Pt XI and reflects the significant changes in the global economic and political climate since 1982. Specifically, it reallocates international and national responsibilities for the management of deep-sea mining.[11] The 1982 Convention came into

[6] I.L.M. 1261 (1982).
[7] See art.309 of the 1982 Convention. For reservations and their effect, see Ch.10, "The Law of Treaties".
[8] The US and the UK were particularly opposed to Pt XI of the Convention. For the UK's objections as expressed in HC, see Hansard, Vol.69, col.642 (6 December 1984).
[9] On 28 July 1994. GA Res. 48/263, 121–0 in favour, seven abstentions, 35 I.L.M. 1309 (1994). The Agreement entered into force on 28 July 1996.
[10] The Agreement has also phased out the Preparatory Commission whose role, inter alia, was to oversee the entry into force of the Convention. The Commission adopted its concluding report in August 1994 at its final meeting.
[11] Certain provisions, which were the source of controversy, such as production limitation and technological transfer, are eliminated.

force on 16 November 1994 and represents an important step in the progressive development and codification of the law of the sea.[12] The 1982 Convention's entry into force confirmed the UN General Assembly's competence as the global forum for review of all developments relating to the law of the sea.[13]

Some of the provisions of the 1982 Convention simply restate provisions of the Geneva Conventions—representing established customary international law. Others, notably those on the Exclusive Economic Zone, mirror what is now customary international law—reflecting state practice before the 1982 Convention was finalised. Other provisions represent a departure from established law and indicate the way in which the law was developing. In subsequent years some parts of the Convention have been developed by other treaties which address, and supplement, specific issues. Any review of the laws of the sea must begin with the Geneva Conventions of 1958.

TERRITORIAL SEA

A coastal state enjoys sovereignty over "a belt of sea adjacent to its coast, described as the territorial sea"[14] which extends "to the air space over the territorial sea as well as its bed and subsoil".[15] Every coastal state possesses a territorial sea:

> "To every State whose land territory is at any place washed by the sea, international law attaches a corresponding portion of maritime territory consisting of what the law calls territorial waters . . . International law does not say to a State: 'You are entitled to claim territorial waters if you want them.' No maritime States can refuse them. International law imposes upon a maritime State certain obligations and confers upon it certain rights arising out of the sovereignty, which it exercises over its maritime territory. The possession of this territory is not optional, not dependent upon the will of the State, but compulsory."[16]

---

[12] For a detailed discussion of the 1994 Agreement, see, generally, J. Charney, "Law of the Sea Forum: The 1994 Agreement on Implementation of the Seabed Provisions of the Convention on the Law of the Sea" and D. Anderson, "Legal Implications of the Entry into Force of the UN Convention on the Law of the Sea" (1995) 44 I.C.L.Q. 313.

[13] There are currently 167 parties (166 states and the European Union) to the 1982 Convention. The US is the only Security Council Permanent Member not to have ratified the Convention.

[14] art.1 of the Geneva Convention on the Territorial Sea and the Contiguous Zone 1958; art.1 of the 1982 Convention on the Law of the Sea.

[15] art.2 of the 1958 Convention; art.2 of the 1982 Convention.

[16] McNair J (dissenting opinion), *Anglo–Norwegian Fisheries* case I.C.J. Rep. (1951) 116 at 160.

Article 3 of the 1982 Convention establishes the breadth of the territorial sea at a limit "not exceeding 12 nautical miles".[17]

Previously, the breadth of the territorial sea had eluded an agreed definition. State practice had been uncertain and varied. Some countries, for example the UK and the US, rigidly maintained the traditional three-mile territorial sea, while certain Latin American countries made extensive claims up to 200 nautical miles. The norm, however, was for states to claim a territorial sea of a width somewhere between 3 and 12 miles. The uncertainty of state practice was reflected at the 1958 and 1960 Geneva Conferences—neither Conference was successful in defining the breadth of the territorial sea. Various permutations were suggested, such as the US formula of six-plus-six, (that is, a six-mile territorial sea with a six-mile fishing zone); an Asian/Latin American sponsored proposal calling for a 12-mile territorial sea; and a Soviet proposal whereby every state would enjoy the discretion to declare the width of its territorial sea as a distance between 3 and 12 miles. None of these proposals were adopted. The 12-mile maximum, which has been widely reflected in state practice, including the UK and the US,[18] is now accepted as customary international law—see the *Guinea/Guinea-Bissau Maritime Delimitation* case.[19] The advent and acceptance of a coastal state's exclusive economic zone (EEZ—see below) has enabled the territorial sea question to be settled independently.

In the 1950s and 1960s, increased fishing activity and advancing technology raised concern for coastal states about fisheries. There was a need for fishing to be controlled, however at that time fisheries jurisdiction was very much an integral aspect of territorial jurisdiction. The failure of the 1958 and 1960 Conferences to reach agreement regarding the territorial sea and fishing zones prompted states to take matters into their own hands and unilaterally extend their fisheries jurisdiction beyond the territorial sea, precipitating the establishment of the exclusive economic zone.

Measurement of the territorial sea

As a general rule, the baseline employed to determine the breadth of the territorial sea is the low-tide water line, as marked on large-scale charts recognised by the coastal state.[20] The outer limit of the territorial sea is the line, every point of which is at a distance from the nearest point of the baseline equal to the breadth of the

---

[17] A nautical mile is equal to 1.1508 miles or 1.852 kilometers. In this chapter the use of the term "mile" refers to a nautical mile.

[18] Territorial Sea Act 1987 (Commencement) Order 1987 (SI 1987/1270).

[19] 77 I.L.R. 636 at 638; 25 I.L.M. 251 (1988) at 272, para.43.

[20] art.3 of the 1958 Convention; art.5 of the 1982 Convention.

territorial sea.[21] Geography can present problems, and so rules to resolve these problems have evolved.

In respect of deeply indented coastlines the 1958 and 1982 Conventions reflect the International Court of Justice's judgment in the *Anglo-Norwegian Fisheries* case.[22] This case came before the Court because the UK challenged the method employed by Norway to measure its territorial sea. Rather than use the low-water mark method, Norway used the straight baseline system. As a result, waters which would otherwise have been high seas were characterised as territorial sea. The Court affirmed the legality of the straight baseline method and thus acknowledged in delimiting Norway's territorial sea, cognisance had to be given to "geographical realities" and the drawing of the baselines had to be adapted to the special conditions pertaining in different regions.[23]

Both the 1958 and 1982 Conventions acknowledge the derogation from the low-water mark allowed by the Court. Straight baselines joining appropriate points may be employed where a coastline is deeply indented,[24] provided that the lines do

> "not depart to any appreciable extent from the general direction of the coast, and the seas lying within the lines must be sufficiently closely linked to the land domain to be subject to the regime of internal waters."[25]

They may not normally be drawn "to and from low-tide elevations" unless "lighthouses or similar installations which are permanently above sea level have been built on them"[26] or "where the drawing of baselines to and from such elevations has received general international recognition".[27] The ICJ has latterly emphasised the use of straight baselines "which is an exception to the normal rules for the determination of baselines [and] may only be applied if a number of conditions are met."[28] However any such exception must be applied restrictively.

Both the 1958 and 1982 Conventions allow account to be taken

---

[21] art.6 of the 1958 Convention; art.4 of the 1982 Convention.

[22] Above, fn.16.

[23] Above, at 128.

[24] art.4(1) of the 1958 Convention; art.7(1) of the 1982 Convention.

[25] art.4(2) of the 1958 Convention; art.7(3) of the 1982 Convention.

[26] art.4(3) of the 1958 Convention.

[27] Added by art.7(4) of the 1982 Convention. See also *Nicaragua v Honduras* I.C.J. Rep. (2007), p.1, at para.141, where the Court noted that "features which are not permanently above water, and which lie outside of a State's territorial waters, should be distinguished from islands."

[28] *Qatar v Bahrain* I.C.J. Rep. (2001), p.40, at para.212.

of a further possible consideration which may be employed in the delimitation of the territorial sea.[29] This was acknowledged by the ICJ when it stated:

"one consideration not to be overlooked, the scope of which extends beyond purely geographical factors: that of certain economic interests peculiar to a region, the reality and importance of which are closely evidenced by a long usage."[30]

The Court recognised that the special economic interests of a region could be taken into consideration. However, such consideration of special economic interests is only supplementary and is at all times optional rather than mandatory. Likewise, under the 1958 and 1982 Conventions, special economic interests may be invoked to support an application of the straight baseline system, but only if their reality and importance are clearly evidenced by long usage.[31]

States are prohibited from applying straight baselines in order to cut off the territorial sea of another state, from high seas or an EEZ, and a state using the straight baseline system must publicise by way of charts the lines being employed. The 1982 Convention requires a coastal state to deposit copies of charts and lists of geographical co-ordinates with the Secretary-General of the United Nations.[32]

Another instance when straight baselines can be used is found in the 1982 Convention which provides:

"Where because of the presence of a delta and other natural conditions the coastline is highly unstable, the appropriate points may be selected along the furthest seaward extent of the low-water line and, notwithstanding subsequent regression of the low-water line, the straight baselines shall remain effective until changed by the coastal State in accordance with this Convention."[33]

Bays

A bay is defined under art.7(2) of the 1958 Convention as a

"well-marked indentation whose penetration is in such proportion to the width of its mouth as to contain landlocked

---

[29] art.4(4) and art.7(5), respectively.
[30] *Anglo–Norwegian Fisheries* case, above, fn.16 at 133.
[31] Both Conventions are silent on what constitutes real and important.
[32] art.4(5) and (6) of the 1958 Convention; art.7(6) and art.16 of the 1982 Convention.
[33] art.7(2) of the 1982 Convention.

waters and constitute more than a mere curvature of the coast. An indentation shall not, however, be regarded as a bay unless its area is as large as, or larger than, that of the semi-circle whose diameter is a line drawn across the mouth of that indentation."

Article 10(2) of the 1982 Convention reiterates this definition.

A special formula has evolved in respect of bays which belong to a single state and are more than mere curvatures of the coast. The salient feature of the formula is that straight baselines may be employed "if the distance between the low-water marks of the natural entrance points of a bay does not exceed 24 miles".[34] In the event of 24 miles being exceeded, a straight baseline of 24 miles may be drawn within the bay in such a manner as to enclose the maximum area of water that is possible with a line of that length.[35]

Neither Convention refers specifically to historic bays, namely bays, the waters of which have been treated as internal waters by the coastal state with the acceptance of other states, such as Hudson Bay and the Gulf of Fonseca.[36] Nor does either Convention refer to bays bordered by more than one state. The legal regime which will be applied in these instances is dependent upon the response of affected states but the position vis-à-vis the latter is one over which there is controversy. The Gulf of Fonseca was discussed by the International Court of Justice in the *Land, Island and Maritime Frontier Dispute (El Salvador/Honduras; Nicaragua intervening)*.[37] Therein the Court, on the basis of particular historical circumstances and the consent of the relevant states, affirmed the Gulf beyond a three-mile maritime belt for the coastal states was historical waters subject to the co-ownership or a condominium of the three coastal states.[38]

Outermost permanent harbour works (which under the 1982 Convention do not include "offshore installations and artificial islands") forming an integral part of the harbour system are to

---

[34] art.7(4) of the 1958 Convention; art.10(4) of the 1982 Convention.

[35] art.7(5) of the 1958 Convention; art.10(5) of the 1982 Convention.

[36] Previous to the 1958 Convention, it had been generally accepted under customary international law that straight baselines could be employed in respect of bays, but there was uncertainty as to beyond what width the closing line could not be employed. The ICJ in the *Anglo–Norwegian Fisheries* case, above, fn.16, rejected, because of inconsistent state practice, the ten-mile rule (which the UK was claiming as the maximum width) and refuted that such a rule had ever acquired the character of international law.

[37] I.C.J. Rep. (1992), p.351.

[38] I.C.J. Rep. (1992), p.601. See in contrast the response to Libya's claim that the Gulf of Sirte (Sidra) was a historical bay in 1973, R. Churchill and V. Lowe, *Law of the Sea*, 3rd edn (Manchester: Manchester University Press, 1999), p.45.

be regarded as part of the coast for the purpose of delimiting the territorial sea.[39]

Islands

An island is defined in art.10 of the 1958 Convention "as a naturally-formed area of land, surrounded by water, which is above water at high tide". The territorial sea of an island is decided in the same way as the territorial sea of mainland territories. The 1982 Convention retains the same definition of an island, but introduces a "regime of islands".[40] This provides that "the territorial sea, the contiguous zone, the exclusive economic zone and the continental shelf of an island are to be determined in accordance with the provisions . . . applicable to other land territory". Rocks which cannot sustain human habitation or economic life of their own are denied both an EEZ and a continental shelf, though they may continue to have a territorial sea.[41] Low-tide elevations, on the other hand, do not have a territorial sea of their own, though the low-water mark on such an elevation, if it is within the territorial sea of a coastal state, may be utilised as a baseline,[42] and art.6 of the 1982 Convention provides:

> "in the case of islands situated on atolls or islands having fringing reefs, the baseline for measuring the breadth of the territorial sea is the seaward low-water line of the reef, as shown by the appropriate symbol on charts officially recognised by the coastal State."

In the *St Pierre and Miquelon* decision, a court of arbitration considered in some detail the role of islands in delimitation and declined to adjust the extent of the maritime rights of the islands by reference to either their political status or special geographical circumstances.[43]

---

[39] art.8 of the 1958 Convention; art.11 of the 1982 Convention.

[40] Pt VIII, art.121.

[41] art.121(3). This provision would deny an EEZ and continental shelf, e.g. to the area referred to as the Island of Rockall. In the *Jan Mayen Case (Denmark v Norway)* I.C.J. Rep. (1993) 38, Denmark asserted that the island in dispute could not sustain economic or human life but appeared to implicitly accept that it could have a continental shelf or fishery zone. The UK had, under the Fishery Limits Act 1976, proclaimed a 200–nautical-mile fishing zone around the Island of Rockall. However, the UK Government withdrew this claim in 1997 on accession to the Law of the Sea Convention.

[42] art.11 of the 1958 Convention; art.13 of the 1982 Convention.

[43] See Court of Arbitration for the *Delimitation of Maritime Areas between Canada and France: Decision in case Concerning Delimitation of Maritime Areas (St Pierre and Miquelon)*, in particular the dissenting opinion of Mr Prosper Weil interpreting the Court's decision 31 I.L.M. 1145 (1992) at 1216–1218. The issue of islands and

Delimitation of territorial seas between opposite or adjacent states

The territorial sea between opposite or adjacent states is determined in one of three ways: by agreement between the states, e.g. the Anglo–French agreement relating to the Delimitation of the Territorial Sea in the Straits of Dover[44]; by the median line, every point of which is equidistant from the nearest points on the baselines from which the breadth of the territorial seas of each of the two states is measured[45]; or by another line required by historic title or other special circumstances.[46] The 1982 Convention envisages that a coastal state "may determine baselines . . . by any of the methods provided for . . . to suit different conditions".[47]

Archipelagic states

Archipelagic states, such as Indonesia, the Bahamas and the Philippines which are made up of a number of islands, have, in the absence of international agreement, drawn straight baselines around the outer limits of their islands. The effect has been to turn what were formerly "high seas" into territorial waters.

International law traditionally sidestepped the problems raised by archipelagic states, and the 1958 Convention makes no provision for special treatment of mid-ocean archipelagos. The 1982 Convention, however, does deal separately with such states.[48] An archipelagic state is, for the purposes of the Convention, constituted wholly of one or more archipelagos and may include other islands including parts of islands, interconnecting waters and other natural features which are so closely interrelated that such islands, water and other natural features form an intrinsic geographical, economic and political entity, or which historically have been regarded as such.[49] The 1982 Convention recognises archipelago baselines joining the outermost points of the outermost islands. Such baselines may "not exceed 100 nautical miles, except that up to three per cent of the total number of baselines enclosing any archipelago may exceed that length, up to a maximum length of 125 nautical miles" and must "not depart to any appreciable extent from the general configuration of the

---

delimitation was also considered in *Jan Mayen*, above, fn.41, in which it was also held that art.121 mirrored "the present status of international law."

[44] Cmnd.557.
[45] Cmnd.557 Guinea and Guinea-Bissau submitted their dispute on the *Delimitation of the Maritime Boundary* to an Arbitration Tribunal, 25 I.L.M. 251 (1986).
[46] art.12 of the 1958 Convention; art.15 of the 1982 Convention.
[47] art.14 of the 1982 Convention.
[48] Pt IV, arts 46–54.
[49] art.46.

archipelago".[50] The territorial sea, the contiguous zone, the EEZ and the continental shelf are drawn from the archipelagic baselines.[51] Archipelagic waters enclosed by the archipelago baselines fall within the territorial sovereignty of the archipelagic state,[52] subject to the right of all states to enjoy the right of innocent passage[53] similar to that enjoyed in territorial waters (see below). An archipelagic state may designate archipelagic sea-lanes for passage and prescribe traffic separation schemes[54] comparable to the right of passage through straits.

The 1982 Convention does not address the issue of straight baselines by continental states with archipelagos. Nevertheless, Canada established baselines round the entire Arctic Archipelago from latitude 60°E to the Beaufort Sea in the west and designated all waters enclosed as Canadian.

Innocent passage

The definition of "passage" contained in art.18 of the 1982 Convention elaborates upon the accepted customary international law definition and that contained in art.14 of the 1958 Convention. Article 18 provides[55]:

> "1. Passage means navigation through the territorial sea for the purpose of:
>
>   (a) traversing that sea without entering internal waters or calling at a roadstead or port facility outside internal waters; or
>
>   (b) proceeding to or from internal waters or a call at such roadstead or port facility.
>
> 2. Passage shall be continuous and expeditious. However, passage includes stopping and anchoring, but only in so far as the same are incidental to ordinary navigation or are rendered necessary by force majeure or distress or for the purpose of rendering assistance to persons, ships or aircraft in danger or distress."

The 1958 Convention recognises what had become established under customary international law, namely, a coastal state's sovereignty over its territorial sea is subject to the obligation to

---

[50] art.47.
[51] art.48.
[52] art.49.
[53] art.52.
[54] art.53.
[55] *Nicaragua (Merits)* case I.C.J. Rep. (1986) 14 at 111.

allow a right of innocent passage to all foreign ships.[56] Innocent passage is defined in a very general way as that which "is not prejudicial to the peace, good order or security of the coastal State".[57] Fishing vessels are required to observe the laws and regulations of coastal states[58] and submarines are required to navigate on the surface and to show their flag,[59] otherwise their passage will not be regarded as innocent. The 1982 Convention is more specific in its definition of "innocent" and enunciates a list of activities which, if occurring in a coastal state's territorial waters, would not be characterised as "innocent". Such activities include: any threat or use of force against the sovereignty, territorial integrity or political independence of a coastal state; any exercise or practice with weapons of any kind, any act aimed at collecting information to the prejudice of the defence or security of a coastal state; any act of propaganda aimed at affecting the defence or security of a coastal state; any fishing activities and the carrying out of research or survey activities.[60] A coastal state is under a duty not to hamper innocent passage.[61] The 1982 Convention, again, is more precise and stipulates that a coastal state shall not

"(a) impose requirements on foreign ships which have the practical effect of denying or impairing the right of innocent passage; or

(b) discriminate in form or in fact against the ships of any State or against ships carrying cargoes to, from or on behalf of any State."[62]

Under both Conventions, coastal states are required to give appropriate publicity of any dangers to navigation of which it has knowledge within its territorial sea.[63]

Article 17 of the 1958 Convention simply provides that foreign ships engaging in innocent passage must comply with a coastal state's laws and regulations. Once more, the 1982 Convention articulates to a greater extent the laws and regulations which a

---

[56] art.5 of the 1958 Convention and art.8 of the 1982 Convention provide where the straight baseline is employed because of an indented coastline, and this has led to territorial waters or high seas being designated internal waters, a right of innocent passage shall exist in those waters.

[57] art.14(4).

[58] art.14(5).

[59] art.14(6).

[60] art.19 of the 1982 Convention.

[61] art.15 of the 1958 Convention.

[62] art.24.

[63] art.15(2) of the 1958 Convention; art.24(2) of the 1982 Convention.

coastal state may adopt. These may, for instance, include measures on the safety of navigation and the regulation of maritime traffic, the protection of navigational aids and facilities and other facilities or installations, the protection of cables and pipelines, the conservation of the living resources of the sea, and the preservation of the environment of a coastal state and the prevention, reduction and control of pollution thereof.[64]

Two new provisions are included in the 1982 Convention. Article 22 provides a coastal state may require foreign ships to use such sea lanes and traffic separation schemes as it (that is, the coastal state) may designate or prescribe for vessels, in particular tankers, nuclear-powered ships and ships carrying nuclear or other inherently dangerous or noxious substances, or materials, engaged in innocent passage. Also art.23, which provides that foreign nuclear-powered ships and ships carrying nuclear or like material shall be required to carry documents and observe special precautionary measures established for such ships by international agreements.

A coastal state may take the steps necessary to prevent passage, which is not innocent[65] and may, without discriminating between foreign ships, suspend innocent passage temporarily in specified areas of its territorial sea if required in the interest of that coastal state's security.[66] If a vessel is proceeding to internal waters, a coastal state may take the steps necessary to prevent any breach of the conditions to which the admission of the ship to internal waters is subject.[67]

Foreign vessels engaged in innocent passage are only subject to a coastal state's criminal and civil jurisdiction in limited defined circumstances. A coastal state may only exercise jurisdiction with regards to any crime committed on board the ship during its passage in the following cases:

(a) if the consequences of the crime extend to the coastal State; or

(b) if the crime is of a kind to disturb the peace of the country, the good order of the territorial sea; or

(c) if the assistance of the local authorities has been requested by the captain of the ship, the consul of the state whose flag the ship flies; or

(d) if it is necessary for the suppression of illicit traffic in

---

[64] art.21.
[65] art.16 of the 1958 Convention; art.25 of the 1982 Convention.
[66] art.16(3) of the 1958 Convention; art.25(3) of the 1982 Convention.
[67] art.16(2) of the 1958 Convention; art.25(2) of the 1982 Convention.

narcotic drugs (or psychotropic substances—1982 Convention only).[68]

Civil jurisdiction may not be exercised against either the ship or against a person on board, save in respect of obligations and liabilities assumed by the ship itself in the course of, or for the purpose of, its voyage through the waters of a coastal state, or if the vessel is passing through the territorial sea, after having left internal waters.[69] Government vessels operated for commercial purposes also come within the ambit of the foregoing provisions. In respect of warships and government vessels operating for non-commercial purposes, the 1982 Convention does not affect the jurisdictional immunities from which they are entitled.

A foreign warship which does not comply with a coastal state's regulations may be required to leave the territorial sea ("immediately" has been added by the 1982 Convention).[70] Although mention is made of warships, neither the 1958 nor the 1982 Convention expressly grants or denies foreign warships a right of innocent passage. The 1982 Convention does provide, however, that the flag state of a vessel shall incur international liability for "any loss or damage to the coastal State resulting from the non-compliance by a warship or other government ship operated for non-commercial purposes with the laws and regulations of the coastal State".[71]

Passage through straits

What is a coastal state's jurisdiction in international straits bordering its coast?

Article 16(4) of the 1958 Convention on the Territorial Sea prohibits a coastal state from suspending innocent passage in territorial sea straits, which are used for international navigation between one part of the high seas and another part of the high seas, or the territorial sea of a foreign state.

The right of innocent passage similar to that provided by art.14 is retained by the 1982 Convention for straits which are formed by an island of a state bordering the strait and its mainland and where there exists seaward of the island a high seas route or an EEZ (see below),[72] and secondly where the strait is between a part of the high seas or an EEZ and the territorial sea of a foreign state, namely where there is only territorial sea at one end of a

---

[68] art.19 of the 1958 Convention; art.27 of the 1982 Convention.
[69] art.20 of the 1958 Convention; art.28 of the 1982 Convention.
[70] art.23 of the 1958 Convention; art.30 of the 1982 Convention.
[71] art.31.
[72] art.38.

strait.[73] A coastal state may not suspend such innocent passage.[74] However, for straits which are used for international navigation between one part of the high seas or an EEZ and another part of the high seas or an EEZ,[75] the 1982 Convention dispenses with the right of innocent passage and provides rather for a right of transit. In other words, the right of transit will only apply in straits which have high seas or an EEZ at both ends.

Article 38(2) defines transit passage as "the freedom of navigation and overflight solely for the purpose of continuous and expeditious transit of the strait". Ships and aircraft are charged with certain duties when travelling through and over a strait, for example proceeding without delay and refraining from any threat or use of force against the sovereignty, territorial integrity or political independence of states bordering the strait.[76] A strait state may, in the interest of safe passage, prescribe sea lanes and traffic separation schemes, but only after its proposals have been referred to and adopted by the "competent international organisation"[77]: the authority of a strait state under the 1982 Convention is thus more restricted than under the 1958 Convention. A strait state may also adopt laws and regulations designed to prevent, reduce or control pollution. However, a strait state is under a duty not to hamper transit passage and is required "to give appropriate publicity to any danger to navigation or overflight within or over the strait of which they have knowledge".[78] There may be no suspension of transit passage.[79]

Why should international straits be subject to a special regime under the 1982 Convention?[80] The result of extended territorial seas has been to bring straits which were previously high seas exclusively within territorial waters. Consequently, maritime powers sought definite guarantees for shipping as a condition to their accepting a 12-mile territorial sea; the 1988 Anglo–French Agreement[81] relating to the Straits of Dover guarantees the right of "unimpeded transit passage for merchant vessels, state vessels and, in particular, warships following their normal mode of navigation". The Geneva Convention is also deficient in that it fails to grant a right of passage to aircraft (under the 1982 Convention

[73] art.45(1)(b).
[74] art.45(2).
[75] art.37.
[76] art.39.
[77] art.41.
[78] art.44.
[79] art.44.
[80] The regime does not apply to straits regulated by treaty, e.g. the 1936 Treaty of Montreux in respect of the Straits of the Bosphorus and Dardanelles.
[81] Cmnd.557.

all aircraft will enjoy the right of transit) and submarines have to navigate on the surface and show their flag. The 1982 Convention appears, with respect to warships in time of peace, to rely upon the International Court of Justice's pronouncement in the *Corfu Channel (Merits)* case[82] that it was generally accepted international custom

> "that States in time of peace have a right to send their warships through straits used for international navigation between two parts of the high seas without the previous authorisation of a coastal State, provided that the passage is innocent."[83]

Contiguous zone

A coastal state, under the 1958 Convention, may claim a zone of the high seas not exceeding 12 miles from the territorial sea baselines contiguous to its territorial sea. A contiguous zone need not be claimed, as in the case of the UK, but if it is it must be done so specifically. Although the status of the contiguous zone remains that of high seas, a coastal state may exercise control to prevent or punish infringement of its customs, fiscal, immigration or sanitary regulations within its territory or territorial sea. The 1982 Convention extends the maximum breadth of the contiguous zone to 24 miles from the territorial baselines.[84]

HIGH SEAS

The high seas constitute "all parts of the sea that are not included in the territorial sea or in the internal waters of a State".[85] This definition has had to be modified with the advent of the EEZ and the recognition of archipelagic waters. The high seas are now constituted by waters not included in the EEZ, the archipelagic waters of an archipelagic state, the territorial waters or internal waters of a state.[86]

According to classical doctrine, the high seas are free and may not be apportioned by any one state. The freedom of the high seas, with qualified jurisdiction over adjacent waters by the coastal state, was articulated by Hugo Grotius in *Mare Liberum* (1609). The freedom principle was initially articulated in an effort to break the monopoly of the Spanish and Portuguese over the

---

[82] I.C.J. Rep. (1949) at p.4.
[83] I.C.J. Rep. (1949) at 28. See also the "Joint Statement by the US and the USSR on Uniform Interpretation of Rules of International Law Governing Innocent Passage 1989" (1989) 28 I.L.M. 1444.
[84] art.33.
[85] art.1 of the Geneva Convention on the High Seas.
[86] art.86 of the 1982 Convention.

seas and was accepted subsequently by the major maritime states, including the UK, the US, the Netherlands and Japan, which all sought to keep the territorial waters narrow and the high seas as broad as possible.

The equality of states, including those without a sea-coast (some 40 states), on the high seas is enshrined in art.3 of the 1958 Convention, which provides "States having no sea-coast should have access to the sea". The right of access of land-locked states to and from the sea and freedom of transit is exclusively elaborated upon in arts 124 and 132 of the 1982 Convention.[87]

The freedoms of the high seas, which are to be enjoyed by both coastal and non-coastal states, are the freedom of navigation, the freedom of fishing, the freedom to lay submarine cables and pipelines and the freedom of overflight.[88] These freedoms are not exhaustive and others which are recognised by the general principles of international law and which may be "exercised by all States with reasonable regard to the interests of other States in their exercise of their freedom of the high seas"[89] may also exist.[90]

The 1982 Convention reaffirms the four freedoms[91] (though the freedom of fishing is now subject to the rules governing the EEZ) and acknowledges two additional freedoms: the freedom to construct artificial islands and other installations permitted by international law and the freedom to undertake scientific research. Under the 1958 Convention, consideration must be given to the rights of other states on the high seas which must be treated "with respect to activities in the area"[92] (that is, the area of the deep seabed and ocean floor and subsoil—see below).

Nuclear testing

The testing of conventional weapons and nuclear weapons may limit other states from exercising the freedom of navigation. The

---

[87] See also the 1965 Convention on Transit Trade of Land-locked States, 597 U.N.T.S. 3; 4 I.L.M. 957 (1965).

[88] art.2 of the 1958 Geneva Convention, art.87 of the 1982 Convention.

[89] Above, art.87 of the 1982 Convention.

[90] Spain instituted proceedings against Canada in the ICJ on 28 March 1995 with respect to a dispute which had arisen relating to the Canadian Coastal Fisheries Protection Act 1985 and various other measures which had been taken on the basis of that legislation, in particular, the boarding on the high seas of a Spanish ship by Canadian officials. Spain contended that these measures seriously affected the principle of the freedom of the high seas and infringed the sovereign rights of Spain. The Court, in December 1998, declared it had no jurisdiction to hear the case by virtue of the reservation contained in para.2(d) of the Canadian Declaration, 10 May 1994.

[91] Above, fn.89.

[92] art.87(2) of the 1982 Convention.

International Court of Justice in the *Nuclear Test* cases,[93] brought by Australia and New Zealand against France, did not address the legality under international law of nuclear testing.[94] Petren J,[95] however, highlighted that, in spite of the 1963 Nuclear Test Ban Treaty,[96] the prohibition on nuclear testing had not evolved into a rule of customary international law. He asserted that the signatories to the 1963 Treaty, (France was not a party to that Treaty) by mutually banning themselves from carrying out further atmospheric nuclear tests, had shown "they were still of the opinion that customary international law did not prohibit atmospheric nuclear tests". In a 1996 Advisory Opinion, the ICJ confirmed that the threat or use of nuclear testing is now considered contrary to contemporary international law.[97] Despite this Opinion, France renewed its nuclear testing activities in the South Pacific in 1996.[98]

Article 88 of the 1982 Convention designates the high seas as an area reserved for peaceful purposes.[99]

Nationality of ships

To benefit from the rule of international law, a ship must fly the flag of a state; its nationality is that of the state whose flag it flies. A state may establish its own conditions for the granting of nationality to a ship, but there

> "must exist a genuine link between the State and the ship; in particular, the State must effectively exercise its jurisdiction and control in administrative, technical and social matters over ships flying its flag."[100]

---

[93] I.C.J. Rep. (1974) at 253 *(Australia v France)*; I.C.J. Rep. (1974) at 457 *(New Zealand v France)*.

[94] The cases were withdrawn following assurances by France in a number of statements that the tests would cease.

[95] I.C.J. Rep. (1985) at 305.

[96] 480 U.N.T.S. 43. For a case dealing with a situation not dealt with under the Convention see *Land and Maritime Boundary between Cameroon and Nigeria* ICJ 10 October 2002, General List No.94.

[97] 35 I.L.M. 809 (1996). See also Ch.11, "The Use of Force".

[98] In response to the actions of France, New Zealand submitted a request to the ICJ on 21 August 1995, for an examination of the situation arising from the proposed nuclear testing in accordance with para.63 of the ICJ's judgment in the *Nuclear Tests* case in 1974. New Zealand argued that renewed nuclear testing action would affect the judgment in that case. The ICJ dismissed the request on the grounds that the basis of its original judgment was not affected by the proposed course of action. (Order of the Court I.C.J. Rep. (1995) at 288).

[99] There are also a number of regional agreements which prohibit nuclear weapons, e.g. Treaty on the South East Asia Nuclear Weapon Free Zone 1995 and the African Nuclear Weapon Free Treaty 1996.

[100] art.5 of the 1958 Convention; art.91 of the 1982 Convention. See also *M/V Virginia G Case (Panama/Guinea-Bissau)* ITLOS (2014).

A ship may sail under the flag of one state only, and a ship

> "which sails under the flags of two or more States, using them according to convenience, may not claim any of the nationalities in question with respect to any other State, and may be assimilated to a ship without nationality."[101]

A ship is not prohibited from sailing without a flag, but if it does sail without one it cannot invoke diplomatic protection for any international wrong it may have allegedly suffered: *Naim Molvan v Attorney-General for Palestine*.[102] A ship may not normally change its flag during a voyage.

The introduction of the genuine link requirement was prompted by the increased use of "flags of convenience" i.e. where ship owners register in a particular state because of less onerous municipal taxation and labour laws. The United Nations attempted to address the issue with the 1986 UN Convention on Conditions for Registration of Ships.[103] The purpose of the Convention was to introduce improved standards of responsibility and accountability, thereby reinforcing the "genuine" link requirement.[104] Obligations incumbent on the flag state under the 1958 and 1982 Conventions include, inter alia: the maintenance of a register of all ships flying its flag; the exercise of effective authority and control over the ships in administrative, technical and social matters; to take those measures necessary to ensure safety at sea, to prevent collisions and to prevent, reduce and control pollution of the marine environment and adopt laws and regulations; and to take such steps as are required to achieve conformity with generally accepted standards, regulations, procedures and practices, and to serve their implementation and observance.[105]

It is not always for economic benefits that a ship may seek to fly the flag of a state other than that of its state of nationality. During the Iran–Iraq conflict, Kuwaiti vessels seeking the military protection of British and American naval vessels patrolling the Gulf re-registered under the UK and the US flags.[106]

---

[101] art.6 of the 1958 Convention; art.92 of the 1982 Convention.

[102] [1948] A.C. 351; see 369–370.

[103] 26 I.L.M. 1236 (1987).

[104] The Convention requires the ratification of 40 countries before it shall enter into force. The ICJ in the *IMCO* case, I.C.J. Rep. (1960), p.150, considered the term "largest ship owning nations" and held the term referred only to registered tonnage. The issue arose in the context of the eligibility of Liberia and Panama to be elected to the Committee of the Inter-Governmental Maritime Consultative Organisation. The ICJ did not consider in-depth the notion of genuine link.

[105] Relevant arts in the 1958 Convention are 5(1), 10, 11, 24 and 25; in the 1982 Convention, 94, 192, 211 and 219.

[106] See *M/V Saiga* (No.2) 120 I.L.R., p.143, wherein the Tribunal for the Law of the

Jurisdiction on the high seas

Jurisdiction over ships on the high seas lies with the flag state. The flag state is, for instance, responsible for the manning of ships and the labour conditions of the crew.[107] The 1982 Convention sets out in greater detail the measures which a flag state is required to take to ensure safety at sea.[108] In respect of a collision on the high seas, neither penal nor disciplinary proceedings may be initiated against either the master or a crew member, except before the judicial or administrative authorities of the flag state or the state of which such person is a national. The ship itself may only be arrested or detained, even for investigation purposes, by the authority of the flag state.[109] Warships and government ships used for other than commercial purposes are accorded sovereign immunity and are subject only to the jurisdiction of their flag state.

Exceptions to the freedom of navigation—interference on the high seas

The most important limitation to the freedom of navigation is

> "every State may seize a pirate ship or aircraft, or a ship taken by piracy and under the control of pirates, and arrest the persons and seize the property on board."[110]

Piracy is strictly defined in international law as

> "(a) any illegal acts of violence, detention or any act of depredation committed for private ends by the crew or the passengers of a private ship or a private aircraft, and directed:
>
> > (i) on the high seas, against another ship or aircraft, or against persons or property on board such ship or aircraft;
> >
> > (ii) against a ship, aircraft, persons, or property in a place outside the jurisdiction of any State;
>
> (b) any act of voluntary participation in the operation of a

---

Sea held that a ships nationality is a factual question to be established on the basis of evidence provided by the parties concerned, (at p.175–176).

[107] art.10 of the 1958 Convention.

[108] art.94.

[109] Hence, the EU's condemnation of Canada's actions directed at Spanish trawlers as "international piracy" in March 1995. art.11 of the 1958 Convention; art.97 of the 1982 Convention; cf. decision in the *Lotus* case P.C.I.J. Rep., ser.A, No.10 (1927).

[110] art.19 of the 1958 Convention; art.105 of the 1982 Convention.

ship or of an aircraft with knowledge of facts making it a pirate ship or aircraft;

(c) any act of inciting or of intentionally facilitating an act described in sub-paragraph 1 or sub-paragraph 2 of this article."[111]

What is necessary in international law for an act to be characterised as piracy is that it be committed for private ends.[112]

The courts of the seizing state are competent to decide the penalties which may be imposed.[113] If the suspicion for the seizure proves groundless, the state making the seizure is liable for any loss or damage it has caused as a consequence.[114] Only warships, military aircraft or other authorised vessels may carry out such a seizure.

Unless provided for by treaty a foreign merchant ship may only be boarded by the crew of a warship if there are reasonable grounds for suspecting

"(a) that the ship is engaged in piracy; or

(b) that the ship is engaged in the slave trade; or

(c) that, though flying a foreign flag or refusing to show its flag, the ship is, in reality, of the same nationality as the warship."[115]

Again, if the suspicions prove unfounded, the boarded ship shall be entitled to receive compensation. In the last decade, renewed piracy activities have brought intense collaboration among states in an effort to tackle this problem. Frequent attacks off the coast of Somalia prompted a series of UN Security Council Resolutions,[116] including authorising states to enter the territorial waters of Somalia in pursuit of pirates and to consider the possibility of establishing specialised piracy courts. Twenty Asian states are

---

[111] art.15 of the 1958 Convention; art.101 of the 1982 Convention.

[112] The hijacking of the Italian liner *Achille Lauro* by four Palestinians in October 1985 did not constitute an act of piracy under international law.

[113] Above, Canada's Criminal Code, e.g. states that it is an offence, punishable by life imprisonment to do "any act that, by the law of nations, is piracy" (s.75). The Code also makes it an offence to carry out "piratical acts", which include stealing a Canadian ship or its cargo, starting a mutiny or inciting others to do so (s.76).

[114] art.20 of the 1958 Convention; art.106 of the 1982 Convention.

[115] art.22 of the 1958 Convention; art.110 of the 1982 Convention—the latter also includes the right of visit in respect of ships suspected of engaging in unauthorised broadcasting.

[116] See, UN Security Council Resolutions 1816 (2008); 1846 (2008); 1851 (2008); 1976 (2011); 2015 (2011); 2020 (2011) and 2125 (2013).

party to the 2005 Regional Co-operation Agreement on Combating Piracy and Armed Robbery against Ships in Asia, which extends the regulation of piracy to include internal waters; territorial seas; and archipelagic waters.[117] In June 2013 African states agreed the Yaoundé Declaration on the Gulf of Guinea Security which addresses piracy and other illegal activities in West and Central Africa. The EU and NATO have set up operations to combat piracy in the affected areas.[118]

The 1982 Convention requires states to co-operate in the suppression of illicit traffic in narcotic drugs and psychotropic substances engaged in by ships on the high seas contrary to international conventions, and provides that a state

> "which has reasonable grounds for believing that a ship flying its flag is engaged in illicit traffic in narcotic drugs or psychotropic substances may request the co-operation of other States to suppress such traffic."[119]

The 1988 Vienna Convention against Illicit Traffic in Narcotics Drugs and Psychotropic Substances[120] supplements this provision.

The *Achille Lauro* incident and fears of escalating maritime terrorism prompted the International Maritime Organisation to produce a Convention for the Suppression of Unlawful Acts against the Safety of Maritime Navigation[121] and a Protocol for the Suppression of Unlawful Acts against the Safety of Fixed Platforms Located on the Continental Shelf.[122]

Article 3 of the above Convention articulates what constitutes an offence for the purposes of the Convention and includes, inter alia, the seizure or exercising of control over a ship by force or threat thereof or any form of intimidation.[123] Contracting Parties are required to take such measures as may be necessary to establish its jurisdiction over the offences identified by the Convention when the offence is committed:

---

[117] 44 I.L.M. 2005, p.829.
[118] The NATO Operation Ocean Shield was approved by the North Atlantic Council on 17 August 2009 and has a mandate until the end of 2016. The European Union Naval Force (EU NAVFOR) Somalia – Operation Atalanta was launched on 8 December 2008 and is set to conclude in December 2016.
[119] art.108.
[120] U.N. Doc. E/CONF.82/15 (1988) / 28 I.L.M.493 (1989).
[121] The Convention entered into force on 1 March 1992.
[122] The Protocol entered into force on 1 March 1992.
[123] art.3.1(a). Note the Convention does not apply to warships, state vessels being used as a naval auxiliary or for customs or police purposes; art.2.

(a) against or on board a ship flying its flag at the time when the offence is committed; or

(b) in its territory, including territorial sea; or

(c) by one of its nationals.[124]

Jurisdiction *may* be exercised by a Contracting Party in the event of the offence:

(a) being committed by a stateless person who is habitually resident in its territory; or

(b) resulting in one of its nationals being threatened, injured or killed; or

(c) being committed in an attempt to compel that state to do or abstain from doing any act.[125]

The Convention requires Contracting Parties to make the relevant offences punishable by penalties appropriate to the gravity of the offences[126] and obliges them to either institute proceedings through the national courts or extradite the offender or alleged offender.[127]

The 1982 Convention also tackles the problem of high seas broadcasting (pirate radio), particularly in art.109(3), which provides that a person

"engaged in unauthorised broadcasting may be prosecuted before the Court of:

(a) the flag State of the ship;

(b) the State of registry of the installations;

(c) the State of which the person is a national;

(d) any State where the transmissions can be received; or

(e) any State where authorised radio communication is suffering interference."

Article 109(4) confirms the right of visit to ships suspected of engaging in unauthorised broadcasting and provides that any person or ship engaged in such activities may be arrested and the

---

[124] art.6.1.
[125] art.6.2.
[126] art.5.
[127] art.10.

broadcasting apparatus seized by any state which has jurisdiction under art.109(3).

The very pressing issue of people trafficking and migrant smuggling has also prompted recent international cooperation. The 1982 Convention is silent on this but it is addressed by the 2000 UN Convention against Transnational Organised Crime,[128] especially the Protocol against the Smuggling of Migrants by Land, Sea and Air, adopted in November 2000.[129]

Fishing activities on the high seas

The 1982 Convention[130] provides for a management and conservation scheme for the living resources of the high seas. These provisions, which consolidate and elaborate on those imposed upon states by the 1958 Geneva Convention on the Fishing and Conservation of Living Resources, are, of course, independent of those provisions in respect of the coastal states' rights in the EEZ.

Hot pursuit

The warships, law enforcement vessels or aircraft (the 1982 Convention requires that such vessels and aircraft should be clearly marked) of a coastal state may pursue a vessel leaving its territorial waters when it suspects it of having violated its laws and regulations.[131] Pursuit must be continuous and must cease immediately the pursued vessel reaches the territorial waters of another state, be it the vessel's own state or a third state. If pursuit is initiated in contiguous waters it must only be because of a violation of the rights for which the contiguous zone was established (see above). Pursuit may only be initiated after the offending vessel has received a visual or auditory signal to stop.

Failure to stop may lead to the use of "necessary and reasonable force for the purpose of effecting the object of boarding, searching, seizing and bringing into port the suspected vessel."[132] The right of hot pursuit has evolved and is now accepted as an established rule of customary international law.

---

[128] 40 I.L.M. 335 (2001) / UN Doc. A/55/383 at 25 (2000)/ [2004] ATS 12.

[129] 40 I.L.M. 384 (2001) / UN Doc A55/383 (Annex III, p.62) / [2004] ATS 11.

[130] arts 116–120.

[131] art.23 of the 1958 Convention; art.111 of the 1982 Convention.

[132] The *I'm Alone* case 3 R.I.A.A. 1607 at 1615; 29 A.J.I.L. 326 (1935)—where, in fact, the sinking of the vessel concerned was held to be excessive action which "could not be justified by any principle of international law". See also *M/V Saiga*, above fn.106, at p.194, confirming that lawful hot pursuit demands the fulfillment of each of the art.111 conditions.

Protection of marine environment against pollution

The concern over the protection of the marine environment against pollution precedes the 1958 Geneva Convention on the High Seas. In 1954, the International Convention for the Prevention of the Pollution of the Sea by Oil (OILPOL)[133] prohibited the discharge of oil or any oily mixture by vessels and made any such violation subject to the jurisdiction of the state of registration. The 1958 Convention requires every state to draw up regulations to prevent pollution of the seas by the discharge of oil from ships or pipelines or resulting from the exploitation and exploration of the seabed and its subsoil, taking account of existing treaty provisions on the subject.[134]

Since then a significant number of treaties have been concluded to address oil pollution damage and compensation, including the 1969 International Convention relating Intervention on the High Seas in Cases of Oil Pollution Casualties[135], which allows parties to take necessary measures in the high seas to prevent, mitigate or eliminate grave and imminent danger faced from pollution; the 1969 International Convention on Civil Liability for Oil Pollution Damage,[136] which establishes that the owners of ships causing oil pollution damage are liable to pay compensation; and the 1973 Convention for the Prevention of Pollution from Ships (MARPOL),[137] which covers not only oil discharges from ships, but discharges such as sewage, garbage and other noxious harmful substances.[138]

Article 25 of the 1958 Convention on the High Seas requires states to take measures to prevent pollution caused by the

---

[133] 327 U.N.T.S. 3.

[134] art.24.

[135] 9 I.L.M. 25 (1969). A 1973 Protocol to the Convention authorises intervention with respect to threats of pollution from substances other than oil, 13 I.L.M. 605 (1974).

[136] 9 I.L.M. 45 (1970). Amending Protocol 1976, 16 I.L.M. 617 (1977). Replaced by the 1992 IMO Convention on Civil Liability for Oil Pollution Damage, and Protocol.

[137] Misc.26 (1974) Cmnd.5748; 12 I.L.M. 1319 (1973).

[138] The MARPOL Convention is the most important international Convention dealing with pollution from ships. Technical difficulties in respect of the provisions dealing with noxious liquid substances acted as an obstacle to the ratification of the 1973 Convention. A Protocol was adopted in 1978 (Misc.26 (1974) Cmnd.5748) to facilitate the entry into force of the regulations pertaining to oil discharge. A number of amendments to the MARPOL Convention were adopted by the IMO Assembly and entered into force on 3 March 1996. The amendments were designed to improve the application of the Convention and apply to four of the Convention's five technical annexes. Ships can now be inspected in the ports of other Contracting Parties so as to ensure that the crews are competent to perform important procedures relating to the prevention of marine pollution.

dumping of radioactive waste as well as co-operating with competent international organisations. Article 5(7) of the 1958 Convention on the Continental Shelf requires coastal states "to undertake, in the safety zones all appropriate measures for the protection of the living resources of the sea from harmful agents." These provisions have been reinforced by other international conventions on dumping and pollution from land-based sources.[139]

The 1982 Convention envisages a comprehensive regime for the protection and preservation of the marine environment.[140] Article 192 places parties under a general obligation to protect and preserve the marine environment, and further to this parties are required to adopt national and international measures. The 1982 Convention further provides, inter alia, for global and regional co-operation, contingency plans against pollution, studies, research programmes, exchange of information and data, and scientific and technical assistance to developing states. States are required to adopt laws and regulations with regard to pollution from land-based sources, seabed activities, dumping, pollution from vessels and pollution from or through the atmosphere. Enforcement is envisaged by flag states, port states and coastal states. Non-fulfilment of international obligations by a party will give rise to international responsibility. The UN Conference on the Environment and Development held in Rio de Janeiro in 1992 endorsed the environmental provisions of the 1982 Convention, and the link between this Convention and Ch.17 of Agenda 21 emphasised the need for international co-operation in this area.

In 2012 at the Rio+20 UN Conference on Sustainable Development, oceans were one of the "7 Critical Issues" identified for discussion. The Summit reiterated the importance of the UN Convention on the Law of the Sea for providing the legal framework for the conservation and the sustainable use of the oceans and their resources, and noted

"with concern that the health of oceans and marine biodiversity are negatively affected by marine pollution, including marine debris, especially plastic, persistent organic pollutants, heavy metals, and nitrogen-based compounds, from a

---

[139] Examples of such include the 1972 Oslo Convention for the Prevention of Marine Pollution by Dumping from Ships and Aircraft (11 I.L.M. 262 (1972)); the 1972 London Convention on the Prevention of Marine Pollution by Dumping of Wastes and Other Material (11 I.L.M. 1291 (1972)); the 1974 Paris Convention for the Prevention of Marine Pollution from Land-based Sources (13 I.L.M. 352 (1974)); and regional arrangements such as the 1976 Barcelona Convention for the Protection of the Mediterranean against Pollution (15 I.L.M. 290 (1976)).
[140] arts 192–238.

number of marine and landbased sources, including shipping and land runoff."[141]

The International Maritime Organisation (IMO) is the principal international organisation concerned with vessel pollution issues. The IMO is responsible for convening conferences and drafting and revising Conventions. The IMO, although one of the smaller UN agencies, has, through its work, achieved considerable success in reducing oil pollution and improving safety at sea. There are 171 Member states and three Associate Members.[142]

EXCLUSIVE ECONOMIC ZONE (EEZ)

The 1982 Convention acknowledges the EEZ as "an area beyond and adjacent to the territorial sea"[143] which "shall not extend beyond 200 nautical miles from the baselines from which the breadth of the territorial sea is measured."[144] UNCLOS III recognised the right to claim an EEZ as one existing under customary international law. Subsequent judicial endorsement for the exercise of this right is found in the *Continental Shelf (Tunisia v Libya)* case.[145]

The concept of the EEZ evolved with the realisation that fishery resources are not inexhaustible and consequently it was imperative to adopt conservation measures.

It was only with the failure of both the 1958 and 1960 Conferences to establish the width of the territorial sea and fisheries zone that the two jurisdictional areas became independent of each other. Fisheries jurisdiction, until then, was an integral part of territorial waters jurisdiction. The failure to reach international agreement saw the development of diverse state practice. Iceland, for example, did not wait for the 1960 Conference but in 1958 extended its exclusive fishery zone to 12 miles by employing the straight baseline method recognised by the International Court of Justice in the *Anglo-Norwegian Fisheries* case, see above.

Throughout the 1960s, the trend was towards recognition of a 12-mile exclusive fishery zone (with, as a general rule, recognition being given to the rights of foreign vessels which had tra-

---

[141] The Future We Want: Outcome document adopted at Rio+20, para.163.

[142] The IMO was established in 1958 and was primarily charged with the task of improving maritime safety. The increase in oil transportation by sea and a number of serious spills in the 1960s led to the IMO's involvement in pollution prevention.

[143] art.55.

[144] art.57.

[145] I.C.J. Rep. 1982, p.18 at 74; *Gulf of Maine* case I.C.J. Rep. 1984 246 at 294–295; *Continental Shelf (Libya v Malta)* case I.C.J. Rep. 1985 13 at 33; *Guinea/Guinea Bissau Delimitation of the Maritime Boundary* 25 I.L.M. 251 (1986) at 272, para.42.

ditionally fished within these waters).[146] By the end of the 1960s, a coastal state's territorial waters and fisheries jurisdiction were no longer synonymous and judicial recognition was accorded to a 12-mile exclusive fisheries zone by the International Court of Justice in 1974, when it concluded in the *Fisheries Jurisdiction (Merits) (United Kingdom v Iceland)* case[147] that the 12-mile fishery zone had in the years subsequent to the 1960 Conference "crystallised as customary international law".[148] Nevertheless, the Court failed to answer explicitly the question addressed to it, that is, whether Iceland's claim to a 50-mile exclusive fishing zone was compatible with international law.[149] Rather the Court characterised Iceland's unilateral extension as "an infringement of the principles enshrined in art.2 of the 1958 Geneva Convention on the High Seas."[150] The door was left open for expansion by coastal states and such expansion occurred throughout the 1970s. The impact of such claims is reflected in the 1982 Convention and in state practice.

The right to claim an EEZ is discretionary, not mandatory, e.g. the UK does not claim an EEZ, as there would be no advantage in doing so as "the United Kingdom already has a fishery zone extending to a maximum of 200 nautical miles and . . . rights over [the UK's] continental shelf (which extends well beyond 200 miles) are inherent and do not have to be proclaimed."[151] The US, on the other hand, does claim an EEZ.

Rights of coastal states within the EEZ

A coastal state does not enjoy complete sovereignty within the EEZ but only sovereign rights "for the purpose of exploring and exploiting, conserving and managing the natural resources, whether living or non-living, of the seabed and subsoil and the superjacent waters" and jurisdiction, inter alia, with regard to

"(i) the establishments and use of artificial islands, installations and structures;

(ii) marine scientific research;

---

[146] See e.g. 1964 European Fisheries Convention 581 U.N.T.S. 57; US legislation Public Law 89–658, 5 I.L.M. 1103 (1966).

[147] I.C.J. Rep. 1974 at p.3.

[148] Above, at 23.

[149] The Icelandic Government implemented its intention to extend Iceland's exclusive fishing zone to 50 miles by the Resolution of the Althing of 15 February 1972 and Regulations of 14 July.

[150] Above, fn.147 at 29.

[151] Hansard, HL Vol.473, Col.46 (7 April 1986).

   (iii) the protection and preservation of the marine
   environment."[152]

A coastal state is responsible for determining both "the allow-
able catch of the living resources in its exclusive economic
zone"[153] and "its capacity to harvest the living resources of the
EEZ."[154] A coastal state's task is to conserve resources within
the EEZ and to this end is charged with adopting measures
which will

> "maintain or restore populations of harvested species at
> levels which can produce the maximum sustainable yield,
> as qualified by relevant environmental economic needs of
> coastal fishing communities and the special requirement of
> developing States"[155]

Account must be taken of "the best scientific evidence available"
with a coastal state co-operating, where appropriate, with the
"competent international organisations, whether sub-regional,
regional or global."[156]

A coastal state's most important task as far as foreign states are
concerned is to decide, in respect of the EEZ's living resources,
the surplus available over its own harvesting capacity.[157] That
surplus, the Convention provides, is to be made available to other
states either through agreements or other arrangements to certain criteria which that coastal state is, especially with regard to
developing states, to take into account. Such criteria include the
"significance of the living resources of the area to the economy
of the coastal state and its other national interests", the interests
of land-locked states and those states "with special geographical
characteristics" and the interests of those states "whose nationals have habitually fished in the zone."[158] The final say remains,
however, with the coastal state.

A coastal state is responsible for regulating fishing by foreign
vessels within the EEZ[159] and is required to give due notice of con-

---

[152] art.56.
[153] art.61(1).
[154] art.62(2).
[155] art.61(3).
[156] art.61(2).
[157] art.61(2).
[158] art.62(2); art.69; art.70; arts 69 and 70 do not apply to coastal states whose economy is overwhelmingly dependent on the exploitation of the living resources
of its exclusive economic zone.
[159] art.62(4) gives a list of the measures, which the coastal state may take, e.g.
licensing of fishermen.

servation and management regulations[160] and to exercise control over foreign vessels granted access.[161] The Convention provides for co-operation in the event of stocks occurring within the EEZ of two or more coastal states.[162] A coastal state enjoys rights within the EEZ, but it is also charged with obligations. A coastal state is not the owner, but rather the guardian of the natural resources within its EEZ.

Rights and duties of other states

Other states enjoy the right of free navigation, overflight and the laying of submarine cables and pipelines in the EEZ, provided they respect the rights and duties of coastal states and comply with the laws and regulations of the latter.[163] The rights of foreign states are reinforced by the obligation on coastal states to pay "due regard to the rights and duties of other states".[164]

Delimitation of the EEZ between states with opposite or adjacent coasts

Article 74(1) of the 1982 Convention provides that the delimitation of the EEZ between states with opposite or adjacent coasts is to be effected "by agreement on the basis of international law as referred to in art.38 of the Statute of the International Court of Justice, in order to achieve an equitable solution." The *Jan Mayen* case affirmed the desirability for a common maritime boundary between the EEZ and the continental shelf. However Oda J, in his dissenting opinion, stated that because of the separate and independent legal regimes of the EEZ and the continental shelf, a common maritime boundary cannot be presumed.[165]

In the *Delimitation of the Maritime Boundary in the Gulf of Maine Area*,[166] the ICJ established an ad hoc Chamber to decide the delimitation of both the continental shelf and the fishery zone between Canada and the US. It was submitted that the criteria to be employed should be those which, by their neutral character, were best suited for employment in a multi-purpose delimitation. In the case before it the Chamber utilised criteria especially derived from geography. Likewise the practical methods to be employed to give effect to the criteria should be "basically

---

[160] art.62(5).
[161] art.73.
[162] art.63(1); art.63(2); art.64.
[163] art.58(1) and (3).
[164] art.56(2).
[165] Above, fn 41. See, also, *Delimitation of Maritime Areas between Canada and France (St Pierre and Miquelon)* 1992 31 I.L.M. 1145.
[166] I.C.J. Rep. (1984) at 246.

founded upon geography and be as suitable for the delimitation of the seabed and subsoil as to that of the superjacent waters and their living resources" and accordingly the Chamber concluded that "only geometrical methods" would be utilised. The Chamber denied that the parties' respective scale of fishing or petroleum exploitation could serve as an equitable criterion unless

> "unexpectedly, the overall result should appear radically inequitable as entailing disastrous repercussions on the subsistence and economic development of the population concerned."[167]

In *Maritime Delimitation in the Black Sea Case (Romania v Ukraine)*,[168] the ICJ drew a single maritime boundary, including both the EEZ and continental shelf, between Romania and Ukraine in the Black Sea. The distinct rules that apply to the delimitation of the EEZ and continental shelf were applied respectively. The Court enunciated its now usual three-stage approach to delimitation,[169] namely (1) drawing a "provisional delimitation line" (using the equidistance or median line), (2) considering any "relevant circumstances" which would require the provisional line to be amended to produce an equitable result, and (3) considering whether the provisional line, amended or not, results in a "marked disproportion" between the ratio of the coastal lengths of the states and the ratio of the maritime areas resulting from the delimitation.

CONTINENTAL SHELF

"Continental shelf" is the geographical term used to describe the gently sloping ledge covered by shallow water projecting from the shoreline of many land masses before a steep descent to the ocean waters. Continental shelves vary considerably in width: off the west coast of the US the shelf is less than five miles whereas the entire area under the water of the North Sea is continental shelf.

In accordance with the principle of the freedom of the high seas, all states equally enjoy the right to explore the seabed. Continental shelves are rich in oil reserves, and by the 1940s states possessed the technology to exploit such resources. Furthermore, economically, exploration had become a viable proposition.

President Truman's Proclamation of 28 September 1945, whereby the US regarded

---

[167] I.C.J. Rep. (1984) at 342.
[168] I.C.J. Rep. (2009) 3.
[169] Above, para 115.

"the natural resources of the subsoil and seabed of the continental shelf beneath the high seas but contiguous to the coasts of the United States as appertaining to the United States, subject to its jurisdiction and control. . . [but that] . . .the character as high seas of the waters above the continental shelf and the right to their free and unimpeded navigation are in no way affected"[170]

precipitated numerous assertions of coastal states' rights over the continental shelf and marked the beginning of the change in the legal status of the continental shelf.

The claims, which followed in the wake of the Truman Proclamation, differed in nature. Some were restrained, while some asserted exclusive sovereignty by the coastal state. Argentina and El Salvador claimed not only the continental shelf but also the superjacent waters and the airspace above, whereas Chile and Peru claimed sovereignty over the seabed, subsoil and water around their coasts to a limit of 200 miles.[171] It was against the background of such claims that the International Law Commission addressed itself to the issue of the continental shelf.

Article 1 of the 1958 Convention on the Continental Shelf defines the continental shelf as referring

"(a) to the seabed and subsoil of the submarine area adjacent to the coast but outside the area of the territorial sea, to a depth of 200 metres or, beyond that limit, to where the depth of the superjacent waters admits of the exploitation of the natural resources of the said areas;

(b) to the seabed and subsoil of similar submarine areas adjacent to the coasts of islands."

Article 76 of the 1982 Convention defines the continental shelf as

"the seabed and subsoil of the submarine areas that extend beyond its territorial sea throughout the natural prolongation of its land territory to the outer edge of the continental margin,[172] or to a distance of 200 nautical miles from the baselines from which the breadth of the territorial sea is measured where the outer edge of the continental margin does not extend up to that distance."

---

[170] 4 Whiteman 756.

[171] Chile and Peru possess no geographical continental shelf.

[172] i.e. the continental margin consists of the continental shelf, slope and rise that separate the landmass from the deep ocean floor (abyssal plain).

The continental shelf extends to 200 nautical miles for all states, but retains an advantage for the geographically favoured. However, art.76(6) provides the continental shelf shall not exceed 350 nautical miles from territorial baselines, and art.76(7) provides the method of delimitation to be employed where the continental shelf exceeds 200 nautical miles.

Regarding a coastal state's rights over the continental shelf, the 1982 Convention essentially reproduces the provisions of the 1958 Convention. A coastal state's rights are not territorial sovereign rights but are, rather, functional rights for the purpose of exploring and exploiting the natural resources of the continental shelf.[173] A coastal state's rights are exclusive, and exploration and exploitation activities may not be undertaken without its consent. Natural resources are defined as the mineral and other non-living resources of the seabed and subsoil, together with living organisms belonging to sedentary species. The 1982 Convention provides that coastal states have the exclusive right to authorise and regulate drilling on the continental shelf for all purposes.[174]

A coastal state's rights in the continental shelf do not affect the status of the superjacent waters as high seas or that of the airspace above those waters,[175] and states in exercising their rights on the continental shelf must not impede the laying or maintenance of submarine cables or pipelines and must not result in

> "any unjustifiable interference with navigation, fishing or the conservation of the living resources of the sea, nor result in any interference with fundamental oceanographic or other scientific research carried out with the intention of open publication."[176]

A coastal state may construct artificial installations on the continental shelf and may establish safety zones around such installations to a maximum of 5,000 metres. Article 82 of the 1982 Convention further restricts the maximum limit of the continental shelf by providing for the payment of contributions in kind by coastal states in respect of the exploitation of the non-living resources when their continental shelf exceeds 200 nautical miles from the territorial baselines. Payments and contributions are to be made five years after production. Developing states that are net importers of a mineral resource produced from its continen-

---

[173] art.2 of the 1958 Convention; art.77 of the 1982 Convention.
[174] art.81.
[175] art.3 of the 1958 Convention; art.78 of the 1982 Convention.
[176] art.5(1) of the 1958 Convention; art.246 of the 1982 Convention applies to research on the continental shelf and the EEZ.

tal shelf will be exempt from making such payments or contributions. The payments or contributions shall be made through the International Seabed Authority, regulated by Pt XI of the Convention (see below) which shall distribute to states which are parties to the Convention "on the basis of equitable sharing criteria, taking into account the interests and needs of developing states, particularly the least developed and land-locked among them."[177]

Delimitations of the continental shelf between states with opposite or adjacent coasts

Articles 6(1) and (2) of the 1958 Convention on the Continental Shelf provide formulae for delimiting the outer limit of the continental shelf between opposite and adjacent states. In both instances the boundary should be determined by agreement between the states concerned, in the absence of which the boundary for opposite coasts "is the median line, every point of which is equidistant from the nearest point of the baselines from which the breadth of the territorial sea of each State is measured." For adjacent coasts "the boundary shall be determined by application of the principle of equidistance from the nearest point of the baselines from which the breadth of the territorial sea of each State is measured." Both rules show a recognised exception, namely that neither the median line nor the principle of equidistance will apply if "another boundary is justified by special circumstances."

However, the 1958 Convention failed to provide any indication of what would constitute "special circumstances". The ICJ in the *North Sea Continental Shelf* cases[178] provided that delimitation was to be "effected by agreement in accordance with equitable principles, and taking account of all the relevant circumstances."[179] Relevant circumstances identified by the Court were, inter alia, the general configuration of the coasts of the parties; so far as known or readily ascertainable, the physical and geological structure and the natural resources of the continental shelf areas involved; the element of a reasonable degree of proportionality, which a delimitation carried out in accordance with equitable principles ought to bring about between the extent of the continental shelf areas pertaining to the coastal state and the length of its coast measured in the general direction of the coastline, account being taken for this purpose of the effects, actual or prospective, of any other con-

---

[177] art.82.
[178] I.C.J. Rep. (1969), p.3.
[179] I.C.J. Rep. (1969) at 46.

tinental shelf delimitations between adjacent states in the same region.[180] Nevertheless, having identified the possible relevant circumstances, the Court concluded that there was

> "no legal limit to the considerations which States may take account of for the purpose of making sure that they apply equitable procedures, and more often than not it is the balancing-up of all such considerations ... rather than reliance on one to exclusion of all others."[181]

Further, in the absence of any "imperative rules" recognised by international law for the delimitation of the continental shelf, resort could be made to "various principles or methods, as may be appropriate, or a combination of them, provided that, by the application of equitable principles, a reasonable result is arrived at."[182]

In the *Continental Shelf (Libyan Arab Jamahiriya v Malta)* case,[183] the parties agreed the delimitation of the continental shelf had to be effected by the application of equitable principles in all the relevant circumstances in order to achieve an equitable result. Certain principles then identified by the Court were: there should be no question of refashioning geography; non-encroachment by one party on areas appertaining to the other; respect for all relevant circumstances; that equity did not necessarily imply equality nor could there be any question of distributive justice.[184] The Court also refuted the respective economic positions of the parties concerned should be taken into account but did acknowledge the existence of economic resource and security and defence interests might be given cognisance.[185]

Note that in *Continental Shelf (Tunisia v Libya)*, economic and political factors were dismissed unless to do so would be "radically inequitable". See also the *Gulf of Maine* case in which such factors were dismissed as "ineligible for consideration".[186]

In the *North Sea Continental Shelf* cases, the Court maintained the equidistance principle was not, in light of the special circumstances exception, a principle of international law but merely an application in appropriate situations of a more general rule.

---

[180] I.C.J. Rep. (1969) at 50–52.
[181] I.C.J. Rep. (1969) at 50.
[182] I.C.J. Rep. (1969) at 49.
[183] I.C.J. Rep. (1985), p.13.
[184] I.C.J. Rep. (1985), p.13.
[185] I.C.J. Rep. (1985), p.13.
[186] Above, fn.166 at 340. The Court acknowledged that they could be relevant to assessment of the equitable character of delimitation, first established on the basis of criteria borrowed from physical and political geography.

In the *English Channel Arbitration*,[187] the Arbitrators held that art.6 did not formulate the equidistance principle and "special circumstances" as two separate rules but rather as a combined equidistance—special circumstances rule.

Relevant circumstances were considered in the *Gulf of Maine* case.[188] The Chamber adopted the stance that the objective of a delimitation of an equitable maritime boundary should (unless the parties agree otherwise) be to attain "an equal division of areas where the maritime projections of the coasts of the States between which delimitation is to be effected converge and overlap."[189] Unless, that is, there were "special circumstances in the case which would make that criterion inequitable."[190] Both parties (the US and Canada) made submissions as to what "relevant circumstances" should embrace. These included, inter alia, environmental (US) and economic (Canada) circumstances. In rejecting the arguments advanced the Chamber stated that, under international law, the equitable criteria for delimitation were to be derived essentially from geographical factors.[191]

The Tribunal in the *Guinea/Guinea Bissau Arbitration* stated that, as it was concerned only with "a contemporary evaluation, it would be neither just nor equitable to base a delimitation on the evaluation of data which changes in relation to factors that are sometimes uncertain"[192] and that its prime objective had been "to avoid that either Party, for one reason or another should see rights exercised opposite its coast or in the immediate vicinity thereof, which could prevent the exercise of its own rights to development or compromise its security".[193] In the *Continental Shelf (Tunisia v Libya)* case the Court maintained "each continental shelf case in dispute should be considered and judged on its own merits, having regard to its peculiar circumstances."[194]

The ICJ has, in doing so, minimised the equidistance principle.[195]

---

[187] 18 I.L.M. 397 (1979).

[188] Above, fn.166 at 246, in which the Chamber was called to decide the "maritime boundary" as between the continental shelves and fishing zones of the two parties. The objective for the establishment of such a boundary was held to be that of attaining "an equitable result".

[189] Above, fn.166 at 327.

[190] Above, at 301.

[191] Above, at 278.

[192] 25 I.L.M. 251 (1986) at 122.

[193] Above, at para.124.

[194] I.C.J. Rep. (1982) 18 at 92; see also *Delimitation of the Maritime Boundary in the Gulf of Maine (Canada v United States of America)*, above, fn.166 at 292 "any agreement or other equivalent solution should involve the application of equitable criteria." The Chamber in this case did not apply the equidistance principle.

[195] The equidistance principle has been used in treaties between states. However, see also *Guinea/Guinea Bissau Arbitration*, above, fn.145, in which the equidistance method was identified as "just one among many and that there is no

This is reflected in the 1982 Convention, which has abandoned the art.6 formula and provides delimitation is to be "effected by agreement on the basis of international law, as referred to in art.38 of the Statute of the International Court of Justice, in order to achieve an equitable solution".[196] What the 1982 Convention envisaged was characterised in the *Gulf of Maine* Case as being "singularly concise", but one which served "to open the door to continuation of the development effected in this field by international case law."[197] The way in which the Chamber arrived at a solution in the *Gulf of Maine* dispute still best represents how delimitation disputes are tackled under contemporary international law. The Chamber acknowledged that there was no "body of detailed rules" in customary international law, nor indeed under general international law, which would "provide a ready made set of rules" for the solution of delimitation rules, and that rather what had to be sought was "a better formulation of the fundamental norm . . . whose existence in the legal convictions not only of the Parties to the present dispute, but of all States, is apparent from an examination of the realities of international legal relations."[198] The fundamental norm in question was identified by the Chamber as meaning:

(a) no maritime delimitation between states may be effected unilaterally by one of the affected states;

(b) delimitation is to be sought and effected through agreement, following negotiation conducted in good faith with a genuine intention of achieving a positive result;

(c) in the absence of agreement recourse should be made to a third party;

and in all instances delimitation is to be effected by:

(a) the application of equitable criteria;

(b) the use of practical methods capable of ensuring, with regard to the geographic configuration of the area and other relevant circumstances, an equitable result.

---

obligation to use it or give it priority, even though it is recognised as having a certain intrinsic value because of its scientific value and the relative ease with which it can be applied" at para.102.

[196] art.83(1); art.74 articulates a similar formula for the delimitation of the EEZ between states with opposite or adjacent coasts. See also, *Maritime Delimitation in the Black Sea Case (Romania v Ukraine)* I.C.J. Rep. (2009) 3.

[197] Above, fn.166 at 252.

[198] Above, at 299.

Subsequent to the foregoing, the ICJ upheld the principle of the equidistance line and acknowledged it may be varied on the basis of special circumstances.[199] In the *Land and Maritime Boundary between Cameroon and Nigeria (Equatorial Guinea intervening)*,[200] the Court reiterated that equitable agreement must be reached. However the Court stressed equity does not represent a method of delimitation but rather an aim to be borne in mind when making the delimitation. The imprecise nature of equitable considerations was highlighted by the Permanent Court of Arbitration in *Barbados/Trinidad and Tobago Maritime Delimitation*[201] where the Tribunal said the role of equity lay within and not beyond the law. The Tribunal gave cognisance to relevant circumstances such as the coastline of the parties and adjusted the provisional equidistance line in the light of these circumstances.

In January 2014, the ICJ further clarified the issue of maritime delimitation in the case of *Peru v Chile*.[202] The Court highlighted that the provisions contained in arts. 74(1) and 83(1) of the 1982 Convention reflect customary international law. The Court reiterates that a three-stage test is used to find an equitable solution to maritime delimitation: first, the Court constructs a provisional equidistance line unless there are compelling reasons which prevent that; second, it considers whether there are relevant circumstances which may call for an adjustment of that line to achieve an equitable result and third, through a disproportionality test, it assesses whether the effect of the line, as adjusted, is such that the parties' respective shares of the relevant maritime area are markedly disproportionate to the lengths of their relevant coasts.

A Commission on the Limits of the Continental Shelf was established pursuant to art.76(8) of the 1982 Convention to deal with the establishment of the outer limits of the continental shelf beyond 200 nautical miles. This Commission is made up of 21 experts elected by the state parties to the 1982 Convention and meets twice a year. Since its inception the Commission has dealt with numerous submissions from various countries parties to the 1982 Convention. The deadline for submissions to the Commission was 13 May 2009.[203] Article 298 of the 1982 Convention provides that states may opt to exclude delimitation disputes from proce-

---

[199] The *Maritime Delimitation on Territorial Questions between Qatar and Bahrain (Qatar v Bahrain)* I.C.J. Rep. (2001) p.40.

[200] I.C.J. Rep. (2002), p.303.

[201] 11 April 2006, Arbitration Tribunal, Permanent Court of Arbitration.

[202] I.C.J. *Maritime Dispute (Peru v Chile)* 27 January 2014 General List No.137, para.180.

[203] Decision of the Eleventh Meeting of the State Parties May 2001 UNSPLOS/72. However owing to the workload of the Commission and the (in)ability of states, in particular those developing, states were allowed to present prelimi-

dures involving a binding decision and may refer them instead to "compulsory" conciliation.

DEEP SEABED

The deep seabed is the area beneath the high seas. The deep seabed and its subsoil are rich in mineral resources, for example manganese nodules, the extraction of which was considered by the 1982 Convention.

Should these resources belong to those relatively few states which, because of a technological and capital advantage, are able to finance deep-sea mining or should the resources of the ocean bed belong to all states and the benefits derived distributed among the international community generally? If the answer is the latter, then what conditions should apply?

The US, for example, regards deep-sea mining as a freedom of the high seas, whereas some developing and technologically disadvantaged states have adopted the view that the deep seabed should be designated an "area" which is the "common heritage of mankind" and the natural resources of which should not be liable to appropriation by any state. The years preceding the sessions of UNCLOS III witnessed the emergence of two groups—one representing developing states, calling for an international body to conduct all exploitation in the deep seabed and the second, that of the developed states maintaining that deep-sea activity should be undertaken by states and/or national companies subject to a registration and licensing system. Both groups did however agree on the need to avoid a "free-for-all". Accordingly, the UN General Assembly Declaration of Principles Concerning the Sea Bed and the Ocean Floor and the Subsoil Thereof, Beyond the Limits of National Jurisdiction 1970[204] provided that the area and its resources "are the common heritage of mankind" and that no state or person, natural or juridical, could "claim, exercise or acquire rights with respect to the area or its resources incompatible with the international regime to be established".[205]

The deep seabed is regulated in Pt XI of the 1982 Convention as modified by the 1994 Implementation Agreement. The regime articulated represents a compromise between the demands of developed and developing states.

nary information regarding a future submission, Decision of the Eighteenth Meeting of the States Parties June 2008, UN SPLOS/183.
[204] GA Resolution 2749 (XXV) 17 December 1970. 10 I.L.M. 230 (1970).
[205] Above, arts 1 and 3.

International Seabed Authority[206]

Under the 1982 Convention all deep seabed exploration and exploitation is to be carried out for the benefit of mankind and is to be carried out and controlled by an International Seabed Authority.[207] The benefits of such exploitation are to be shared equitably by the Authority. The Authority has signalled several areas of interest but there has been no exploitation activity, mainly due to seabed mining not being commercially profitable as yet. Activities in the Clarion-Clipperton Zone of the Pacific Ocean and the Central Indian Ocean Basin are, for now, limited to exploration and research.

The organs of the International Seabed Authority are the Assembly,[208] the Council and the Secretariat. The Assembly, with a representative from each member state, is the supreme policy-making organ, adopting decisions by a two-thirds majority. The Council is made up of 36 Member States elected by the Assembly representing various special interest groups, such as the largest investors in sea mining, land-locked nations and potential producers. The executive organ of the Authority is the Council, which will take decisions, depending on the subject, by two-thirds majority, three-quarters majority or consensus. The Secretariat is responsible for conducting the activities of the Authority.

The 1982 Convention also provides for the compulsory settlement of deep seabed disputes, either by judicial settlement (by reference to the International Tribunal for the Law of the Sea) or by commercial arbitration. Pursuant to art.283 of the 1982 Convention in the event of a dispute arising the parties concerned are to advance "expeditiously to an exchange of views regarding its settlement by negotiation or other peaceful means." Article 284 provides the options for parties to invoke conciliation procedures by way of establishing a conciliation commission which in turn will produce a non-binding report. In the event of a failure to reach settlement the compulsory procedures prescribed in Pt XV of the 1982 Convention s.2 apply.

INTERNATIONAL TRIBUNAL FOR THE LAW OF THE SEA

The International Tribunal for the Law of the Sea[209] was established under the 1982 Convention as an independent judicial body to hear disputes relating to the interpretation and application of

---

[206] arts 156–188.

[207] art.153.

[208] The Assembly of the Authority was inaugurated by the UN Secretary-General in Kingston, Jamaica on 16 November 1994 and held its first session on 27 February to 17 March 1995.

[209] art.287 in accordance with Annex VI.

the Convention.[210] The Tribunal sits in Hamburg, Germany, and has 21 members. Members are independent and are elected from persons who have a high reputation for fairness and integrity and have a recognised competence in the law of the sea. Each state party may nominate up to two candidates. No two members of the Tribunal may be nationals of the same state and an equitable geographical distribution is sought. Members are elected for nine years and may be re-elected. Elections are staggered with one-third of members being elected every three years.[211] The Tribunal was granted observer status by the UN General Assembly on 17 December 1996.[212] The Tribunal's jurisdiction extends to all disputes submitted in accordance with the 1982 Convention and any other agreements which specifically confer jurisdiction on the Tribunal. The parties to the 1982 Convention can choose to submit their disputes to the Tribunal for the Law of the Sea, the International Court of Justice, or an arbitral tribunal constituted in accordance with the Convention. Unless provided to the contrary the Tribunal's jurisdiction is mandatory in respect of the prompt release of vessels and crews,[213] provisional measures[214] and in certain circumstances the Tribunal may also give advisory opinions. There are also some limitations on the Tribunal's jurisdiction, for instance disputes arising from a coastal state exercising its sovereign rights or jurisdiction in the EEZ.[215]

The first case before the Tribunal was the *M/V Saiga* case (*Saint Vincent and the Grenadines v Guinea*) in which the Tribunal ordered the prompt release of the tanker *Saiga* and its crew from detention by Guinea. The Tribunal went on to hold that Guinea had violated the rights of St Vincent and the Grenadines by arresting their tanker, and the Tribunal awarded compensation of over $2 million. To date 23 cases have been referred to the Tribunal, including the dispute between Ireland and the UK as to whether the mixed oxide fuel (MOX) facility at Sellafield, UK, would have detrimental effects on the marine environment of the Irish Sea, as alleged by Ireland. An order for provisional measures was granted whereby both parties were required to co-operate, consult, exchange information and to monitor the risks involved.[216] Ireland withdrew its

---

[210] art.288.
[211] In the absence of a national judge on the Tribunal a party to a dispute may chose an ad hoc judge to participate in the settlement of the dispute, art.17.
[212] Resolution A/RES/51/204 of 17 December 1996.
[213] art.292. See *Juno Trader* (*Saint Vincent and the Grenadines v Guinea-Bissau*), Prompt Release, 18 December 2004.
[214] art.290, and pending the creation of an arbitral Tribunal when the parties have decided to submit their dispute to such a body (para.5).
[215] art.297 (1).
[216] Order 18 December 2001.

claim in 2007. The Tribunal's first case relating to the delimitation of a maritime boundary was *Dispute Concerning Delimitation of the Maritime Boundary between Bangladesh and Myanmar in the Bay of Bengal (Bangladesh/Myanmar),*[217] in which the Tribunal relied upon relevant jurisprudence of the ICJ in this area in making its decision. In April 2015, the Tribunal handed down its second advisory opinion, in *Request for an advisory opinion submitted by the Sub-Regional Fisheries Commission (SRFC).*[218] This advisory opinion clarified the rights and duties of states with regard to illegal, unreported and unregulated fishing in the EEZ of the Sub-Regional Fisheries Commission states.

The Tribunal has, under its Statute, formed the following Chambers:

- Chamber of Summary Procedure;

- Chamber for Fisheries Disputes;

- Chamber for Marine Environmental Disputes; and a

- Chamber for Maritime Delimitation Disputes, which can be formed to deal with specific disputes at the request of the parties involved.[219]

In January 2015, the Tribunal formed a special chamber to deal with the *Dispute Concerning Delimitation of the Maritime Boundary between Ghana and Côte d'Ivoire in the Atlantic Ocean* which concerned oil exploration and exploitation in an area disputed by the two states. The Chamber delivered its order at the end of April 2015, which called on Ghana to refrain from any activity in the area which would be prejudicial to Côte d'Ivoire.[220]

Disputes relating to the activities in the International Seabed Area are brought before the Seabed Disputes Chamber of the Tribunal. Any party to a dispute within the competence of the Seabed Disputes Chamber may ask that an ad hoc chamber be constituted from 3 of the 11 judges who make up the Chamber. The Chamber is also competent to give advisory opinions.[221] The

---

[217] Judgment 14 March 2012.

[218] Advisory Opinion 2 April 2015.

[219] Art.15(2) of the Statute of the Tribunal. The first time this Chamber was formed was with regards the case Concerning Conservation and Sustainable Exploitation of Swordfish Stocks in the South-Eastern Pacific Ocean, a dispute between Chile and the European Union. The case was withdrawn in 2009.

[220] *Delimitation of the Maritime Boundary in the Atlantic Ocean (Ghana/Côte d'Ivoire), Provisional Measures,* Order of 25 April 2015, ITLOS Reports 2015, to be published.

[221] This Chamber delivered the Tribunal's first Advisory Opinion on 1 February 2011, *Responsibilities and Obligations of States Sponsoring Persons and Entities with*

jurisdiction of the Tribunal is only compulsory with regard to disputes arising over deep seabed mining under Pt XI of the 1982 Convention.[222]

CONCLUSION

The international legal regime that governs the uses and protection of the seas and oceans is a complex web of customary norms, multilateral, regional and bilateral agreements with the 1982 Convention at its centre. The 1982 Convention reinforces many of the established customary and convention laws regulating the law of the sea. However it also gave the hallmark of law to the EEZ and articulates a legal regime applicable to the deep seabed. In doing this, it also emphasises that the seas should be the "heritage of all mankind", imposing limits on the eagerness of states to claim sovereignty as well as to explore and exploit the oceans.

Respect to Activities in the Area, Case No. 17, Advisory Opinion (ITLOS Seabed Disputes Chamber, 1 February 2011), 59 I.L.M. 458 (2011).

[222] See Oda J of the ICJ, "Dispute Settlement Prospects in the Law of the Sea" (1995) 44 I.C.L.Q. 863.

8. STATE RESPONSIBILITY

State responsibility in international law denotes liability—that of one state to another for non-observance of the obligations imposed by the international legal system. A state may incur liability for injury to another state when, for example, there is a breach of a treaty obligation or for injury to another state's nationals or their property.

State responsibility is a complex issue which has received attention from the International Law Commission (ILC) since it initiated a study of state responsibility in 1949. Its early efforts to produce a draft Convention proved inconclusive,[1] however the Commission's work culminated in the adoption of the Draft Articles on the Responsibility of States for Internationally Wrongful Acts on August 2001 (the Draft Articles) and General Assembly Resolution 56/83 recommended the text of the Draft Articles to governments.[2] Notwithstanding the absence of a

---

[1] I.L.C. Drafts arts on State Responsibility, 1979, II Y.B.I.L.C., (Pt II), p.90; 1980, II Y.B.I.L.C., (Pt II), pp.14, 70; arts 1–32, 18 I.L.M. 1568 (1979); arts 33–35, 74 A.J.I.L. 962 (1980). Revised Draft Articles were adopted by the Commission in 1996 and were more detailed than the draft adopted in 1969.

[2] 10 December 2001. International Law Commission Commentary, Official Records of the G.A., 53rd session, Supplement No.10 (A/56/10 Ch.IV.E.1). The Articles and the Commentaries of the International Law Commission are

convention, there is now consensus that some of the Draft Articles reflect international customary law. These Draft Articles "seek to formulate, by way of codification and progressive development, the basic rules of international law concerning the responsibility of States for internationally wrongful acts".[3] The emphasis is on the secondary rules of state responsibility, the general conditions under international law for a state to be considered responsible for wrongful actions or omissions and legal consequences which flow there from. The Draft Articles do not attempt to define the content of international law obligations, breaches of which gives rise to responsibility; this is the function of primary rules:

> "The Articles take the existence and content of the primary rules of international law as they are at the relevant time; they provide the framework for determining whether the consequent obligations of each State have been breached, and with what legal consequences for other States."[4]

The Draft Articles are limited in scope and deal with the responsibility for internationally wrongful conduct. They do not address instances of state responsibility arising from the injurious consequences of conduct which is not prohibited and may even be allowed under international law. The Draft Articles are concerned only with state responsibility and they do not address the issue of responsibility incurred by international organisations or other non-state actors.

The Draft Articles are comprised of four parts. Part One, the Internationally Wrongful Act of a State, sets out the requirements necessary for international responsibility to be incurred; Part Two, Content of the International Responsibility of a State, focuses primarily on the legal consequences for the responsible state for any internationally wrongful acts, particularly regarding cessation and reparation; Part Three, the Implementation of the International Responsibility of a State; and Part Four deals with the general provisions applicable to the Draft Articles as a whole.

Draft art.1 spells out the basic rule, namely, "[e]very internationally wrongful act of a State entails the international responsibility of that State." This article is supplemented by draft art.2, which provides:

contained in Crawford, J, *The International Law Commission's Articles on State Responsibility, Introduction, Text and Commentaries*, Cambridge University Press, 2002. In 2013 the General Assembly deferred the consideration of the adoption of a Convention on state responsibility to its seventy-first session in 2016. See A/RES/104 (2103).

[3] Above, p.74, Commentaries 1.

[4] Above, p.75.

"There is an internationally wrongful act of a State when conduct consisting of an action or omission:

(a) is attributable to the State under international law; and
(b) constitutes a breach of an international obligation of the State."

Thus draft art.2 specifies the conditions required to establish the existence of an internationally wrongful act of the state, i.e. the constituent elements of such an act.

Draft art.3 provides "the characterisation of an act of a State as internationally wrongful is governed by international law. Such characterisation is not affected by the characterisation of the same act as lawful by internal law".

Breaches of international obligations by states are dealt with in draft art.12 "when an act of the State is not in conformity with what is required of it by that obligation, regardless of its origin or character." However, "An act of State does not constitute a breach of an international obligation unless the State is bound by the obligation in question at the time the act occurs."[5]

Liability will also be attributed to a state if implicated in the wrongful acts of another state: that is by assisting, controlling or coercing the activities of the "offending" state.[6] A state cannot relieve itself of responsibility by invoking either provisions or omissions of its domestic legislation.[7] In a federal state, such as Canada or the US, the federal government is responsible on the international plane and will incur international liability for any actions or omissions of its constituent provinces/states which result in international injury. A federal government may not exonerate itself from responsibility by submitting that individual provinces/states are independent or autonomous.[8]

Recognised defence pleas, which may be utilised by a state to deny responsibility, are consent, self-defence, counter measures, force majeure, distress and necessity.[9]

NATURE OF LIABILITY

A notable absence from the Draft Articles is the distinction between international delict and international crimes, which were

---

[5] Draft art.13.
[6] Draft arts 16 and 17.
[7] *Free Zones of Upper Savoy and the District of Gex* P.C.I.J.Rep., ser.A/B. No.46 at 167 (1932), Draft art.3.
[8] e.g. Franco-Italian Conciliation Commission, *Heirs of Duc de Guise* (1951) 13 RIAA 161.
[9] See draft arts 20–25; also note draft art.26, regarding compliance with peremptory norms.

previously identified in draft art.19 of the 1996 version of the Draft Articles.[10] The more generally framed draft art.12 is designed to define what constitutes a breach of an international obligation.

The origin of an internationally unlawful act is, as noted above, irrelevant. The origin neither affects the characterisation of the act as unlawful nor does it affect the international responsibility of the state concerned.[11] The basic principle contained in draft art.1 spells out a rule of customary international law; this rule was acknowledged in *Chorzow Factory (Indemnity) (Merits)*,[12] when the Permanent Court of International Justice maintained "any breach of an engagement involves an obligation to make reparation."[13] See also draft art.31 and below.

Is state responsibility absolute or must there be fault? Is liability strict or must there be a degree of blameworthiness which can be attributed to the state? Must there be intention, recklessness, or negligence?

Customary international law on these questions is not clear. While evidence in the form of arbitral and judicial decisions can be found in support of both standpoints, conclusive evidence in support of either theory is absent. Fault liability appears to have received support in the *Home Missionary Society Claim*[14] and the *Corfu Channel (Merits)* case,[15] while the Claims Commission in the *Caire Claim*[16] supported absolute liability. State practice throws little light on the issue which is essentially theoretical and one of largely academic interest. It is true that certain primary obligations may well require that fault be shown before there can be a breach of that obligation and ensuing state responsibility, for example, the 1948 Genocide Convention requires acts to be "committed with intent" in order to qualify as genocide.[17] The proliferation of state organs and agencies has witnessed an increased application of strict liability. Fault liability has, because of the growth of state activities, become too complicated to apply in practice. However it is noteworthy that draft art.39 of the Draft Articles states "[i]n the determination of reparation, account shall be taken of the contribution to the injury by wilful or negligent

---

[10] The 1996 version of the Draft Articles can be found in the Yearbook of the International Law Commission, 1996, A/CN.4/SER.A/1996/Add.l (Pt 2).

[11] See draft art.12, above.

[12] P.C.I.J. Rep., ser.A, No.17 (1928).

[13] Above, at 29.

[14] 6 R.I.A.A. 42 (1920).

[15] I.C.J. Rep. 1949 p.4.

[16] 5 R.I.A.A. 516 (1929).

[17] This was reiterated by the ICJ in the *Case Concerning Application of the Convention on the Prevention and Punishment of the Crime of Genocide (Croatia v Serbia)*, Judgement, 3 February 2015.

action or omission of the injured State or any person or entity in relation to whom reparation is sought." In the *La Grand* case, the ICJ recognised that the conduct of the claimant state could be pertinent in determining what reparation is due.[18]

Imputability

Imputability in the context of state responsibility means acts or omissions attributable to a state. It is dealt with in Ch.II of the Draft Articles, where draft art.4 sets out the basic rule that "the conduct of any State organ shall be considered an act of that State under international law". Draft art.5 deals with the conduct of entities other than an organ of the state, but which is empowered to exercise elements of governmental authority and thereby "shall be considered an act of the State under international law, provided the person or entity is acting in that capacity in the particular instance". Draft art.6 addresses the special case where an organ of one state is placed at the disposal of another state and acts temporarily for the benefit of that state and under its authority. Draft art.7 makes it clear that the conduct of organs or entities empowered to exercise governmental authority is attributable to the state even if that conduct exceeded the authority of the organ or person concerned or was contrary to instructions. Draft articles 8–11 are concerned with certain additional cases where conduct, not that of a state organ or entity, is nonetheless attributed to the state in international law. Draft art.8 deals with conduct carried out on the instructions of a state organ or under its direction or control. Draft art.9 focuses on certain conduct involving the exercise of elements of governmental authority carried out in the absence of the official authorities and without any actual authority to do so. Draft art.10 concerns the special case of responsibility in defined circumstances for the conduct of insurrectional movements, namely when that insurrectional movement subsequently becomes the new government of the state or succeeds in establishing a new state. Draft art.11 deals with conduct not attributable to the state under one of the earlier draft articles which is nonetheless adopted by the state, expressly or by conduct, as its own.[19]

A state is only responsible for acts or omissions which can be attributed to it as its own. What, for the purposes of state responsibility, constitutes the state?[20]

---

[18] *LaGrand (Germany v United States)* 40 I.L.M. 1069 (2001).
[19] See also the judgment in the *Nicaragua (Nicaragua v The United States) (Merits)* I.C.J. Rep. 1986 p.14 and also case IT-94-1, *Prosecutor v Tadic* 38 I.L.M. 1518 (1999).
[20] "Without a fixed prescription for State authority, international law has to accept,

In international law a state is responsible for the actions of:

(a) its government;

(b) any political sub-division of the state;

(c) any organ, agency official employee or other agent of its government or of any sub-division acting within the scope of their employment.

Imputability is a legal fiction attributing the acts of those identified above to the state as if they were its own.

A state is not responsible for acts committed by one of its nationals (provided, that is, he or she is a private individual acting in a private capacity and is not, for example, an on-duty police officer) against a foreigner. The individual may, of course, be liable to prosecution in the domestic courts and indeed the government concerned may be held internationally liable if it fails to discharge its duty "of diligently prosecuting and properly punishing".[21] A distinction can be made between direct responsibility—where acts of individuals become those of a state—and indirect responsibility—where a state breaches a primary obligation to control the conduct of individuals. Acts of private persons performed on their own initiative in an emergency, e.g. a natural disaster, may be attributable to a state.[22] Individuals may be held responsible for certain crimes under international law.[23]

A state cannot deny responsibility for an international wrong on the grounds that the act is ultra vires under its domestic law. As already noted, a state can be held liable for the conduct of an official, even when official competence has been exceeded, provided that is the official acted with apparent authority as a competent official or organ, and the powers or methods used were appropriate to this official authority.[24] For example, in 1993 the International Centre for Settlement of Investment Disputes rejected the argument submitted by Egypt that it was not responsible for the acts of certain high-ranking officials, as the officials

by and large, the actual systems adopted by States, and the notion of attribution thus consists primarily of a renvoi to the public institutions or organs in place in the different states": ILC, "Report of the ILC on the Work of its 25th Session" (7 May –13 May 1973) UN Doc. A/CN.4/SER.A/1973/Add.1, 190, para.8.

[21] *Noyes Claim* 6 R.I.A.A. 308 at 311 (1933); see also the *Zafiro* case 6 R.I.A.A. 160 (1925).

[22] Draft art.8.

[23] See the Statutes of the ICTY, ICTR and ICC. See further Chs 4 and 9.

[24] Draft art.7; *Caire Claim*, above fn.16 and *Velasquez Rodriguez* case Inter-Am. C.t H.R., Series C, No.4 (1989), at para.170.

had not followed the correct procedures required under Egyptian law.[25] The Tribunal stated:

> "the principle of international law which the Tribunal is bound to apply is that which establishes the international responsibility of States when unauthorized or ultra vires acts of officials have been performed by State agents under cover of their official character. If such unauthorized or ultra vires acts could not be ascribed to the State, all State responsibility would be rendered illusory."[26]

In the *Youmans Claim*,[27] Mexico was held liable for the conduct of certain members of its militia who acted in defiance of orders and, instead of affording protection to a group of US citizens, opened fire on the house where the latter were seeking refuge. The United States–Mexican General Claims Commission maintained that the Mexican Government was liable for the soldiers' unlawful acts, even though the soldiers had exceeded their powers.

A state is responsible for the acts of all its officials irrespective of their rank[28] and, as is illustrated by the *Rainbow Warrior* case,[29] that includes responsibility for the acts of its security services. However, as highlighted previously, a state is not held liable for the activities of insurrectionaries,[30] but should the insurrectionaries be successful in their objective and become the subsequent government, they (as the legitimate government) will be held liable for any wrongful act committed during their struggle for power.[31] A state is not responsible for the acts of individuals who act as state organs when they act in a private capacity.[32] Pursuant to draft art.13 of the Draft Articles a state will only be held responsible for an international obligation, which it was bound by at the time the act occurred. Draft art.13 reflects the general principle of intertemporal law.[33] Draft art.17 deals with derived responsibility and namely the circumstances in which "one State is responsible for the internationally wrongful act of

---

[25] *Southern Pacific Properties (Middle East) Ltd v Arab Republic of Egypt* 32 I.L.M. 933.

[26] Above. See further Chs 4 and 9.

[27] 4 R.R.A.A.110. *Caire Claim*, above, fn.16.

[28] *Massey (US v Mexico)*, 4 R.I.A.A. 155 at 157 (1927).

[29] 26 I.L.M. 1346 (1987).

[30] *Sambaggio (Italy v Venezuela)*, 10 R.I.A.A. 499 at 513 (1903).

[31] art.10. See *Short v Iran* (1987) 16 Iran–USCTR 76; cf. *Yeager v Iran* 17 Iran–USCTR 92.

[32] e.g. the *Bensleys* case: see ILC, "Report of the ILC on the Work of its 25th Session" (7 May–13 May 1973) UN Doc. A/CN.4/SER.A/1973/Add.1, 192, para 9.

[33] See statement of Judge Huber in the *Island of Palmas* case, R.I.A.A., Vol.II, p.829 [1949], at p.845.

another State".[34] The legal consequences of an internationally wrongful act are primarily twofold, namely the responsible state should cease from the wrongful conduct and secondly make full reparation for the injury as stated in draft arts 30 and 31. It should also be noted draft art.41 provides that states are charged with co-operating to "bring to an end through lawful means any serious breach within the meaning of [draft] Article 40 [namely a serious breach of an obligation arising under a peremptory norm of general international law]."[35] Furthermore, "No State shall recognize as lawful a situation created by a breach within the meaning of [draft] Article 40, nor render aid or assistance in maintaining that situation."[36]

Erga omnes obligations

While the foregoing is concerned with the obligation owed by one state to another, contemporary international law also recognises the concept of *erga omnes*—that is, obligations owed by every state to the international community as a whole. These obligations were identified by the ICJ in the *Barcelona Traction* case[37] as deriving from "the outlawing of acts of aggression, and of genocide" and from "rules concerning the basic rights of the human person, including protection from slavery and racial discrimination."[38] *Erga omnes* obligations are contained in peremptory norms of international law.[39] Such obligations are, by their nature, the concern of all states and because of the importance of the rights involved all states have a legal interest in their protection. This decision prompted the ILC to include in the 1996 version draft art.19, which distinguished between civil and criminal liability but, as already noted in this chapter, this distinction was omitted in the 2001 version of the Draft Articles. What the Draft Articles recognise, as discussed in the accompanying Commentary, is that there are

---

[34] Liability will be incurred if: a) a state acts in the knowledge of the circumstances of the internationally wrongful act; and b) the act would be internationally wrongful if committed by that state.

[35] Draft art.41(1).

[36] Draft art.41(2). The obligations in draft art.41(1) and (2) can be seen in operation in *The Legal Consequences of the Construction of a Wall in the Occupied Palestinian Territory* (Advisory Opinion) 2004, para.159.

[37] I.C.J. Rep. 1970 p.3.

[38] Above, at p.32 at para.34. See also *East Timor (Portugal v Australia)* case I.C.J. Rep. (1995) p.90; "Legality of the Threat or use of Nuclear Weapons" I.C.J. Rep. (1996) p.226; *Application of the Convention on the Prevention and Punishment of the Crime of Genocide (Preliminary Objections)*, I.C.J. Rep. (1996) p.595.

[39] See also Chs 2 and 10.

"certain consequences flowing from the basic concepts of peremptory norms of general international law and obligations
to the international community as a whole within the field
of State responsibility. Whether or not peremptory norms of
general international law and obligations to the international
community as a whole are aspects of a single basic idea, there
is at the very least substantial overlap between them. The
examples which the International Court has given of obligations towards the international community as a whole all concern obligations which, it is generally accepted, arise under
peremptory norms of general international law. Likewise the
examples of peremptory norms given by the Commission in
its commentary to what became [draft] art.53 of the Vienna
Convention [on the Law of Treaties] involve obligations to
the international community as a whole. But there is at least
a difference in emphasis while peremptory norms of general
international law focus on the scope and priority to be given
to a certain number of fundamental obligations, the focus
of obligations to the international community as a whole is
essentially on the legal interest of all States in compliance—
i.e., in terms of the present articles, in being entitled to invoke
the responsibility of any State in breach. Consistently with
the difference in their focus, it is appropriate to reflect the
consequences of the two concepts in two distinct ways. First,
serious breaches of obligations arising under peremptory
norms of general international law can attract additional consequences, not only for the responsible State but for all other
States. Secondly, all States are entitled to invoke responsibility for breaches of obligations to the international community
as a whole."[40]

Draft art.40 defines the scope of the breaches covered by Ch.III and
distinguishes "serious breaches of obligations under peremptory
norms of general international law" from other types of breaches.
The obligation breached must be derived from a peremptory norm
and the breach must be serious. A breach of such an obligation is
serious if it involves a gross or systematic failure by the responsible state to fulfil the obligation.[41] However, draft art.40 does not
provide any illustrative examples of peremptory norms.[42] Draft
art.42 provides that the implementation of state responsibility is
the entitlement of "an injured state" and recognises a state may

---

[40] I.L.C. Commentaries, pp.244–245.
[41] Draft art.40(2).
[42] See Ch.2 "Sources" for discussion of art.53 Vienna Convention on the Law of
Treaties.

be responsible to a group of states including the injured state or to the international community as a whole. The latter is dealt with in draft art.48. In 2012, the ICJ confirmed that a special interest is required before a state can invoke the responsibility of another state for failing to comply with an obligation *erga omnes*.[43]

Reparation

The state which has committed the internationally wrongful act is under an obligation to make full reparation for the injury caused. This is in line with the Permanent Court of International Justice decision in the *Chorzow Factory* case, namely "it is a principle of international law that the breach of an engagement involves an obligation to make reparation in an adequate form".[44]

The object of reparation should be to wipe out, as far as possible, "all the consequences of the illegal act and re-establish the situation which would, in all probability, have existed if that act had not been committed."[45] Reparation is designed to restore conditions to how they were or, if this is not possible, to compensate for the injury itself.[46]

Reparation may be awarded through restitution in kind and if restitution is not possible, through

> "payment of a sum corresponding to the value which a restitution in kind would bear; the award, if need be, of damages for loss sustained which would not be covered by restitution in kind or payment in place of it—such are the principles which should serve to determine the amount of compensation due for an act contrary to international law."[47]

Reparation may also be by way of diplomatic negotiation, which may produce an apology or an assurance that the offending breach of international law will not recur.

Draft art.35 details two exceptions to the obligation to provide reparation: where it is materially impossible, and where it involves a burden out of all proportion to the benefit deriving

---

[43] See also ICJ, *Questions Relating to the Obligation to Prosecute or Extradite (Belgium v Senegal)*, Merits, 20 July 2012, para.68–70.

[44] *Chorzow Factory* case, Jurisdiction, 1927, P.C.I.J., Series A, No.9. However, note any conduct whereby the injured state has contributed to that injury will be taken into account, see Draft art.39.

[45] *Chorzow Factory (Indemnity) (Merits)* P.C.I.J. Rep., ser.A, No.17 (1928) at 47. See also arts 34 and 35.

[46] Draft art.36(1) expresses the primacy of restitution over compensation, as the latter will only apply to the extent that damage "is not made good by restitution".

[47] Above, fn.45.

from restitution instead of compensation. Restitution in kind is infrequent.[48] More frequently monetary compensation is awarded to cover the cost of the injury suffered.

The ICJ held in the *Case concerning the Gabčíkovo-Nagyamaros Project*:

> "It is a well established rule of international law that an injured State is entitled to obtain compensation from the State which has committed an internationally wrongful act for the damage caused by it."[49]

In *Chorzow Factory (Indemnity)*,[50] the Permanent Court of International Justice held the rules of law governing reparation should be

> "the rules of international law in force between the two States concerned, and not the law governing relations between the State which has committed a wrongful act and the individual who has suffered damage. Rights or interests of an individual the violation of which rights causes damage are always in a different plane to rights belonging to a State, which rights may also be infringed by the same act. The damage suffered by an individual is never therefore identical in kind with that which will be suffered by a State; it can only afford a convenient scale for the calculation of the reparation due to the State."[51]

Compensation is normally a matter of negotiation. There is no established principle for calculating the sum to be paid. In respect of material loss, the sum awarded is generally commensurate with the loss sustained and will take account of "loss of profits as compared with other owners of similar property".[52] Draft art.36 provides that the compensation shall cover any financially assessable damage including loss of profits in so far as it is established. Draft art.36 deals only with financially assessable damage and draft art.37 deals with non-material injury. However, while damages

---

[48] Restitution in kind was ordered in *Martini (Italy v Venezuela)* 2 R.I.A.A. 975, 1002 (1930), the Temple Case, I.C.J. Rep. 1962 p.6, and *Case concerning the Arrest Warrant of 11 April 2000 (Democratic Republic of Congo v Belgium)* 2002 I.C.J. Rep. 3, para.76.

[49] *Case concerning the Gabčíkovo-Nagyamaros Project (Hungary v Slovakia)* 1997 I.C.J. Rep p.7, para.152.

[50] Above, fn.45. See also art.31 above, and for various forms of reparation. See art.34 and art.37 for reparation in the form of an apology.

[51] Above, at 28.

[52] *Norwegian Shipowners Claim (Norway v U.S.)* 1 R.I.A.A. 307 at 338 (1922).

have been awarded for non-material loss international tribunals have been reluctant to grant exemplary or punitive damages:

> "Counsel has failed to point us to any money award by an international arbitral tribunal where exemplary, punitive, or vindictive damages have been assessed against one sovereign nation in favor of another presenting a claim on behalf of its nationals."[53]

In the *Lusitania* case, the United States–Germany Mixed Claims Commission refused to award punitive damages. The Commission did not impose a penalty and only awarded reparation in respect of the injury suffered. However, in the *I'm Alone* case,[54] between the US and Canada, the US was ordered to pay compensation as a "material amend in respect of the wrong suffered by Canada".

A state will be liable to another state if it, inter alia, breaches a treaty obligation, violates its territorial integrity, injures its diplomatic representatives, mistreats one of its nationals or causes injury to the property of one of its nationals.

TREATMENT OF ALIENS

If an individual allegedly sustains injury while in a foreign state, redress may only be sought through the individual's state of nationality (see nationality of claims rule below). An individual cannot force a state to espouse a claim on his or her behalf. It is a matter of state discretion whether a claim is taken up, and if a state does pursue a claim on behalf of an individual, it is not required to hand over any damages which may be received.[55] Nor can an individual prevent a state from exercising its rights of diplomatic protection if the state feels its right to have its nationals treated properly has been violated

> "an alien . . . cannot deprive the government of his nation of its undoubted right of applying international remedies to violations of international law committed to his damage. Such government frequently has a larger interest in maintaining the principles of international law than in recovering damage for one of its citizens in a particular case, and manifestly such

---

[53] *Lusitania (United States v Germany)* 7 R.I.A.A. 32 at 38–44 (1956).

[54] *(Canada v United States)* 3 R.I.A.A. 1609 (1933/35); 29 A.J.I.L. 326 (1935).

[55] *Civilian War Claimants Association v The King* [1932] A.C. 14. Cf. Draft art.19 Draft Articles on Diplomatic Protection 2006 proposes a "recommended practice" that the state exercising diplomatic protection "transfer to the injured person any compensation obtained for the injury from the responsible State subject to any reasonable deductions".

citizen cannot by contract in this respect, tie the hands of his Government."[56]

In espousing a claim on behalf of an individual, a state is protecting a state right which must be respected in international law, namely that its nationals be treated in a particular manner. This is called diplomatic protection. Once a state has taken up a claim on behalf of an individual, the state enjoys exclusive control over the handling and presentation of the claim[57] which becomes one between two states

> "it is true that the dispute was at first between a private person and a State ... Subsequently, the Greek Government took up the case. The dispute then entered upon a new plane; it entered the domain of international law, and became a dispute between two States ... Once a State has taken up a case on behalf of one of its subjects before an international tribunal, in the eyes of the latter the State is sole claimant."[58]

In 2006, the ILC adopted a set of Draft Articles on Diplomatic Protection.[59] These represent both codification and progressive development of existing customary international law on diplomatic protection. Given the varied definitions of diplomatic protection, the ILC opted for a rather strict definition:

> "For the purposes of the present draft articles, diplomatic protection consists of the invocation by a State, through diplomatic action or other means of peaceful settlement, of the responsibility of another State for an injury caused by an internationally wrongful act of that State to a natural or legal person that is a national of the former State with a view to the implementation of such responsibility."[60]

Standard of treatment

A state is not required to admit foreign nationals. Immigration control is a matter of national law although groups of states may make specific regional agreements, e.g. in the European Union,

---

[56] *North American Dredging Co. (U.S./Mexican)* 4 R.I.A.A. 26 at 29 (1926).
[57] See e.g. *Administrative Decision No.V (U.S. v Germany)* 7 R.I.A.A. 119 (1924).
[58] *Mavrommatis Palestine Concessions* case, P.C.I.J. Rep., ser.A, No.2 (1924) at 12.
[59] ILC, "Report of the ILC on the work of its 58th Session" (1 May – 9 June and 3 July – 11 August 2006) (2006) UN Doc A/61/10, Ch.IV. The question of whether to adopt the Draft Articles on Diplomatic Protection is still being considered by the General Assembly.
[60] art.1, Draft Articles on Diplomatic Protection 2006.

nationals of Member States may only be denied admission to other Member States in specifically defined circumstances. Once non-nationals are admitted, should a state then fail to treat them in a particular way, the host state will be in breach of an international obligation. This was endorsed by the UN General Assembly in 1985, in the Declaration on the Human Rights of Individuals who are not Nationals of the Country in which They Live,[61] which articulates the fundamental human rights to be observed by the host state. The Declaration was an effort to clarify and compile the existing international customary law on the matter. It states that non-nationals are assured of certain rights, such as the right of equality within the judicial process and protection from torture, cruel or inhuman treatment. As international human rights norms have evolved it is clear that they apply both to aliens and nationals, therefore the need to codify these customary laws has become less pressing. Aliens are, of course, required to observe the laws of the host state and to respect the host state's customs and traditions.

By what standard is the treatment to be gauged? There are two views, one generally representing that of developing states and the other representing that of developed states.

The national treatment standard

Originally supported by Latin American countries during the 19th and early-20th centuries, this view is favoured today primarily by developing states. According to the national treatment standard, non-nationals are to be treated in the same way as nationals of the host state. Obviously, if applied consistently, this would be advantageous to non-nationals.

The disadvantage of the national treatment standard is obvious. A state could subject a non-national to inhuman treatment and justify such treatment on the grounds that nationals could be similarly treated. In response to this international arbitration tribunals and developed states have denied that a state can exonerate itself by pleading that nationals are treated in the same way should the treatment of non-nationals falls short of the international minimum standard.[62]

International minimum standard

The international minimum standard is difficult to define. International law has not provided a definition, although an

---

[61] GA Res. 144 (XL), G.A.O.R., 49th Sess., Supp.53, p.253.
[62] *Roberts Claim* 4 R.I.A.A. 77 (1926). See also *Asian Agricultural Products Ltd* case (1990) 30 I.L.M. p.577.

attempt at such was made in 1957 when the ILC debated the Second Report on State Responsibility of its Special Rapporteur.[63] In the Report, an article which embraced both the national minimum standard and the international minimum standard was proposed. States were to afford to a non-national the same treatment as that enjoyed by nationals but in no circumstances was such treatment "to be less than the 'fundamental human rights' recognized and defined in contemporary international instruments". However, the proposal was too far-reaching and since then the ILC has concentrated its attention on the codification of general principles of responsibility.

To violate the international minimum standard, a state's treatment of foreign nationals must fall so short of established acceptable behaviour "that every reasonable and impartial man would readily recognize its insufficiency".[64]

A state may incur responsibility if a non-national is physically ill-treated,[65] or if his or her property is damaged.[66] A state may also incur responsibility if a non-national suffers a maladministration of justice, for example is denied assistance of counsel[67] or denied adequate protection. However liability will only be incurred if the lack of protection has been either wilful or a consequence of neglect.[68]

States are required to afford a higher degree of protection to internationally-protected persons[69] than to "ordinary" non-nationals.

Although international law is against the arbitrary and unjustified expulsion of non-nationals,[70] states do enjoy discretion to deport non-nationals if their presence is a threat to the public interest. Article 18 of the Treaty on the Functioning of the European Union prohibits discrimination between the nationals of Member States on the grounds of nationality and arts 45–48 of that Treaty

---

[63] Y.B.I.L.C., 1957, II, p.104.

[64] *Neer Claim* 4 R.I.A.A. 60 at 62 (1926).

[65] *Roberts Claim*, above, fn.62; *Quintanilla Claim (Mexico v U.S.)* 4 R.I.A.A. 101 (1926).

[66] *Zafiro* case, above, fn.21 Draft art.9, Harvard Draft Convention on the International Responsibility of States for Injuries to Aliens 1961, 55 A.J.I.L. 548 (1961).

[67] *Pope* case, 8 Whiteman 709.

[68] *Noyes Claim (US v Panama)*, above, fn.21; *Janes Claim (U.S. v Mexico)* 4 R.I.A.A. 82 (1926).

[69] See the Convention on the Prevention and Punishment of Crimes Against Internationally Protected Persons including Diplomatic Agents 1973, 13 I.L.M. 42 (1974); Misc.19 (1975) Cmnd.6176.

[70] See art.3 1955 European Convention on Establishment, 529 U.N.T.S. 141; Fourth Protocol of the European Convention of Human Rights 1963, Misc.6 (1964) Cmnd.2309; 58 A.J.I.L. 334 (1964).

provide for the free movement of workers. Member States can only deny the exercise of that right on the grounds of public health, public security or public order. However, when deported the individual concerned should be advised of the reasons for his or her deportation, except if to do so would be contrary to national security.[71]

Nationals

If a national of a state is expelled from another state, the state of nationality is obliged to receive the individual, unless he or she is willing to go to another state and that state is willing to admit him or her.

Refugees

International law does not require a state to admit asylum seekers,[72] nevertheless under the 1951 Convention Relating to the Status of Refugees[73] and the 1967 Protocol Relating to the Status of Refugees,[74] Contracting Parties undertake to accord refugees treatment no less favourable than that accorded to non-nationals generally. Also no individual may be expelled to territory "where his life or freedom would be questioned".[75] To fall within the ambit of the Refugee Convention, the individual must show a well-founded fear of persecution because of race, religion, nationality, membership of a particular social group or political opinion, and is outside the country of nationality and is unable or unwilling to invoke the protection of that country.[76] The Office of the United Nations High Commissioner for Refugees (UNHCR) was created in December 1950 and has responsibility for providing international protection to refugees and also to finding long-term solutions to the displacement of refugees.[77] Of particular contem-

---

[71] Directive 2004/38 on the right of citizens of the Union and their family members to move and reside freely within the territory of the Member States OJ 2004 L 158.

[72] Significantly, art.14 of the United Nations Declaration of Human Rights was omitted from further international instruments. However see the European Charter of Fundamental Rights OJ 2000 C 3641.

[73] 189 U.N.T.S. 150; 39 (1954) Cmnd.9171.

[74] 606 U.N.T.S. 267; 6 I.L.M. 78 (1967); 63 A.J.I.L. 385 (1969). Currently two-thirds of the international community have ratified either or both the Convention and the Protocol.

[75] See art.33 of the Refugee Convention which spells out the principle of *non-refoulement*.

[76] art.1A(2) of the Convention Relating to the Status of Refugees 1951.

[77] See 87 A.J.I.L. 157 (1993). The Cairo Declaration was adopted by consensus at the ILA Conference in Cairo, 20–26 April 1992. See also Statute of the Office of the United Nations High Commissioner for Refugees, GA Res 5/428, annex,

porary concern to UNHCR is the displacement of civilians in their own country of origin. Globally it is estimated there are some 38 million internally displaced persons (IDPs).[78] There are no specific international instruments affording IDPs protection, however, in 1998 the United Nations presented its Guiding Principles on Internal Displacement, which contains 30 pointers for governments. The Principles are not legally binding, however UN members have been urged to accept them as "the basic international norm for protection" of IDPs.[79]

The 1993 Vienna Declaration reaffirmed the right of an individual to seek asylum from persecution in other countries and the right to be able to return home. The granting of refugee status is a matter for individual states subject to art.33(1) of the 1951 Convention.[80] The 1951 Convention dealt with a specific problem arising in Europe in the wake of the Second World War. Regional organisations have promulgated refinements of the 1951 Convention refugee definition, for example as by the Organisation of American States,[81] the Organisation of African Unity[82] and the European Union. The EU has developed the Common European Asylum System, which attempts to provide a common procedure for the determination of asylum claims and a uniform status valid throughout the Union for persons granted asylum.[83]

International Refugee Law is not static and continues to evolve to address issues such as gender-related persecution, unaccompanied minors and the scope and meaning of the term "particular social group" as found in the 1951 Convention.[84] A major refugee crisis has taken place since the beginning of the Syrian civil war in 2011 and hundreds of thousands of people have fled Syria, Iraq and Afghanistan. Other countries where there is conflict or where populations live in poverty in the Middle East, Africa and Asia have also contributed to this mass movement of people. This crisis,

G.A.O.R. 5th Sess., Supp.20 p.46, UN Doc A/1775 (1950) adopted December 1950. The office came into existence on 1 January 1951.

[78] UNHCR's estimate of the global position at the end of 2014. It is, however, impossible to calculate the number of IDPs accurately.

[79] UN Secretary-General Kofi Annan in his 2005 Report to the UN *In larger freedom: towards development, security and human rights for all*, para.210.

[80] See art.32(1). Art.32(1) will not apply if the "individual is reasonably suspected of being a security risk or having been finally convicted of a particular serious crime, constitutes a danger to the Community"—art.33(2).

[81] Definition of Refugee Status (Cartagena Declaration) OAS/SER.I/ V/II.66, doc.10, rev.1, pp.190–193, adopted by 10 Latin American states in 1986.

[82] (OAU) Convention Governing the Specific Aspects of Refugee Problems in Africa, UNTS.14, 691 entered into force 20 June 1974.

[83] For a detailed discussion on the developments of the European asylum system see, G. Clayton, *Textbook on Immigration and Asylum Law*, 6th edn, (Oxford: Oxford University Press, 2014).

[84] Further examination of these topics is outwith the scope of this text.

the most acute since World War II, is testing immigration rules, at national, regional and international level, as never before.

Expropriation of the property of non-nationals

Expropriation is the compulsory taking of private property by the state. Initially the definition of property was said to include "all moveable and immovable property, whether tangible or intangible, including industrial, literary and artistic property, as well as rights and interests in any property"[85] but not, however, rights derived from contracts. Nevertheless, the jurisprudence of the United States–Iran Claims Tribunal, established in 1981, has extended the definition to include contractual rights.[86]

Expropriation extends beyond the actual physical taking of property to include any action, which unreasonably interferes with "the use, enjoyment or disposal of property".[87] The application of taxation and regulatory measures designed specifically to deny the effective use of private property may be referred to as "creeping", "constructive" or "indirect" expropriation.[88]

Expropriation, particularly in the post-colonial period, became an important issue in international law. Possibly more than any other issue, expropriation highlighted the opposing views of capitalist developed countries, socialist states and developing states. At the time capitalist developed countries required a guarantee of protection and security before investing abroad, while the latter (that is, socialist and developing states) were more reluctant to allow too much foreign investment for fear of undermining control of their own resources. Developed and developing states recognise that every state has a legitimate right to expropriate property. However, developed states of the western tradition maintain that expropriation is only legitimate if it complies with an international minimum standard and if, in particular, it is accompanied by effective compensation. Developing states refute this.

General Assembly Resolution 1803 on Permanent Sovereignty over Natural Resources reflects the position of the capitalist developed states.[89] The Resolution recognises the right of peoples and nations "to permanent sovereignty over their natural wealth and resources".[90]

---

[85] Draft art.10(7), 1961 Harvard Draft Convention, above, fn.66.
[86] See e.g. *Starrett Housing Corp v Iran* (Interlocutory Award) 4 Iran-USCTR 122; 23 I.L.M. 1090 (1984); *Amoco International Finance Corp v Iran* 15 Iran-USCTR 189; 82 A.J.I.L. 358 (1986).
[87] Draft art.10(3)(a), 1961 Harvard Draft Convention, above, fn.66.
[88] See the *Starrett* case, above, fn.86.
[89] (1962) G.A.O.R., 17th Session, Supp.17, p.15.
[90] Above.

Paragraph 4 of the Resolution reinforces customary international law by providing

> "nationalization, expropriation or requisitioning shall be based on grounds or reasons of public utility, security or the national interest which are recognized as overriding purely individual or private interests, both domestic and foreign. In such cases the owner shall be paid appropriate compensation in accordance with the rules in force in the State taking such measures in the exercise of its sovereignty and in accordance with international law."

To be valid expropriation should be for public purposes, should not be discriminatory (not specified but implied in para.4) and should be accompanied by compensation assessed in accordance with the rules in force in the appropriate state and international law.

Public purpose

The requirement that nationalisation should be for a public purpose for it to be valid under international law was identified in the *Certain German Interests in Polish Upper Silesia* case[91] and in *Amoco International Financial Corp v Iran*.[92] The concept of a "public purpose" whereby expropriation is lawful remains undefined and consequently states enjoy considerable discretion in its application. In the *BP* case of 1974,[93] the UK challenged Libyan nationalisation measures on the grounds that, inter alia, they were not motivated by considerations of a political nature related to the international well-being of the taking state. In that case, the arbitrator confirmed the measures in question violated international law, as they were made for purely extraneous political reasons.[94] However, three years later in the *Liamco* case,[95] the arbitrator dismissed the independent public purpose requirement on the grounds "it is the general opinion in international law that the public utility principle is not a necessary requisite for the legality of a nationalisation."[96] In practice, public purpose has not been predominant in international claims and has only been of secondary importance. Public purpose is a broad concept which does not easily submit to objective examination.

---

[91] P.C.I.J. Rep., ser.A, No.7, (1929), p.22.
[92] Above, fn.86.
[93] 53 I.L.R. 297 (1974).
[94] Above, at 329.
[95] 20 I.L.M. 1 (1981).
[96] Above, 58–59.

Discrimination

Nationalisation[97] which discriminates against foreigners, foreigners of a particular nationality and/or particular foreigners has been regarded by developed states as contrary to international law.[98] Discrimination is difficult to prove. There may, for example, be no comparable enterprises owned either by local nationals of other countries. Like public purpose, arguments inferring discrimination have not been predominant when expropriation has been challenged. In the *Amoco* case,[99] although acknowledged as being prohibited, an element of discrimination may be tolerated in certain circumstances, e.g. being reasonably related to the public purpose.[100]

Compensation

What has been decisive has been whether or not compensation has been paid and whether, if paid, it complies with the standard prescribed by international law. To comply with international law as represented by Resolution 1803 compensation must be "prompt, adequate and effective".[101] These terms have been used in many bilateral commercial treaties. The expression "appropriate compensation" was adopted in Resolution 1803 and has been subsequently endorsed in the *Texaco* case[102] and the *Aminoil* case[103] as reflecting the standard demanded under customary international law. "Appropriate compensation" is, according to the Tribunal in the latter case, to be assessed in the light of the circumstances specific to the particular case. Compensation has traditionally been considered as payment equivalent to the full value of the property taken, possibly with a margin allowed for future loss of profits. Payment should be made in a readily convertible currency (that is, the recipient should be in a position to use and benefit from the compensation) either before or at the time of the takeover. Deferred payment will only be allowed if the amount to be paid is fixed promptly and provision is made for the payment of interest.

---

[97] Nationalisation is used synonymously with expropriation and requisitioning.
[98] See UK's objections in the *Anglo–Iranian Oil Co* case I.C.J. Rep. (Pleadings) 1951 at 81; also in the *BP* case, above, fn.93; US's argument in the *Liamco* case, above, fn.95, also arbitrator's findings in that case.
[99] Above, fn.86.
[100] Above, at para.145.
[101] See *Anglo–Iranian Oil Co* case, above, fn.98 at 105.
[102] 53 I.L.R. 389 (1977); 17 I.L.M. 1 (1978).
[103] *Kuwait v American Independent Oil Co* 21 I.L.M. 976 (1982). More recently, in *Southern Pacific Properties (Middle East) Ltd v Arab Republic of Egypt* 32 I.L.M. 933 (1993), the International Centre for Settlement of Disputes held "fair" compensation was the standard that should be applied when assessing compensation in a lawful expropriation.

This traditional approach has been challenged and, to some extent, rejected by developing states whose position is reflected particularly in art.2(c) of the 1974 Charter of Economic Rights and Duties of States.[104] This provides "appropriate compensation should be paid by the State adopting such measures, taking into account its relevant laws and regulations and all circumstances, that the State considers pertinent." Article 2(c) further provides that in the event of a dispute arising over compensation it should be decided, unless otherwise mutually agreed, by the domestic law of the nationalising state. However, note that the 1974 Charter has, as yet, been denied the status of customary international law.[105]

In the *Amco Indonesia* case,[106] it was stated that compensation should be awarded for the loss suffered (*damnum emergens*) and expected profits (*lucrum cessans*).

It is important to distinguish between expropriation which is lawful and that which is unlawful. The distinction was highlighted in the *Amoco* case as being necessary "since the rules applicable to the compensation to be paid by the expropriating State differ according to the legal characterisation of the taking".[107] In accordance with the established rules of state responsibility, unlawful expropriation should merit full restitution in kind or, alternatively, the equivalent pecuniary value and, in some instances, a payment for loss or expected loss of profits. On the other hand, lawful expropriation would only warrant compensation reflecting the value of the property taken at the time of takeover. However, a by-product of the collapse of the former communist powers was the removal of considerable ideological opposition to the payment of compensation.[108]

Settlement of disputes

The uncertainty regarding the customary international law of expropriation prompted bilateral treaties between developed and developing states guaranteeing compensation in the event of expropriation. The US and other developed western capital-exporting countries also operate insurance schemes for nationals engaged in foreign investment.

Frequently, disputes will be resolved by a compromise settlement, whether settlement is by straightforward negotiation

---

[104] GA Res.3281 (XXIV) 14 I.L.M. 251 (1975); see also GA Res.3171 (XXVIII) 1973, 68 A.J.I.L. 381 (1974); GA Res.3201 (S-VI) Declaration on the Establishment of a New International Economic Order 1974, 13 I.L.M. 765 (1974).

[105] See Arbitrator's finding in the *Texaco* case, above, fn.102.

[106] *Amco Asia Corporation v The Republic of Indonesia* 24 I.L.M. 1022 (1985).

[107] *Amoco International Finance Corp v Iran*, above, fn.86 at 246.

[108] See O'Brien, *International Law*, (London: Cavendish Publishing, 2001), p.385.

between the parties or by a "lump-sum settlement" agreement. Lump-sum settlement agreements have found increasing favour since the late 1940s, e.g. United Kingdom–USSR Agreement on the Settlement of Mutual Financial and Property Claims. Under lump-sum settlements, the expropriating state agrees to pay the investor state a lump sum in respect of all subsisting claims by nationals of the investor state. The investor state is then responsible, normally via a national claims commission for adjudicating upon and settling, in accordance with international law, individual claims.[109]

In 1981, an international tribunal was established at The Hague to settle the claims of US nationals against Iran and the claims of Iranian nationals against the US.[110] Another example of a compensation fund was the United Nations Claims Commission established in 1991 to settle war claims against Iraq arising from the hostilities in the Gulf. The UN Claims Commission concluded payments to individuals in 2007.[111]

In 1965, the Convention on the Settlement of Investment Disputes between States and Nationals of Other States[112] established the International Centre for the Settlement of Investment Disputes (ICSID) in Washington, DC. The Convention, through the Centre, provides for parties who agree procedures for the settlement of disputes between contracting parties and companies of the nationality of a contracting party. The procedures established by way of the ICSID, which are not limited to cases of expropriation, have been endorsed by states as an appropriate mechanism for the settlement of investment disputes. This is reflected in the provisions of an increasing number of Bilateral Investment Agreements (BIAs).

Breach of contract

Contracts between a state and a non-national as a rule are governed by the national law of the former and consequently seldom involve international law. A state will only therefore incur liability if it denies the non-national concerned access to an effective domestic forum for adjudication of the alleged dispute.

A contract between a state and a non-national, however, can be "internationalised". A contract may be "internationalised" if a

---

[109] Examples of such national claims commissions are the Foreign Compensation Commission in the UK and in the US the Foreign Claims Settlement Commission of the United States.

[110] The Tribunal was set up under the Claims Settlement Declaration made on 19 January 1981 by the Governments of Iran and the US. See 20 I.L.M. 230 (1981).

[111] 30 I.L.M. 846 (1996), see also p.292.

[112] 575 U.N.T.S. 159; 4 I.L.M. 532 (1965).

state legislates to abolish or repudiate its contractual obligations. The state can, by its unilateral action, place itself on a different level than the other party to the contract. In the *Norwegian Loans* case,[113] such was the alleged effect of Norwegian legislation on the contract between Norway and French bondholders.[114] Others maintain the insertion of a clause that a concession agreement is to be governed not by the law of the state party to the agreement, but e.g. by "general principles of the law of nations" or "principles of the law of the concessionary State not inconsistent with international law", removes the contract from the municipal plane and "internationalises" it. One view, for example, is such a clause transforms the agreement into an international agreement and breaches of contract into breaches of international law.[115] Developing states in particular refute such arguments and do not accept such clauses as valid, as they deny a state its sovereign right to control its natural resources. Accordingly, the norm is that a contract between a state and a non-national will be governed by the municipal law of the state concerned.

The Calvo Clause

The Calvo Clause, named after an Argentinian jurist and statesman, was frequently included in agreements between Latin American states and foreigners. Under the Calvo Clause nonnationals accepted in advance that, in the event of a dispute, they would not attempt to invoke the assistance of their national state. The Calvo Clause purported to deny a state its right of exercising diplomatic protection on behalf of one of its nationals. The validity of the Calvo Clause has been debated by international tribunals, which have maintained that an individual is not competent to fetter his or her state in such a way, and the right of diplomatic protection and its exercise belong exclusively to the state of nationality.[116] The requirements to exhaust local remedies still exist.[117]

Nationality of claims rule

Nationality is important in the context of state responsibility. A state may only espouse a claim against another state on behalf of one of its nationals. Pursuant to art.3 of the Draft Articles on

[113] I.C.J. Rep. 1957 p.9.
[114] The Court did not decide on the merits of the case, but individual judges considered the internationalisation of the contract; Read J at 87–88; Lauterpacht J at 38.
[115] See e.g. Arbitrator in *Texaco* case, above, fn.102.
[116] *North American Dredging Co Claim* (1926), above, fn.56 at 29.
[117] See below, pp.228–229.

Diplomatic Protection 2006 the state entitled to exercise diplomatic protection is the state of nationality. International law provides no definition of nationality, as the granting of nationality is exclusively a matter of domestic law.[118] A state is free to decide as to whom it deems to be its nationals.[119] In spite of this prima facie unfettered discretion, a state may have its grant of nationality challenged should it attempt to raise a claim against another state. A state's right to afford diplomatic protection may be challenged on the grounds that the link between it and its alleged national is tenuous and not genuine. In the absence of such a link, a claimant state will be prohibited from proceeding with an international claim. The need for there to be an obvious genuine link between the claimant state and the individual concerned was emphasised in the *Nottebohm* case. In that case, Liechtenstein attempted to exercise diplomatic protection, on behalf of Nottebohm, against Guatemala. Nottebohm had become a naturalised Liechtenstein citizen after only residence of a few weeks in that state and Guatemala challenged Liechtenstein's right to espouse a claim on his behalf. The ICJ maintained

> "a State cannot claim that the rules it has thus laid down are entitled to recognition by another State unless it has acted in conformity with this general aim of making the legal bond of nationality accord with the individual's genuine connection with the State".[120]

The ICJ characterised nationality as

> "a legal bond having as its basis a social fact of attachment, a genuine connection of existence, interests and sentiments, together with the existence of reciprocal rights and duties. It may be said to constitute the juridical expression of the fact that the individual upon whom it is conferred, either directly by the law or as the result of an act of the authorities, is in fact more closely connected with the population of the State conferring nationality than with that of any other State."[121]

---

[118] Nationality may be acquired in a variety of ways but the two most common ways of attaining nationality are: (i) by descent from parents (*jus sanguinis*); or (ii) by birth in the territory of the state (*jus soli*) art.4. Draft Articles on Diplomatic Protection 2006 states that nationality is acquired "in accordance with the law of that State, by birth, descent, naturalization, succession of States or in any other manner, not inconsistent with international law."

[119] art.1 of the 1930 Hague Convention on Certain Questions Relating to the Conflict of Nationality Laws, 179 L.N.T.S. 89.

[120] *Nottebohm* case (Second Phase), I.C.J. Rep. 1955 p.4 at 23.

[121] Above.

The *Nottebohm* case emphasised an individual must possess the claimant state's nationality, and also that the nationality must be effective. The *Nottebohm* judgment extended the concept of "genuine connection", which previously had been utilised to resolve problems of dual nationality,[122] to the issue of diplomatic protection generally. However, in the *Diallo (Guinea v Democratic Republic of Congo)*[123] case the concept of "genuine link" did not feature. In that case the DRC accepted Diallo's Guinean nationality, notwithstanding his residency in DRC for the whole of his adult life.

The general rule is a state will only espouse a claim on behalf of an individual if the latter is a national both at the time when the injury occurs and at the time when the claim is presented.[124]

In respect of an individual possessing dual nationality, the traditional view is that a claim by one national state against another national state will not be entertained. Some states however, such as the UK, have conceded that a claim may be taken up against the state of nationality if the other state of nationality has treated the claimant as a national of the proposed espousing state.[125]

In respect of claims against a third state on behalf of an individual with dual nationality, it is not altogether clear which of the national states has the right to espouse the claim. In the *Merge Claim*,[126] it was suggested only the state with which the individual had the closest connection could espouse a claim on his or her behalf, whereas in the *Salem* case[127] it was suggested that both states could do so and the Iran–United States Claims Tribunal has employed the terms of "dominant and effective nationality" as a basis for exercising jurisdiction.[128] The UK attitude is that although the government of the day may take up a claim on behalf of an individual possessing dual nationality, it prefers to do so jointly with the other national state.[129] The Draft Articles on Diplomatic Protection, 2006, provide that one state or two or more

---

[122] See *Canevaro* case *(Italy v Peru)* 11 R.I.A.A. 397; 6 A.J.I.L. 746 (1912) Translation.

[123] *Diallo Case (Preliminary Objections) Guinea v Democratic Republic of Congo* (2007) I.C.J. Rep. 2007.

[124] See e.g. Rule I of the Rules Regarding International Claims issued by the British Foreign and Commonwealth Office 1985, (1998) 37 I.C.L.Q. 1006. See also Draft art.5, Draft Articles on Diplomatic Protection 2006.

[125] Rule III, above. See also Draft art.7 above, which provides for a claim against one state by another in respect an individual who is a national of both states, where that individual is "predominantly" the national of the claimant state both at the time of injury and at the date the claim is presented.

[126] 22 I.L.R. 443.

[127] *(Egypt v U.S.)* 2 R.I.A.A. 1161 (1932).

[128] Iran–United States No.A/18 (1984) 5 Iran-U.S.C.T.R. 251.

[129] Rule III, above, fn.124. See also Draft Articles on Diplomatic Protection arts 5 and 6.

states jointly may exercise diplomatic protection in respect of a dual national against a third state.[130]

The absence of nationality, that is statelessness, means that a state which inflicts injury against a stateless person cannot be held internationally responsible nor is any state competent to intervene on such a person's behalf.[131] An element of progressive development in the Draft Articles on Diplomatic Protection, 2006, relates to stateless persons and refugees. Article 8 provides that states *may* exercise diplomatic protection in respect of stateless persons and refugees who, at the date of injury and the date of presentation of claim, are "lawfully and habitually resident in that State".

The concept of a "genuine link" is not limited to individuals in that "ships have the nationality of the State whose flag they are entitled to fly. There must exist a genuine link between the State and the ship."[132]

Companies and shareholders

Which state may espouse a claim on behalf of a corporation? A company has traditionally been regarded as having the nationality of "the State under the laws of which it is incorporated and in whose territory it has its registered office".[133] However, these are not the only two criteria whereby a link between a company and a state may be evidenced. For example

> "it has been the practice of some States to give a company incorporated under their law diplomatic protection solely when it has its seat (siège social) or management or centre of control in their territory, or when a majority or a substantial proportion of the shares has been owned by nationals of the State concerned."[134]

The ICJ concluded in the *Barcelona Traction* case, with respect to "the diplomatic protection of corporate entities, no absolute test of the 'genuine connection' has found general acceptance".[135] In this case the question confronting the ICJ was whether Belgium could intervene on behalf of Belgian nationals and shareholders in a company, Barcelona Traction, which was incorporated

---

[130] Above, Draft art.6.
[131] *Dickson Car Wheel Company case (US v Mexico)* (1931) 4 R.I.A.A. 669, but note ILC Draft Articles on Diplomatic Protection, Draft art.7.
[132] art.5 of the Geneva Convention on the High Seas 1958—see above and art.91 of the 1982 Law of the Sea Convention. See also Chicago Convention 1944, arts 12 and 18.
[133] *Barcelona Traction, Light and Power Co* case, I.C.J. Rep. 1970 p.3 at 42.
[134] Above.
[135] Above.

and maintained its registered office in Canada. The losses sustained were a result of measures taken by Spain, the country in which the company operated. Canada initially intervened, but subsequently withdrew and did not proceed with a claim. The Court upheld Spain's objection to Belgian intervention on the grounds that Canada's failure to act did not increase Belgium's right. According to the ICJ's judgment, the state whose nationality a company possesses, even if it operates in a foreign country and is controlled by foreign shareholders, has the right to make the claim on its behalf. It was the company which had suffered the injury, but the company was not defunct and, therefore, whether or not to espouse a claim on behalf of the company remained within Canada's discretion.

Regarding shareholders, the general rule is that a state may not pursue a claim on behalf of nationals who suffer injury as a consequence of a measure taken against foreign companies in which they own shares. The ICJ in the *Barcelona Traction* case concluded that to recognise diplomatic protection on behalf of shareholders would result in confusion, as the shares of international companies are "widely scattered and frequently change hands".[136] The ICJ did admit one exception to the general rule, namely if the company ceased to exist. In such circumstances, the ICJ recognised that the state of the shareholders' nationality could initiate a claim on behalf of the shareholders for losses sustained by them as a consequence of the injury to the company.[137] The ICJ's judgment failed to acknowledge that a state in which a company is incorporated may have little interest in pursuing a claim on that company's behalf. A company may be incorporated in a particular state as a matter of convenience. In that event, the state whose nationals are shareholders may indeed have considerable interest in espousing a claim.

In the *Diallo* case the ICJ was again faced with the issue of the substitution of the state of nationality of the company with the state of nationality of its shareholders. The Court concluded the "substitution doctrine" is not a rule of customary international law.[138] The Court did, however, leave open the possibility that a more limited rule of substitution exists, allowing substitution where incorporation in the state of wrongdoing was a precondition to doing business there.[139]

Article 9 of the Draft Articles on Diplomatic Protection, 2006, states:

[136] Above, at 49.
[137] Above, at 41.
[138] Above, para.89.
[139] Above, para.93.

> "For the purposes of diplomatic protection of a corporation, the State of nationality means the State under whose law the corporation was incorporated. However, when the corporation is controlled by nationals of another State or States and has no substantial business activities in the State of incorporation, and the seat of management and the financial control of the corporation are both located in another State, that State shall be regarded as the State of nationality."

As with nationality of natural persons, a state's entitlement to exercise diplomatic protection is subject to the rule of continuous nationality.[140] The Draft Articles also provide a general rule that states shall not be entitled to exercise diplomatic protection on behalf of shareholders. However, draft art.11 provides two exceptions; first, as in the *Barcelona Traction* case, where "the corporation has ceased to exist according to the law of the State of incorporation for a reason unrelated to the injury",[141] and second, where "the corporation had, at the date of injury, the nationality of the State alleged to be responsible for causing the injury, and incorporation in that State was required as a precondition for doing business there".[142]

Exhaustion of local remedies

It is an established rule of customary international law that before diplomatic protection is afforded, or before recourse may be made to international arbitral or judicial processes, local remedies must be exhausted. The raison d'être of the rule is:

(a) to allow the state concerned the opportunity to afford redress within its own legal system for the alleged wrong;

(b) to reduce the number of possible international claims; and

(c) respect for the sovereignty of states.

"Local remedies" means

> "not only reference to the courts and tribunals, but also the use of the procedural facilities which municipal law makes available to litigants before such courts and tribunals. It is the whole system of legal protection, as provided by municipal law".[143]

---

[140] Draft art.10, Draft Articles on Diplomatic Protection 2006.
[141] Above, Draft art.11(a).
[142] Above, Draft art.11(b).
[143] *Ambatielos Arbitration* (Greece v UK) 12 R.I.A.A. 83 (1956); 23 I.L.R. 306 (1956).

An individual must, therefore, employ "all administrative, arbitral or judicial remedies".[144] Only effective remedies which could affect the final outcome of the case need to be exhausted.[145] The exhaustion of local remedies has been strictly applied, but local remedies need not be exhausted if it is evident that there is no justice to exhaust, or where it is apparent that any attempt to seek redress would be thwarted.[146] The exhaustion of local remedies is not required when the alleged wrong is a direct injury by one state against another state. Exhaustion of local remedies may be dispensed with by treaty, but this must be explicitly stated and not merely implied. This generally reflects the position adopted by the Draft Articles on Diplomatic Protection, 2006.[147]

STATE RESPONSIBILITY FOR THE ENVIRONMENT

Increasing concern for the environment has led to the realisation that protection, to be effective, demands international co-operation. "States shall co-operate in a spirit of global partnership to conserve, protect and restore the health and integrity of the Earth's eco system."[148] The focus of the international community has increasingly been on preventative measures rather than on the traditional international law approach whereby responsibility is attributed to the state deemed to have caused the harm. The expansion of international/regional environmental norms is reflected in the weight afforded to environmental law in the increasing number of academic programmes.

International regulation of the environment has increased dramatically in the last 50 years, and the preventative approach is reflected in a plethora of arrangements both at an international and regional level (see below). The UN in 1972 established the United Nations Environment Programme (UNEP) to implement the Action Programme adopted at the Stockholm Conference on Human Environment that year. This international "legislative" activity has been accompanied by regional developments. Initially, the international community tackled responsibility for the environment by way of customary international law and imposed certain restrictions on the enjoyment of a state's recognised right

---

[144] See Draft art.19, 1961 Harvard Draft Convention on International Responsibility of States for Injuries to Aliens.

[145] *Finnish Ships Arbitration* 3 R.I.A.A. 1479 (1934); cf. *El Oro Mining and Railway Co case (Great Britain v Mexico)* 5 R.I.A.A. 191 (1931); *Interhandel* case (Preliminary Objections) I.C.J. Rep. 1959 6 at 26–29.

[146] *Robert E. Brown* case 6 R.I.A.A. 120, 129 (1923).

[147] Draft art.14, Draft Articles on Diplomatic Protection. See further Draft art.15 for a comprehensive list of situations in which local remedies do not need to be exhausted.

[148] Principle 7 Rio Declaration (see below fn.151).

"in accordance with the Charter of the United Nations and the principles of international law, ... to exploit their own natural resources pursuant to their own environmental policies".[149] The responsibility incumbent on states under customary international law is expressed in Principle 21 as being "to ensure that activities within their jurisdiction or control do not cause damage to the environment of other States or of areas beyond the limits of national jurisdiction"[150] It is currently reiterated in Principle 2 of the Rio Declaration.[151] Article 30 of the Charter of Economic Rights and Duties of States also provides:

> "The protection, preservation and enhancement of the environment for the present and future generations is the responsibility of all States. All States shall endeavour to establish their own environmental and developmental policies in conformity with such responsibility ... All States have the responsibility to ensure that activities within their jurisdiction or control do not cause damage to the environment of other States or of areas beyond the limits of national jurisdiction. All States should co-operate in evolving international norms and regulations in the field of the environment."[152]

Article 24 of the 1981 African Charter on Human and Peoples' Rights (the Banjul Charter) heralds as a right of all people "a general satisfactory environment favourable to their development".

The extent and scope of a state's responsibility under customary international law is reflected in two cases involving the US and Canada, namely the *Trail Smelter Arbitration*[153] and *Gut Dam Arbitration*.[154]

The *Trail Smelter Arbitration* dealt with damage caused in the state of Washington by sulphur dioxide emitted from a smelter plant at Trail on the Columbia River, ten miles from the US/Canadian border on the Canadian side.

In the Tribunal's final decision in 1941, a general principle of international law was recognised, namely "a State owes at all times a duty to protect other States against injurious acts by

---

[149] Declaration on the Human Environment (Stockholm, 1972) 11 I.L.M. 1416 (1972), Principle 21.
[150] Above.
[151] The Rio Declaration on the Environment was adopted on 14 June 1992, at the UN Conference on Environment and Development, Rio de Janeiro, 3–14 June 1992. It was attended by 176 states; see 31 I.L.M. 814 (1992).
[152] It may be recalled that the status of the Charter under international law is not fully established.
[153] 3 R.I.A.A. 1905.
[154] 8 I.L.M. 118 (1969).

individuals from within its jurisdiction".[155] The Tribunal concluded from decisions of the US Supreme Court relating to disputes between Member States of the Union and there existed in US law and international law a principle that

> "no State has the right to use or permit the use of its territory in such a manner as to cause injury by fumes in or to the territory of another or the properties or persons therein, when the cause is of serious consequences and the injury is established by clear and convincing evidence."

The Gut Dam, on the border between the US and Canada, raised the water levels of Lake Ontario between 1947 and 1952 resulting in considerable damage being sustained to properties on the lakeshore. On the re-establishment of an International Arbitral Tribunal, Canada agreed to pay compensation in respect of the damage caused to the property of US citizens.

Similarly in the *Corfu Channel* case[156] it was maintained that incumbent on every state is the duty "not to allow knowingly its territory to be used for acts contrary to the rights of other States".[157]

In 1972 the UN passed the Declaration on the Human Environment, known as the Stockholm Declaration, when it convened its first international conference on the environment. Principle 22 of the Stockholm Declaration emphasised state co-operation in the further development of international law on liability and compensation for the victims of pollution and extra-territorial damage, while Principle 24 called upon states to act in a co-operative spirit for the protection and improvement of the international environment. The requirement to co-operate is a recurring theme in contemporary international agreements.[158]

In 1992, the UN convened a second global conference on the environment, the Conference on Environment and Development (UNCED) in Rio de Janeiro. The Conference was in response to the growing recognition that environmental problems should

---

[155] 3 R.I.A.A. 1905, at 1963.

[156] I.C.J. Rep. 1949 p.4.

[157] Above, at 22. See also the ICJ acknowledgment a state's territorial sovereignty is restricted by obligations towards the environment. This is now part of the corpus of international law relating to the environment, as was stated in the *Nuclear Weapons* case, per Weeramantry J. See also the separate opinion of Weeramantry J in the *Nagymaros* case.

[158] e.g. art.5 of the 1979 Long-Range Transboundary Air Pollution Convention; and Vienna Convention on Early Notification of a Nuclear Accident 1986—see below.

be addressed at an international level. In between these two conferences states assumed obligations on specific issues regarding the protection of the environment (see below), but it was the UNCED which introduced the concept of sustainable development[159] in its Declaration on Environment and Development (the Rio Declaration). The Rio Declaration introduced a number of general principles, namely, the obligation on states to take precautionary measures (Principle 15); the polluter pays principle (Principle 16); and environmental impact assessment (Principle 17). These principles generally now govern international environmental law. The Declaration also contains obligations for states to notify emergencies and engage in consultation where there is a risk of transboundary pollution.

A follow up to the 1992 Rio Conference was held in June 2012, Rio+20, which identified seven key areas of focus, namely, jobs, energy, cities, food, water, oceans and disasters. The Conference, in which all UN Member States participated, agreed an outcome document, *The Future we Want*, which laid out plans for sustainable development and measures to tighten environmental protection. However, civil society groups and campaigners who had attended Rio+20 criticised the document for lacking the detail and ambition necessary to address the deteriorating environment and growing inequality.

One of the Millennium Development Goals (MDGs), adopted in 2000, was to achieve environmental sustainability by 2015. In September 2015 world leaders approved the new Sustainable Development Goals (SDGs), which should guide international policy for the next 15 years.[160] Of the 17 SDGs several deal directly with protecting the environment. Goals 13, 14 and 15 are, respectively, to take urgent action to combat climate change and its impacts; to conserve and sustainably use the oceans, seas and marine resources for sustainable development; and to protect, restore and promote sustainable use of terrestrial ecosystems, sustainably manage forests, combat desertification and halt and reverse land degradation, and halt biodiversity loss. A significant difference between the MDGs and the recently articulated SDGs is that the former were addressed only to developing coun-

---

[159] Sustainable development can be described simply as meeting the needs of present generations without compromising the ability of future generations to do the same. See, the Bruntland Report of the World Commission on Environment and Development (WCED) 1987, titled *Our Common Future*. With the population of the earth set to double in the next 50 years, sustainable development is regarded as vital to the survival of the planet. See Ch.39 of Agenda 21 generally.

[160] *Transforming Our World by 2030: A New Agenda for Global Action* (Zero draft of the outcome document for the UN Summit to adopt the Post-2015 Development Agenda).

tries, whereas the latter are commitments expected from all states, irrespective of their stages of development.

As mentioned above, together with global policy documents states have developed norms on specific topics. Issues of priority for the international community relating to the environment include desertification, transboundary air pollution, global warming/depletion of the ozone layer, the transfer and disposal of hazardous waste and control of nuclear activities. Special conditions and environmental problems which some developing countries face have been recognised by the United Nations in a Convention to Combat Desertification in those Countries Experiencing Serious Drought and/or Desertification, particularly in Africa.[161] The purpose of the Convention is to identify the factors contributing to desertification, the practical measures necessary to combat it and the mitigation of the effects of drought through international co-operation and partnership agreements. The problem of drought has far-reaching repercussions for economic growth, social development and poverty eradication.[162]

The 1979 Convention on Long-Range Transboundary Air Pollution and the eight subsequent Protocols[163] tackle the problem of transboundary air pollution and Contracting Parties agree to "endeavour to limit and, as far as possible, gradually reduce and prevent air pollution including long-range transboundary air pollution". The Convention defines transboundary air pollution as that which originates

> "within the area under the national jurisdiction of one State and which has adverse effects in the area under the jurisdiction of another State at such a distance that it is not generally possible to distinguish the contribution of individual emission sources or groups of sources."

The Convention does not address the issue of liability for pollution across state frontiers, but rather emphasises research and the exchange of information.[164]

In a further effort to minimise transboundary pollution, the UN adopted a Convention on Environmental Impact Assessment in 1991.[165] The obligation incumbent on Contracting Parties is to "either individually or jointly, take all appropriate and effective measures to prevent, reduce and control significant

---

[161] 33 I.L.M. 1328 (1994). Entered into force 26 December 1996.
[162] See Ch.12 of Agenda 21 generally.
[163] All eight Protocols are in force. The last entering into force on 17 May 2005.
[164] 18 I.L.M. 1442 (1979).
[165] 30 I.L.M. 800 (1991).

adverse transboundary environmental impact from proposed activities".[166]

Throughout the 1980s, the issue of global warming and the depletion of the ozone layer was widely recognised by governments and individuals alike as requiring urgent attention. The need to protect the ozone layer precipitated an international response, which culminated in the 1985 Vienna Convention for the Protection of the Ozone Layer,[167] the 1987 Montreal Protocol on Substances that Deplete the Ozone Layer,[168] and the 1989 Helsinki Declaration on the Protection of the Ozone Layer.[169] The 1985 Vienna Convention entered into force in 1988 and essentially provides for co-operation, scientific research and the exchange of information, while the 1987 Protocol, as amended in 1990, entered into force in 1990 and stipulates maximum consumption levels of chlorofluorocarbons and imposes a freeze on the use of halons. However, the 1989 Helsinki Declaration required a phasing out of CFCs by the year 2000 and, as soon as practical, other ozone-harming materials.

One of the most pressing environmental issues is climate change. The first instrument addressing the protection of climate was the Hague Declaration on the Environment 1989,[170] calling for the establishment of an international body exclusively dedicated to the consideration of such issues. The most relevant international instrument to date is the Framework Convention on Climate Change adopted in 1992 and its subsequent protocol, the Kyoto Protocol, adopted in 1997.[171] The primary objective of the Framework Convention is to stabilise greenhouse gas concentrations in the atmosphere while recognising some climate change

---

[166] Above, art.2.1. See also *Responsibilities and Obligations of States Sponsoring Persons and Entities with Respect to Activities in the Area*, Case No.17, Advisory Opinion (ITLOS Seabed Disputes Chamber, 1 February 2011), 59 I.L.M. 458 (2011) in which the Tribunal endorsed a legal obligation on states to conduct environmental impact assessments.

[167] 26 I.L.M. 1516 (1987).

[168] Above, at 1541. The 1987 Montreal Protocol was amended at the Fourth Meeting of the Parties to the Protocol at Copenhagen in 1992. Besides shortening the deadlines for already scheduled substances, the adjustments also provided for new rules on other substances. See UN: Montreal Protocol on Substances that Deplete the Ozone Layer—Adjustments and Amendments, Copenhagen, 23–25 November 1992 32 I.L.M. 874 (1993).

[169] 28 I.L.M. 1335 (1989).

[170] Above, 1308 (1989).

[171] The Convention was signed by 155 states and entered into force on 24 March 1994. It was the first international environmental agreement to be negotiated by almost all of the international community. 31 I.L.M. 849 (1992). The Kyoto Protocol to the Convention was adopted on 10 December 1997, amended by the Marrakesh Accords and Declaration in 2001, FCCC/CP/2001/13, 21 January 2002. It entered into force on 16 February 2005.

was inevitable. Although the Framework Convention did not impose binding provisions on the reduction of emissions, states are required to adopt national measures to limit the emission of greenhouse gases. These measures are then to be reviewed at an international Conference by all parties.[172] Under the Kyoto Protocol, developed states are required to limit or reduce their greenhouse gas emissions according to legally-binding, individual targets which differ for developed and developing countries.

In December 2015, 196 states met in Paris in the Climate Summit to renew their commitments under the Framework Convention and the Kyoto Protocol. They adopted, by consensus, the Paris Agreement. The ambitious text calls for zero greenhouse gas emissions to be reached during the second half of the 21st century and for all parties to "pursue efforts to" limit the temperature increase to 1.5°C. The Agreement will become legally binding once is it signed and ratified by at least 55 countries which together are responsible for at least 55% of global greenhouse emissions. The goal is for it to be ratified by April 2017.

The UN Convention on Biological Diversity was negotiated under the auspices of UNCED[173] and was designed to protect the planet's biodiversity by promoting its sustainable use (art.2). The Convention imposes a number of obligations upon states, including national monitoring of biological diversity, national *in situ* and *ex situ* conservation measures, environmental impact assessments and national reports, from countries concerned, on the steps they have taken to implement the Convention.

A number of international measures regulate the transfer and dumping of hazardous waste,[174] e.g. the 1989 Basel Convention on the Control of Transboundary Movements of Hazardous Wastes and Their Disposal[175] controls and in certain circumstances prohibits the transfer of such material between Contracting Parties. A Protocol to the Basel Convention was adopted on 10 December 1999, namely the Basel Protocol on Liability and Compensation for Damage Resulting from Transboundary Movements of Hazardous Waste and Their Disposal.[176]

In 1992, the UN adopted a Convention on the Transboundary Effects of Industrial Accidents.[177] The Convention applies to

---

[172] art.7 of the Convention establishes the Conference of the Parties as the body responsible for monitoring the implementation of the Convention and of taking any necessary decisions to ensure implementation is effected.

[173] 31 I.L.M. 818 (1992) entered into force on 29 December 1993.

[174] For those relating to the protection of the marine environment, see Ch.7 above.

[175] 28 I.L.M. 649 (1989).

[176] This Protocol is not yet in force and will enter into force on the ratification of 20 parties.

[177] Adopted 17 March 1992, in Helsinki, 31 I.L.M. 1330 (1992).

the prevention of and response to industrial accidents capable of causing transboundary effects, including the effects of such accidents caused by natural disasters. An industrial accident is defined as an event resulting from an uncontrolled development in the course of any activity involving hazardous substances (art.1(a)) either in an installation (art.1(a)(i)) or during transportation (art.1(a)(ii)). The Convention also sought to promote international co-operation concerning mutual assistance, research and development, exchange of information and exchange of technology in the area of industrial accidents. It does not apply to, inter alia, nuclear accidents or oil spillages.[178]

International watercourses and their use, the protection of ecosystems and the marine environment[179] were the subject of Draft Articles[180] produced by the ILC in 1994. These Draft Articles culminated in the 1997[181] Convention on the Law of Non-navigational Uses of International Watercourses. A Convention on the Protection and Use of Transboundary Watercourses and Lakes was adopted in 1992 under the auspices of the UN Economic Commission for Europe.[182] The 1992 Convention codifies regional rules concerning the protection and use of watercourses and contributes to the progressive development of the law relating to the conservation and restoration of ecosystems and pollution control, e.g. the polluter pays principle.

The ILC, on 5 August 2008, adopted draft articles for an international framework convention on transboundary aquifers. The Draft Articles emphasise the principle of equitable and reasonable utilisation as well as the obligation not to cause significant harm. It further emphasises the need to cooperate. In 2009 the UN General Assembly adopted a Resolution on the Law of Transboundary Aquifers[183] which endorsed the Draft Articles compiled by the ILC.

Nuclear and conventional weapons and nuclear energy and the environment

The International Atomic Energy Agency (IAEA), created in 1957, is the main international organisation promoting peaceful use of nuclear energy and trying to prevent its military use, including through the use of nuclear weapons. It was created as an

---

[178] See art.2 generally.
[179] See Pts II and IV of the Draft Articles.
[180] For a commentary of these Draft Articles, see Reports of the Commission in II Yearbook of the ILC (1993) and (1994).
[181] Approved by a General Assembly Resolution, GA Res.51/229, 21 May (1997).
[182] 31 I.L.M. (1992) 1312.
[183] A/RES/63/124, 11 December 2009.

independent organisation but it reports to the Security Council and the UN General Assembly.

The 1963 Treaty Banning Nuclear Weapons Tests in Outer Space and Under Water[184] was prompted by the fear of radioactive fall-out. Article 1(1)(b) of the Treaty forbids testing "in any . . . environment if such explosion causes radioactive debris to be present outside the territorial limits of the State under whose jurisdiction or control such explosion is conducted".[185]

Australia in the *Nuclear Tests* cases[186] advanced the argument that there existed a rule of customary international law prohibiting atmospheric nuclear testing and the prohibition was expressed in absolute terms, thus constituting an obligation *erga omnes*.[187] The ICJ declared, in 1996, that the threat or use of nuclear weapons is "contrary to the rules of international law applicable in armed conflict"[188] and there is now a customary obligation upon states to negotiate in good faith for nuclear disarmament.[189]

The 1986 Chernobyl incident highlighted the risks of non-military uses of nuclear energy and the inadequacies of the international nuclear safety regime and brought an almost immediate international response in the form of the Vienna Convention on Early Notification of a Nuclear Accident[190] and the Convention on Assistance in the Case of a Nuclear Accident or Radiological Emergency.[191]

The Convention on Nuclear Safety was opened for signature by the General Conference of the International Atomic Energy Agency (IAEA) in Vienna, 1994.[192] The Convention does not establish an internationally binding regime and was originally intended as a framework Convention introducing a system of accountability whereby states are required to take appropriate measures in order to implement their obligations under the Convention. Responsibility for nuclear safety rests with the state having jurisdiction over a nuclear installation, e.g. a nuclear

---

[184] 480 U.N.T.S. 43.
[185] Discussed further in Ch.7. See also Ch.11, "The Use of Force".
[186] I.C.J. Rep. 1973, Pleadings, at 333–336.
[187] The ICJ, on the basis of France's undertakings to refrain from any further testing, declined to give a ruling on the claims presented—see I.C.J. Rep. 1974 253.
[188] 35 I.L.M. 809 (1996). This was in response to a request from the GA. The ICJ in 1993 was asked by WHO to give an advisory opinion concerning the legality of the use of nuclear weapons in armed conflict on the grounds that the request as submitted by WHO "did not relate to a question within the scope of [the] activities of that Organisation."
[189] Above. See Declaration of President Bedjaoui. See also Ch.11 for further discussions on nuclear weapons.
[190] 25 I.L.M. 1370 (1986).
[191] Above, at 1377.
[192] 33 I.L.M. 1514 (1994).

power plant. Discussions around strengthening the international regulatory regime in respect of nuclear energy were renewed following the 2011 Fukushima Daiichi incident. The IAEA published an Action Plan on Nuclear Safety that same year where it specifically established the need to improve the effectiveness of the international legal framework. In 2015 it approved the Vienna Declaration, which established a series of guiding principles for safety assessment and for national law to take into account the IAEA safety standards.

States are not relieved of their responsibilities to the environment during times of conflict. The 1977 Convention on the Prohibition of Military or Any Other Hostile Use of Environmental Modification Techniques[193] and Protocol 1 of the 1980 Conventional Weapons Treaty[194] prohibits modes of warfare having a severe and long-term effect on the environment and requires respect to be shown for the natural environment and its protection from severe widespread and lasting damage. In 1993, the UN adopted a Convention on the Applicability of the Development, Production, Stockpiling and Use of Chemical Weapons and on their Destruction, the purpose of the Convention being to prohibit and eliminate all chemical weapons[195] and para.39.6(a) of Agenda 21 also highlights this issue by calling on states to adopt measures which address the problem of large-scale destruction of the environment during international armed conflict.[196] The Prohibition of the Use, Stockpiling, Production and Transfer of Anti-personnel Mines and Their Destruction was adopted in Ottawa 1997.

International liability for the injurious consequences of acts not prohibited by international law

Similar to responsibility, but not identical to it, is the possible liability of states for the injurious consequences of acts which are not prohibited by international law. The distinction between responsibility and liability is that the prerequisite to the former is an act breaching international law, while the latter is concerned with harmful effects of an activity which is not, per se, a violation of international law. The ILC has been considering this since 1978 with much of its work focused on such liability for harm to the environment. At the 53rd Session, 2001, the ILC adopted Draft Articles on the Prevention of Transboundary Harm from Hazardous Activities. The UN General Assembly adopted

[193] 16 I.L.M. 88 (1977).
[194] 19 I.L.M. 1529 (1980).
[195] Adopted in Paris, 13 January 1993, 32 I.L.M. 800 (1993).
[196] UN GA Res.47/191, 22 December 1992.

a Resolution in 2006 endorsing the Draft Articles.[197] The activities to which the Draft Articles apply are those "not prohibited by international law which involve a risk of causing significant transboundary harm through their physical consequences."[198] These Draft Articles only apply to instances where there is risk of significant harm arising in the territory of a state other than the state in which the activity is undertaken. The Commentaries to the Draft Articles provide valuable insight into the interpretation of the terms used within the Convention, e.g. the Commentary highlights

> "that the element of 'risk' is concerned with future possibilities and thereby implies some element of assessment or appreciation of risk. The notion of risk is thus to be taken objectively as denoting an appreciation of possible harm resulting from an activity which a properly informed observer had or ought to have had."[199]

States remain reluctant to pursue claims against other states for environmental damage despite there being a solid legal basis for such an action, e.g. the Chernobyl incident in 1986. International conventions that have sought to address this issue have tended to focus on liability for oil pollution.

CONCLUSION

The rules governing responsibility in international law, as evidenced by the above, are complex and evolving. Notwithstanding the complexity in a world of increasing globalisation rules as to the attribution of, and recompense for, legal wrongdoings on the international stage are a necessary element for state accountability and co-existence. International environmental issues are now recognised as requiring international co-operation seeking prevention. The international agenda for the next 15 years has a very specific focus on sustainable development and the responsibility of all states to achieve it.

---

[197] A/RES/61/36, 18 December 2006.
[198] Draft art.1.
[199] Commentaries to the Draft Articles on Prevention of Transboundary Harm from Hazardous Activities, p.385, Report of the International Law Commission on the work of its fifty-third session, Official Records of the General Assembly, 56th session, Supplement No.10 (A/56/10), Ch.V.E.2.

9. HUMAN RIGHTS

"All human rights are universal, indivisible and interdependent and interrelated."[1]

The field of human rights is a prime example of how international law has developed its own specialisms.[2] In the years since the 1948 Universal Declaration of Human Rights there has developed a corpus of norms affording protection to individuals which has led to the growth of procedural apparatus whereby individuals may seek redress against alleged violations of human rights. The substantive norms encompass a wide range of rights recognised at the international level and which have permeated to regional and national levels. Acknowledgement of accountability for violations of human rights has culminated in the establishment of, for example, the International Criminal Court (ICC) and a large number of national human rights commissions.

---

[1] Pt I, para.5 of the Vienna Declaration and Programme of Action, adopted following the UN World Conference on Human Rights, Vienna, June 1993.
[2] For the purpose of this text this chapter focuses only on the basic principles and how they are implemented.

WHAT ARE HUMAN RIGHTS?

Generally human rights are regarded as those fundamental and inalienable rights essential for life as a human being. Human rights were born out of the need to protect the individual from an abuse of state authority. However international law has recognised that the actions of non-state actors may impact, and indeed impact adversely, on the lives of individuals. Notwithstanding their everyday use, human rights have escaped a universally acceptable definition, which presents a problem to international regulation. Of course as the international community has grown so has the debate between universalism and cultural relativism.

Universalism reflects a position by which all human rights must be treated in an equal manner and with the same emphasis independently of the specific circumstances of the State. As the Vienna Declaration resulting from the UN World Conference on Human Rights in June 1993 (The Vienna Conference) states:

> "While the significance of national and regional particularities and various historical, cultural and religious backgrounds must be borne in mind, it is the duty of States, regardless, of their political, economic and cultural systems, to promote and protect all human rights and fundamental freedoms" (Principle 5).[3]

Contrary to that, the relativist theory maintains human rights differ from state to state fashioned by a state's values, cultural and religious traditions. Adherents to the relativist theory frequently criticise international human rights instruments as simply reinforcing accepted traditional views of western concepts and values under the guise of universal rights. At its simplest, the difference between the universality approach and that of the relativist is the emphasis on the individual. The emphasis in universalism is on the individual, whereas relativists place the emphasis on the state. Relativists accept the rights pertaining to individuals but emphasise that individuals are defined in terms of their relations with others and as a part of society. As with all theories, there are varying degrees of observance. At its strictest, cultural relativists maintain human rights are inapplicable to non-western societies whereas others accept human rights are universal but that differences in societies should be reflected within international human rights instruments and their implementation. The debate between universalism and cultural relativism has increased in intensity

---

[3] Vienna Declaration and Programme of Action, A/CONF.157/23, 12 July 1993, art.5, see also R.M.M. Wallace, *International Human Rights, Text and Materials*, 2nd edn (London: Sweet & Maxwell, 2001), p.589.

with the development of human rights and the "chipping away" at state sovereignty and domestic jurisdiction.

An international human rights instrument which highlights sensitivity to cultural diversity is the 1989 UN Convention on the Rights of the Child.[4] Article 20 para.3 identifies Kafala in Islamic law as an alternative care system alongside foster care and adoption, thereby acknowledging that adoption is not recognised within every society. This is the most widely signed and ratified Convention in the international legal system.

Traditionally human rights have been sub-divided into three classifications: first, second and third generation rights. According to this classification "first generation" rights are those which may be characterised as civil and political rights; economic, social and cultural rights, as "second generation"; and group rights as "third generation" or "solidarity" human rights. The distinguishing feature of the latter is the particular focus on collective rights as opposed to the emphasis on individual rights of the first and second generation classifications. The right to development and the right to self-determination are two principal examples of "third generation" rights. However the right to peace and the right to a healthy environment are often also included in this category. The Vienna Conference affirmed, for example, the right to development as a fundamental human right. This was endorsed by the then UN Secretary-General, Boutros Boutros-Ghali, who pledged his personal commitment in his "Agenda for Development",[5] which has since been reaffirmed in the Millennium Development Goals and again in the Sustainable Development Goals agreed in September 2015.[6] The concept of "third generation" rights originated in the 1970s and remains controversial with the primary protagonists being developing states. The definition and enforcement of third generation rights has given rise to considerable academic debate with, for example, a denial of such rights as human rights to their acceptance as a sub-category of human rights.

---

[4] 1989 28 I.L.M. 1448.
[5] Report of the Secretary-General A/48/935, 6 May 1995. In response to the Secretary-General's Agenda, the General Assembly adopted a resolution, which created an ad hoc open-ended working group with the specific purpose of "elaborating further an action-oriented comprehensive agenda for development." A/Res/49/126, 20 January 1995.
[6] The Millennium Development Goals were drawn up in 2000 as a result of world leaders committing their nations to a new global partnership to reduce extreme poverty and setting out a series of time-bound targets, with a deadline of 2015. In September 2015 states met again to revise these goals and adopt a new set of global goals to end poverty, protect the planet, and ensure prosperity for all as part of a new sustainable development agenda. The Sustainable Development Goals, or Global Goals, adopted contain 17 new goals with specific targets for the following 15 years.

The classification of human rights by generations is somewhat artificial as it perpetrates a difference between rights, which should be avoided. For instance, the classification of rights even as political, civil, economic, social and cultural has prompted debate, and a recurring theme has been the normative relationship between the various suggested categories of rights as to whether both categories merit characterisation as "rights proper". One view is that civil and political rights alone merit the term human rights, whereas social, economic and cultural rights are only aspirations. An alternative argument is that social, economic and cultural rights are rights proper as they alone are vehicles of social change, whereas civil and political rights only maintain the status quo. A counter argument to this however is that the exercise of civil and political rights do challenge, and perhaps even bring down, the status quo, for example the protests that led to the collapse of the Berlin Wall in 1989, and of those in Tunisia in December 2010 which precipitated further protests in the region which became known as "the Arab Spring".

A further distinction sometimes made is that civil and political rights only require a state to abstain from doing something whereas economic, social and cultural rights demand positive action. However this assertion is unsustainable as all rights involve responsibility whether it be monetary or require the political will to deliver the rights in question. If a right is a right it remains a right, irrespective of how it is to be realised.

Notwithstanding the foregoing, any distinction between civil and political rights and economic, social and cultural rights is at odds with the position of the Committee on Economic Social and Cultural Rights and in particular General Comment No.2, where it is stated:

> "efforts to promote one set of rights should also take full account of the other. The United Nations agencies involved in the promotion of economic, social and cultural rights should do their utmost to ensure that their activities are fully consistent with the enjoyment of civil and political rights."[7]

In other words civil and political rights and economic, social and cultural rights are indivisible and interdependent. This was reaffirmed by the Vienna Declaration (Principle 5). However, it is true that different conditions prevail and different priorities in respect of human rights are inevitable—inevitable because the world's resources are not perfectly distributed. States have and will have different priorities. Societies at different stages in their

---

[7] 2 February 1990, para.6. See HRI/GEN/1/Rev. 7 (ESC) 12 May 2004.

development will emphasise the realisation of certain rights as being more important than others. Notwithstanding this, certain rights still remain core, inherent in all human beings because of their humanity and transcending all boundaries—geographical, historical, cultural, religious, political and economic. These core rights are those from which no derogation is allowed even in times of public emergency.[8]

However the term "human rights" is defined, the issue of human rights is high on many agendas. There is an increasing plethora of international instruments purporting to guarantee wide-ranging rights and the provisions of these instruments have ramifications for states. In the international arena, overcoming the challenges posed by globalisation for the promotion and protection of human rights was assumed as a general goal for the United Nations in the last decade of the 20th century. Former Secretary-General, Kofi Annan, in his Millennium Report[9] called for the international community to adopt as global challenges the distribution of the benefits of globalisation and the organisation of the opportunities it offers to the service of the individual.[10] This brings on to the international stage non-state actors with a responsibility for the protection of human rights. These actors include international organisations, financial and economic institutions, the private sector and civil society.[11]

A major contributing difficulty, beyond definitional, in the realisation of human rights has been that many states regard human rights as falling within domestic jurisdiction and, therefore, not a matter to be tackled by international law. In other words, treatment of one's own nationals should not, according to those states, be the focus of external review. The international law position is that severe violations of human rights can no longer fall within the exclusive jurisdiction of states. There is an acknowledgment

---

[8] For an example of core rights and the prohibition on derogation see art.4 para.2 of the International Covenant on Civil and Political Rights (see below).

[9] "We the Peoples: The role of the UN In the 21st Century" UN Doc. A/54/2000, 27 March 2000.

[10] Above.

[11] Above, fn.9, p.46 or see Resolution of the Human Rights Commission Globalisation and its Consequences for the Effective Enjoyment of Human Rights 2002/28, 22 April 2002. In 2008 the UN Special Representative of the Secretary-General on Business and Human Rights approved its Framework on Business and Human Rights establishing the state duty to protect human rights from corporate violations, business responsibility to respect human rights and the need for remedies to victims. *Protect, Respect and Remedy: a Framework for Business and Human Rights*, UN Doc. A/HRC/8/5, 7 April 2008. Business responsibilities remain a social expectation of the international community, not a legal obligation under international law. See also the call in 2012 by the UN Committee on the Rights of the Child for contributions to the General Comment on Child Rights and the Business Sector.

that under international human rights law four principal duties are required of states, viz, to respect, protect, promote and fulfil human rights. Respecting rights requires that a state does not breach human rights either through actions or omissions and that the state addresses any harm should a violation occur. The promotion of rights involves raising awareness so as to inform, publicise and create a human rights culture. Fulfilling rights refers to the provision of resources so as to facilitate the realisation of rights, which often may be done progressively. Protection is now frequently interpreted so as to protect individuals within a state's jurisdiction from human rights breaches perpetrated by non-state actors. However for the state to incur responsibility there must be evidence of some act or omission by the state demonstrating failure to exercise due diligence in fulfilling the duty to protect.[12]

Human rights law is now undoubtedly a subject of contemporary international law and the efforts to regulate human rights at an international level has increasingly gained momentum post-Second World War. Human rights are not static, as was highlighted by the European Court of Human Rights in the *Selmouni* judgment regarding the characterisation of treatment which previously would have escaped such a label.[13] The importance of human rights on the political agenda is reflected in state practice, e.g. the Foreign and Commonwealth Office (FCO) of the UK Government has, since 1998, published an annual report detailing the FCO's activities in promoting human rights globally.

Rights of the individual recognised by international law

Pre-1945

Prior to the Second World War, minority groups and foreign nationals were in a privileged position vis-à-vis majority groups and nationals of the host state. They were recognised as deserving at least a minimum standard of treatment, whereas such a guarantee was not afforded to the host state's nationals. Minority groups, i.e. those people of a different race, religion or language from the majority group within a state, came to be guaranteed certain rights, at least on paper, such as equality of treatment, by way of minority treaties, e.g. those concluded in Albania, Finland and Poland. Nevertheless, minority treaties were not renewed after the Second World War. Freedom from slavery has been rec-

---

[12] Inter-American Court of Human Rights, *Velasquez Rodriguez v Honduras*, Series C, Case No. 4 (1988); *Rantsev v Cyprus and Russia*, Application no. 25965/04, Council of Europe: European Court of Human Rights, 7 January 2010, Final 10 May 2010.

[13] *Selmouni v France*, European Court of Human Rights, 25803/94, 28 July 1999.

ognised under customary international law since 1815 and was in international Conventions, such as the 1926 Slavery Convention[14] and the 1956 Supplementary Convention on the Abolition of Slavery, the Slave Trade and Institutions and Practices Similar to Slavery.[15] Trafficking of women and children was similarly prohibited by Convention,[16] but with the exception of such isolated ad hoc interventions, there was no attempt to regulate human rights at an international level until after 1945.

Post-1945

The signing of the United Nations Charter marked the formal realisation that human rights are a matter for international concern. One of the purposes for which the United Nations was founded was "to achieve international co-operation ... in promoting and encouraging respect for human rights and for fundamental freedoms for all without distinction as to race, sex, language or religion."[17] Articles 55 and 56 charge the United Nations and Member States with achieving, inter alia, "universal respect for, and observance of, human rights and fundamental freedoms for all without distinction as to race, sex, language and religion." The language of the Charter is vague and although Members pledged themselves to the realisation of human rights, they were not required to do so within a particular time period. The UN Charter acknowledges certain benefits individuals should enjoy, however it does not confer rights upon them.[18]

UNITED NATIONS

An early resolution of the UN General Assembly was the Universal Declaration of Human Rights,[19] adopted on 10 December 1948. The Declaration spells out a series of political, civil, economic, social and cultural rights. As a resolution it is, of course, not legally binding. It was never intended to be, but rather was to act as a "common standard of achievement for all peoples of all nations."[20] The Declaration has been tacitly accepted by

[14] 60 L.N.T.S. 253.

[15] 266 U.N.T.S. 3.

[16] e.g. International Convention for the Suppression of Traffic in Women and Children, 60 U.N.T.S. 416; the 1947 Protocol 53 U.N.T.S. 13.

[17] art.1(3) of the UN Charter.

[18] See *Sei Fujii v California* (1952) 19 I.L.R. 312; and *Filartiga v Pena-Irala* 630 F (2d) 876 (1980); 19 I.L.M. 966 (1980).

[19] GA Res.217 (III), G.A.O.R., 3rd Session, Pt I, Resolutions, p.71. 10 December is celebrated annually as Human Rights Day.

[20] As stated by Eleanor Roosevelt, the US representative to the General Assembly and Chairman of the United Nations Commission on Human Rights during the drafting of the Declaration.

all Member States and has served as the blueprint for the constitutions of many newly independent states. Arguably many, if not all, the rights and freedoms enunciated in the Charter have become accepted as customary international law.

The rights spelt out in the Universal Declaration are diverse and include, inter alia, the right to life, liberty and security of the person; freedom from slavery or servitude; freedom from torture or cruel, inhuman or degrading treatment or punishment; recognition as a person before the law; the right to nationality; the right to own property; freedom of thought, conscience and religion; the right to participate in government; the right to social security; the right to work and the right to education. The rights and freedoms are to be enjoyed without "distinction of any kind, such as race, color, sex, language, religion, political or other opinion, national or social origin, property, birth or other status"[21] and are only to be curtailed by

> "such limitations as are determined by law solely for the purposes of securing due recognition and respect for the rights and freedoms of others and of meeting the just requirements of morality, public order and the general welfare in a democratic society."[22]

The rights and freedoms set out in the Universal Declaration have been articulated more precisely in two separate international Covenants; the Covenant on Civil and Political Rights 1966 (ICCPR),[23] which entered into force in March 1976; and the Covenant on Economic, Social and Cultural Rights 1966 (ICESCR),[24] which entered into force in January 1976. Moreover, a General Assembly Resolution was adopted in 1985 regarding the human rights of individuals who are not nationals of the country in which they live.[25]

Under the Covenant on Civil and Political Rights, contracting parties undertake "to respect and to ensure to all individuals within its territory and subject to its jurisdiction the rights recognised in the present Covenant".[26] Whereas the Covenant

---

[21] art.2.

[22] art.29(2).

[23] 6 I.L.M. 368 (1967). One right that is not contained is the right to seek asylum. However, states are under an obligation not to return an individual to a country in which his/her life or his/her freedom would be threatened. See art.33 of the UN 1951 Convention Relating to the Status of Refugees. See also, Ch.8, pp.216–218.

[24] 6 I.L.M. 360 (1967).

[25] GA Res.144 (XL), G.A.O.R., 49th Session, Supp.53, p.253; see also Ch.8, p.212.

[26] ICCPR art.2(1).

on Economic, Social and Cultural Rights requires a Contracting Party "to take steps . . . to the maximum of its available resources, with a view to achieving progressively the full realisation of the rights recognised in the present Covenant."[27]

An initial difference between the two Covenants is the timing of the obligations assumed by a state on becoming a contracting party. Under the Covenant on Civil and Political Rights the rights are required to be implemented immediately upon ratification of the Covenant by a state, while the Covenant on Economic, Social and Cultural Rights provides that the realisation of the rights it recognises may be achieved progressively. However, note the view of the Committee on Economic, Social and Cultural Rights in General Comment No.3:

> "The concept of progressive realization constitutes a recognition of the fact that full realization of all economic, social and cultural rights will generally not be able to be achieved in a short period of time. In this sense the obligation differs significantly from that contained in article 2 of the International Covenant on Civil and Political Rights which embodies an immediate obligation to respect and ensure all of the relevant rights. Nevertheless, the fact that realization over time, or in other words progressively, is foreseen under the Covenant should not be misinterpreted as depriving the obligation of all meaningful content. It is on the one hand a necessary flexibility device, reflecting the realities of the real world and the difficulties involved for any country in ensuring full realisation of economic, social and cultural rights. On the other hand, the phrase must be read in the light of the overall objective, indeed the *raison d'être*, of the Covenant, which is to establish clear obligations for States parties in respect of the full realisation of the rights in question. It thus imposes an obligation to move as expeditiously and effectively as possible towards that goal. Moreover, any deliberately retrogressive measures in that regard would require the most careful consideration and would need to be fully justified by reference to the totality of the rights provided for in the Covenant and in the context of the full use of the maximum available resources."[28]

The three UN instruments mentioned above: the Universal Declaration of Human Rights, the Covenant on Civil and Political Rights and the Covenant on Economic, Social and Cultural

---

[27] ICESCR art.2(1).
[28] The nature of States parties' obligations (art.2, para.1): 14/12/90. CESCR General Comment 3.

Rights, constitute what is referred to as the International Bill of Rights. These instruments have been complemented by other Conventions designed to protect specific rights of groups of people, as will be seen below.

Even if these sets of rights appear to have developed independently of each other, human rights remain indivisible. The 1993 Vienna Conference, convened to further the protection and promotion of human rights in the international community,[29] established that "all human rights are universal, indivisible, interdependent and interrelated."

This Conference provided an opportunity for an extensive analysis of the international human rights system and the machinery used to afford such protection. The Vienna Conference culminated in a Declaration on Human Rights and the adoption of an Action Programme,[30] which identified particularly vulnerable groups of individuals as being women, minorities, children, refugees, indigenous people, prisoners and persons with disabilities. The Action Programme emphasised the need for frequent review and appraisal of the measures taken by the international community to ensure the rights of these groups are adequately protected.[31] The Vienna Declaration and the Programme of Action were reviewed in 1998.[32] The conclusion reached was that implementation of human rights throughout the world remains inconsistent. Nonetheless, the end of apartheid in South Africa and the break-up of the Soviet Bloc and the emergence of democratic governments in Central and Eastern Europe symbolise advances made towards "making human rights a reality".[33]

Challenges to human rights realisation have continued to arise particularly in the wake of the terrorist attacks of 11 September 2001, ensuing and ongoing military actions and post-conflict situations. Some are being addressed by way of such instruments as Resolution 1325[34] whereby the UN Security Council unanimously adopted the first resolution specifically to address the impact of war on women, and women's contributions to conflict resolution and sustainable peace. Also the events of 2011 in the Middle East and North Africa, deemed the "Arab Spring", have witnessed

---

[29] The conference marked the 45th anniversary of the Declaration of Human Rights. See 32 I.L.M. 1661 (1993).

[30] Adopted by the Conference on 25 June 1993, by 171 representatives.

[31] For the relevant international instruments protecting the rights set out in the Vienna Declaration, see below, p.260.

[32] Note by the UN Secretary-General, 11 September 1998 on presenting the Report of the UN High Commissioner for Human Rights, to the General Assembly, A/53/372.

[33] Above, para.104.

[34] S.C. Res. 1325 (2000).

calls for the recognition of human rights in a region where it had previously not been high on the political agenda. Unfortunately while many of the uprisings in the region brought the prospect of a possible shift to a more democratic and human rights respecting culture, conflict continues, for example there is civil war in Syria, a lack of state authority in Libya, a military dictatorship in Egypt and continued repression in Bahrain. Only Tunisia seems to be heading towards peaceful democratic reform.

Rights protected by the ICCPR and ICESCR

The rights protected by the Covenant on Civil and Political Rights include the right to life, to liberty and security, to equality before the courts, to peaceful assembly, to marry and found a family and to vote; whereas the freedoms articulated include those of association and, of thought, conscience and religion. The Covenant explicitly prohibits torture, cruel, inhuman or degrading treatment or punishment,[35] slavery, servitude and forced or compulsory labour.

The exercise of a right may be subject to restriction, but these limitations must be provided by law and must be necessary to protect national security, public order, public health or morals, or the rights and freedoms of others, for example art.12(3) which concerns limitations on freedom of movement and residence within a country and the right to leave a country. Derogation is allowed in times of public emergency, e.g. in 1989, the UK intimated a notice of derogation with respect to Northern Ireland and the detention of suspects. At such times parties to the Covenant may take

> "measures derogating from their obligations to the extent strictly required by the exigencies of the situation, provided that such measures are not inconsistent with their obligations under international law and do not involve discrimination solely on the ground of race, colour, sex, language, religion or social origin."

Article 4(2) prohibits derogation in respect of arts 6, 7, 8 (paras 1 and 2), 11, 15, 16 and 18. The Human Rights Committee in General Comment No.29, States of Emergency (art.4) para.6[36]:

> "The fact that some of the provisions of the Covenant have been listed in article 4 (paragraph 2), as not being subject to

[35] This guarantee is supplemented by the UN Convention Against Torture and Other Cruel, Inhuman or Degrading Treatment or Punishment (New York, 4 February 1985), 23 I.L.M. 1027 (1984); for amended text 24 I.L.M. 535 (1985).

[36] CCPR/C/21/Rev.1/Add.11, 31 August 2001.

derogation does not mean that other articles in the Covenant may be subjected to derogations at will, even where a threat to the life of the nation exists. The legal obligation to narrow down all derogations to those strictly required by the exigencies of the situation establishes both for States parties and for the Committee a duty to conduct a careful analysis under each article of the Covenant based on an objective assessment of the actual situation."

However the qualification of a Covenant provision as a non-derogable one does not mean that no limitations or restrictions would ever be justified, e.g. as in art.18(3).[37]

In 1989, the Second Optional Protocol to the Covenant Aiming at the Abolition of the Death Penalty[38] was adopted and entered into force in July 1991 on receipt of the 10th ratification.[39]

The Covenant on Economic, Social and Cultural Rights guarantees those rights originally spelt out in arts 22–27 of the Universal Declaration, for example the right to work, to just and favourable conditions of work and rights to medical and social services and social security. Article 4 of the Covenant provides that these rights are subject "only to such limitations as are determined by law only in so far as this may be compatible with the nature of these rights and solely for the purpose of promoting the general welfare in a democratic society."

Both Covenants recognise the right of all peoples to self-determination and the right to "freely dispose of their natural wealth and resources." These provisions do not appear in the Universal Declaration.

Implementation machinery

The Covenants establish the following implementation mechanisms:

- *Reporting system*—common to both Covenants.

- *Inter-State complaint*—art.41 of the Covenant on Civil and Political Rights.

- *Individual communication to the Committee of Human Rights*—(First) Optional Protocol to the Covenant on Civil and Political Rights.

---

[37] Above, para.7.
[38] For the First Optional Protocol, see below, p.255.
[39] There are currently 75 parties.

Reporting system

A reporting system as a medium for enforcing the rights guaranteed is common to both Covenants. States are required to submit periodic reports to the relevant Committees. Article 40 of the Covenant on Civil and Political Rights requires states to submit periodic reports to the Human Rights Committee on the measures adopted to give effect to the rights recognised by Covenant and on the progress made in the enjoyment of those rights. These reports have to be submitted within one year of the entry into force of the Covenant for the reporting state. Article 40 is the only compulsory supervisory system to which states submit on ratifying the Covenant.

The Human Rights Committee is a body of 18 individuals elected by the contracting parties, but who sit as individuals, not as government representatives. The Committee's task is to study the reports received and transmit a report and "such general comments as it may consider appropriate to the States Parties." Additional information may be requested from the state by the Committee and will be provided either by a state representative who will be present at the Committee's discussions or at a later date to the government concerned.

The reporting system is essentially a means of providing information which may provide the basis for the Committee to issue General Comments on the scope of the obligations contained in the Covenant.[40] These General Comments have concerned, inter alia, freedom of speech, freedom from torture as guaranteed by the Covenant[41] and the interpretation of discrimination for the purposes of the Covenant. Although for the most part non-controversial, the Committee, in the Second General Comment on the right to life as guaranteed by art.6, stated that nuclear weapons, their production, testing, possession and deployment should not only be prohibited but should be "recognised as crimes against humanity", a sentiment not shared, at least, by those states with a nuclear arsenal. General Comments have been of considerable importance in augmenting the jurisprudence evolving in respect of the Covenant and in particular elaborating upon the views of the Committee issued in accordance with the Optional Protocol procedure.

However, the Committee has noted that few states submit reports on time.[42] Most states have submitted reports with delays ranging from a few months to several years. Indeed some states

---

[40] art.40(4).

[41] arts 19 and 7, respectively. As of August 2015 there have been 35 General Comments.

[42] General Comment No. 30: Reporting Obligations of States parties under art.40 of the Covenant: 18/09/2002. CCPR/C/21/Rev.2/Add.12, General Comment No. 30. (General Comments). Guidelines for reporting were issued by the

parties are still in default, despite repeated reminders, thus the Committee has made the following provision:

> "In cases where the Committee has been notified under rule 69, paragraph 1, of these rules of the failure of a State to submit under rule 66, paragraph 3, any report under article 40, paragraph 1 (a) or (b), of the Covenant and has sent the corresponding reminders to the State party, the Committee may, at its discretion, notify the State party through the Secretary-General that it intends, on a date or at a session specified in the notification, to examine in a public session the measures taken by the State party to give effect to the rights recognized in the Covenant, and to proceed by adopting concluding observations."[43]

State parties to the Covenant on Economic, Social and Cultural Rights are also required to submit reports to the specialised Committee on Economic, Social and Cultural Rights (the Committee). The Committee was formally established in 1985 by ECOSOC. It is composed of 18 independent experts in the field of human rights. Its main task is to examine the reports submitted by states in accordance with art.16 of the Covenant. Reports are examined with a view to ensuring that states are adopting suitable measures to implement the rights set out in the Covenant. Originally states reported in "stages" in respect of the rights contained within the Covenant, however as of 1988 this was amended with the effect that states had to report on all rights within the confines of one report. Regrettably many states fail to submit reports, or when submitted they are long overdue.[44] The Committee makes concluding observations in which a state's performance will be praised and/or criticised. The Committee also submits an annual report to the ECOSOC Council. The Committee has also issued 21 General Comments on topics ranging from the nature of states parties' obligations to the rights to water and for all to participate in cultural life.

Inter-state complaint—Article 41, Covenant on Civil and Political Rights

Article 41 is not compulsory for states. Acceptance of this procedure by a state is independent to its ratification of the Covenant.

Committee in General Comment No. 02: Reporting guidelines: 28/07/81. CCPR General Comment No. 2. (General Comments).

[43] Rules of Procedure of the Human Rights Committee, CCPR/C/3/Rev, 11 January 2012, r.70, para.1.

[44] In November 2008, the Committee issued new reporting guidelines which take account of the harmonised guidelines on reporting under international human rights treaties, (HRI/GEN/2/Rev.5).

Article 41 provides for optional inter-state petitions. A state may accept the right of other states to bring before the Human Rights Committee a claim alleging a violation of the Convention. The initiation of the art.41 procedure is dependent upon:

(a) the condition of reciprocity—both states, the one alleging the violation and the alleged offender, must have accepted art.41; and

(b) the exhaustion of local remedies.

Under the art.41 procedure the Human Rights Committee shall make its good offices available to the states, and within 12 months will submit a report indicating the facts and solution reached. In the absence of a solution the Human Rights Committee's report will be confined to the facts accompanied by the submissions of the two parties. In the event of no solution being reached the Committee may, with the prior consent of the states concerned, appoint an ad hoc Conciliation Commission.[45] If the Conciliation Commission is used, but a solution is not achieved, the Conciliation Commission produces a report which is not binding but in which it may indicate "its views on the possibilities of an amicable settlement."[46] Compared to certain regional provisions, which establish judicial mechanisms for redress,[47] art.41 lacks teeth. There is no provision for reference to a judicial body or for the taking of a decision in accordance with judicial procedures. Conciliation remains the primary aim. Article 41 entered into force on 28 March 1979 but has not yet been utilised.

Individual communications to the Human Rights Committee—(First) Optional Protocol to the Covenant on Civil and Political Rights[48]

Under the First Optional Protocol to the Covenant on Civil and Political Rights,[49] the Human Rights Committee is competent to receive and consider communications from individuals who claim to be victims of a violation by a state party to the Covenant, provided the latter is a party to the Optional Protocol.

A communication must:

---

[45] art.42.
[46] art.42(7)(c).
[47] See below other systems of protection of human rights.
[48] 6 I.L.M. 383 (1967); 61 A.J.I.L. 870 (1967). The Optional Protocol entered into force in March 1976 and has been adopted by 114 parties. Neither the UK nor the US has accepted the Optional Protocol.
[49] art.1 of the Covenant; the Committee is also competent under art.5 of the Second Optional Protocol (1989).

- not be anonymous;

- concern an alleged violation of one of the rights provided for in the Covenant;

- not relate to a matter which is under consideration in any other international forum (this provision is designed to prevent the simultaneous consideration of petitions by the Human Rights Committee and, e.g. the European Commission of the Council of Europe); and

- all domestic remedies must have been exhausted, unless the application of such remedies is unreasonably prolonged.[50]

The Optional Protocol makes no provision for reference to a court nor does the Human Rights Committee perform a conciliatory role. The Committee's function is simply to receive applications, examine them and subsequently "forward its views to the State Party concerned and the individual" on whether the Covenant has been breached. It considers applications in private and there are no oral hearings. The Committee's views, which are not binding, are published as annexes to its annual report.[51] The Human Rights Committee has considered applications against a number of states and has developed a body of decisions amounting to quasi-jurisprudence. One of the first cases was against Uruguay, the *Weinberger* case.[52] The following year in the *Lovelace* case,[53] a provision of Canada's Indian Act, denying an Indian woman from returning to her native Indian reserve on the break-up of her marriage to a non-Indian, was held to be in violation of art.27 of the Covenant.

In the *Mauritian Women* case,[54] Mauritian legislation placing Mauritian women married to foreign husbands, but not Mauritian men married to foreign women, at risk of deportation was found to be contrary to arts 2(1), 3 and 26 in relation to arts 17(1) and 23(1) of the Covenant. As for compliance, Uruguay made little consistent effort, whereas Canada and Mauritius amended their "offending" legislation. In an effort to tackle the problem of non-adherence to the Human Rights Committee's views a Special Rapporteur for the Follow up "on views" has been appointed.

---

[50] arts 3 and 5 of the Covenant.
[51] See General Comment No.33 For the Obligations of States Parties under the Optional Protocol to the International Covenant on Civil and Political Rights, CCPR/C/GC/33, 5 November 2008.
[52] 1980 Selected Decisions H.R.C. 57.
[53] 1981 2 Selected Decisions H.R.C. 28.
[54] 1981 1 Selected Decisions H.R.C. 67.

The Economic, Social and Cultural Committee, following protracted consideration, adopted an Optional Protocol to the Covenant on Economic, Social and Cultural Rights on 10 December 2008.[55] The Optional Protocol provides that communications may be submitted by, or on behalf of, individuals or groups of individuals under the jurisdiction of a state party claiming there has been a breach to their rights as protected by the Covenant. The principle of reciprocity and the need to exhaust local remedies remain applicable.

The Human Rights Council

The UN machinery provides for other general implementation mechanisms common to all human rights. The main UN implementation body is the Human Rights Council[56] established in 2006, by General Assembly Resolution 60/251. The Council comprises representatives from 47 Member States, chosen by secret vote by the majority of members of the General Assembly. It depends directly on the Assembly. The first members of the Council were elected in September 2008. The Council was created to overcome some of the problems of its predecessor, the Commission on Human Rights, mainly that of its partiality and potential polarisation. The Commission on Human Rights was made up of 53 state representatives, which on occasion included representatives of states accused of gross human rights violations. These members allegedly made use of their seats on the Commission to avoid international sanction of their government's policies. Council members are elected on the basis of their knowledge, experience, independence, impartiality, personal integrity and objectivity.

The Human Rights Council has a very broad mandate. In general, it fulfils a double function of promoting and protecting human rights. This is done through the promotion of universal respect for human rights and drawing attention to situations in which human rights are violated, including situations of severe and systematic violations, and the promulgation of recommendations. The Council does this through a series of special public procedures, a confidential complaints procedure and a universal periodic review, analysed below. The Human Rights Council has an Advisory Committee which is composed of 18 independent experts. Its mandate is to advise the Council and develop studies and investigations in specific

---

[55] This Optional Protocol entered into force on 5 May 2013, following the receipt of the tenth ratification in February 2013.
[56] The Human Rights Council replaces the Commission on Human Rights which had been established by ECOSOC in 1946.

topics but it does not enjoy the competence to adopt resolutions or decisions. [57]

The special procedures

Thematic and country procedures

Through the thematic and country procedures the Human Rights Council addresses specific country situations where human rights are grossly and systematically being violated or considers thematic issues. These procedures are diverse but they are all public. They can be created with the consent of the state concerned but such consent is not mandatory.

Thematic issues include: enforced or involuntary disappearances; arbitrary detention; the right to education; the right to food; the sale of children, child prostitution and pornography; the situation of human rights and fundamental freedoms of indigenous populations, etc. Country mandates have focused on countries or territories such as Burundi, Cambodia, Haiti, Burma, North Korea, Palestinian Occupied Territories, Somalia and Sudan.

Special procedures involve the appointment of either an individual or a working group. An individual will assume the name of "Special Rapporteur", "Special Representative of the Secretary-General", "Representative of the Secretary-General" or "Independent Expert". Working groups are usually composed of five members, one representing each geographical region. Individuals involved in this procedure have to be independent and impartial. Their mandate normally consists of the examination, monitoring, advice and public reporting on human rights situations in the specific countries or issue in question. They can also carry out country visits.

The complaints procedure

Under this procedure the Human Rights Council considers situations of consistent patterns of gross human rights abuses. This procedure is confidential and relies on the cooperation of the state subject to the claim and on the victim having exhausted all domestic remedies. The claims are studied by two working groups: first by the Working Group on Communications and then by the Working Group on Situations.

This mechanism substitutes the previous individual complaints

[57] The Advisory Committee substitutes the former Sub-Commission on the Promotion and Protection of Human Rights which was the main subsidiary body of the Commission on Human Rights. It was previously known as the Sub-Commission on Prevention of Discrimination and Protection of Minorities. The name change was made in 1999.

procedure of the Commission on Human Rights, established in ECOSOC Resolution 1503 (XLVIII), 27 May 1970. This procedure allowed the Commission on Human Rights to deal with individual communications of human rights violations by considering them as part of a wider pattern of gross violations in one country or region. This procedure was very limited and had been criticised for its lack of efficiency.

Universal Periodic Review

This procedure is distinct to the Human Rights Council, having not been within the mandate of the Commission on Human Rights. It consists of a regular review of the human rights records of all 193 UN Member States. This system is based on the cooperation of those states which report to the Council and indicate the actions they are taking to improve the human rights situation in their countries in order to fulfil their human rights obligations. As well as states, NGOs and national human rights institutions are invited to submit information to be considered during the review.

Ban Ki-moon, the current UN Secretary-General, has described the Universal Periodic Review as having "great potential to promote and protect human rights in the darkest corners of the world."[58] The Human Rights Council completed the first cycle of reviews of all Member States by 2011, and the second cycle is underway, due to be completed in 2016. It was agreed that this second, and subsequent cycles, of the Universal Periodic Review should focus on, inter alia, the implementation of the accepted recommendations and developments in the human rights situation in the state being reviewed.[59]

United Nations High Commissioner on Human Rights

Together with the Human Rights Council, an important body within the United Nations rights protection system is the High Commissioner for Human Rights. This post was created by the General Assembly in 1993 to promote and protect civil, cultural, economic, political and social rights.[60] The first UN High Commissioner for Human Rights was Mr Jose Ayala–Lasso, the Ecuadorian Ambassador to the United Nations at the time. The current Commissioner is Zeid Ra'ad Al Hussein of Jordan who was appointed in 2014. Other previous incumbents of the position

[58] Secretary-General's video message for the opening of the Fourth Session of the Human Rights Council, Geneva, Switzerland, 12 March 2007.
[59] Resolution 16/21 and Decision 17/119 on 25 March 2011. This Resolution and Decision also established that the timetable of the review for the second and subsequent cycles will be four and a half years, instead of four.
[60] A/Res.48/141 adopted 20 December 1993.

were Navanethem Pillay (South Africa), Mary Robinson (Ireland), Louise Arbour (Canada) and Sérgio Viera de Mello (Brazil) who was assassinated in an attack against the United Nations in Iraq in 2003 while serving as the UN Secretary-General's Special Representative in Baghdad. The Office of the High Commissioner for Human Rights provides the personnel, logistical and research assistance to support the Human Rights Council.

OTHER UNITED NATIONS CONVENTIONS GUARANTEEING PARTICULAR HUMAN RIGHTS

A number of International Conventions guaranteeing specific human rights have been concluded under the auspices of the United Nations. Such Conventions include the 1948 Genocide Convention,[61] 1966 Convention on the Elimination of All Forms of Racial Discrimination (CERD),[62] 1973 Convention on the Suppression and Punishment of the Crime of Apartheid,[63] 1979 Convention on the Elimination of All Forms of Discrimination Against Women (CEDAW),[64] 1984 Convention Against Torture and Other Cruel, Inhuman or Degrading Treatment or Punishment (CAT),[65] 1989 Convention on the Rights of the Child (CRC), supplemented by two additional protocols, namely the Optional Protocol to the Convention of the Rights of the Child on the involvement of Children in Armed Conflict[66] and the Optional Protocol to the Convention on the Rights of the Child Concerning the Sale of Children, Child Prostitution and Child Pornography,[67] the 1990 Convention on the Protection of the Rights of All Migrant Workers and Members of Their Families,[68] the 2006 Convention on the Rights of People with Disabilities (CRPD)[69] and the 2006 Convention for the Protection of All Persons from Enforced Disappearance (CED).[70]

Some of these instruments have evolved from years of advocacy from victims of human rights abuses and human rights groups. A long struggle has been that of the rights of women. In 1993 the Vienna Conference confirmed, as a priority, the full and

---

[61] 79 U.N.T.S. 277; see also Chs 4 and 6, above.
[62] 60 U.N.T.S. 195.
[63] 13 I.L.M. 50 (1974).
[64] 19 I.L.M. 33 (1980).
[65] 23 I.L.M. 1027 (1984); 24 I.L.M. 535 (1985).
[66] GA Resolution A/RES/54/263, 25 May 2000 which came into force on 12 February 2002.
[67] GA Resolution A/RES/54/263, 25 May 2000 which came into force on 18 January 2002.
[68] 28 I.L.M. 1448 (1989).
[69] A/RES/61/106, Annex I, 13 December 2006.
[70] Doc.A/61/488, 20 December 2006.

equal participation of women in political, civil, economic, social and cultural life at national, regional and international levels and the eradication of all forms of discrimination on grounds of sex was an important objective.[71] At the same time, a Declaration on the Elimination of Violence against Women was issued.[72] The Fourth UN Conference on Women, held in Beijing in September 1995, looked specifically at areas of particular concern to the advancement of women and adopted a Platform of Action to tackle these issues.[73] The Platform of Action "is an agenda for women's empowerment"[74] and includes actions to eradicate poverty, eliminate violence and inequality in education, promote women's human rights and ensure access to relevant health care.[75] In June 2000, Beijing Plus Five was discussed in a special session of the General Assembly, which concluded with a political declaration, adopted by consensus, confirming the political will to implement the Beijing Declaration and Platform for Action. In July 2010 the UN General Assembly created UN Women by merging four previously distinct parts of the UN system that had individually focused on gender issues.[76] UN Women has identified six focus areas in which to ensure women's participation and empowerment, all of which involve the protection and promotion of women's human rights. The strands are: violence against women; peace and security; leadership and participation; economic empowerment; national planning and budgeting; and the Millennium Development Goals.[77]

Of equal international concern has been, and continues to be, the rights of indigenous peoples. In 2007 the General Assembly adopted the Declaration on the Rights of Indigenous Peoples which sets out their individual and collective rights, including those pertaining to culture, identity, language, health and education.[78]

The monitoring of the human rights treaties which deal with these specific rights is primarily by the submission of reports from contracting parties to the relevant Committee and, for certain

[71] Pt I, para.18 of the Declaration.
[72] A/RES/48/104, 20 December 1993.
[73] A/CONF.177/20, 17 October 1995; 35 I.L.M. 401 (1996).
[74] Ch.1, Mission Statement.
[75] See Ch.IV, paras 45–285, which contain the Strategic Objectives and Actions.
[76] A/RES/64/289, 2 July 2010. The four sections were the Division for the Advancement of Women; the International Research and Training Institute for the Advancement of Women; the Office of the Special Adviser on Gender Issues and Advancement of Women; and United Nations Development Fund for Women (UNIFEM).
[77] Above, fn.6.
[78] A/RES/61/295, 2 October 2007.

conventions, a system of inter-state and individual complaints. Eight human rights conventions have Optional Protocols or other mechanisms allowing for individual complaints or communications to the relevant monitoring treaty body. These are: the ICCPR,[79] CERD,[80] CAT,[81] CEDAW,[82] CRPD,[83] CED,[84] ICESCR[85] and CRC.[86]

The CAT is one of the treaties that provides for inter-state and individual petition, subject to the state concerned accepting the competence of the Committee in this respect. An Optional Protocol to CAT[87] provides a "two-pillar" visiting mechanism to places of detention whereby an expert international visiting body, a Sub-Committee to the UN Committee against Torture, funded by the UN, is competent to conduct periodic visits to all state parties and maintain contact with both the state party and the national visiting body. States ratifying the Optional Protocol must establish or maintain a visiting body, known as National Preventative Mechanisms (NPMs), to visit places of detention.

Of particular note is the procedure contained in the CERD, which provides for an optional system of individual petition whereby an individual, or group of individuals, can lodge a complaint within the Convention (art.14). This can only occur if the alleged offending state has accepted the optional individual complaint procedure. An instance in which the right of individual petition was employed successfully is *Yilmaz-Dogan v Netherlands*.[88] There is a compulsory inter-state complaint procedure in the Convention (art.11), but this has never been utilised.

The Committee on the Elimination of All Forms of Racial Discrimination, a body of 18 independent experts, is central to the enforcement of the Convention. It receives reports from contracting parties and forwards to the General Assembly suggestions and general recommendations as it sees fit. Article 22 of the Convention provides for compulsory reference to the International Court of Justice in the event of any "dispute between two or more States Parties with respect to the interpretation or application of this Convention unless the disputants agree to another mode of

---

[79] Above, fn.48.
[80] As per art.14 of the Convention.
[81] U.N.T.S., vol. 2375, p.237, entered into force 22 June 2006.
[82] U.N.T.S., vol. 2131, p.83, 6 October 1999, entered into force 22 December 2000.
[83] A/61/611, 13 December 2006, entered into force 3 May 2008.
[84] As per art.31 of the Convention.
[85] Above, fn.55.
[86] A/RES/66/138, 19 December 2011, entered into force 14 April 2014.
[87] Above, fn.81.
[88] C.E.R.D. Report, G.A.O.R., 43rd Session, Supp.18, p.59 (1988).

settlement." This represents an interesting attempt at strengthening international enforcement. However, the lodging by states of reservations to this provision undermines its potential.

In 2008, Georgia raised an action against Russia at the ICJ, alleging a breach of the CERD based on Russian actions in the regions of South Ossetia and Abkhazia. In its initial application to the ICJ, Georgia argued that the ICJ enjoyed jurisdictional competence based on, inter alia, art.22 of CERD. In April 2011, however, the Court dismissed the case for lack of jurisdiction, based on procedural reasons.

OTHER HUMAN RIGHTS PROTECTION SYSTEMS

The international protection of human rights does not lie exclusively with the United Nations. Regional instruments include the European Convention on Human Rights and Fundamental Freedoms (ECHR) and the American Convention on Human Rights.[89] Both Conventions have sophisticated enforcement mechanisms, including judicial mechanisms: the European Court of Human Rights and the Inter–American Court of Human Rights respectively. These judicial bodies have spawned extensive jurisprudence on the scope of the rights protected by both conventions. States have concluded other human rights treaties in the framework of each regional system for the protection of specific rights such as the rights of women and protection against torture. Other regional conventions include the Banjul Charter on Human and Peoples Rights[90], which rights can be enforced through the African Court of Human and Peoples' Rights, and the Arab Charter on Human Rights.[91]

Human Rights also feature on the agenda of other bodies, for example the International Red Cross, the Organization for Security and Cooperation in Europe (OSCE) and certain of the specialised agencies of the United Nations, e.g. the International Labour Organisation.

HUMAN RIGHTS AND INTERNATIONAL CRIMINAL TRIBUNALS

Individuals are the holders of human rights, but of course they may also be the perpetrators of human rights violations. The international legal system has moved increasingly towards

---

[89] ECHR–213 U.N.T.S. 221 and ACHR–O.A.S. Treaty Series No. ECOSOC Resolution 1503 (XLVIII).

[90] Adopted by the then Organisation of African Unity (now the African Union), and came into force in 1986.

[91] Adopted in 1994, revised in January 2004 and entered into force on 15 March 2008.

providing mechanisms whereby individuals can be held account-
able. The first international attempt to make individuals responsible for serious crimes committed during war was the Treaty
of Versailles, which provided for the criminal responsibility of
German state officials during the First World War. However it
was not until the end of the Second World War that those responsible for atrocities committed during war could be brought to justice at the Nuremberg and Tokyo trials. Subsequent trials of war
criminals in courts took place in the allies' domestic courts. This
system of ad hoc justice was far from ideal and early in the life of
the UN the establishment of a permanent criminal court to judge
those responsible for the most heinous crimes and the drafting of
a code of international crimes featured high on the agenda. The
Cold War made it impossible for states to agree on the creation of
such a body.

In the 1990s, televised reports of war camps, rape and ethnic
cleansing in what was then Yugoslavia, as well as the horrific
images of the Rwandan genocide, shocked the international
community. This contributed to the creation of two ad hoc
Tribunals by the UN Security Council, under the powers of
Ch.VII of the UN Charter: the International Criminal Tribunal
for the Former Yugoslavia (ICTY), created by UNSC Resolution
827, 25 May 1993,[92] and the International Criminal Tribunal for
Rwanda (ICTR), by UNSC Resolution 955, 8 November 1994.[93]
Both Tribunals have jurisdiction to prosecute those perpetrators
responsible for the most serious crimes.[94] The ICTY has jurisdiction under its Statute to prosecute individuals responsible
for grave breaches of the Geneva Conventions of 1949, violations of the laws or customs of war, genocide and crimes against
humanity. The ICTR has jurisdiction over genocide, crimes
against humanity and violations of art.3 common to the Geneva
Conventions and Protocol II.

Both Tribunals are bound by their respective Statutes, not by
human rights conventions. They should however proceed by
respecting the human rights of both victims and the accused. For
both Tribunals the rules of evidence and procedure reflect international human rights standards, particularly those enshrined
in the International Covenant on Civil and Political Rights,
e.g. art.21(a) which deals with the accused's right to be present at
his or her trial and art.25 which provides the accused with a right

---

[92] S.C.Res 827, UN SCOR, 48th Year, 3217th mtg at 1, reprinted in 32 I.L.M.
1203 (1993).
[93] S.C.Res. 955, UN SCOR, 49th year, 3453d mtg at 1. UN Doc.S/RES/955
(1994).
[94] See Ch.6 for jurisdictional issues.

of appeal.[95] The Statutes also confer sentencing powers on the judges who must make their decisions public along with a reasoned opinion. Convicted persons may be imprisoned but there is no death sentence.

After 20 years of work, both the ICTY and ICTR have wound down their activities. In December 2010, the UN Security Council established the Mechanism for International Criminal Tribunals (MICT)[96] which will finish any remaining work the Tribunals have outstanding once their mandates have been completed.

The ICTY has indicted 161 perpetrators, of which 64 were sentenced for their crimes, including some of those most responsible for war crimes, crimes against humanity and genocide in the Former Yugoslavia. The ICTY has continued in order to conclude the trials of two of the key figures of the war: Radovan Karadžić, the former Bosnian Serb leader, and Radko Mladić, the ex-Bosnian Serb military commander. Karadžić's trial concluded in October 2014 and in March 2016 he was found guilty and sentenced to 40 years' imprisonment. Mladić's trial is ongoing with a judgement not expected until March 2017. No accused remain at large.

The ICTR, which officially closed on 31 December 2015, has indicted 93 individuals for genocide and other serious violations of international humanitarian law. Nine suspects still remain at large, but these cases have been transferred to Rwandan or MICT jurisdiction. This is in line with the completion strategies of both Tribunals which has seen the ICTY and ICTR transferring cases to relevant national jurisdictions, which include Bosnia and Herzegovina, Croatia, Serbia and Rwanda.

A third ad hoc international criminal court was established by the UN with the creation of a Special Court for Sierra Leone. This Special Court is distinct from the ICTY and the ICTR in that it is a treaty-based Court established by agreement between the UN and Sierra Leone. The Special Court is composed of international judges and Sierra Leonean judges, prosecutors and staff. It is therefore a "hybrid court". The subject matter of the Special Court's jurisdiction includes certain crimes recognised under Sierra Leone's domestic law, but unlike the ICTY and the ICTR the Special Court does not have jurisdiction over the crime of genocide. This omission was because there was no evidence the mass killing in Sierra Leone was perpetrated against

---

[95] Rules and Procedure and Evidence, adopted pursuant to art.15 of the Statute of the Tribunal, which came into force, 14 March 1994; 33 I.L.M. 484 (1994). They have been amended on several occasions since, e.g. see 35 I.L.M. 1342 (1996).

[96] Security Council Resolution 1966 (2010), 22 December 2010, S/RES/ 1966(2010).

an identifiable national, ethnic, racial or religious group with the intention of annihilation of the group as required by the 1948 Genocide Convention. The agreement between Sierra Leone and the UN, which was signed in January 2002, provided the Court jurisdiction to prosecute persons for crimes committed in the territory of Sierra Leone since 30 November 1996.[97] Thirteen people from all sides involved in the conflict have been indicted by the Prosecutor of the Special Court. The Special Court had intended to have completed its work by 2007, but this deadline proved unrealistic. In December 2011 the Government of Sierra Leone, in agreement with the UN, established the Residual Special Court[98] to continue any outstanding work of the Special Tribunal after the latter ceased operation in 2013.

On 13 May 2002, the UN General Assembly adopted a Resolution approving the proposal of an agreement between the UN and Cambodia on the prosecutions of crimes committed between 1975 and 1979 in Cambodia.[99] The Cambodian Parliament ratified the agreement on 4 October 2004. The resulting tribunal, the Extraordinary Chambers in the Courts of Cambodia for the Prosecution of Crimes Committed during the Period of Democratic Kampuchea (ECCC), is part of the Cambodian judiciary system and is composed of Cambodian and foreign legal experts, with Cambodians in the majority. The ECCC can only prosecute two categories of alleged perpetrators for suspected crimes committed between 17 April 1975 and 6 January 1979, namely senior leaders of the then Democratic Kampuchea, and those believed to be most responsible for grave violations of Cambodian national and international law. There have been four cases brought before the ECCC. In August 2014 the ECCC found Nuon Chea, who had been Deputy Secretary of the Communist Party of Kampuchea, and Khieu Samphan, who had held several party roles, guilty of crimes against humanity. Both men were sentenced to life imprisonment.

Hybrid tribunals or similar mechanisms have been used in other scenarios, such as the East Timor Special Panels for Serious Crimes, established by the UN Transitional Administration in June 2000, to deal with crimes against humanity, war crimes and other atrocities; and the special panels created by the UN Mission

---

[97] The Statute of the Special Court was annexed to the agreement and on 7 March 2002, Sierra Leone enacted the Special Court Agreement 2002, Ratification Act, 2002 to implement the Statute.

[98] The Residual Special Court was established pursuant to an agreement between the United Nations and the Government of Sierra Leone on 11 August 2010. It was ratified by Parliament on 15 December 2011 and signed into law on 1 February 2012.

[99] A/Res./57/228B.

in Kosovo in 2000 and Bosnia's War Crimes Chambers, also composed of national and international judges, prosecutors and other staff.

In 2013 the Extraordinary African Chambers were constituted within the Senegalese court system, in agreement with the African Union, for the purpose of prosecuting the former Chadian president Hissène Habré. He was charged with the crimes of genocide, crimes against humanity, war crimes and torture committed during his rule, between 7 June 1982, and 1 December 1990. The Extraordinary African Chambers were created following the ruling of the ICJ in the case *Questions relating to the obligation to prosecute or extradite (Belgium v Senegal)*, 20 July 2012,[100] which demanded Senegal prosecute or extradite Habré. There are two chambers; the Trial Chamber and the Appeals Chamber which both have two Senegalese judges and a president from another African Union Member State. Habré was convicted of crimes against humanity, and torture and rape on 30 May 2016.

The Special Tribunal of Lebanon is also an internationalised Tribunal, however its jurisdictional remit is more restricted to the investigation and prosecution of just one event: the assassination of former Lebanese Prime Minister Rafiq Hariri and 22 other people travelling with him in February 2005.

Notwithstanding certain criticisms regarding, for example, inadequate funding arrangements and a backlog of cases accumulated by such Tribunals, their establishment was undoubtedly a significant step towards the creation of a permanent international criminal tribunal. The operation of such ad hoc tribunals endorsed a willingness among UN Security Council members to co-operate in apprehending and prosecuting alleged perpetrators of international crime.

A permanent International Criminal Court

In 1937, the League of Nations initiated a Convention for the Creation of an International Criminal Court; however, this never came to fruition. The experience of both the ICTY and the ICTR refreshed calls for the creation of a permanent criminal court.[101] The UN General Assembly adopted a resolution on 16

---

[100] ICJ Report 2012, p.422.
[101] See the Draft Statute for an International Criminal Court, in the Report of the International Law Commission on its Forty-sixth Session, UN G.A.O.R., 49th Sess., Supp.No.10 at 43, UN Doc.A/49/10 (1994). See 33 I.L.M. 253 (1994). The ILC had also been asked in the context of its work on the Draft Code of Crimes Against the Peace and Security of Mankind to address the question of a permanent International Criminal Court. GA Res.48/31 UN G.A.O.R., 48th Sess., Supp.No.49, at 328, UN Doc.A/48/49 (1993).

January 1997, which confirmed its commitment to establish an International Criminal Court (the ICC). The General Assembly renewed the mandate of the Preparatory Committee[102] and decided to convene a diplomatic conference of plenipotentiaries in Italy in 1998 with the task of finalising and adopting a Convention on the establishment of a permanent International Criminal Court.[103]

The Convention,[104] once finalised and opened for signature, received the requisite number of ratifications for entry into force on 1 July 2002.[105] The establishment of the Court is regarded as making good a deficiency in the international legal system. It also removes the need for further ad hoc tribunals such as those discussed above and guards against what has been referred to as "tribunal fatigue". Delays are characteristic of any ad hoc system, but expeditious procedures are essential in criminal law. Otherwise memories fade and, as a consequence, evidence is difficult to obtain.

The ICC is situated in The Hague, the Netherlands, and is made up of 18 judges elected for a 9-year term. The jurisdiction of the Court is set out in art.5.1 and covers genocide, crimes against humanity, war crimes and crimes of aggression. The various terms are defined in art.6 (genocide), art.7 (crimes against humanity), and art.8 (war crimes) and crimes of aggression.[106] The Court has jurisdiction in respect of crimes which occur after 1 July 2002. As of May 2016, 26 cases in 10 situations have been brought before the Court. The situations are in the Democratic Republic of Congo; Darfur, Sudan; Uganda; two in the Central African Republic; Libya; Kenya; Côte d'Ivoire; Mali; and Georgia. There are also currently preliminary examinations taking place in relation to situations in Afghanistan, Colombia, Nigeria, Guinea, Honduras, Iraq, Ukraine and Palestine.

The first case to be heard in the Court was that of Thomas Lubanga Dyilo, the former leader of the Congolese militia, Union of Congolese Patriots (UPC), who was charged with the recruitment of child soldiers, under the age of 15 to actively partici-

---

[102] The Preparatory Committee was established by GA Res.50/46, 11 December 1995 with the specific task of preparing the text of an international Convention for a permanent International Criminal Court.

[103] 51st session, UN GA Res.A/Res/51/207, 16 January 1997.

[104] The Statute of the International Criminal Court General Assembly Resolution ICC-ASP/2/Res.3, 12 September 2003.

[105] The US is not a state party to the ICC, however since November 2009, it has participated in an observer capacity in meetings of the ICC Assembly of States Parties.

[106] See further, Ch.6, "Jurisdiction", at p.137, in particular with reference to the 2010 Rome Statute Review Conference and the subsequent Kampala Declaration.

pate in combat. On 14 March 2012 the Court unanimously found Lubanga guilty. He was subsequently sentenced to 14 years' imprisonment.

The establishment of the Court is evidence that the international community recognises that there is a role for a permanent international legal regime to prosecute the most egregious crimes committed by individuals. To be effective, this demands the recognition that certain crimes are of international concern and arguably are more effectively dealt within an international forum. However, as highlighted, "No provision . . . relating to individual criminal responsibility shall affect the responsibility of States under international law."[107]

CONCLUSION

Human rights in the 21st century must be seen in the international global context. The picture is not palatable and certainly does not suggest a world which universally respects, protects, promotes and fulfils human rights. The task confronting the international community is to work together to achieve a world in which there is mutual respect for all individuals as individuals, an absence of arbitrary discrimination and protection from human rights violations. International human rights instruments in themselves will not prove the ultimate panacea but hopefully, in time, their principles will permeate all strata of society and provide, at the very least, a minimum standard which will be the universal norm rather than the exception.

---

[107] art.25.4 of the Statute.

10. THE LAW OF TREATIES

Treaties regulate relations between international persons, and the expansion in the content of international law is reflected in the diversity of subject matter now regulated by treaty. The importance of treaties has been acknowledged in the context of the sources of international law.

Treaty law is, for the most part, non-controversial. As the international law of contract, it is essentially "lawyers' law". What is a treaty? How is a treaty concluded? How is a treaty to be interpreted?

The law relating to these questions has to be considered against the backcloth of the 1969 Vienna Convention on the Law of Treaties.[1] The 1969 Convention, which entered into force in January 1980, was the culmination of some 20 years of work by the International Law Commission (ILC). The 1969 Convention represents a mixture of codification of existing customary international law[2] and progressive development.[3]

The 1969 Convention does not have retroactive effect. However the 1969 Convention spells out established customary rules, and

---

[1] 8 I.L.M. 679 (1969); A.J.I.L. 875 (1969).
[2] See *Fisheries Jurisdiction* case, I.C.J. Rep. 1973 p.3 at 14.
[3] For example, art.53 which renders a treaty void if it conflicts with a peremptory norm of general international law.

the rules therein may be applied to agreements which pre-date it, for example as in the League of Nations Mandate in the *Namibia (South West Africa)* case,[4] and in the *Beagle Channel Arbitration*,[5] where the Convention's rules were applied to the 1881 Argentina/ Chile Treaty.[6]

The 1969 Convention is limited to treaties made between or among states. A Convention on the Law of Treaties between States and International Organisations or between International Organisations was adopted on 21 March 1986.[7] The 1986 Convention's provisions closely parallel those of the 1969 Convention, but has yet to enter into force, however, it is generally accepted as reflecting the applicable law on the matter.

DEFINITION OF A TREATY

"Treaty" is the generic term which covers convention, agreement, arrangement, protocol, and exchange of notes.[8] International law does not distinguish between agreements identified as treaties and other agreements. The name accorded to an agreement is not important and has no legal effect.[9]

A treaty, for the purposes of the 1969 Convention, is "an international agreement concluded between States in written form and governed by international law".[10]

The 1969 Convention is concerned only with written agreements. But can states enter into oral agreements?

It cannot be stated unequivocally that an oral agreement has no legal significance and oral statements have been held to have binding effect.

In 1919, the Danish Government informed the Norwegian Government, through the Danish representative in Norway,

---

[4] I.C.J. Rep. 1971 p.16 at 47.

[5] 17 I.L.M. 632 at 645 (1978).

[6] See also U.S. Department of State letter to the U.S. President (1971) 5 Exec. Doc. L92nd Cong. 1st Sess. 1.

[7] Misc. 11 (1987) Cm.244; 25 I.L.M. 543 (1986).

[8] For definitions of key terms used in the United Nations Treaty Collection, including "treaty", "convention", "charter", etc, see *http://treaties.un.org/Pages/ Overview.aspx?path=overview/definition/page1_en.xml* [accessed 26 May 2016]

[9] Within a national system "treaty" may have a specialised meaning, e.g. in the US.

[10] art.2(1)(a). Note the comments of the I.C.J. in the *Maritime Delimitations and Territorial Questions case (Qatar v Bahrain)* 1994 I.C.J. Rep. p.112 with respect to what may constitute an international agreement at pp.121–122. Particular caution should be taken in respect of agreements termed memorandum of understanding. A memorandum of understanding is a less formal agreement see the International Law Commission Yearbook 188 para.2. For further discussion of Memorandum of Understanding see A. Aust, *Modern Treaty Law and Practice*, 2nd edn (Cambridge: Cambridge University Press, 2007), pp.26–46.

that Denmark would not raise any objection at the Paris Peace Conference to the Norwegian claim over Spitzbergen, if Norway would not challenge Danish claims of sovereignty over Greenland. The then Norwegian Foreign Minister, M. Ihlen, subsequently reported to his Danish counterpart "the Norwegian Government would not make any difficulty." Denmark argued before the Permanent Court of International Justice in the *Legal Status of Eastern Greenland*[11] that Norway had, by the "Ihlen Declaration", recognised Danish sovereignty. The Court denied the "Ihlen Declaration" constituted recognition of Danish sovereignty, but nevertheless maintained that Norway had assumed a legally binding obligation to refrain from contesting Danish sovereignty over Greenland. The Court did not characterise the "Ihlen Declaration" as an oral agreement, nor did it define the circumstances, if any, in which a unilateral statement could be binding. The Court rather emphasised the contemporaneous acceptance by Denmark of the Norwegian claims over Spitzbergen.

The International Court of Justice (ICJ) was confronted with the legal nature of unilateral declarations in the *Nuclear Tests* cases,[12] in which Australia and New Zealand sought a decision from the Court against France, that the latter's testing of nuclear weapons in the atmosphere of the South Pacific was contrary to international law. The Court found that the series of public statements made by France announcing restrain from further testing was sufficient to commit France and negate Australian and New Zealand objections.

The legal consequences flowing from statements were discussed by the ICJ in the *Case Concerning the Application of the Convention on the Prevention and Punishment of the Crime of Genocide (Bosnia and Herzegovina v Serbia and Montenegro)*.[13] The ICJ concluded that the statement in question, which had been made by the new Serbian authorities relating to the Srebrenica genocide, was of a political nature and it was clearly not intended to have legal effect. Accordingly the Court maintained that the statement did not constitute an admission of Serbian responsibility for the massacres in Srebrenica.[14]

---

[11] P.C.I.J. Rep. ser.A/B, No.53 (1933).
[12] I.C.J. Rep. 1974 253, 457. See also comments of the ICJ in the *Frontier Dispute case (Burkina Faso v Mali)* I.C.J. Rep. 1986, 554, in which the Court stated that unilateral statements could only bind a state where it was apparent the state intended to be bound, i.e. only in exceptional circumstances.
[13] Judgment of 27 February 2007.
[14] Above, at para.378 p.135 see however dissenting opinion of Judge Al-Khasawneh at p.16 paras 57–8. For further discussion on the case see Ch.8, "State Responsibility".

The capability of states to create legal obligations through unilateral declarations was addressed by the ILC culminating in the adoption of 10 Guiding Principles in 2006.[15] The Principles acknowledge that declarations publicly made, orally or in writing, and expressing the will to be bound may create legal obligations. When these conditions are met, the binding character of such declarations is based on good faith. States concerned may then take these declarations into consideration and rely on them, and are entitled to expect that such obligations be respected. The legal effect of such declarations will depend on the factual circumstances in which they are made and will only bind the state internationally if made by an authority with the requisite power.

Not all written agreements necessarily establish binding relations. The Charter of Paris for a New Europe, adopted at the Conference on Security and Co-operation in Europe,[16] is such an instance and is soft law.[17]

Article 102 of the UN Charter provides for the registration of treaties.[18] Every treaty and international agreement entered into by any member state of the UN should be registered with the Secretariat of the UN. Only treaties or international agreements so registered can be invoked before any organ of the UN. Registration provides tangible evidence that the agreement is to be regarded as a treaty and that is the intention of the parties concerned. The Charter of Paris for a New Europe[19] provides that the Charter is "not eligible for registration under art.102 of the Charter of the United Nations". Nonetheless, non-registration or late registration does not affect the binding nature of the agreement between the parties concerned.[20]

If the 1969 Vienna Convention is to apply to an international agreement, the agreement must be in written form, reflect the intention of the parties to be bound and must be governed by international law.[21]

---

[15] Text adopted by the ILC at its 58th session in 2006 and submitted to the General Assembly as a part of the Commission's report covering the work of that session (A/61/10). For the report see the Yearbook of the International Law Commission 2006, Vol.11, Pt 2.

[16] 30 I.L.M. 190 (1991).

[17] See Ch.2, "Sources", pp.31–32.

[18] UN Treaties Series (UNTS) contains over 158,000 treaties and related subsequent actions.

[19] Above, fn.16.

[20] Above, fn.10, at 122.

[21] Treaties may be employed as a vehicle for the expression of soft law.

TREATY-MAKING COMPETENCE

National law

States enjoy discretion as to the allocation of treaty-making competences and the constitutional arrangements for the ratification of treaties. These arrangements vary widely. However a state may not plead a breach of its constitutional provisions relating to treaty-making competence so as to invalidate an agreement, unless such a breach was manifest and "objectively evident to any State conducting itself in the matter in accordance with normal practice and in good faith."[22]

International law

A state representative may conclude a treaty on behalf of a state if (a) he or she possesses full powers or (b) if it can be deduced he or she enjoys full powers from the practice of the states concerned or from other circumstances.

"Full powers" refers to a document

> "emanating from the competent authority of a State designating a person or persons, to represent the State for negotiating, adopting or authenticating the text of a treaty, for expressing the consent of the State to be bound by a treaty, or for accomplishing any other act with respect to a treaty."[23]

Heads of state, heads of government and foreign affairs ministers are regarded as possessing, by virtue of their office, "full powers".[24]

An act relating to the conclusion of a treaty performed by a person who cannot be considered as enjoying "full powers" and thereby authorised to represent a state for that purpose is without legal effect, unless afterwards confirmed by that state.[25]

Adoption and confirmation of the text of a treaty

The text of a treaty may be adopted by the consent of all states participating in the drafting, by the majority vote of two-thirds of states present and voting, or by a different procedure if the two-thirds majority so agree.[26]

---

[22] art.46.
[23] art.2(1)(c).
[24] In *Qatar v Bahrain*, above, fn.10 at 121–122, the Court denied the claim of Bahrain's Foreign Minister that he had no authority under Bahrain's constitution to conclude a treaty as the existence of a valid treaty had to be determined objectively.
[25] art.8.
[26] art.9.

Expression of consent

A state may indicate its consent to be bound by a treaty in a variety of ways, e.g. signature, signature *ad referendum*, ratification and accession.

Simple signature may be sufficient to bind parties, but frequently signature *ad referendum* is employed, that is signature subject to later ratification. Although lacking legal effect, *ad referendum* implies political approval and a moral obligation to seek ratification. Ratification in international law refers to the subsequent formal confirmation (subsequent to signature) by a state that it is bound by a treaty. Ratification is employed most frequently by those states (e.g. the US) which are required to initiate some parliamentary process to gain approval for the state being bound by the international agreement in question. Between signature and ratification, a state is under an obligation to refrain from acts which would defeat the object and purpose of the treaty.[27]

Accession

A state may, by acceding to a treaty, express its consent to be bound by the terms of the treaty, that is, a non-signatory state may subsequently become a party under a procedure provided by the treaty concerned. The term "adhesion" may also be encountered. Adhesion is distinct from accession in that it refers to a state's acceptance of either only certain aspects of the treaty or certain principles contained within it.

Reservations

Treaties may be likened to legislation, but unlike national law, which generally applies to all, international law allows a state to become a party to a treaty while opting out from the application of certain provisions.

Article 2(1)(d) of the Vienna Convention defines a reservation as a

> "unilateral statement, however phrased or named, made by a State, when signing, ratifying, accepting, approving or

---

[27] art.18(a). See for example the US statement that it did not intend to become party to the ICC Statute: the US "has no legal obligations arising from its signature on 31 December 2000. The United States requests that its intention not to become a party be reflected in the depositary's status lists relating to this treaty" (US Dept. of State Press Statement, 6 May 2002). See also *R v O* (Court of Appeal) (Criminal Division) 2 September 2008 *Times Law Reports* 2 October 2008 where it was held that the UK was obliged by art.18 of the Vienna Convention on the Law of Treaties to refrain from acts which would defeat the purpose of the 2005 Convention on Action against Trafficking in Human Beings.

acceding to a treaty, whereby it purports to exclude or to modify the legal effect of certain provisions of the treaty in their application to that State."

A reservation is distinct from an "interpretative declaration" in that the latter is simply a statement by a party to the treaty as to the position it adopts concerning some aspect of the treaty. However, only a reservation allows a state to derogate from an application of the treaty.[28]

Reservations only apply in respect of multilateral treaties. They cannot apply to bilateral treaties, as the rejection of a proposed provision is in effect the refusal of an offer made which then demands re-negotiation.[29]

Traditionally, it was maintained that a reservation could only be inserted if all contracting parties to the treaty consented. In the absence of unanimous agreement, the reservation was null and void. However, with the increase in the number of states and the simultaneous growth in the complexity of treaty subject matter, obtaining the unanimous consent of states became increasingly difficult. What was required, if states were not to reject treaties in whole if they contained a particular provision to which states took exception, was a more flexible approach to reservations. The ICJ's *Reservations to the Convention on Genocide* Advisory Opinion [30] heralded the necessary change in approach.

The ICJ expressed the view that a state making a reservation to which one or more but not all parties to the Convention had raised an objection could be regarded as a party to the Convention *provided* the reservation was compatible with the object and purpose of the Convention. As to the effect of a reservation between the reserving state and (i) those objecting and (ii) those accepting the reservation, the Court's response was

---

[28] For further discussion, see D. McRae 49 B.Y.I.L. 155 (1978) and the case of *Belilos v Switzerland* E.C.H.R., Series A, No.132, Judgment of 20 April 1988. See also *Loizidou v Turkey* (Preliminary Objections) E.C.H.R. Series A Number 301 (1995). See also the general comments of the UN Human Rights Committee on the effect of reservations made to the International Covenant on Civil and Political Rights and the Optional Protocols, General Comment 24/52, 2 November 1994, 34 I.L.M. 1995, 839, 840; International Law Commission—Preliminary Conclusions on Reservations to Normative Multi-lateral Treaties including Human Rights Treaties, 1997, Report of the I.L.C. on its 49th Session, A/52/10, pp.126–7.

[29] For distinction between bilateral and multilateral see Ch.2 p.22. Also note there the terms "bipartite" and "multipartite" which are technically correct but seldom used.

[30] I.C.J. Rep. 1951 15. Note the Genocide Convention does not contain a reservation clause.

"(a) that if a party to the Convention objects to a reservation which it considers to be incompatible with the object and purpose of the Convention, it can in fact consider that the reserving State is not a party to the Convention;

(b) that if, on the other hand, a party accepts the reservation as being compatible with the object and purpose of the Convention, it can in fact consider that the reserving State is a party to the Convention."[31]

The Court's opinion introduced the test of compatibility. This test, which is applied by states themselves, is a matter of subjective interpretation. The Court's opinion marked a sharp contrast to the previous approach, namely one of unity and a minimising of deviance from treaty provisions. This opinion opened up the possibility of different legal relationships existing between parties to the same agreement.

The 1969 Vienna Convention allows reservations unless

"(a) the reservation is prohibited by treaty;" for example Art.64 of the European Convention on Human Rights prohibits "reservations of a general character";[32]

"(b) the treaty provides that only specified reservations, which do not include the reservation in question, may be made"; or

"(c) in cases not falling under sub-paragraphs (a) and (b), the reservation is incompatible with the object and purpose of the treaty."[33]

Incompatibility with the object and purpose of the treaty can relate either to substantive provisions of the treaty, or to the nature and spirit of the treaty. For a case involving the "object and purpose" issue, see the *Restrictions to the Death Penalty* case.[34] A convention may provide a mechanism for deciding whether

[31] Above, at 29–30.
[32] See *Belilos v Switzerland*, above, fn.28 in which the Swiss reservation was declared invalid because, inter alia, it was "couched in terms that are too vague or broad for it to be possible to determine their exact scope or meaning", thus it was a "reservation of a general character".
[33] art.19. In the *Effect of Reservations Case*, 22 I.L.M. (1983), it was stated that art.75 of the American Convention on Human Rights 1969 had impliedly incorporated art.19(c) and thus allowed reservations which were not "incompatible with the object and purpose of the treaty." art.75 provides the American Convention on Human Rights "shall be subject to reservations only in conformity with" the Vienna Convention on the Law of Treaties.
[34] 23 I.L.M. 320 (1983).

a provision is compatible or not, e.g. the UN Convention on the Elimination of all Forms of Racial Discrimination 1966 deems a reservation to be incompatible if at least two-thirds of Contracting Parties object.[35]

Acceptance of and objection to reservations

A reservation which is expressly authorised by a treaty does not demand the subsequent approval of other Contracting Parties unless required by the treaty.

If, however, it is apparent from the limited number of states concerned and from the object and purpose of the treaty "the application of the treaty in its entirety between all the parties is an essential condition of the consent of each one to be bound by the treaty", then any reservation must be accepted by all the parties.

In respect of a treaty which is the constituent instrument of an international organisation, a reservation, unless it is other-wise provided, must be accepted by the competent organ of the relevant organisation.

The general rules to be followed in other cases are

"(a) acceptance by another contracting State of a reservation constitutes the reserving State a party to the treaty in rela-tion to that other State if or when the treaty is in force for those States;

(b) an objection by another contracting State to a reserva-tion does not preclude the entry into force of the treaty as between the objecting and reserving States unless a contrary intention is definitely expressed by the objecting State;

(c) an act expressing a State's consent to be bound by the treaty and containing a reservation is effective as soon as at least one other contracting State has accepted the reservation."[36]

If a state does not object to a reservation, (a) within 12 months of having been informed of the reservation, or (b) within 12 months of having expressed consent to be bound by the treaty—depend-ing on which is later—that state will be deemed to have expressed its consent to be bound by the treaty.[37]

---

[35] art.20 of the International Convention on the Elimination of All Forms of Racial Discrimination 1966.
[36] art.20(4).
[37] art.20(5).

Legal effects of reservations and of objections to reservations

The effect of a reservation established with regard to another party is that it

> "(a)　modifies for the reserving State in its relations with that other party the provisions of the treaty to which the reservation relates to the extent of the reservation; and
>
> (b)　modifies those provisions to the same extent for that other party in its relations with the reserving State."[38]

If a state objects to a reservation, but does not oppose the entry into force of the treaty between itself and the reserving state, the provisions to which the reservation relates do not apply between the two states to the extent of the reservation. The provisions of the treaty for the other Contracting Parties are not modified by the reservation.[39] The effect of art.21(3) is illustrated by the Arbitration Tribunal's decision in the *English Channel Arbitration*[40]

> "the combined effect of the French reservations and their rejection by the United Kingdom is neither to render Art.6 [that is, art.6 of the 1958 Geneva Convention on the Continental Shelf] inapplicable *in toto*, as the French Republic contends, nor to render it applicable *in toto*, as the United Kingdom primarily contends. It is to render the Article inapplicable as between the two countries to the extent of the reservations."[41]

The effect in practice is that a multilateral agreement becomes fragmented. States will be parties to the same agreement, but in effect one agreement will exist between some Contracting Parties while another agreement will exist between other parties. In other words, under the umbrella of one multilateral convention, several separate agreements may emerge. The overall purpose of the reservation system is to induce as many states as possible to adhere to a multilateral agreement.

A reservation and an objection to a reservation must be expressed in writing but may be withdrawn at any time, unless otherwise provided for in the treaty. The withdrawal of a

---

[38] e.g. Libya's reservation to the Vienna Convention on Diplomatic Relations, whereby the diplomatic bag could be intercepted in suspicious circumstances, would by the operation of the principle of reciprocity have entitled the UK to exercise the same right; see Libyan People's Bureau Incident, above Ch.6, pp.148–149.

[39] art.21(3).

[40] 18 I.L.M. 397 (1979).

[41] Above, at 341.

reservation becomes operative only when the state(s) concerned receive notice of the withdrawal. Similarly, the withdrawal of an objection to a reservation only has effect when received by the reserving state.[42] An express acceptance of a reservation must also be formulated in writing.

The ILC adopted a *Guide to the Practice on Reservations to Treaties* in 2011, which deals with the formulation and withdrawal of acceptances and objections as well as the procedure for acceptance of reservations together with commentaries. This Guide is supplementary to the provisions on reservations contained in the 1969 Vienna Convention.[43]

Entry into force

A treaty enters into force in such a manner and upon such a date as it may provide, or as the negotiating states may agree.[44] A multilateral treaty normally comes into force following receipt of a stipulated number of ratifications or accessions, e.g. the 1969 Vienna Convention provided for its own entry into force "on the thirtieth day following the date of deposit of the thirty-fifth instrument of ratification or accession."[45] Once the required number of ratifications have been received, a treaty will normally provide how soon after receipt of consent an agreement enters into force at the international level for the states concerned. For example, the 1982 Law of the Sea Convention entered into force one year after the 60th ratification, namely on 16 November 1994; the 1998 Rome Statute, establishing the International Criminal Court, entered into force on 1 July 2002, 60 days after the 60th state became a party to the Statute; and the 2006 International Convention for the Protection of All Persons from Enforced Disappearance entered into force on 23 December 2010, 30 days after the 20th state ratification or accession.

OBSERVANCE AND APPLICATION OF TREATIES[46]

States are charged with performing and fulfilling their treaty obligations, which are binding in good faith—*pacta sunt servanda* is the maxim which expresses this basic canon of treaty observance. As a rule, treaties do not have retroactive effect. If they are to have such effect, this will be expressly stated.

---

[42] See *Democratic Republic of the Congo v Rwanda* I.C.J. Rep. 2006, paras 41-42.

[43] For text of Guidelines see International Law Commission's Annual Reports, G.A.O.R., A/50/10 to A/58/10.

[44] art.16.

[45] art.84(1).

[46] art.26.

Unless otherwise provided, a treaty applies to all the territory of a Contracting Party.[47] The 1969 Convention does not address itself to the question of dependencies, but an agreement may spell out the dependencies to which it is to apply. If silent, e.g. under US law, an agreement will be held as applying to all dependencies of the US. Parties to a multilateral treaty may agree to conclude a new treaty and accordingly negate any preceding agreement.

If all states consent then no problem arises, however there may be parties to the old treaty which do not accede to the new agreement. The relationship between two such states will be governed by the treaty to which both states are parties (that is, the former).[48]

TREATY INTERPRETATION

How is a treaty to be interpreted? There are three main approaches in international law to treaty interpretation:

(a) the "objective" approach—interpretation in accordance with the ordinary use of the words of the treaty[49];

(b) the "subjective" approach—interpretation in accordance with the intention of the parties to the treaty; and

(c) the "teleological" approach—interpretation in accordance with the treaty's aims and objectives.

Although characterised as distinct, the three approaches are in practice not mutually exclusive. Credence may be given to the principles found in the three approaches, as is reflected in the international jurisprudence which has emerged.

The 1969 Convention adopts an integrated approach to interpretation, but nevertheless gives emphasis to the ordinary meaning approach. Article 31 of the 1969 Convention sets out the general rule of interpretation as being:

---

[47] The issue of the extraterritorial application of treaties is well is well illustrated by reference to the European Convention on Human Rights. Art.1 of that Convention states "the High Contracting Parties shall secure to everyone within their jurisdiction the rights and freedoms defined in Section I of this Convention." The European Court of Human Rights has consistently held that the terms of the Convention may be applicable in situations beyond the territory of a state party, e.g. *Al-Skeini v The United Kingdom* (no. 55721/07) and *Al-Jedda v The United Kingdom* (no. 27021/08).

[48] art.30(4)(b).

[49] As reflected in the ICJ's statement in Competence of the General Assembly for the Admission of a State to the United Nations, I.C.J. Rep. 1950, pp.4 at 8.

"A treaty shall be interpreted in good faith in accordance with the ordinary meaning to be given to the terms of the treaty in their context and in the light of its object and purpose."

Article 31 allows the use of the teleological approach, but only to shed light on the ordinary meaning of the words of the treaty provisions.[50] It may be invoked as an ancillary aid in interpretation and not as an independent approach to interpretation. A special meaning may be given to a term if it is evident that is what the concerned parties intended. "Context" includes the text of the treaty, the preamble, any annexes and also

"(a) any agreement relating to the treaty which was made between all the parties in connection with the conclusion of the treaty;

(b) any instrument which was made by one or more parties in connection with the conclusion of the treaty and accepted by the other parties as an instrument related to the treaty."[51]

In addition, account may be taken of

"(a) any subsequent agreement between the parties regarding the interpretation of the treaty or the application of its provisions;

(b) any subsequent practice in the application of the treaty which establishes the agreement of the parties regarding its interpretation;

(c) any relevant rules of international law applicable in the relations between the parties."[52]

If giving the ordinary meaning in the terms of the treaty would lead to an ambiguous or obscure meaning, or would produce a manifestly absurd and unreasonable approach, supplementary means of interpretation may be invoked.[53] Supplementary means

---

[50] The ICJ recognised the provisions of art.31 as customary international law in *Territorial Dispute (Libya v Chad)* I.C.J. Rep. 1994 6; see also the *Kisikili/Sedudu Island (Botswana v Namibia)* case, ICJ 13 October 1999 I.C.J. Rep. 1045.

[51] art.31(2).

[52] art.31(3). See, e.g. *Application of the Interim Accord of 13 September 1995 (Former Yugoslav Republic of Macedonia v Greece)* I.C.J. Rep 2011, 644.

[53] The ICJ has rejected supplementary evidence when the text of the treaty is clear, see the *Maritime Delimitation and Territorial Questions* case. See above, fn.10.

include "the preparatory work of the treaty and the circumstances of its conclusion."[54]

Preparatory work—*travaux préparatoires*—is not defined in the 1969 Convention, but the term, it is accepted, refers to records documenting the treaty's drafting and includes the records of negotiations between the participating drafting states. A treaty is to be interpreted in the context of the circumstances prevailing at the time the treaty was concluded.[55] However account may be taken of "the present day state of scientific knowledge, as reflected in the documentary material submitted to it by the parties."[56]

In certain cases, the opinion of expert bodies may also be utilised. "Circumstances" of its "conclusion" refer not only to contemporary circumstances but also to the historical context against which the treaty was concluded, e.g. *Anglo-Iranian Oil Co* case.[57]

Interpretation of treaties authenticated in two or more languages

A text is equally authoritative in each language, unless the agreement provides and the parties agree that, in the case of divergence, a particular text shall prevail. One text may be designated as authoritative while other versions may only be recognised as having the status of "official texts" (that is, a text signed by the negotiating states, but not adopted as authoritative). In the event of any doubt as to the meaning between texts, the more limited interpretation and the one which will least restrict a state's sovereignty is preferred.

THIRD STATES

Pacta tertiis nec nocent nec prosunt—a treaty does not create either obligations or rights for a third state without its consent. This rule of customary international law is spelt out in art.34 of the 1969 Convention. This does not preclude a provision contained in a treaty from becoming law for a non-party when the provision has crystallised into customary international law. The non-party is bound, not by the treaty, but rather by customary international law.[58] Article 34 contains the general rule, however there are exceptions, and special territorial arrangements may

---

[54] art.32.
[55] See *Cameroon v Nigeria*, I.C.J. Rep., 2002, p.303.
[56] *Botswana/Namibia*, I.C.J. Rep., 1999, p.1045 at 1060.
[57] I.C.J. Rep. 1952 p.3 at 105.
[58] art.38. See also *North Sea Continental Shelf* Case, I.C.J. Rep. 1969, 3. Cf. *Military and Para Military Activities in and Against Nicaragua (Merits)*, I.C.J. Rep., 1986, p.14.

produce obligations which third parties are obliged to respect (e.g. in the case of the Aaland Islands). Article 2(6) of the UN Charter provides:

> "the Organisation shall ensure that States which are not Members of the United Nations act in accordance with these Principles so far as may be necessary for the maintenance of international peace and security."

Article 2(6) is regarded as being customary international law, and any state acting contrary to art.2(6) would be violating customary international law.

A treaty can produce obligations for a third state "if the parties to the treaty intend the provisions to be the means of establishing the obligation and the third State expressly accepts that obligation in writing."[59] A third state may derive rights from a treaty, e.g. those guaranteeing freedom of passage through the Suez and Kiel Canals, if that is the intention of the parties to the treaty and the assent of the third state has been secured. In contrast, however, to the assent of states on which an obligation is incumbent, the assent of a benefiting state "shall be presumed so long as the contrary is not indicated, unless the treaty otherwise provides."[60]

AMENDMENT AND MODIFICATION

Both amendment and modification relate to a revision of treaty terms by parties. Amendment is the more formal process involving at least, prima facie, all parties to the treaty, whereas modification is a "private arrangement" between particular parties and in respect of particular provisions.

Amendment

In a bilateral treaty, the amendment process is straightforward but in a multilateral treaty the agreement of all states to a proposed amendment may be difficult to secure. Article 40 of the 1969 Convention lays down the procedure which, if not provided for by the treaty, should be followed. Article 40 allows for amendment by fewer than all Contracting Parties to the original treaty by permitting amendment between those parties in agreement *after* all states have been given the opportunity to participate in considering amendment proposals. An amending agreement does not bind a state which, although a party to the original treaty, fails to become a party to the amending agreement.

---

[59] art.35.
[60] art.36(1).

Modification

Article 41 allows two or more parties to a multilateral treaty to conclude a modifying agreement between themselves, provided the possibility of modification:

- is recognised by the treaty,
- is not prohibited by the treaty,
- does not affect the rights of other parties,
- nor relates to "a provision [or] derogation which is incompatible with the effective execution of the object and purpose of the treaty as a whole."[61]

VALIDITY OF TREATIES

The 1969 Convention stipulates five grounds on which the validity of an agreement may be challenged. The Convention is exhaustive as regards the grounds which may be raised. A state may not invoke other grounds of invalidity. The five grounds are:

(a) non-compliance with national law requirements;

(b) error;

(c) fraud and corruption;

(d) coercion;

(e) *jus cogens*.

Non-compliance with national law requirements

See above at p.275.

Error

Error is of limited significance and its role has been markedly less than that of error in the municipal law of contract. Error may only be invoked by a state if "the error relates to a fact or situation which was assumed by that state to exist at the time when the treaty was concluded and formed an essential basis of its consent to be bound by the treaty."[62]

Error has been invoked almost exclusively in respect of boundary questions. A state which contributed by its behaviour to the error, or should have known of a possible error, cannot relieve

---

[61] art.41(1)(b)(ii).
[62] art.48(1).

itself subsequently of its treaty obligations.[63] An error in the wording of a treaty is not a ground for invalidating the treaty. Such an error must be corrected in accordance with art.79 of the 1969 Convention and most frequently by a quite informal procedure.

Fraud and corruption

Fraud and corruption, like error, are of little significance. Article 49 provides that a treaty may be invalidated "if a State has been induced to conclude a treaty by the fraudulent conduct of another negotiating State". Article 50 provides a treaty may be invalidated if a state's consent to a treaty "has been procured through the corruption of its representative directly or indirectly by another negotiating state". "Corrupts", "fraudulent conduct" and "corruption" are not defined in the 1969 Convention or by international jurisprudence.

Coercion

A treaty will be of no *legal effect* if a state's consent "has been procured by the coercion of its representative through acts or threats".[64] The use of coercion against a state's representative is rare, especially as art.51 is concerned with coercion of the representative's person, rather than with coercion by way of a threat of action against the state.

Acceptance of a treaty through coercion, and the threat of coercion against a state "in violation of the principles of international law embodied in the Charter of the United Nations", renders a treaty void.[65] Article 52 of the 1969 Convention reflects modern international law's prohibition on the use of force. The 1969 Convention refers explicitly to the use of force as per art.2(4) of the Charter of the United Nations and does not extend to political and economic coercion.[66]

Jus cogens

Jus cogens refers to peremptory norms of international law. A peremptory norm is defined, for the purposes of the 1969 Convention,

---

[63] art.48(2); see also the *Temple* case, I.C.J. Rep. 1962 p.6 at 26.
[64] art.51.
[65] art.52.
[66] However see acknowledgement of moral and political pressures in *Fisheries Jurisdiction* Case, I.C.J. Rep., 1973, p.3. Where it was noted "there are moral and political pressures which cannot be proved by the so called documentary evidence, but which are in fact indisputably real and which have, given rise to treaties and conventions claimed to be freely concluded and subjected to the principle of *pacta sunt servanda*." at 47. For further discussion on the interpretation of force see Ch.11, p.300.

as one which is "accepted and recognised by the international community of States as a whole", and from which "no derogation is permitted and which can be modified only by a subsequent norm of general international law having the same character."[67] Any treaty which conflicts at the time of its conclusion with such a norm will be void. Should a new peremptory norm of general international law develop, any existing treaty which is contrary to that norm becomes void and terminates.[68]

The 1969 Convention acknowledges that there are certain rules of international law which enjoy a superior status and as such cannot be affected by treaty. The 1969 Convention does not identify peremptory norms and, as already highlighted, such norms must not only be accepted by the international community, but must also be accepted as having peremptory force.[69] It is accepted that the prohibition on genocide, slavery, torture and the use of force, as well as the right to self-determination all fall within the classification of *jus cogens*. However, international law is still developing, and no list of *jus cogens* norms could be exhaustive.

TERMINATION OF A TREATY

A treaty may be terminated as provided for by the treaty or by the consent of the parties. Material breach by one of the parties may also terminate or suspend a treaty, as may a supervening impossibility or a substantial change in circumstances.

Termination by treaty provision or consent

A treaty may provide for termination. A treaty which is silent regarding termination may not be denounced unless it is apparent that the parties intended to admit the possibility of denunciation or withdrawal, or where such a right may be implied by the nature of the treaty.[70] Two or three parties to a multilateral treaty may at any time conclude an agreement suspending the operation of certain provisions temporarily between them provided the treaty allows it; it does not restrict the rights of other parties; and it is not incompatible with the object and purpose of the treaty.[71] It is common for a treaty either to be for a fixed term,[72] or to provide that a party may withdraw after giving a certain period of notice. If all parties to a treaty conclude a later treaty relating to the same

---

[67] art.53.
[68] art.64.
[69] For further discussion thereof, see Ch.2, "Sources".
[70] art.56.
[71] art.58(1).
[72] e.g. the treaty establishing the European Coal and Steel Community had a term of 50 years and ended in July 2002.

subject matter, the original treaty will be considered terminated. Similarly, this will be the case where it appears the matter should be governed by the later treaty, or where the provisions of the later treaty "are so far incompatible with those of the earlier one that the two treaties are not capable of being applied at the same time."[73]

Material breach

A mere breach of a treaty provision is not sufficient to terminate a treaty.[74] Article 60(3) of the 1969 Vienna Convention defines a material breach as one constituting either

"(a) a repudiation of the treaty not sanctioned by the present Convention; or

(b) the violation of a provision essential to the accomplishment of the object or purpose of the treaty."

In a bilateral treaty, material breach may be invoked by the "innocent" party to terminate the treaty or suspend its operation in whole or in part. Material breach of a multilateral treaty allows the "innocent" parties to suspend, by unanimous agreement, the operation of the treaty, in whole or in part, or to terminate it either "(i) in the relations between themselves and the defaulting State, or (ii) as between all the parties."

The party particularly affected by the breach may invoke the breach as reason for suspending the operation of the treaty in whole or in part in relations between itself and the defaulting state. Any party other than the defaulting state may rely on the breach so as to suspend the treaty's operation in whole or in part with respect to itself. This may be done if the treaty is of such a character that a material breach of its provisions by one party radically changes the position of every party with respect to the further performance of its obligations under the treaty. Neither the definition of material breach nor the consequences of such a breach apply to

"provisions relating to the protection of the human person contained in treaties of a humanitarian character, in particular to provisions prohibiting any form of reprisals against persons protected by such treaties."[75]

---

[73] art.59(1).
[74] See, e.g. *Application of the Interim Accord of 13 September 1995 (Former Yugoslav Republic of Macedonia v Greece)* I.C.J. Rep 2011, 644 at 691.
[75] art.60(5).

The 1949 Geneva Conventions are instances of such treaties. Article 46 of Geneva Convention I states "Reprisals against the wounded, sick, personnel, buildings, or equipment protected by the Convention are prohibited."[76]

The breach by one party of its obligation under a humanitarian or human rights convention does not entitle other parties to either terminate or suspend their own obligations arising from the convention. As to whether there has been a breach each party may decide for itself, except where the treaty provides a procedure for that purpose.

Supervening impossibility of performance

Article 61 of the 1969 Vienna Convention, which provides for termination of a treaty on the grounds of a supervening impossibility of performance, was designed to cover such relatively rare happenings as the "submergence of an island, the drying up of a river or the destruction of a dam or hydro-electric installation indispensable for the execution of a treaty."[77] Performance may become impossible because a party ceases to exist as a state (for the position when this occurs see "State Succession", below). If the impossibility is temporary, it may be invoked only as a ground for suspending the operation of the treaty. A party may not invoke impossibility of performance if that party has been responsible for making performance impossible.

Fundamental change of circumstances

The doctrine of *rebus sic stantibus* may be invoked to terminate a treaty. The operation of this doctrine, which literally means "things remaining as they are", rests on the assumption that a treaty may be denounced if circumstances change profoundly from those prevailing at the time of the treaty's conclusion. In the *Fisheries Jurisdiction* case,[78] Iceland challenged the ICJ's jurisdiction to hear the dispute between Iceland, the UK and Germany on the grounds that there had been a fundamental change of circumstances since the conclusion of the 1961 Exchange of Notes. These Notes contained, inter alia, a compromissory clause providing for reference to the ICJ, and Iceland alleged that there had been a fundamental change of circumstances as a consequence of changes in fishing techniques. The Court identified the changes of circumstances which would be recognised as fundamental or vital as those

---

[76] See below, Ch.11, "The Use of Force".
[77] Y.B.I.L.C. 1966, II, p.256.
[78] *Fisheries Jurisdiction* case (Jurisdiction), I.C.J. Rep. 1973 at p.3.

"which imperil the existence or vital development of one of the parties."[79]

The Court held, however

> "the apprehended dangers for the vital interests of Iceland, resulting from changes in fishing techniques, cannot constitute a fundamental change with respect to the lapse or subsistence of the compromissory clause establishing the Court's jurisdiction,"[80]

and for a change of circumstances to justify termination of a treaty, there would have to be

> "a radical transformation of the extent of the obligations still to be performed. The change must have increased the burden of the obligations to be executed to the extent of rendering the performance something essentially different from that originally undertaken."[81]

The changed circumstances doctrine will only be invoked successfully when it applies to circumstances which were not contemplated by the parties when the treaty was concluded. In the *Fisheries Jurisdiction* case, the Court maintained that not only had the jurisdictional obligation not been radically transformed, it had remained precisely as it was in 1961. The compromissory clause indeed anticipated a dispute such as the one that had arisen. Similarly in the *Danube Dam* case,[82] the Court held that the prevailing political conditions were not sufficiently related to the object and purpose of the Treaty so as to constitute an essential basis of the consent of the parties. Thus, although changed, it did not radically alter the extent of the objectives to be performed; the same was also held to be true of the economic system in force at the time the said treaty was concluded in 1977. The Court also denied that advances in environmental law were completely unforeseen. *Rebus sic stantibus* may not be invoked in respect of a boundary settlement or by a state which has caused the fundamental change.

Severance of diplomatic or consular relations

The severance of diplomatic or consular relations between parties to a treaty does not affect legal relations between the parties,

---

[79] Above, at 19.
[80] Above, at 20.
[81] Above, at 21.
[82] *Gabčikovo-Nagymaros Project (Hungary v Slovakia)* (1997) I.C.J. Rep. p.7; 38 I.L.M. 162. See also for application of art.61.

except in so far as the existence of diplomatic or consular relations is vital for the treaty's application.[83]

Termination of an agreement normally applies to the treaty as a whole, unless the treaty provides otherwise. This is the norm reflected in art.44. Exception is admitted if the ground for termination relates to particular clauses which can be separated from the rest of the treaty. These clauses may be terminated if their acceptance was not an essential basis of the consent of the other parties to be bound, and if continued performance of the remainder of the treaty would not be unjust. A party, a victim of fraud or corruption, has the option of invalidating the agreement as a whole or in part. Such an option is not available in respect of the use or threat of force or violation of *jus cogens*.

A state loses its right to initiate a claim for invalidating, terminating, withdrawing from or suspending the operation of a treaty if, subsequent to becoming aware of the fact, it has expressly agreed the treaty is valid, or, by its conduct, it can be said to have acquiesced in the validity of the treaty.[84]

CONSEQUENCES OF INVALIDITY, TERMINATION OR SUSPENSION

A treaty which is established as invalid is void. The provisions of a void treaty have no legal force. If, however, acts have been performed in reliance upon such a treaty

"(a) each party may require any other party to establish as far as possible in their mutual relations the position that would have existed if the acts had not been performed;

(b) acts performed in good faith before the invalidity was invoked are not rendered unlawful by reason only of the invalidity of the treaty."[85]

The above does not apply "with respect to the party to which the fraud, the act of corruption or the coercion is imputable."[86]

Termination of a treaty, unless otherwise provided, releases the parties concerned from any future obligations, but does not affect any right, obligation or legal situation of the parties created through the execution of the treaty prior to its termination. If a treaty is declared void under art.53 of the 1969 Vienna Convention (conflict with a peremptory norm) the parties are charged with

---

[83] art.63.
[84] art.45.
[85] art.69(2).
[86] art.69(3).

eliminating as far as possible the consequences of any act performed in reliance on the offending provision, and with bringing their mutual relations into conformity with the peremptory norm of general international law. If art.64 is invoked to terminate a treaty, the parties are released from any further obligation to perform the treaty, but the rights, obligations and legal situation of the parties created prior to the treaty's termination are not affected, provided "those rights, obligations or situations may thereafter be maintained only to the extent that their maintenance is not itself in conflict with the new peremptory norm of general international law."[87]

Suspension has, for the period of suspension, a similar effect to termination. During the period of suspension, parties are to refrain from acts which would be likely to obstruct the resumption of the treaty's operation.

Parties to the 1969 Convention are called to seek a peaceful solution to disputes relating to the validity of treaties. This general rule is reinforced by art.66, which provides that if a solution is not achieved on the lapse of 12 months, the parties shall submit to the ICJ, to arbitration or to the consultation procedure provided for in the Convention's Annex.

STATE SUCCESSION

What happens to a state's treaty obligations when it is replaced by another state on the international plane? In 1978, the ILC produced the Vienna Convention on the Succession of States in Respect of Treaties.[88] The 1978 Convention reflects predominantly the views of the "newer" states and, as such, represents progressive development rather than a codification of existing law. Essentially, the "clean-slate" view is favoured with respect to successor states. That is, a state is not to be tied by the obligations of its predecessor. The obligations maintained by a state's predecessor by way of bilateral or multilateral agreements are not automatically incumbent on the new state. A state has the option of assuming the multilateral treaties of its predecessor, nevertheless, it is not required to do so. The continuance of a bilateral treaty depends upon agreement, either express or implied, between the parties, that is, the successor state and the other Contracting State.

There is, however, an exception to this general rule. It does not apply in respect of treaties establishing boundaries, territorial regimes and to those imposing restrictions on a territory for the

---

[87] art.71(2).
[88] 1978 I.L.M. p.1488. The Convention entered into force on 6 November 1996.

benefit of another state. To apply the clean-slate principle in such instances would prove too disruptive. Accordingly a successor state is bound by treaties of that type to which its predecessor has been a party. In the event of states uniting or separating, the 1978 Convention stipulates that treaties continue in force for the territory concerned unless the parties have agreed otherwise, or the result would be inconsistent with the object and purpose of the treaty and would radically change the conditions for its operation.[89] State property, archives and debts are dealt with in the 1983 Vienna Convention on Succession of States in Respect of Property, Archives and Debts.[90]

Under art.11 of the German Unification Treaty,[91] West and East Germany took the position that international treaties of the Federal German Republic would remain in effect, and rights and obligations arising therefrom would also apply in the former German Democratic Republic. Under art.12, international treaties of the German Democratic Republic were to be reviewed with the Contracting States as to their applicability, modification or termination, with due regard to the aspects of *pacta sunt servanda*, the interests of the Contracting States and the contractual obligations of West Germany and the European Communities.

The transfer of Hong Kong to China in 1997 presented a unique situation in international treaty law; namely, the continued application of Hong Kong's treaty obligations. Arrangements for the application of multilateral and bilateral international agreements after the transfer of the government of Hong Kong to China on 30 June 1997 were established in the 1984 Sino–British Joint Declaration on the Question of Hong Kong. The 1984 Declaration provides the Hong Kong Special Administrative Region (HKSAR) with a high degree of autonomy, able to conclude international agreements with states, regions and relevant international organisations in a number of areas, using the name "Hong Kong China".[92] Hong Kong therefore continues to have some treaty-making competence in the international legal system, independent of China. The recent independence of South Sudan has sparked another, as yet unresolved, controversy with regard to treaty succession, in particular on whether South Sudan should be bound by the 1929 and 1959 Nile Waters Agreements.

---

[89] State succession raises issues other than those raised by succession to treaties, but these are outside the subject matter of this text.

[90] UN DOC. A/Conf. 117/14 (1983) 12 I.L.M. 306.

[91] FRG: GDR: Treaty on the Establishment of German Unity, at Berlin, 31 August 1990, entered into force on 29 September 1991; 30 I.L.M. 457 (1991).

[92] Foreign and Commonwealth Office, London. Paper on the Application after 30 June 1997 of Multilateral and Bilateral International Agreements, Hong Kong Department, April 1996, para.26 of the Joint Declaration.

Notwithstanding the position of newer states, there is increasing argument in favour of treaties relating to human rights, binding successor states. In the *Case Concerning the Application of the Convention on the Prevention and Punishment of the Crime of Genocide*[93] Judges Weeramantry and Shahabuddeen expressed the view that state succession applies to conventions such as the Genocide Convention. Judge Shahabuddeen was of the view this was demanded if the Genocide Convention was to fulfil its object and purpose. The views of both Judges resonate with the views of the UN Human Rights Committee as expressed in General Comment (No.26). Namely

> "once the people are accorded the protection of the rights under the Covenant, such protection devolves with territory and continues to belong to them, notwithstanding change in government of the State Party, including dismemberment in more than one state or state succession or any subsequent action of the State Party designed to divest them of their rights guaranteed by the Covenant."[94]

Although the ICJ did not specifically address the continued application of human rights treaties the issue is one of contemporary importance. Of course, beyond the realm of treaty law, new states are bound by customary human rights law.

CONCLUSION

Treaties are used extensively and the subject matter they encompass is wide ranging. They are the most tangible evidence of states' obligations. Treaty law is itself governed by the 1969 Vienna Convention on the Law of Treaties which also illustrates the link between customary international law and treaties, and how the former is frequently mirrored in a subsequent treaty. As international law expands, its subject matter states rely on treaties to regulate their bilateral and multilateral relations as the preferred means of establishing international obligations.

---

[93] *Bosnia and Herzegovina v Yugoslavia* (Preliminary Objections) I.C.J. Rep. 1996, p.595.
[94] Human Rights Committee General Comment 26 (61), UN Doc. A/53/40, Annex VII, 8 December 1997, para.4.

11. THE USE OF FORCE

The use of force, or *jus ad bellum*,[1] as a way to deal with disputes between states is generally prohibited in contemporary international law. The UN Charter requires Member States to settle disputes among themselves by peaceful means, and to refrain in their international relations with each other from either the threat of or the use of force.[2] Nevertheless, international law does provide certain exceptions where the use of force is permitted. The international rules on the use of force are designed to regulate its use, and there is an accepted distinction between the lawful and unlawful use of force. This, however, has not always been the case.

THE LAW PRE-1945

Historically a "just war" was regarded as a legitimate use of force. St Augustine (AD 354–430) articulated the "just war" as one designed to avenge injuries which had been sustained and which "the nation or city against which warlike action is to be directed has neglected either to punish wrongs committed by its own citizens or

---

[1] *Jus ad bellum*, which translates as the right to wage war, is to be distinguished from *jus in bello* (international humanitarian law) relating to the conduct of hostilities—discussed below, p.322.

[2] UN Charter, arts 2(3) and 2(4).

to restore what has been unjustly taken by it." The "just war" was founded in theological doctrine but with the breakdown of the Church's authority power was assumed by the sovereign nation state, and the right to use force was recognised as an inherent right of every independent sovereign state. International law placed no restraints on the use of force; factors other than legal considerations affected a state's decision to resort to force and the use of force was regarded as a legitimate action for all states to adopt.

The unprecedented devastation of the First World War prompted states to establish an international forum in which it was hoped states would discuss their problems rather than resort to force. Consequently the League of Nations was founded. The Covenant of the League of Nations, signed in 1919, did not prohibit war, but rather placed limitations upon the use of force. In the event of a dispute which was potentially disruptive, Member States agreed under the Covenant to submit the dispute to arbitration, judicial settlement or to inquiry by the Council of the League. War was not to be resorted to until three months after the award by the arbitrator, the judicial decision, or the Council's report. In this way the Covenant provided a "cooling-off" period for protagonists. Members also agreed not to go to war with fellow members of the League who complied with an arbitral award, judicial decision or with a unanimous report of the Council. The Covenant required Member States "to respect and preserve as against external aggression the territorial integrity and political independence of all Members of the League."[3]

In 1928, the international community was, for the first time, successful in agreeing to a comprehensive ban on war as an instrument of national policy. Sixty-three states signed the General Treaty for the Renunciation of War (also known as the Kellogg–Briand Pact or the Pact of Paris),[4] in which parties agreed to seek a peaceful solution to all disputes arising between them. Nevertheless, the right of self-defence still existed as an exception to this general ban. The Treaty, although never having been terminated, has been superseded by art.2(4) of the United Nations (UN) Charter. Treaties, however, cannot simply by their existence prevent wars, and the Second World War broke out in 1939 only 11 years after the signing of the Kellogg-Briand Pact.

THE LAW POST-1945

Article 2(3) of the UN Charter requires all Member States "to settle their international disputes by peaceful means in such a

---

[3] art.10 of the Covenant, U.K.T.S. 4 (1919) Cmd.153.
[4] 94 L.N.T.S. 57.

manner that international peace and security, and justice are not endangered". While art.2(4) demands that all Member States

> "shall refrain in their international relations from the threat or use of force against the territorial integrity or political independence of any state, or in any manner inconsistent with the purposes of the United Nations."

Article 2(4), as a provision of the UN Charter, is addressed to all members of the United Nations; however, the prohibition on the use of force as contained in art.2(4) is firmly established as a principle of customary international law, which has attained the character of *jus cogens*, and as such is addressed to all members of the international community.[5]

Extent of the prohibition contained in Article 2(4)

Article 2(4) prohibits the use of force. It is not concerned only with the outlawing of war: art.2(4) does not distinguish between war and the use of force falling short of war, e.g. reprisals.[6]

Article 2(4) thus embraces all threats and acts of violence without distinction. The article specifically refers to the threat or use of force "against the territorial integrity or political independence of any State". Can force be used to enforce a right when force is not employed against territorial integrity or political independence? Can force be used to protect human rights? Article 2(4) should be read as a whole within the context of the UN Charter. Force contrary to "the purposes of the United Nations" is also prohibited. The purposes of the UN are spelt out in art.1 of the Charter. The purposes include respect for the principle of equal rights and self-determination and respect for human rights, but nevertheless the overriding purpose of the UN remains

> "to maintain international peace and security, and to that end: to take effective collective measures for the prevention and removal of threats to the peace, and for the suppression of acts of aggression or other breaches of the peace, and to bring about by peaceful means, and in conformity with the principles of justice and international law, adjustment or

---

[5] Endorsed by the International Court of Justice in the case *Concerning Military and Paramilitary Activities in and against Nicaragua (Merits)* I.C.J. Rep. 1986 p.14 at 100.

[6] A declaration of war is seldom made by state parties to hostilities. War is a technical term. Acknowledgment of war produces consequences under international law, e.g. role of neutral states and the application of national law, e.g. regarding the status of non-nationals. For reprisals see below pp.300–301.

settlement of international disputes or situations which might lead to a breach of the peace".[7]

The emphasis is on the maintenance of international peace and security and on resolving both potential and actual conflict by peaceful means.

Article 2(4) has been supplemented by the 1970 General Assembly Declaration on Principles of International Law Concerning Friendly Relations and Co-operation among States in Accordance with the Charter of the United Nations (the 1970 Declaration).[8] The 1970 Declaration is not legally binding on Member States; however, it is regarded as representing the consensus of the international community on the legal interpretation to be given to the principles enunciated in the UN Charter. This Declaration adds flesh to the prohibition on the use of force, reinforcing the duty to refrain from the threat or use of force to violate the existing international boundaries of another state or as a means of solving international disputes, including territorial disputes and problems concerning frontiers of states and declaring a war of aggression as a crime against the peace for which there is responsibility under international law.[9]

What constitutes force?

Reprisals

Reprisals (now more commonly referred to as countermeasures) are the acts adopted by a state in response to having been the victim of an unlawful act by another state. They are illegal under international law. They were defined in the *Naulilaa* case[10] as

"acts of self-help by the injured State, acts in retaliation for acts contrary to international law on the part of the offending State, which have remained unredressed after a demand for amends. In consequence of such measures, the observance of this or that rule of international law is temporarily suspended in the relations between the two States. They are limited by considerations of humanity and the rules of good faith, applicable in the relations between States. They are illegal unless

---

[7] UN Charter, art.1.1.
[8] G.A. Res.2625 (XXV), 24 October 1970—see also Resolution on the Definition of Aggression 1974, G.A. Res. 3314 (XXIX); 69 A.J.I.L. 480 (1975) and The Declaration on the Enhancement of the Effectiveness of the Principle of Refraining from the Threat or Use of Force in International Relations 1987, G.A. Res.42/22, G.A.O.R., 42nd Sess., Supp., 49, p.287 (1987).
[9] GA Res.2625 (XXV), 24 October 1970.
[10] 2 R.I.A.A. 1012 (1928).

they are based upon a previous act contrary to international law. They seek to impose on the offending State reparation for the offence, the return to legality and the avoidance of new offences."[11]

Reprisals involving armed force now have to comply with the contemporary international law on the use of force otherwise they will be contrary to international law. The 1970 Declaration expressly prohibits reprisals and provides that states "have a duty to refrain from acts of reprisal involving the use of force."[12]

Retorsions

Retorsions are distinct from reprisals/countermeasures in that they are acts which in themselves, although unfriendly, are not unlawful. They are a lawful means of expressing displeasure at the conduct of another state, e.g. the severance of diplomatic relations or foreign aid.

Aggression

The 1970 Declaration states that a war of aggression constitutes a crime against the peace for which there is responsibility under international law. The 1974 General Assembly Resolution on the Definition of Aggression[13] defined it as "the use of force by a State against the sovereignty, territorial integrity, or political independence of another State, or in any other manner inconsistent with the Charter of the United Nations". Examples of acts that would be identified as aggression include the invasion or armed attack by one state against the territory of another state; the blockade of the ports or coasts of a state by the armed forces of another state and the sending by or on behalf of a state of armed bands, groups, irregulars or mercenaries, to employ armed force against another state.[14]

In 1998 the Rome Statute of the International Criminal Code codified aggression as an international crime which, together

---

[11] Above at 1026. See also *Air Services Agreement* case 18 R.I.A.A. 416.
[12] See the International Law Commission's Draft Articles on Responsibility of States for Internationally Wrongful Acts, 2001, Ch.2, art.49 to art.52, which deal with the taking of counter-measures against another state.
[13] GA Res.3314 (XXIX) above, fn.8, note there is a distinction between a "war of aggression" which is characterised as a crime against international peace and "aggression" which gives rise to international responsibility, art.5(2). See also ILC Draft Code of Crimes against the Peace and Security of Mankind 1996, art.16, which deals with the individual responsibility for the crime of aggression, Report of the ILC, A/51/10, 1996, p.9.
[14] Above, art.3.

with genocide, war crimes and crimes against humanity, gives rise to international individual responsibility. The Statute did not contain a definition of aggression, which was later adopted by consensus of the State Parties to the Statute in 2010 in its Review Conference in Kampala. Article 8 *bis* of the reviewed Rome Statute contains the following definition:

> "an act of aggression is defined as the use of armed force by one State against another State without the justification of self-defense or authorization by the Security Council. The definition of the act of aggression, as well as the actions qualifying as acts of aggression contained in the amendments are influenced by the UN General Assembly Resolution 3314 (XXIX) of 14 December 1974".

Among the acts listed in art.8 *bis* are invasion by armed forces, bombardment and blockade of ports and the sending by or on behalf of a state of armed bands, groups, irregulars or mercenaries to carry out acts of armed force another state. This last example is in line with the 1970 Declaration and the ruling of the ICJ in the *Nicaragua* case.[15] The 1970 Declaration states that:

> "every State has the duty to refrain from organising or encouraging the organisation of irregular forces or armed bands, including mercenaries, for incursion into the territory of another State" and "to refrain from organising, instigating, assisting or participating in acts of civil strife or terrorist acts in another State or acquiescing in organised activities within its territory, directed towards the commission of such acts, when the acts involve a threat or use of force".

Economic and political pressure

In everyday usage force does not necessarily have to refer to armed force, but can also be economic and/or political. Does art.2(4) confine itself to prohibiting only the use of armed force or are other categories of force similarly prohibited?

The preamble of the UN Charter and art.51—on a state's inherent right of self-defence, considered below—specifically mentions "armed force". The 1970 Declaration, in the section on the principle of non-intervention contained therein, is inconclusive. It emphasises the duty of states to refrain, in their international relations, from military, political, economic or any other form of coercion. However in the section regarding the use of force,

---

[15] Above, fn.5.

force is not qualified. The imprecise definition reflects the dichotomy which existed primarily between developed and developing states. The latter would have interpreted force to encompass economic and political force,[16] while the former maintained it was only armed force which was outlawed. The former group of states did concede that economic and political pressure might constitute illegal intervention. Economic coercion, although prohibited in the 1970 Declaration's section on non-intervention, remains undefined and in the *Nicaragua* case the ICJ denied that American economic sanctions against Nicaragua constituted "a breach of the customary law principle of non-intervention."[17]

As far as art.2(4) and the legal regime envisaged by the UN Charter are concerned, the prohibition is one aimed at outlawing armed force and "gunboat diplomacy" in the relations between states.

Exceptions to the prohibition on the threat or use of force

The use of force only remains legitimate under international law in particularly well-defined circumstances: in self-defence either individual or collective—in accordance with art.51 of the UN Charter; collective measures taken under the auspices of the UN; or if authorised by a competent organ of the UN.

Self-defence

Customary international law recognises a state's right of self-defence, but the extent of that right was ill-defined for a long time. It was only as states imposed restrictions on the employment of force that the need to articulate the concept of self-defence in international law became more imperative.

Under customary international law, the use of force had to be justified if states were at peace. The use of force by one state against another with which it was not at war was, prima facie, unlawful. The circumstances which allowed for the exercise of self-defence were articulated in the now famous communication of the US Secretary of State Webster to the UK Government following the *Caroline* incident.[18]

The *Caroline* was a vessel which operated from US territory supplying rebel insurrectionaries in Canada. A British force destroyed the *Caroline* and two US citizens were killed. A British subject, McLeod, was charged with murder and arson.

---

[16] See also para.4(e) of the 1974 Declaration on the Establishment of a New International Economic Order, 13 I.L.M. 715 (1974).
[17] Above, fn.5, at 126.
[18] 29 B.F.S.P. 1137–1138; 30 B.F.S.P. 195–196.

In his letter, Secretary Webster emphasised the success of the UK Government's defence was dependent on it establishing that such action was justified on grounds of "a necessity of self-defence and preservation". It had to be demonstrated that the need for self-defence was "instant, overwhelming, leaving no choice of means, and no moment for deliberation." It was also necessary for the UK to show that the Canadian authorities had done nothing "unreasonable or excessive; since the act, justified by the necessity of self-defence, must be limited by that necessity, and kept clearly within it."

To summarise, the exercise of force in self-defence was justified under customary international law provided the need for it was:

(a) instant;

(b) overwhelming;

(c) immediate; and

(d) there was no viable alternative action which could be taken.

The *Caroline* incident also affirmed that the extent of force used in self-defence should be commensurate with the violation against which the self-defence is being used, that is to say proportionate.[19] These criteria have come to be described as "the Webster formula", and still apply today as is confirmed by the *Nicaragua* case[20] and *Oil Platforms (Merits)* case,[21] and the *Legality of the Threat or Use of Nuclear Weapons, Advisory Opinion.*[22]

Article 51, United Nations Charter

Article 51 of the UN Charter acknowledges the right of self-defence as an inherent right of every state:

"Nothing in the present Charter shall impair the inherent right of individual or collective self-defence if an armed attack occurs against a Member of the United Nations, until the Security Council has taken measures necessary to maintain international peace and security. Measures taken by Members in the exercise of this right of self-defence shall be immediately reported to the Security Council and shall not in

---

[19] e.g. the intervention by Israel into Lebanon in 2006 was criticised by members of the Security Council for being disproportionate in nature, see Verbatim Record, Security Council 5489th meeting, UN Doc S/PV.5489.

[20] Above, fn.5, para.194.

[21] *Iran v United States* I.C.J. Rep. 2003 p.161, para.43 and 73–77.

[22] I.C.J. Rep. 1996, p.226, para.41.

any way affect the authority and responsibility of the Security Council under the present Charter to take at any time such action as it deems necessary in order to maintain or restore international peace and security."

Self-defence is permissible if an armed attack has taken place and art.51 confines itself to self-defence only in this situation. When does such an attack occur, and what constitutes an armed attack?

In the *Nicaragua* case the ICJ confirmed the nature of self-defence as an inherent right under customary international law and established that an armed attacked includes

"not merely action by regular armed forces across an international border, but also 'the sending by or on behalf of a State of armed bands, groups, irregulars or mercenaries, which carry out armed force against another State of such gravity as to amount to' (inter alia) an actual armed attack conducted by regular forces, 'or its substantial involvement therein . . .'"

Furthermore

"the Court does not believe that the concept of 'armed attack' includes not only acts by armed bands where such acts occur on a significant scale but also assistance to rebels in the form of the provision of weapons or logistical or other support. Such assistance may be regarded as a threat or use of force, or amount to intervention in the internal or external affairs of other States."[23]

Can only states commit armed attacks? This issue has contemporary relevance given the increasing power of non-state actors, including armed groups and global terrorist groups such as Al-Qaeda and the group calling themselves Islamic State in Iraq and the Levant (ISIL, also known as Da'esh). Article 51 does not identify the perpetrator of an armed attack, and the Article's *travaux préparatoirs* do not provide any guidance in this respect. Traditionally, art.51 has been interpreted as requiring a state to commit an armed attack. To date the ICJ appears to take the view that self-defence may only be between states in nature,[24] however the Court has not been unanimous on this point.[25]

---

[23] Above, fn.5 at 103–104.
[24] *Case Concerning Armed Activities on the Territory of the Congo (Democratic Republic of the Congo v Uganda)*, Judgment of the 19 December 2005, para.146.
[25] See the Separate Opinions of Judge Simma (paras 4–16) and Judge Kooijmans (para.29), above. See also the Separate Opinions of Judge Higgins (para.33), Judge Kooijmans (paras 35–36) and Judge Buergenthal (paras 4–6)

However, states are increasingly using self-defence as the grounds to exercise force against terrorist groups. In 2001, following the attacks of 11 September upon the World Trade Centre in New York and the Pentagon in Washington DC, a series of UN Security Council Resolutions referred to the right of self-defence, and declared international terrorism to be a threat to international peace and security with regards to which such a right is operative.[26] When the US notified the Security Council of the action it was taking in Afghanistan against Al-Qaeda it declared it was exercising its right to self-defence. Equally, when in 2015 the UK commenced a campaign of air strikes against ISIL, the UK Government notified the Security Council that it had taken the measure in exercise of the inherent right of individual and collective self-defence.

Can a state resort to force in anticipation of an armed attack? Anticipatory self-defence is excluded from art.51, but does that mean it is prohibited? The right of self-defence, which art.51 acknowledges as "inherent", exists under customary international law—that is, independently of art.51. Therefore, does the right of anticipatory self-defence exist under customary international law?

States do employ force in anticipation of an alleged armed attack, for example Israel's strike on the United Arab Republic in June 1967. The justification for anticipatory self-defence can be reconciled with the obligation on UN Member States to refrain from either "the threat or use of force". States which are threatened with the use of force may take appropriate anticipatory measures to repel such a threat, however such measures can only be justified if:

(a) a state is the target of hostile activities of another state;

(b) the threatened state has exhausted all alternative means of protection;

(c) the danger is imminent;

(d) the defensive measures are proportionate to the pending danger.

States enjoy the right of self-defence in the event of an armed attack under art.51 of the UN Charter. Under customary international law they also enjoy the right to use force in circumstances

---

in *Legal Consequences of the Construction of a Wall in the Occupied Palestinian Territories, Advisory Opinion* (9 July 2004), I.C.J. Rep. 2004, p.136.

[26] UN SC Resolutions 1368 (2001) and 1373 (2001).

falling short of an armed attack—the ICJ did not feel it necessary to address the issue of anticipatory self-defence in the *Nicaragua* case. The existence of such a right was reaffirmed in the wake of the terrorist attack of 11 September 2001. Security Council Resolution 1368 and Security Council Resolution 1373 both recognise and reaffirm the inherent right of individual and collective self-defence as recognised by the Charter of the UN.

It was against this background that the then US President George W. Bush argued in his 2002 National Security Strategy, that modern technology and weapons of mass destruction rendered traditional deterrents ineffective. Thus, in what has become known as the Bush Doctrine, he postulated that states be allowed more discretion in the use of anticipatory self-defence. This failed to gain general acceptance by the international community and the legality of the US-led coalition intervention in Iraq in 2003 is still questioned.

However, whatever rights states enjoy with respect to the use of force, they are at all times required by the UN Charter and customary international law to settle their disputes by peaceful means.

Collective self-defence

The right of collective self-defence is recognised by art.51. Collective self-defence is something of a misnomer, as it refers to the right of each state to use force in defence of another state. The force is therefore employed on behalf of another state.

Collective self-defence refers, strictly speaking, to collective defence rather than self-defence. All measures adopted by Member States in self-defence must be reported to the Security Council, and the use of force in individual or collective self-defence should only be employed until the Security Council has taken appropriate measures to maintain international peace and security. The right of collective self-defence was recognised by the ICJ in the *Nicaragua* case as existing under customary international law, but its legitimate exercise depended on (a) a declaration by the alleged victim state that it had been attacked; and (b) a request by that state for assistance.[27] In the same case, the ICJ held that intervention by a third state could only be regarded as lawful "when the wrongful act provoking the response was an armed attack."[28] Following the invasion of Kuwait by Iraq in 1990, the Kuwaiti Government appealed for assistance from other states, therefore it has been argued that the armed response (Operation

---

[27] *Nicaragua* case, above, fn.5 at 110.
[28] Above.

Desert Storm) to liberate Kuwait could be considered as the exercise by that state of its legal right to collective self-defence.[29]

Article 51 is the legal basis of collective agreements such as the NATO Alliance, in which an attack on one member is treated as an attack on all. Under art.5 of the North Atlantic Treaty,[30] the Contracting Parties

> "agree that an armed attack against one or more of them in Europe or North America shall be considered an attack against them all; and consequently they agree that, if such an armed attack occurs, each of them, in exercise of the right of individual or collective self-defence recognized by Article 51 of the Charter of the United Nations, will assist the Party or Parties so attacked, by taking forthwith, individually, and in concert with the other Parties, such action as it deems necessary, including the use of armed force, to restore and maintain the security of the North Atlantic area."

NATO invoked art.5 for the first time in its history following the terrorist attacks against the US on 11 September 2001. The principle of collective defence was also discussed in the NATO context after Russia's military aggression against Ukraine and the annexations of part of the territory of the latter by the former in 2014 and certain measures were taken in 2015 to strengthen NATO positions in the region in anticipation of further crisis and in order to strengthen collective defence.

Regional arrangements

The right of states to make regional arrangements to deal with matters of international peace and security is protected by the UN Charter and, in particular, by art.52.

Article 52(1) provides:

> "Nothing in the present Charter precludes the existence of regional arrangements or agencies for dealing with such matters relating to the maintenance of international peace and security as are appropriate for regional action, provided that

---

[29] The armed action was taken, in January 1991, pursuant UN SC Res. 661 (1990), in which the Security Council recognised for the first time that collective self-defence applied, even when the assisting state had not been attacked and there was no special treaty arrangement to provide help. UN Doc.S/Res/661, 6 August 1990.

[30] U.N.T.S. 243. The Eastern European countries, Poland, the Czech Republic and Hungary were admitted into NATO in July 1997. Further enlargement of NATO occurred in March 2004 when another seven Eastern European countries joined.

such arrangements or agencies and their activities are consistent with the Purposes and Principles of the United Nations."

Article 52(2), however, charges members of regional organisations with making

> "every effort to achieve pacific settlement of local disputes through such regional arrangements or by such regional agencies before referring them to the Security Council."

Action taken via regional organisations will only be legitimate if it is consistent with the purposes and principles of the UN Charter, and does not amount to "enforcement action", unless this has been authorised by the Security Council. The Security Council must, under art.54, be kept fully informed at all times "of activities undertaken or in contemplation under regional arrangements or by regional agencies for the maintenance of international peace and security."

Regional organisations can play a vital role in the maintenance of international peace and security, as will be analysed below when referring to peacekeeping and peacebuilding.

Use of force to protect nationals abroad

What if a state's nationals or property are harmed abroad? Does that state have a right to intervene to defend its nationals when its territory has not been the object of an armed attack?

The Anglo–French invasion of Suez (1956), the Israeli raid on Entebbe Airport (1976), the abortive US rescue mission of the hostages in Iran (1980) and the US intervention in both Grenada (1983) and Panama (1989) are instances of force being used by the intervening state to protect its nationals. More recently, the protection of nationals abroad was used as a justification by Russia in respect of its intervention in Crimea in 2014.[31] The legitimacy of intervention to afford such protection is not firmly established in international law. Such intervention can be reconciled with the doctrine of self-defence if the basic concept underlying diplomatic protection is stretched, so that an imminent threat of danger to nationals abroad may be regarded as an imminent threat to the state of nationality itself. By invoking this legal fiction, intervention on behalf of the state's nationals can be reconciled with self-defence.

---

[31] See speech by the Ambassador of the Russian Federation to the UN, Mr. Churkin, at a Security Council debate on the situation in Ukraine, UN Doc. S/PV.7125, 3 March 2014.

Non-fulfilment by the host state of its international duty to safe-guard, to at least a minimum international standard, the interests of non-nationals, may lend support to intervention by the state of nationality. Thus, in the Security Council debate held in July 1976 on the Entebbe incident, an Israeli representative maintained Uganda had "violated a basic tenet of international law in failing to protect foreign nationals on its territory."[32]

Intervention to protect nationals is open to obvious abuse, par-ticularly as it involves a subjective interpretation by a state of when nationals are in danger. Even if protective intervention is accepted, it must be recognised as the exception rather than the norm, not least because it involves violations of another state's territorial integrity and sovereignty. Protective intervention is more likely to be accepted by the international community if the danger to the rescuing state's nationals can be shown to be overwhelming. A successful mission, although it should not be legally condoned, is more likely to be accepted as expedient than one which fails. For example, compare the Entebbe raid with the US abortive mission to rescue the American hostages in Iran. As with self-defence, the force used in such circumstances must be proportionate to the danger posed.

Collective measures through the UN: Chapter VII of the UN Charter

Security Council

Under the UN Charter the primary responsibility for the mainte-nance of peace lies with the Security Council.[33] Member states agree, under art.25, to accept and carry out the decisions of the Security Council. The Security Council can act either under Ch.VI or Ch.VII of the UN Charter.

Under Ch.VI arts 33–38, the Security Council can make recom-mendations with the objective of achieving a peaceful settlement to disputes. Chapter VII arts 39–51 deals with the enforcement measures which the Security Council can adopt. Under art.39, the Security Council is authorised to determine "the existence of any threat to the peace, breach of the peace, or act of aggression".

Following an affirmative decision under art.39, the Security Council can make recommendations or decide what measures are to be taken in accordance with the Charter to maintain inter-national peace and security. In practice, the Security Council seldom discusses the issue of whether it possesses jurisdiction under art.39, and consequently, upon which aspect (that is,

[32] See 15 I.L.M. 1228 (1976).
[33] art.24.

"aggression", "threat to the peace" or "breach of the peace") it is basing its action is not identified.

Aggression has been defined above. "Threat to the peace", which should be read as international peace, has been interpreted extensively and has evolved to encompass situations which previously would have been designated "internal" and thereby protected by art.2(7) of the UN Charter. "Threat to the peace" has been applied to take measures, for example, in respect of the Middle East conflict (1948), Southern Rhodesia (1966), Somalia (1992), Liberia (1992), Rwanda (1994), Sudan (regarding the situation in Darfur) (2004) and Libya (2011). "Threat to the peace" was also employed by the Security Council to the Libyan Government's failure to demonstrate "by concrete actions its renunciation of terrorism." in 2003.[34]

Although there have been arguments put forward to extend a "threat to the peace" to encompass issues such as climate change[35] and HIV/AIDS[36] and the effects they could have on security, the current position remains that the term a "threat to the peace" applies only in instances where there is an imminent risk of armed conflict.

A "breach of the peace" has only been specifically identified in four cases: Korea (1950), the Falklands (1982), Iran–Iraq (1987) and in the invasion of Kuwait by Iraq (1990–91), which was characterised as an act breaching "international peace and security".[37]

Before making recommendations or taking measures in accordance with the Charter to address the act of threat to peace, breach of peace or aggression, art.40 provides that the Security Council may call upon the parties concerned to comply with such provisional measures as it deems necessary or desirable. For example, the Security Council could call for a cease-fire.

The enforcement action which the Security Council may consider necessary may be either:

(i) measures not involving the use of force (art.41); or

(ii) armed force (art.42).

Article 41

Acting under art.41, the Security Council may call upon members of the UN to employ economic sanctions or diplomatic

---

[34] S.C. Res.748 (1992). Libya subsequently denounced terrorism in December 2003.

[35] UN Doc S/PRST/2011/15, 20 July 2011.

[36] S.C. Res.1308 (2000).

[37] S.C. Res.660, (1990) adopted 2 August 1990 by 14–0 (Yemen abstained), 29 I.L.M. 1325 (1990).

sanctions against a "defaulting" state. The economic sanctions imposed against Iraq, following its invasion of Kuwait, represent a most comprehensive action of the UN under art.41. UN Security Council Resolution 661[38] called upon Member States to abstain from the importation of all commodities and products originating in Iraq or Kuwait and the exportation to those states of all products, save those "supplies intended strictly for medical purposes, and, in humanitarian circumstances, foodstuffs". Supervision of Resolution 661 was entrusted to a Committee established by the Security Council and, under Resolution 666,[39] the Committee was charged with overviewing the supply of foodstuffs designated as falling within the humanitarian exception. Such supervision was undertaken in co-operation with humanitarian agencies such as the International Committee of the Red Cross. Resolution 665[40] called upon those Member States with maritime forces in the region

> "to use such measures commensurate with the specific circumstances to halt all inward and outward maritime shipping in order to inspect and verify their cargoes and destinations."

This was for the purpose of enforcing the sanctions. Subsequently, Iraq's continued presence in Kuwait led to stricter measures, namely the requirement that all states deny clearance (that is, permission to take off from, or fly over) to cargo-carrying aircraft bound for either Iraq or Kuwait.[41] The sanctions remained in force after the cease-fire[42] and continued in force, though mitigated to some extent by the "Oil for Food Programme".[43] The lifting of economic sanctions against Iraq was approved by the Security Council in May 2003.[44]

Resolution 748, adopted on 31 March 1992, requiring Libya to comply with Resolution 731 (namely to co-operate in determining responsibility for the activities which culminated at Lockerbie), was also adopted under Ch.VII, as was the mandatory arms embargo established against Yugoslavia by Security Council Resolution 713 in September 1991, and also Security Council Resolution 1373 (2001) in relation to the 11 September 2001 attacks.

---

[38] (1990) adopted by 13–0 (Cuba and Yemen abstained) 6 August 1990; 29 I.L.M. 1325 (1990).
[39] (1990) adopted 13 September 1990, above, at 1330.
[40] (1990) adopted 25 August 1990, above, fn.38 at 1329.
[41] S.C. Res. 670 adopted 25 September 1990, above, fn.38 at 1334.
[42] S.C. Res. 687 (1991), which set out the terms of a permanent cease-fire.
[43] S.C. Res. 986 (1995), the "Oil for Food Programme" was further modified in S.C. Res. 1284 (1999), S.C. Res. 1409 (2002) and S.C. Res. 1472 (2003).
[44] S.C. Res. 1483 (2003).

Article 42

If the Security Council considers that art.41 measures would be, or have proved inadequate, it may take such action by air, sea or land forces as may be necessary to maintain or restore international peace and security. Such action may include demonstrations, blockades and other operations by air, sea, or land forces of members of the UN.

Article 42 is supplemented by art.43, according to which states undertake to provide, under special agreements with the Security Council, armed forces assistance and facilities, including rights of passage, to the extent necessary for maintaining peace and security.

The veto

Every member of the Security Council has one vote.[45] Procedural issues, in order to be adopted, must receive the affirmative vote of nine members, while non-procedural matters require nine votes, including the concurring vote of the five Permanent Members (China, France, the UK, the US and the Russian Federation). Absence and abstention are taken as concurrence.[46] The decision as to whether a matter is or is not procedural is itself a non-procedural issue, that is, the concurring vote of the five Permanent Members is required.

The possibility of exercising a double veto is therefore open to a Permanent Member. If, because of the veto, the Security Council is unable to make any decisions, then the General Assembly, with residual authority for the maintenance of peace, can assume the responsibility which the Security Council is unable to discharge.

General Assembly

Under the UN Charter, the General Assembly may discuss any questions relating to the maintenance of international peace and security, provided the matter is not before the Security Council.[47] The Security Council makes decisions, however the General Assembly can only make recommendations. The UN Charter ascribed a less active role to the General Assembly than

---

[45] art.27.

[46] In *Legal Consequences for States of the Continued Presence of South Africa in Namibia (South West Africa) Notwithstanding Security Council Resolution 276 (1970)* (Advisory Opinion) I.C.J. Rep., 1971, p.16, the ICJ found "abundant evidence" that rulings of the President of the Security Council and Members of the Security Council do not regard voluntary abstention by a Permanent Member as vetoing the adoption of a resolution.

[47] arts 11 and 12.

that given to the Security Council. During the Cold War era the Security Council was, through the use of the veto, less effective and this led to a more active role being assumed by the General Assembly.

The inability of the Security Council to take further action for the management of the Korean campaign (because of the return to his seat of the Soviet Union representative and his consequent use of the veto) led to the Uniting for Peace Resolution in November 1950.[48] This Resolution provided that, in the event of the Security Council being unable, because of a lack of unanimity of the Permanent Members, to discharge its primary responsibility for the maintenance of international peace and security, the General Assembly could, where there appears to be a threat to the peace, breach of the peace or act of aggression

> "consider the matter immediately with a view to making appropriate recommendations to Members for collective measures, including in the case of a breach of the peace or act of aggression the use of armed force when necessary, to maintain or restore international peace and security."

If the General Assembly is not in session at the time, an emergency session may be called. An emergency session may be requested by the Security Council on the vote of any nine members, or by a majority of the members of the UN. The General Assembly has invoked the Uniting for Peace Resolution on a number of occasions, e.g. the Suez Question (1956), the Congo Question (1960), the Pakistan Civil War (Bangladesh) (1972), Afghanistan (1980), Namibia (1981) and alleged violations of the fourth Geneva Convention relating to the protection of civilian persons in times of war—Israel (1999). The Uniting for Peace Resolution was more effective in allowing issues to be discussed in the General Assembly, rather than as a means of preventing crises and preserving international peace and security. The demise of the cold war allowed the Security Council to act more frequently in the way envisaged by the UN Charter unhampered by the use of the veto. This has been reflected in the consequential overshadowing of the General Assembly.

It is generally accepted that the current membership of the Security Council does not accurately reflect the balance of power within the international community but rather still reflects, essentially, the global power structure of 1945. A UN-appointed high-level panel on "Threats, Challenges and Change" proposed two models for the enlargement of the Security Council,

---

[48] Res. 377 (V), 3 November 1950; G.A.O.R., 5th Session, Supp.20, p.10.

in December 2004[49]; in both models the Security Council would be increased to 24 members. In one model there would be an additional six permanent seats with no veto and three new two-year termed elected seats. The alternative proposal would create a new category of eight semi-permanent seats renewable every four years and one new two-year non-renewable seat. However, neither the panel nor Kofi Annan's Report "Enlarging Freedom" expressed any preference and the panel felt the existing five Permanent Members should keep their seats and their veto. On 14 September 2015, the UN General Assembly adopted a decision to advance efforts to reform and increase the membership of the Security Council in its 70th session.[50]

The structure of the Security Council however remains as it has been since it was established, and potential reform remains on the agenda. Criticism of the status quo continues and is directed at both the general configuration of the Security Council and at specific decisions. An example of the former is the lack of an African presence among the Permanent Members. Criticisms of the latter situation include calls for the five Permanent Members to give up their veto rights on issues involving mass atrocities, because of the danger of stalemate and inaction by the Council, for example, the case of Syria in 2012. The lack of agreement towards the actions to take against the repressive measures of the Syrian Government following the uprisings during the so-called Arab Spring in 2011 and the subsequent civil war in the country meant that the war intensified and in 2016 continues. This war has created the greatest influx of refugees since the Second World War and seen some of the worst acts of violence and desperate humanitarian situations in recent years.

The UN Secretary-General

The UN Secretary-General has an important role to play in the maintenance of international peace and security. One of the most vital roles played by the Secretary-General is to prevent international disputes from arising, escalating and spreading through the use of his "good offices". These are the steps taken both in public and in private, drawing upon the independence, impartiality and integrity of the position to bring the parties of an escalating conflict closer for a peaceful resolution. Since 1992, when Dr. Boutros Boutros-Ghali published his Report entitled "An Agenda for Peace",[51] the UN Secretary General has played a decisive role in

---

[49] The panel was made up of 16 veteran diplomats and politicians under the chairmanship of the former Thai Prime Minister Anand Panyarachun.

[50] See U.N. Doc. A/69/L.92, 11 September 2015.

[51] An Agenda for Peace: *"Preventative Diplomacy, Peacemaking and*

defining the collective action of the United Nations to prevent and bring to an end conflicts, as well as rebuilding countries and administering justice after conflict.

"An Agenda for Peace" identified important interconnected UN security functions, inter alia:

(a) preventative diplomacy;

(b) peacemaking;

(c) peace building in its differing contexts;

(d) rebuilding institutions and infrastructures of nations divided by civil war and strife; and

(e) addressing the causes of conflict, for example economic deprivation, social injustice and political oppression.

The Secretary-General also called for the creation of permanent peace-enforcement units under art.43 of the UN Charter with the ability to respond to aggression immediately, but this recommendation has not been implemented and the troops under the emblem of the UN, which intervene in conflict and post-conflict countries, continue to be national troops under their own command. Peacekeeping and peacebuilding activities are analysed below.

Peacekeeping and peacebuilding

An important area of activity of the UN related to armed conflict is that of peacekeeping and, increasingly, peacebuilding, and the UN is the main organisation delivering these missions, although regional organisations are increasingly taking a greater role. The UN Charter does not provide for those peacekeeping forces—i.e. forces which are designed to maintain peace rather than take enforcement action—which have made an important contribution in major crises. Peacekeeping forces, which consist of troops given voluntarily by UN Member States, must remain impartial at all times. The UN has been involved in peacekeeping since its creation, but peacekeeping operations have evolved significantly since the end of the Cold War. Peacekeeping forces have been responsible for supervising a cease-fire, e.g. the UN Emergency Force (UNEF) in the Middle East in 1956. They have also been responsible for the UN Iran–Iraq Military Observer Group (UNIMOG), established in 1988; assisting a return to

Peacekeeping" 17 June 1992 31 I.L.M. 953 (1992) U.N.Doc.A/47/277, S/24111 (1992).

peace with the UN Force in the Congo (ONUC) in 1960, and the UN Protection Force in Yugoslavia (UNPROFOR) 1992, in patrolling a buffer zone. They participated in the supervision of the attainment of independence, UN Transition Assistance Group (UNTAG established 1978, operational 1989) with respect to Namibia. The UN and African Union set up a hybrid peace-keeping operation in Darfur (UNAMID)[52] in 2007, primarily to protect civilians; and a UN peacekeeping force was established for Mali in 2013 to contribute to supporting political stability (MINUSMA).[53]

Peacekeeping, as opposed to peace enforcing and humanitarian intervention, explained below, is based on state consensus. In principle, UN peacekeeping forces can only operate in a territory as long as the host state consents. At the end of the Cold War, the international community attempted to extend its capacity to intervene in civil conflicts through enforcement action and imposed several peace operations on countries without the consent of the parties in the conflict.

The constitutionality of peacekeeping forces was affirmed in the *Certain Expenses of the United Nations* case.[54] The ICJ was requested by the General Assembly to give an Advisory Opinion on the legality of expenses levied on members for the purpose of financing the UN forces in the Middle East (UNEF) and the Congo (ONUC), following the refusal of a number of states, including the Soviet Union and France, to make their contributions. The ICJ held the expenses were legitimate as they were made for the fulfilment of a purpose of the UN.[55]

Regarding the respective roles of the Security Council and General Assembly in the maintenance of international peace and security, the ICJ emphasised that, while the Security Council enjoyed a primary responsibility, its responsibility was not exclusive. The ICJ did, however, acknowledge that only the Security Council could "require enforcement by coercive action against an aggressor."[56] In other words, the authorisation of enforcement measures involving the use of force is the prerogative of the Security Council. The General Assembly's competence is, in the light of the Court's opinion, limited to action which falls short of enforcement action per se. The General Assembly may not be competent to authorise enforcement measures which involve the use of force, but it can nevertheless recommend

---

[52] S.C.Res.1769 (2007).
[53] S.C.Res.2100 (2013).
[54] I.C.J. Rep. 1962 p.151.
[55] Above, at 172.
[56] Above, at 163.

action when that does not involve "enforcement action" but rather the establishment of a peacekeeping force designed to maintain the peace.

Under the UN regime, although the Security Council is the organ exclusively competent to authorise the use of force, the General Assembly enjoys residual competence to recommend action falling short of coercive or enforcement action.

There have been several instances in which the international forces have, under the mandate of the UN, intervened to keep the peace without the consent of the states involved. This is generally referred to as peace enforcement. Situations such as those of the former Yugoslavia and Somalia, highlight the complexity of the tasks confronting UN deployment forces.

In "Agenda for Peace", Secretary-General Boutros Boutros-Ghali recommended the deployment of "peace-enforcement units from member states, which would be available on call and would consist of troops that have volunteered for such service",[57] the idea being that UN military forces would provide an effective means of deterring aggression and containing humanitarian crises.[58] As they evolved, peacekeeping operations became increasingly complex and multifaceted. In March 2000, Secretary-General Kofi Annan convened a high-level panel to undertake a review of the UN peace and security activities with a view to presenting a clear set of specific, concrete and practical recommendations. This panel produced a series of recommendations contained in what is known as the Brahimi Report.[59] The report recommended that peacekeeping operations had civilian components alongside military ones in order to move beyond just keeping the peace to building a sustainable stable environment that permitted durable peace and development. Since then peacekeeping operations have included in their mandates, together with the classical monitoring of a ceasefire, the disarmament, demobilisation and reintegration of excombatants; security sector reform and rule of law reform, including legislative reform and justice system reform; capacity building and training; and human rights goals. In 2005, a Peacebuilding Commission was created by the UN General Assembly and Security Council with the mandate to bring together all relevant actors involved in peacebuilding and focus attention on reconstruction and institution-building for post-conflict recovery,

---

[57] Agenda for Peace doc, above, fn.51.

[58] Note, jurisdictional immunity from the ICC for personnel participating in situations authorised by the UN now exists. Exemption applies to personnel from countries that do not accept the jurisdiction of the ICC, e.g. the US. See S.C. Res. 1422 (2002).

[59] A/55/305-S/2000/809, 17 August 2000, 39 I.L.M. 2000, p.1432.

as well as sustainable development.[60] Two decades on, the Peacebuilding Commission continues its work.

Humanitarian intervention and the responsibility to protect

Humanitarian intervention refers to the intervention of a state or group of states in representation of the international community in a conflict in another country. These tend to be civil wars. Civil wars are not prohibited by international law. Article 2(4) prohibits the use of force in respect of international relations only. International law does, however, have something to say on participation by states in another state's civil war. The general rule is one of non-intervention. The General Assembly's 1981 Declaration on the Inadmissibility of Intervention in the Domestic Affairs of States and the Protection of their Independence and Sovereignty[61] prohibits any state from intervening

> "directly or indirectly, for any reason whatever, in the internal or external affairs of any other State ... no State shall organize, assist, foment, finance, incite or tolerate subversive, terrorist or armed activities directed towards the violent overthrow of the regime of another State, or interfere in civil strife in another State."

The prohibitions enunciated in the General Assembly's 1965 Declaration on the Inadmissibility of Intervention in Domestic Affairs of State[62] were reaffirmed in the 1970 Declaration on Principles of International Law.[63]

States may, for a variety of political reasons, intervene to support the rebels, or alternatively to support the established authorities. Policy rather than law has been determining a state's decision to intervene. However, in recent years the so-called Responsibility to Protect doctrine has been evolving and there is a debate on whether there is an international obligation to intervene in a conflict for humanitarian reasons, in order to protect the civil population.

Humanitarian intervention is distinct from protective intervention in that it involves intervention to protect another state's nationals (or a group of nationals) and possibly those of the territorial state. The intervening state is, in other words, not protecting its own rights. Although it may be contended that, at least

---

[60] A/RES/60/180, 30 December 2005 and S/RES/1645 (2005), 20 December 2005.
[61] A/RES/36/103, 9 December 1981.
[62] General Assembly Res. 2131 (XX).
[63] General Assembly Res. 2625 (XXV).

prima facie, the intervening state is playing a more objective role than when intervening to protect its own nationals, humanitarian intervention is equally open to abuse. The intervening state may ostensibly intervene to promote an altruistic interest, but in reality, political motives and an anxiety to secure for itself some perceived interest may prompt intervention.

The demise of the Cold War transferred the spotlight to the increasing number of internal conflicts which remain a constant feature of the contemporary global landscape. Enhanced media technology heightened public awareness of the human suffering experienced by civilians in areas of conflict and increased the calls for international intervention in civil conflicts. Humanitarian intervention remains at odds with art.2(4) of the UN Charter and the existence in contemporary international law of such an exception is contested. However, notwithstanding this, in certain circumstances a particular situation has demanded at least tacit acceptance of intervention, e.g. the NATO military intervention in Kosovo (Operation Allied Force) in 1999 prompted by the repression of the ethnic Albanian population within Kosovo.[64] NATO also intervened in Libya in 2011 providing military assistance to the rebel groups fighting Colonel Gaddafi's regime and to ease the provision of humanitarian assistance to Libya.[65] In 2013, the UK Government took the position that humanitarian intervention in Syria, in light of the use of chemical weapons by the Syrian Government, would be legal.[66]

In 2000, the International Commission on Intervention and State Sovereignty (ICISS), an independent international body, was established by the Canadian Government, with the aim of building "broader understanding of the problem of reconciling intervention for human protection purposes and [State] sovereignty".[67] In particular, it attempted to move towards

---

[64] Security Council Resolution 1199, 23 September 1998. The NATO intervention was challenged by FRY (Federal Republic of Yugoslavia) in the *Legality of Use of Force* cases brought before the ICJ against NATO member states, see for example *Legality of the Use of Force case (Yugoslavia v US) Provisional Measures*, 2 June 1999, I.C.J. Rep. 1999, p.916.

[65] The Libya case can be contrasted with Kosovo as unlike the latter case, with regard to Libya the Security Council passed resolution 1973 (2011), authorising UN Member States "to take all necessary measures to protect civilians under threat of attack in the country". It has therefore been argued that, without considering humanitarian intervention as a legal basis for military force, the use of force in Libya was lawful as it was authorised by the Security Council under Ch.VII of the UN Charter.

[66] (2013) B.Y.I.L. 806. Despite the UK Government's position on the legality of humanitarian intervention, the British Parliament voted against military action.

[67] Report of the International Commission on Intervention and State Sovereignty, "The Responsibility to Protect", December 2001, para.1.7.

"global political consensus"[68] on the issue of how to deal with humanitarian intervention. In December 2001, the ICISS elaborated the doctrine of responsibility to protect.[69] The ICISS identified three elements to responsibility: to prevent conflict and other crises that put populations at risk; to react to situations of compelling human need; and to rebuild, particularly after a military intervention.

In 2004, the UN Secretary-General appointed a High-Level Panel on Threats, Challenges and Change, to assess current threats to international peace and security; evaluate how these threats have been dealt with; and make recommendations to strengthen the UN collective security system. The Report of the High-Level Panel endorsed "the emerging norm that there is a collective international responsibility to protect".[70] The doctrine of Responsibility to Protect was endorsed by the General Assembly at the 2005 World Summit,[71] reaffirmed by the Security Council[72] and subsequently reiterated in the Secretary-General's report of January 2009.[73] A number of states ostensibly support the doctrine of Responsibility to Protect, including the UK and Canada, however its recognition as a rule of international law remains uncertain and support may be dependent on political factors and circumstances.

Domestic jurisdiction limitation

Article 2(7) of the UN Charter prohibits the UN from intervening in matters which are essentially within the jurisdiction of any state. This limitation does not apply in respect of Ch.VII enforcement action. Domestic jurisdiction has been interpreted restrictively and art.2(7) has not impeded the work of the UN.[74]

For instance, severe violations of human rights are no longer considered to be solely within a state's domestic jurisdiction and

---

[68] Above.
[69] Above.
[70] Report of the High-Level Panel on Threats, Challenges and Change, "A more secure world: our shared responsibility", para.203. See also paras 201–202.
[71] "2005 World Summit Outcome Document", UN Doc A/60/L.1, paras 138–139.
[72] Security Council Res 1674, UN Doc S/RES/1674 (2006), Operative para.4; Security Council Res 1706, UN Doc S/RES/1706 (2006), Preamble, para.2.
[73] The Report to the General Assembly 63rd session, 12 January 2009 A/63/670.
[74] For example, UN S.C. Res. 687 (1991), which was passed in the aftermath of the Gulf crisis, was considered particularly intrusive and authorised the destruction of Iraq's nuclear, chemical and biological weapons. See Lawrence D. Roberts, "United Nations Security Council Resolution 687 and its Aftermath: The Implications for Domestic Authority and the Need for Legitimacy" [1993] 25, International Law and Politics 593.

are therefore excluded from an application of art.2(7).[75] During Security Council debate concerning UN Resolution 688 (1991), it was declared that art.2(7) does not apply to matters which are not fundamentally domestic, such as human rights protection.[76] Intervention by the international community to prevent human suffering is, however, beset with conceptual difficulties. What constitutes human suffering, and how widespread would it need to be before intervention would be triggered?

Certainly, the principles of state sovereignty and non-interference in internal affairs are no longer sacrosanct in a world where increased international telecommunications prevent governments from hiding behind the shield of the sovereign state.

Force authorised by a competent organ of the UN

A state may be authorised by the Security Council to use force, even in circumstances when the use of force would otherwise be illegal. This is the conclusion to be drawn from the Security Council Resolution 221 (1966), which called upon the UK

> "to prevent by the use of force if necessary . . . vessels reasonably believed to be carrying oil destined for Rhodesia, and . . . to arrest and detain the tanker known as the Joanna V upon her departure from Beira in the event her oil cargo is discharged there."[77]

Apparently, as art.42 authorises the Security Council to use force in circumstances where force would normally be illegal, the Security Council can authorise states to do likewise. Other instances where art.42 has been invoked in support of sanctions imposed under art.41 include Iraq (1990 and 1991), Former Yugoslavia (1992) and Haiti (1993 and 1994).

JUS IN BELLO

In the event of states turning from the procedures prescribed by international law for the settlement of their disputes by peaceful means, hostilities may occur. However, there still exists a legal regime which states are required to respect—*jus in bello* (the laws of war). These fall into two categories—those relating to the actual conduct of hostilities and those which afford a minimum

---

[75] On human rights as an international concern beyond the domestic jurisdiction of states, see M. N. Shaw, *International Law*, 7th edn (Cambridge: Cambridge University Press, 2014), p.194.

[76] See UN Doc.S/PV 2982 at 58 (1991) (providing text of the Resolution debates).

[77] S.C.O.R., 21st year, Resolutions and Decisions, p.5; 5 I.L.M. 534 (1966).

protection to individuals. The former are to be found principally in the Hague Conventions 1899 and 1907, and are referred to as "the Law of The Hague", while the Four Geneva Conventions 1949 and two Additional Protocols adopted in 1977 comprise the latter, and are known as "The Law of Geneva". However, as noted by the ICJ the two "have become so closely inter–related that they are considered to have gradually formed one single complex system, known today as international humanitarian law."[78]

Conduct of hostilities during armed conflict

Declarations of war are generally no longer issued. The UN Charter does not distinguish between war and other modes of armed force, nor do the Geneva Conventions or the 1977 Protocols, and the expression "armed conflict" is today frequently employed. However, a characterisation of the nature of the conflict may be important for neutral states and determining the status of aliens.

The promulgation of the Lieber Code[79] in 1863 by US President Lincoln represents the first official statement on the laws relating to the conduct of hostilities. The Code, although originally adopted by the President for application during the American Civil War, continued to govern US practice for some 50 years, as well as influencing the conduct of other states. The Code served as a blueprint for the Brussels Conference when considering the law of land warfare. Although the Declaration emanating from the Conference in 1874 was never ratified, its importance is evident in its contribution to the 1899 International Convention with respect to the Laws and Customs of War on Land[80] and the subsequent 1907 Convention Concerning the Laws and Customs of War on Land[81] and the regulations attached thereto. These constitute the core rules on the conduct of armed conflict in contemporary international law, and are recognised as customary international law.[82]

Essentially, the law restricts the manner of injuring the enemy by prohibiting unnecessary calculated suffering by the employment of arms, projectiles, or materials.

The Hague Conference of 1899 adopted two Conventions

---

[78] *Advisory Opinion on the Legality of the Threat or Use of Nuclear Weapons* I.C.J. Rep. 1996, p.226.
[79] Called after its principal author, Professor Francis Lieber.
[80] The Hague, 29 July 1899; T.S. 11 (1901); Cd.800.
[81] The Hague, 18 October 1907; T.S. 9 (1910); Cd.5030.
[82] For a more in-depth look at the laws of war see Ingrid Detter, *The Law of War* (3rd edn, Ashgate, 2013) and for a synopsis of the laws of war, see, Jochnick and Normand, "The Legitimisation of Violence: A Critical History of the Laws of War" (1994) 35 Harvard International Law Journal 1.

relating directly to the conduct of war and forbidden weapons,[83] a number of Declarations outlawing the discharge of projectiles and explosives from balloons, the use of asphyxiating gases and expanding bullets.

A further 13 Conventions were adopted at the 1907 Hague Conference. These related, inter alia, to the opening of hostilities, the rights and duties of neutral powers, the conversion of merchant ships into warships, the laying of automatic submarine contact mines and bombardments by naval forces in time of war.[84] The only Convention which was not ratified was the 12th, on the establishment of an International Prize Court.

States have attempted to regulate the use of chemical and biological weapons since early in the 20th century. In 1925 The Geneva Protocol[85] forbade the employment of asphyxiating, poisonous or other gases as well as bacteriological methods of warfare. The two main instruments in this area are the 1972 Biological and Toxin Weapons Convention,[86] prohibiting the development, production and stockpiling thereof and the 1993 Chemical Weapons Convention, regulating the development, production, stockpiling and use of such weapons.[87] The Chemical Weapons Convention is the first disarmament agreement negotiated within a multilateral framework which provides for the elimination of chemical weapons under the control of an international agency.[88]

However, the use of chemical weapons remains an issue of concern for the international community. For example, at the early stages of the Syrian civil war, there was evidence that the Syrian Government was using them against its own population. Following intense international pressure, and to avoid a US-led effort of humanitarian intervention, the Syrian Government acceded the Chemical Weapons Convention on October 2013 and agreed to an accelerated destruction schedule of its stock, endorsed by the UN SC Resolution 2118 (2013).[89] The effectiveness of the 1972 Biological and Toxin Weapons Convention[90] is severely restricted by the absence of monitoring compliance, and agreement as to what compliance mechanisms should be established.

---

[83] Hague Conventions I and II.
[84] Hague Conventions III, V, VII, VIII and IX.
[85] Geneva, 17 June 1925; T.S. 24 (1930) Cmd.3604.
[86] London, Moscow and Washington, 10 April 1972; T.S. 11 (1976) Cmnd.6397.
[87] 13 January 1993, 32 I.L.M. 800 (1993). In force as of 29 April 1997.
[88] The Convention establishes a permanent agency, the Organisation for the Prohibition of Chemical Weapons, which has its seat in The Hague.
[89] S/RES/2118 (2013), 27 September 2013.
[90] 1015 UNTS 163.

International efforts have also concentrated on tackling the devastating effects of landmines.[91] These weapons are particularly devastating due to the disproportionate harm they cause to civilians, many of whom are women and children working or playing in the fields in which the weapons have been planted. Also they render areas of land unusable long after a conflict is over, which has serious negative consequences for the recovery of communities by limiting their ability for instance to farm and access forests or other resources for shelter. The main instrument regulating landmines is the 1997 Convention on the Prohibition on the Use, Stockpiling, Production and Transfer of Anti-Personnel (AP) Mines and on their Destruction (the Ottawa Convention). The Ottawa Convention prohibits the use of AP landmines and the gradual destruction of stockpiles and mines already in the ground. The Treaty entered into force on 1 March 1999 and it is today one of the most widely ratified international treaties. All types of conflict are covered, civil war and international; this is in recognition of the increasing use of land mines in civil wars (amendment to Protocol II of the 1980 Convention).[92]

The use of landmines has decreased, many areas have been successfully demined and stockpiles destroyed. Despite this, Landmine and Cluster Munitions Monitor, a civil society organisation which investigates and records the use of landmines and cluster munitions with a view to eliminate their use, reported a global total in 2014 of 3,678 casualties, a 12% increase compared with the previous year.[93]

Similarly to the international effort to ban landmines, concern over the civilian suffering and casualties caused by cluster munitions, as well as the dangers presented by the large scale national stockpiling of cluster munitions for operational use, provided the impetus for the adoption of a treaty banning the use and stockpiling of cluster munitions. In May 2008, the Convention on Cluster

---

[91] In 1993, the UN GA unanimously adopted a resolution calling for a moratorium on the export of landmines A/Res/48/75K, November 1993. Other resolutions passed by the UN in 1993 were, inter alia—strengthening of UN assistance to mine clearance efforts (A/Res/48/7) and additional protection of children against the effects of mines (A/Res/48/157).

[92] The Organization of American States (OAS) also adopted a resolution which provides for the establishment of a continent-wide zone free of all landmines at its 26th General Assembly in Panama City in June 1996. The resolution asks states to declare a moratorium on the production, use and transfer of all anti-personnel mines and to ratify the 1980 UN Convention on Certain Conventional Weapons and the amended Protocol. It further provides for the opening of a register at the organisation's General Secretariat to record information on existing stocks and the mine-clearing situation.

[93] Landmine Monitor 2015, LMM15.

Munitions was adopted.[94] The Convention requires each state party to undertake never under any circumstances to

> "(a) Use cluster munitions;
>
> (b) Develop, produce, otherwise acquire, stockpile, retain or transfer to anyone, directly or indirectly, cluster munitions;
>
> (c) Assist, encourage, or induce anyone to engage in any activity prohibited to a State Party under this Convention".[95]

The Convention has, however, been opposed by a number of states that produce and stockpile cluster munitions, including the US, China, Russia, India, Israel, Pakistan and Brazil.

The trade in conventional weapons remains a major problem globally and contributes to the fuelling of conflicts as well as inflicting extensive suffering on the civilian population as there is a lack of internationally agreed standards to ensure that arms are only transferred for appropriate use. In 2009 the UN General Assembly called for a Conference to be held in July 2012 to negotiate a comprehensive arms treaty which would serve as "a legally binding instrument on the highest possible common international standards for the transfer of conventional arms".[96] After long and often difficult negotiations, the Arms Trade Treaty, which will regulate the trade of conventional weapons from small arms to large combat aircraft and ships, entered into force on 24 December 2014.[97]

Nuclear Weapons

The control of nuclear weapons has been on the international agenda since the establishment of the UN. In 1946, the UN General Assembly adopted the first Resolution addressing the need for options to eliminate atomic weapons from national armaments. A number of multilateral treaties currently make up the legal regime for the prevention of nuclear proliferation and testing and nuclear disarmament. These include the Limited Test Ban Treaty (LTBT) 1963[98]; the Treaty on the Non-Proliferation of

---

[94] CCM/77, 30 May 2008. As of August 2015, 93 states are party to the Convention which entered into force on 1 August 2010.

[95] art.1 Convention on Cluster Munitions.

[96] UN Office for Disarmament Affairs.

[97] Arms Trade Treaty, New York, 2 April 2013, entered into force 24 December 2014, 90 days following the date of the deposit of the fiftieth instrument of ratification, as per art.22. As of August 2015 the Treaty has 72 parties.

[98] 480 U.N.T.S. 43.

Nuclear Weapons (Non-Proliferation Treaty) 1968[99]; the Treaty for the Prohibition of Nuclear Weapons in Latin America 1967 and Additional Protocols I and II.[100]

The LTBT prohibits nuclear tests in the atmosphere, in outer space and underwater. Also prohibited is any such explosion by a state in any other environment if that would result in the presence of radioactive debris outside its territory.

Under the Non-Proliferation Treaty "nuclear weapons parties" undertake not to transfer to any recipient nuclear weapons or devices, or to assist any "non-nuclear weapon State" to manufacture, acquire or control such weapons or devices. "Non-nuclear weapon parties" undertake corollary obligations, whereas the Treaty of the Prohibition of Nuclear Weapons in Latin America and its Protocols established Latin America as a denuclearised region.

Strategic Arms Limitation Talks and the Strategic Arm Reduction Talks

The Strategic Arms Limitation Talks held between 1969 and 1972 produced a number of agreements, namely; the 1971 Agreement on Measures to Reduce the Risk of Outbreak of Nuclear War (the Accidents Agreement), the 1971 Agreement on Measures to Improve the Direct Communications Link (the Hot-Line Upgrade Agreement) and the 1972 Treaty on the Limitation of Anti-Ballistic Missile Systems (ABM). The SALT II negotiations did not prove as fruitful as only one treaty was produced; the 1979 Treaty on the Limitation of Strategic Offensive Arms, and this has never been ratified by the US.

The 1980s witnessed the initiation of new talks—the Strategic Arms Reduction Talks (START) and Reduction of Intermediate-Range Nuclear Forces (INF). Treaties were signed, respectively, in July 1991 by Presidents Bush and Gorbachev (START I) and January 1993 by Presidents Bush and Yeltsin (START II). Negotiations on a START III Treaty were never concluded. The emphasis is now more on reduction than elimination. On 24 May 2002, the US President, George W. Bush, and the Russian President, Vladimir Putin, signed a Nuclear Arms Reduction Treaty (the Moscow Treaty). The Treaty was designed to substantially reduce deployed, strategic, nuclear warhead arsenals by 31 December 2012. In April 2010, the New START Treaty was signed by the US and Russia in Prague. New START entered into force in February 2011 and replaces the Treaty of Moscow. It is expected

---

[99] 729 U.N.T.S. 161; 7 I.L.M. 809 (1968). Extended indefinitely in 1995.
[100] 6 I.L.M. 533–534 (1967).

to last until at least 2021 and commits the US and Russia to reduce by half their strategic nuclear missile launchers. It also establishes a new inspection and verification regime.

A comprehensive Nuclear Test Ban Treaty was opened for signature in September 1996 after it received majority support in the General Assembly. The Treaty seeks to impose an international ban on all nuclear testing. However, a problem besetting its entry into force is the need for those states known to possess nuclear reactors to sign before the Treaty can become law.[101]

The ICJ considered the legality of the use of nuclear weapons in 1996. In the *Advisory Opinion on the Legality of the Threat or Use of Weapons*, the ICJ expressed the view "[T]here is in neither customary nor conventional international law any specific authorisation of the threat or use of nuclear weapons."[102] The ICJ did not give a conclusive opinion on the use of nuclear weapons in self-defence but observed that the requirements of a lawful self-defence would have to be met, e.g. proportionality. Nor could the ICJ conclude definitively that the use or threat of nuclear weapons could legitimately be used in the extreme circumstances of self-defence if the very survival of the State were at stake. However, the ICJ found, unanimously, that an obligation did exist to negotiate in good faith, and also bring to a conclusion those negotiations that would lead to nuclear disarmament under strict and effective international control.

The control of nuclear weapons is a crucial contemporary international issue, given their destructive capacity. Several countries have refused to engage in talks regarding their possession and use of such weapons, and of particular concern have been North Korea and Iran. Following years of international economic sanctions, Iran entered into negotiations with the US to dismantle its capacity to produce nuclear weapons and in July 2015 the Joint Comprehension Plan of Action between Iran, the five Permanent Members of the UN Security Council, plus Germany, and the European Union was agreed. In exchange for lifting the international sanctions, Iran will practically eliminate its stockpile of enriched-uranium under the monitoring of the International Atomic Energy Agency.

HUMANITARIAN LAW

The first expression of protection for the individual involved in armed conflict was the 1864 Geneva Convention for the Amelioration of the Condition of the Wounded and Sick of

---

[101] Annex 2; for full text, see 35 I.L.M. 1439 (1996).
[102] Re UN General Assembly Res. 49/75K. See 35 I.L.M. 809 (1996).

Armed Forces in the Field.[103] However, the bulk of contemporary humanitarian law is contained in the four 1949 Geneva Conventions and the two 1977 Additional Protocols,[104] which are now largely regarded as customary international law. Sick, wounded and shipwrecked military personnel are afforded protection by Conventions I and II. The third Convention sets out the minimum treatment to be afforded to prisoners of war. The fourth articulates the protection of civilian persons (this represented an advance, in that earlier protection to civilians had been relatively limited, being contained in the Hague Regulations and customary international law).

The Geneva Conventions originally applied only to all international armed-conflict situations, but this definition was extended in 1977 to include wars of "self-determination" (Protocol I) and victims of "non-international armed conflicts" (Protocol II). The latter builds on art.3, which is common to the four Conventions, and provides that certain minimum provisions apply in "armed conflict not of an international character."[105] Specifically excluded are instances of "internal disturbances and tensions, such as riots, isolated and sporadic acts of violence and other acts of a similar nature."[106]

The Convention for the Protection of Cultural Property in the event of Armed Conflict,[107] adopted in 1954, should also be mentioned. This Convention aims at protecting cultural objects and religious places, as well as objects designated vital to the survival of the civilian population—drinking-water supplies, foodstuffs, agricultural areas for production thereof and irrigation works (provided they are not used exclusively by the armed forces or in furtherance of military action).

Spies and mercenaries are denied the general protection which is enjoyed by either prisoners of war or combatants. Mercenaries are those who sell their fighting services for personal gain, and their recruitment is contrary to international law. See, for example the Declaration on Principles of International Law Concerning Friendly Relations and Co-operation among States in Accordance with the Charter of the United Nations 1970.

---

[103] Geneva, 22 August 1864; 129 C.T.S. 361; 55 B.F.S.P. 43.

[104] U.N.T.S. 31; 16 I.L.M. 1391 (1977).

[105] The ICJ decision in *Nicaragua (Merits)* I.C.J. Rep. 1986 p.3, at 114 regarding the application of Common art.3 as a "minimum yardstick" applicable in international armed conflicts. See also *Tadic* case no. I.T-94-1-AR 72 in which it was held art.3 of the ICTY Statute provided jurisdiction in respect of "violations of the laws or customs of war, regardless of whether they occurred within an internal or an international armed conflict."

[106] Above, art.1(2).

[107] The Hague, 14 May 1954; 249 U.N.T.S. 215; Misc.6 (1956) Cmd.9837.

Contracting Parties to the four Geneva Conventions and the additional Protocols are under a duty "to respect and to ensure respect" for the provisions contained therein "in all circumstances." Article 8 of the ICC Statute defines a grave breach of the Geneva Conventions as a war crime over which the ICC has jurisdiction, and therefore grave breaches of the Convention call for individual criminal accountability. Rape, sexual slavery, enforced prostitution and forced pregnancy or any other forms of sexual violence are now also characterised as a grave breach of the Geneva Conventions.[108]

International Red Cross

Any survey of humanitarian law would be incomplete without reference to the International Red Cross. The International Red Cross is made up of the International Red Cross Committee (ICRC), national Red Cross Societies and a co-ordinating body, the League of the Red Cross. The ICRC, which each of the Geneva Conventions recognise as "an impartial humanitarian body", has been responsible for developing much of substantive humanitarian law. Such work is evidenced in the international conference convened in Geneva in September 1993, specifically to discuss ways to protect war victims caught up in armed conflicts.[109] The Declaration adopted at the conference condemned, inter alia, violations of international humanitarian law and called for the establishment of an intergovernmental group of experts to "study practical means of promoting full respect for and compliance with that law".[110] Another study conducted by the International Red Cross has identified "161 rules of customary international humanitarian law that offer legal protection for people affected by war".[111]

CONCLUSION

Force, save in the accepted exceptions acknowledged by international law, is prohibited by contemporary international law. The use of and resort to force is an all too frequent feature of the

---

[108] art.8(2)xxii.

[109] International Conference for the Protection of War Victims: Declaration for the Protection of War Victims 33 I.L.M. 297 (1994).

[110] Above, at 302. The Vienna Declaration on Human Rights (1993) also confirmed "effective international measures to guarantee and monitor the implementation of human rights standards should be taken in respect of people under foreign occupation, and effective legal protection against the violation of their human rights should be provided, in accordance with human rights norms and international law." 32 I.L.M. 1661 (1993) at para.3 for the text of the Declaration.

[111] See Jean-Marie Henckaerts, "Study on customary international humanitarian law: A contribution to the understanding and respect for the rule of law in armed conflict." (2005) 87 International Review of the Red Cross, Number 857.

international scene. International law cannot prevent the use of force; it can only seek to regulate its use, and in the event of force being employed provide a legal framework for its conduct. The use of force should be a last resort, as the employment of force is to turn from legal processes to an alternative, which is ultimately an untenable medium for the conduct of international relations.

12. ARBITRATION AND JUDICIAL SETTLEMENT OF INTERNATIONAL DISPUTES

States are under an obligation to "settle their international disputes by peaceful means in such a manner that international peace and security, and justice, are not endangered".[1] States have traditionally been reticent to submit disputes to independent, impartial adjudication and have been cautious about agreeing in advance to the compulsory jurisdiction of an independent judicial body. The majority of inter-state disputes—that is, "a disagreement on a point of law or fact, a conflict of legal views or of interests between two persons" (that is, international persons)[2]—are settled by direct negotiation. Negotiation is the primary vehicle for attaining settlement on the international scene, as peaceful co-existence and conciliation are regarded as being more important than the characterisation of one state as "guilty" and another as "innocent". The *North Sea Continental Shelf* cases[3] endorsed the

---

[1] art.2(3) of the UN Charter—also recognised as a rule of customary international law; see also art.33 of the UN Charter; 1970 Declaration on Principles of International Law Concerning Friendly Relations and Co-operation Amongst States (G.A. Res., 2625 (XXV)), 1982 Manila Declaration on the Peaceful Settlement of International Disputes (G.A. Res., 37/590), 21 I.L.M. 449 (1982).

[2] *Mavrommatis Palestine Concessions* case P.C.I.J. Ser.A, No.2 at 11–12 (1924).

[3] I.C.J. Rep. 1969 p.3.

obligation to enter into negotiation when the International Court of Justice (ICJ) declared

> "parties are under an obligation to enter into negotiations with a view to arriving at an agreement . . .; they are under an obligation so to conduct themselves that the negotiations are meaningful, which will not be the case when either of them insists upon its own position without contemplating any modification of it."[4]

However, negotiations "do not of necessity always presuppose a more or less lengthy series of notes and dispatches; it may suffice that a discussion has been commenced, and . . . a deadlock is reached, or if finally a point is reached at which one of the Parties definitely declares himself unable, or refuses, to give way."[5]

International agreements may require that negotiation be attempted before other settlement procedures are initiated. Negotiations as a rule are conducted through normal diplomatic channels involving only the parties to the dispute. These negotiations should be conducted in good faith,[6] and must not be mere formalities.[7]

Other methods involve the participation of a third party, i.e. a state, a group of states or an individual, may be employed if the states party to the dispute consent. Such methods include good offices, conciliation, mediation and commissions of inquiry.[8]

Good offices

Good offices take place when a third party brings the disputing states to the negotiating table and suggests the general framework for producing a settlement.

Mediation

Mediation similarly involves a third party, namely the mediator. The mediator may assume a more active role than the provider of good offices and may attempt to reconcile the positions and claims of the respective interested parties. Mediation has been employed in a number of instances, including the dispute between Chile and Argentina with regard to the Beagle Channel; in the former Yugoslavia, leading ultimately to the

---

[4] Above, at para.85.
[5] Above, fn.2 at 13.
[6] *Cameroon v Nigeria* I.C.J. Rep., 2002 p.303, para.244.
[7] *Lac Lanoux Arbitration*, 24 I.L.R., 101–119.
[8] All such methods are identified in art.33 of the UN Charter.

conclusion of the Dayton/Paris Agreement; and in respect of Kosovo. Suggestions of the third party do not have binding effect.

Conciliation

The task of a Conciliation Commission is to examine the claims of the parties and make proposals to the parties for a friendly solution. If agreement is not reached, the Commission produces a report containing observations, conclusions and recommendations. The Commission's findings or proposals are not binding upon the parties. Conciliation as a means of dispute settlement may be by way of treaties, for example the 1969 Vienna Convention on the Law of Treaties and the 1982 Convention on the Law of the Sea. The dispute regarding the continental shelf between Iceland and the island of Jan Mayen[9] is another instance of the conciliation procedure having been employed.

Commission of Inquiry

The primary function of a Commission of Inquiry is to establish the facts pertaining to the dispute, for example by the hearing of witnesses or visiting the area where the alleged breach of international law has allegedly occurred. Dispute settlement may also be initiated either in or by international organisations, for example as the Security Council of the United Nations did in 1982, when a fact-finding Commission was established following an attempted coup in the Seychelles. Specialised agencies of the United Nations, such as the International Labour Organisation (ILO)[10] and the International Civil Aviation Organisation (ICAO)[11] have also initiated inquiries. A Commission of Inquiry refers to a type of international tribunal introduced by the Hague Convention.[12]

The common denominator reflected in all such dispute settlement methods discussed above is the consent of the parties involved. The success of these methods cannot be denied, however it is only by arbitration and judicial settlement that adjudication is carried out in accordance with legal principles and culminates in a decision accepted as binding on the contesting parties.

---

[9] 20 I.L.M. 1981, 797.
[10] In respect of labour conventions.
[11] e.g. in respect of the shooting down of a South Korean aircraft over Soviet territory, KE007 Incident 1093.
[12] See the Hague Convention for the Pacific Settlement of Disputes (1899), arts 9–14; U.K.T.S. 9 (1901) Cd.798; see also the 1907 Hague Convention for the Pacific Settlement of Disputes 54 L.N.T.S. 435.

ARBITRATION

The International Law Commission has defined arbitration as "a procedure for the settlement of disputes between states by a binding award on the basis of law and as a result of an undertaking voluntarily accepted."[13]

The essential difference between arbitration and judicial settlement is that arbitration parties are more active in deciding, for instance, the law to be applied and the composition of the tribunal, whereas parties submitting to judicial settlement must accept an already constituted tribunal with its jurisdictional competence and procedure laid down in statute. Arbitration allows parties a degree of flexibility denied to them in judicial settlement.

The idea of entrusting an impartial authority with finding a legally based solution to international disputes is not new, and examples of arbitration settlement date back to ancient Greece, China and early Arabian tribes. However, the modern history of arbitration and the rekindling of an interest in arbitration as a mode of settlement can be traced from the 1794 Jay Treaty between the US and Great Britain. That Treaty provided for the establishment of three mixed Commissions to which both states nominated an equal number of members, presided over by an "umpire". Although, strictly speaking, the Commissions were not organs of third party adjudication, they were intended to function to some extent as tribunals, e.g. the Commissions were to decide for themselves whether a claim fell within their jurisdictional competence. Throughout the 19th century, arbitration was frequently utilised, with each party to the dispute nominating two representatives to serve on the tribunal. In 1871, under the Treaty of Washington, the US and Britain agreed to submit to arbitration alleged breaches of neutrality by Britain during the American Civil War. The Treaty provided that, while the US and Britain were to nominate a member of the tribunal of five, so also were Brazil, Italy and Switzerland. The nomination and involvement of three independent states was an innovation and the *Alabama Claims Arbitration*[14] heralded the increasing use of arbitration, with many treaties providing for recourse to arbitration in the event of a dispute.

The 1899 Convention for the Pacific Settlement of International Disputes[15] adopted by the First Hague Peace Conference marked a new era in arbitration settlement with the Convention providing for the creation of a Permanent Court of Arbitration (PCA). In 1907,

---

[13] Y.B.I.L.C. 1953 11 at 202.
[14] Moore, 1 Int.Arb. 495 (1872).
[15] U.K.T.S. 9 (1901) Cd.798.

following a Second Hague Conference, a further Convention was adopted revising its predecessor, but maintaining the Court.[16]

The PCA, established in 1900, began functioning in 1902. It is still in existence, but it is neither a court nor a permanent institution. It is rather a panel of some 300 persons (four nominated by each Contracting Party to the 1899 and 1907 Conventions) from whom states may select one or more arbitrators to constitute a tribunal for the settlement of a particular dispute. Only the Bureau of the Court, which acts as a registry, is permanent. What was established in 1899 was essentially the machinery to call tribunals into being. Since its inception, the PCA has provided the mechanism for the hearing of over 40 cases, including some of considerable importance, e.g. the *Island of Palmas* case.[17]

Arbitration presupposes and depends upon the willingness of the states involved to submit to adjudication and their desire to reach a settlement. A state is not required to submit a dispute to arbitration, and consent is a prerequisite. Consent can be on an ad hoc basis, as in the *Canada/France Maritime Delimitation* case[18] and the *Guinea/Bissau Maritime Delimitation* case.[19] The identity of the arbitrators; the formulation of the question to be submitted to the tribunal; the rules of law to be applied; and the time limit within which an award be made, must be agreed upon by the states concerned. Such issues are spelt out in a special agreement between the parties, known as the *Compromis*. The functioning of the Permanent Court therefore presupposes that the states not only have a desire to reach a settlement, but they reach agreement on the issues which are the content of the *Compromis*.

Model rules on arbitration procedure, which were adopted by the 1899 Convention, were considerably revised in 1907. Arbitration agreements may refer to these, while others may refer to the General Act on the Pacific Settlement of International Disputes adopted under the auspices of the League of Nations in 1928 and revised by the United Nations in 1949.[20] "Model Rules on Arbitral procedures" were submitted by the International Law Commission to the General Assembly and adopted in 1958. Normally awards of arbitration tribunals are binding and will be provided for expressly in the *Compromis*.[21]

Compliance with arbitration awards has been high. Rejection

---

[16] U.K.T.S. 6 (1971) Cmnd.4575.

[17] 2 R.I.A.A. 829 (1928).

[18] 31 I.L.M. 1145 (1992).

[19] 77 I.L.R. 636 (1985).

[20] 71 U.N.T.S. 101.

[21] A dispute may be referred to arbitration for an advisory report, in which case the parties to the dispute will normally be charged with putting that report into effect.

of an award has only occurred when the tribunal has allegedly exceeded its jurisdiction or has been guilty of a manifest procedural error.

Arbitration via the PCA has been used in several occasions for delimiting borders between states, for example in the dispute settlement between Eritrea and Yemen in 2001 on questions of territorial sovereignty and delimitation of maritime boundaries[22]; and was invoked by the Government of Sudan and the Sudan People's Liberation Movement/Army with regards to the territorial sovereignty over the region of Abyei.[23] Increasingly the PCA serves as registry or to provide administrative support for investment disputes between states and between states and companies. This arbitration is normally conducted under the rules of free trade agreements, such as the North American Free Trade Agreement (NAFTA) or the rules of the United Nations Commission on International Trade Law (UNCITRAL), adopted in 1976 and revised in 2010.

The use of arbitration as a medium of dispute settlement has declined, especially as disputes between states and treatment of aliens were increasingly solved by a "lump sum settlement agreement".[24] Nevertheless, arbitration has continued to be employed,[25] e.g. the Convention on the Settlement of Investment Disputes between States and Nationals of Other States 1965[26] makes available conciliation and arbitration procedures for the settlement of cases between contracting parties and companies of the nationality of a contracting party when both sides consent, as did the Iran/United States Claims Tribunal, established in 1981.[27] In 1996, the UN Compensation Commission (the UNCC) delivered its first decision concerning the corporate–governmental claims in the Iraq–Kuwait conflict. The UNCC specifically deals with, among other things, the costs to Kuwait of extinguishing

---

[22] see PCA, *Eritrea–Yemen Arbitration* (first stage: territorial sovereignty and scope of dispute) (9 October 1998) 40 I.L.M. 900 (2001) and Permanent Court of Arbitration (PCA): *Eritrea–Yemen Arbitration* (second stage: maritime delimitation) (17 December 1999) 40 I.L.M. 983 (2001).

[23] Government of Sudan and the Sudan People's Liberation Movement/Army Abyei (22 July 2009) 48 I.L.M. 1254 (2009). Arbitration Award.

[24] Discussed in Ch.8, "State Responsibility".

[25] See, for instance, the decision of the Iran–US claims Tribunal: *Partial Award Containing Settlement Agreements on the Iranian Bank Claims Against the United States* and the International Court of Justice case *Concerning the Aerial Incident of July 3, 1988*—35 I.L.M. 553 (1996).

[26] 575 U.N.T.S. 159; 4 I.L.M. 532 (1965).

[27] 20 I.L.M. 223 (1981). For background information on these claims, see David Caron, "The Nature of the Iran–United States Claims Tribunal and the Evolving Structure of International Dispute" Resolution (1990) 84 A.J.I.L. 1990 104.

the fires started by Iraqi troops in Kuwait's oilfields during the Gulf crisis. The UNCC has granted awards to the sum of $52.4 billion.[28]

Representatives from a third of the world's countries have sat on the UNCC's governing Council and all decisions taken have been adopted by consensus.

It was only with the establishment of a judicial organ by and through the League of Nations[29] that a permanent international judicial institution was created, that is, a court in the real sense of the term, ready to function at any time. What was created was the Permanent Court of International Justice (PCIJ). A state could, by unilateral application, bring a dispute against another state, calling upon the latter to appear before the PCIJ. Prior agreement did not need to be reached on the composition of the tribunal or the questions to be submitted to it, provided, that is, the latter state accepted the jurisdiction of the Court.

The PCIJ was the forerunner of the International Court of Justice.[30] The PCIJ sat for the first time at the Peace Palace in The Hague on 15 February 1922. The Court's activities were interrupted by the outbreak of the Second World War and the Court ceased to exist in 1946 on the dissolution of the League of Nations.

THE INTERNATIONAL COURT OF JUSTICE

The ICJ is the principal judicial organ of the United Nations and, as such, is an integral part of the organisation with its Statute annexed to the UN Charter.[31] Although favouring the creation of a new Court, the delegates at the San Francisco Conference wished to maintain continuity with the PCIJ and the Statute of the ICJ is essentially the same as that of its predecessor. In addition, the ICJ adopted, without any substantial amendment, the Rules of Court of the PCIJ.[32] At the last meeting of the PCIJ the necessary

---

[28] The UNCC was established on 3 April 1991 by S.C. Res. 687 as a subsidiary organ of the UN SC, 30 I.L.M. 846 (1991).

[29] The Court was never an integral part of the League of Nations. There was a close association between the two bodies, e.g. the League Council and Assembly elected the members of the Court and both the Council and the Assembly were competent to request an Advisory Opinion from the Court.

[30] Both Courts are frequently referred to as the World Court.

[31] art.92 of the UN Charter.

[32] The Rules of Court have since been substantially amended. The most recent amendments entered into force in 2005. However the Court, having looked at ways of improving its working methods and accelerating its procedures, adopted Practice Directions in 2001, which were amended in January 2009. These Directions do not involve any alterations to the Rules of Court but are supplementary to the Rules and are to be employed by states appearing before it. This was an innovative step for the Court, designed to address the problem of a growing caseload within increasing budgetary constraints. Further measures

steps to ensure the transfer of the archives and effects to the ICJ were taken. The judges of the PCIJ resigned on 31 January 1946, and at the first meeting of the UN General Assembly the judges to the ICJ were elected. The PCIJ was formally dissolved in April 1946.

Composition of the International Court of Justice

Fifteen judges sit on the ICJ. The judges, of whom no two may be nationals of the same state, are elected by an absolute majority at separately and, in theory, simultaneously held meetings of the Security Council and the General Assembly. In practice, the frequent disagreement and political bargaining over the appointment of judges means the Security Council is aware of what the General Assembly is doing and vice versa. Candidates for election are nominated by the national groups in the Permanent Court of Arbitration or by specially constituted groups for those UN members who are not represented in the Permanent Court of Arbitration. Persons eligible for election are those "of high moral character, who possess the qualifications required in their respective countries for appointment to the highest judicial offices, or are jurisconsults of recognised competence in international law."[33] The Court's Statute provides that judges are to be elected without regard to nationality and there is no entitlement on the part of any one state to membership. In practice, an equitable geographical distribution is sought and the five Permanent Members of the Security Council, save China, have always been represented.[34] Judges are appointed for a nine-year term and may be re-elected. Elections are staggered with five judges being elected every three years. This is designed to ensure continuity. A judge who is elected to fill an unexpected vacancy holds office only for the remainder of his or her predecessor's term. A President and Vice-president are elected by fellow judges for three years and both may be re-elected.[35]

A judge may only be dismissed from office when he or she is considered no longer fit to discharge his or her function and only then on the unanimous vote of the other judges, but this

to streamline procedures have been introduced by way of an amendment to art.45 para.1 regarding pleadings. Any amendments to the Rules of Court or Practice Directions, once they have been adopted by the Court, are published on the Court's website and its yearbook.

[33] art.2 of the ICJ Statute.

[34] China was not represented from 1967 to 1984, when no candidate was put forward.

[35] The current President is the French judge, Judge Ronny Abraham, elected 6 February 2015. The Vice President is Judge Abdulqawi Ahmed Yusuf of Somalia.

has never happened. During his or her term in office, a judge may not perform any political or administrative function, nor may he or she act as counsel, agent, or advocate in any suit or participate in the decision of a case in which he or she has represented one of the parties involved. Nevertheless, a judge is not barred from sitting on the bench even if he or she has previously participated in an international forum when what is essentially the subject matter of the case was being discussed. For example in *Legal Consequences for States of the Continued Presence of South Africa in Namibia (South West Africa) Notwithstanding Security Council Resolution 276 (1970)*,[36] members of the bench, including the President, had been members of the Security Council when it had condemned South Africa's continued presence in Namibia. In spite of South African representations the Court refused to withdraw those concerned.

A judge is not prohibited from sitting on a case in which the state of his or her nationality is a party. The Rules of Court do specify that if the President is a national of one of the parties to a case before the Court, then he or she will refrain from exercising his or her functions as President for that particular case. If a state to a dispute does not have a representing judge, an ad hoc (for that purpose only) judge may be appointed. If the bench includes no judge of the nationality of the parties involved, each of the parties may select an ad hoc judge. An ad hoc judge need not be of the same nationality as the nominating state. Cases are conducted in either of the Court's two official languages, English and French,[37] and are decided by a majority of the judges sitting. In the event of a split vote the President has the casting vote, which may be different from his or her initial vote. Dissenting judgments and separate opinions are published in full. Cases may be heard by either a full Court (a quorum of nine being sufficient) or by a Chamber of three or more judges constituted for handling a particular case or a particular category of case. The Court's Statute also makes provision for the establishment of Chambers.[38] In January 1982 the Court approved, for the first time, the creation of a Chamber to deal specifically with the dispute between Canada and the US over the Gulf of Maine area.[39] This procedure has been repeated in *Frontier Dispute (Burkina Faso v Mali)*,[40] the *Land, Island and Maritime Frontier Dispute (El Salvador v Honduras)*[41] and the *Elettronica Sicula S.p.A. (ELSI) (US*

---

[36] (Advisory Opinion) I.C.J. Rep. 1971 at 16.
[37] A party may be authorised by the Court to use another language.
[38] art.34 of the ICJ Statute.
[39] I.C.J. Rep. 1984 at p.246.
[40] I.C.J. Rep. 1985 at p.6.
[41] I.C.J. Rep. 1987 at p.10.

v Italy).[42] On 6 August 1993, the Court established a Chamber for Environmental Matters pursuant to art.26(1) of the Statute. The agreement of all parties involved is required before a matter may be brought before the Chamber rather than the plenary court. The Chamber is constituted of seven judges, elected by secret ballot. However after being in existence for 13 years no state had ever brought a case before it, and so in 2006 the Court decided not to hold elections for a Bench for the Chamber for Environmental Matters.

Jurisdiction of the court

The Court can hear contentious cases and deliver advisory opinions.

Contentious cases

Ratione personae (locus standi before the court). Only states have locus standi and may be party to a contentious case before the Court.[43] In the case concerning the *Application of the Convention on the Prevention and Punishment of the Crime of Genocide (Bosnia and Herzegovina v Yugoslavia Serbia and Montenegro)* (Indication of Provisional Measures in 1993),[44] the Court had to consider whether either state had locus standi in the action, as the statehood of both countries was in dispute at that time. The Court ultimately decided that both were competent under art.35(2) of the ICJ Statute because they were parties to the Genocide Convention, which provides for a reference to the ICJ on disputes arising from the Convention.

All members of the United Nations are ipso facto parties to the Court's Statute. A non-UN member may become a party to the Court's Statute on conditions determined by the UN General Assembly pursuant to a Security Council recommendation. These conditions are (i) an acceptance of the provisions of the Court's Statute; (ii) an agreement to accept and enforce the Court's judgments (that is, an acceptance of art.94, UN Charter); and (iii) an undertaking to contribute to the Court's expenses as may be assessed by the General Assembly.[45]

Access to the Court may also be available to a state which is neither a member of the United Nations nor a party to the Court's Statute, if that state lodges a special declaration with the Court's

---

[42] I.C.J. Rep. 1989 at p.15.
[43] art.34 of the ICJ Statute.
[44] I.C.J. Rep. 1993 at p.325.
[45] States which have availed themselves of this are Switzerland and Nauru. Both are now members of the UN.

Registry accepting the obligations of the Court's Statute and art.94 of the UN Charter. A declaration may be either particular or general. A particular declaration accepts the Court's jurisdiction in respect of a particular dispute or disputes which have already arisen. A general declaration accepts the Court's jurisdiction in respect of all disputes, or of a particular class or classes of dispute(s) which have already arisen or which may arise in the future.

A state may be entitled to appear before the International Court of Justice, but no state, unless it has expressed its consent, is required to appear in proceedings before the Court. This was affirmed in the case *Concerning East Timor (Portugal v Australia)*[46] in which Portugal objected to a treaty between Australia and Indonesia. The Court was unable to exercise jurisdiction to adjudicate upon the dispute because Indonesia had not accepted the jurisdiction of the Court.[47] The Security Council can recommend, but *only* recommend, that states in dispute refer to the Court.[48] Such a recommendation does not confer jurisdiction on the Court independently of the wishes of the disputing parties. A state must have agreed that the dispute, or the class of dispute, should be dealt with by the Court.

Acceptance of the Court's jurisdiction may be expressed in different ways.

Article 36(1)

Article 36(1) of the Court's Statute provides that the Court has jurisdiction in all cases "which States in a dispute may agree to refer to it and all matters specially provided for in the Charter of the United Nations or in treaties and conventions in force." States need not express consent to the Court's jurisdiction in advance or in any particular form.[49] States may agree by special agreement ("*compromis*") to submit an already existing dispute to the Court and thereby recognise the Court's jurisdiction over that particular case. The Court may entertain the case once the special agreement has been lodged with the Court. Examples of cases which have come before the Court via a special agreement are the *Asylum* case,[50] *Minquiers and Ecrehos* case,[51] *Continental Shelf*

---

[46] 34 I.L.M. 1581 (1995).
[47] To do so would have meant the Court's deciding on whether or not the treaty between Indonesia and Australia was lawfully concluded. It was unable to do so given that Indonesia was not a party to the case. The Court thus reinforced the position it had taken previously in *Monetary Gold Removed from Rome in 1943*, I.C.J. Rep., 1954, p.32.
[48] art.36 of the UN Charter.
[49] *Corfu Channel* (Preliminary Objection) case I.C.J. Rep. 1948 15 at 27.
[50] I.C.J. Rep. 1950 at p.266.
[51] I.C.J. Rep. 1953 at p.47.

(Tunisia v Libya) case,[52] *The Danube Dam* case[53] and *Kasikili/Sedudu island (Botswana/Namibia)*.[54]

Forum prorogatum

Occasionally the Court has prorogated jurisdiction. This arises when, at the initiation of proceedings, only one state has expressly consented to the Court's jurisdiction for that particular dispute. However the other party, by its conduct, has inferred consent. The absence of express consent by one party has not acted as an obstacle to the Court being seised of the case, as consent can be implied. A letter from the Albanian Deputy Minister for Foreign Affairs was taken by the Court in the *Corfu Channel (Preliminary Objection)* case[55] as expressing Albania's consent, while consent to submit to the Court has been inferred through the acts of a state.[56] Jurisdiction may not be implied, however, from a consistent denial of the Court's jurisdiction.[57]

Prorogatum jurisdiction is rare, as states not wishing to submit to the Court's jurisdiction will refrain from behaviour from which consent could be deduced.

Attempts by one state to bring unilateral application proceedings against another state, when the former acknowledges that the latter has not recognised the Court's jurisdiction, have proved unsuccessful. The Applicant state, relying on the doctrine of *forum prorogatum*, invites a positive reaction from the Respondent state; that is, a subsequent acceptance of the Court's jurisdiction.[58]

The Court's Rules, art.38(5) provides:

> "where the applicant State proposes to found the jurisdiction of the Court upon a consent thereto yet to be given or manifested by the State against which such application is made, the application shall be transmitted to that State. It shall not however be entered in the General List, nor any action be taken in the proceedings, unless and until the State against which such application is made consents to the Court's jurisdiction for the purpose of the case."[59]

---

[52] I.C.J. Rep. 1982 at p.18.
[53] *Gabćikovo-Nagymaros Project (Hungary v Slovakia)* (1997) I.C.J. 7; 38 I.L.M. 162.
[54] I.C.J. Rep. 1999 p.1045.
[55] Above, fn.49.
[56] See e.g. "The Rights of Minorities in Polish Upper Silesia", P.C.I.J. Rep., ser.A, No.15 (1928); the *Monetary Gold* case, I.C.J. Rep. 1954 at 19.
[57] See *Anglo–Iranian Oil Co* case I.C.J. Rep. 1952 93 at 114.
[58] e.g. *Treatment in Hungary of Aircraft of the U.S.A.* I.C.J. Rep. 1954 at 99, at 103; the *Antarctica* cases, I.C.J. Rep. 1956 p.12, at 15.
[59] See Liberia's application to the Court in a dispute with Sierra Leone concerning an international arrest warrant issued by the Special Court for Sierra

Note also art.35(2) of the Rules provides that the basis for the Court's jurisdiction should be specified "as far as possible."

Jurisdiction is also conferred on the Court by treaties which states have negotiated. Many bilateral and multilateral treaties contain compromissory clauses providing for recourse to the Court in the event of a dispute.[60] Compromissory clauses are found in treaties which are of two types: (i) those designed specifically to promote the pacific settlement of disputes between two or more states and which frequently provide, not only for judicial settlement, but for the employment of conciliation and arbitration, e.g. Revised 1928 General Act for the Pacific Settlement of International Disputes 1949[61] and the European Convention for the Pacific Settlement of Disputes 1957[62]; and (ii) those on a particular subject which contain a provision for recourse to the Court in the event of a dispute arising over the interpretation or application of the treaty, e.g. the 1971 Convention for the Suppression of Unlawful Acts Against the Safety of Civil Aviation (the "Montreal Convention") 1971[63] and the 1982 UN Convention on the Law of the Sea.[64] For an example of the Court establishing jurisdiction on such a basis, see the *Nicaragua* case.[65] Treaties with such compromissory clauses are registered with the UN Secretariat, while the Yearbook of the ICJ publishes the text of the compromissory clauses.[66]

Leone against the Liberian President (filed 4 August 2003). For an application of art.38(5) see *Certain Criminal Proceedings in France (Republic of the Congo v France)* Provisional Measure, Order 17 June 2003, I.C.J. Rep. 2003, p.102 and the *Case of Certain Questions of Mutual Assistance in Criminal Matters (Djibouti v France)*, I.C.J. Rep. 2008 p.177.

[60] e.g. *Territorial Dispute (Libya v Chad)* I.C.J. Rep. 1994 p.6 was referred to the Court under a jurisdictional clause in a bipartite treaty whereas the *Prevention of Genocide* case, above, fn.44, was brought before the Court under the multipartite Genocide Convention.

[61] 71 U.N.T.S. 101.

[62] 320 U.N.T.S. 243.

[63] 10 I.L.M. 1151 (1971).

[64] 21 I.L.M. 1261 (1982).

[65] *Case Concerning Military and Paramilitary Activities in and against Nicaragua* I.C.J. Rep. 1984 p.392 at 429 in respect of the 1956 Treaty of Friendship, Commerce and Navigation. Libya's application to the Court in March 1992 was based on art.14(1) of the Montreal Convention, which provides for submission to the Court of a dispute between two or more contracting parties, which cannot be settled through negotiation. See *Questions of Interpretation and Application of the 1971 Montreal Convention Arising from the Aerial Incident at Lockerbie. (Jurisdiction and admissibility)* (1998) I.C.J. Rep. p.3.

[66] art.37 of the ICJ's Statute stipulates that in respect of compromissory clauses which conferred jurisdiction on the PCIJ, the ICJ is to be substituted, thus preventing such clauses from losing their effectiveness.

Article 36(2)—The optional clause

States may accept the Court's jurisdiction by way of a declaration under art.36(2):

> "The States Parties to the present Statute may at any time declare that they recognize as compulsory ipso facto and without special agreement, in relation to any other State accepting the same obligation, the jurisdiction of the Court in all legal disputes concerning:
>
> (a) the legal interpretation of a treaty;
> (b) any question of international law;
> (c) the existence of any fact which, if established, would constitute a breach of an international obligation;
> (d) the nature or extent of the reparation to be made for the breach of an international obligation."

States are not required to make a declaration under art.36(2).[67] Declarations under art.36(2) are optional, but once the Court's jurisdiction has been accepted, reference to the Court is compulsory. Such declarations, being unilateral acts, obviate the need for agreement. The effectiveness of art.36(2) depends on the participation of many states. States have been reluctant to make declarations; 72 states have currently made a declaration under art.36(2). Declarations must be lodged with the UN Secretary-General and copies transmitted to parties to the Statute and the Registrar of the Court. States which have made a declaration accepting the Court's jurisdiction, in principle, possess the right to bring before the Court another state accepting the same obligation.

Conversely a state, by a declaration pursuant to art.36(2), undertakes to appear before the Court should proceedings be initiated against it. The subject matter of the dispute must fall within the terms of the acceptance lodged by both parties, as the Court only has jurisdiction to the extent that the declarations coincide. Common ground is not always easy to find, as art.36(3) provides that declarations may be made "unconditionally or on condition of reciprocity on the part of several or certain states or for a certain time."

Reservations are found in most declarations and the Court's jurisdiction over a case is restricted to those disputes that states have not excluded from its jurisdiction.[68] If, for example,

---

[67] In the *Jan Mayen* case (*Denmark v Norway*), Denmark invoked art.36(2), the first time compulsory jurisdiction has been exercised in a maritime delimitation case.

[68] Hence, the Court found it had no jurisdiction to adjudicate in the dispute

state A has accepted the compulsory jurisdiction of the Court as of 2 April and state B accepts the Court's jurisdiction but excludes all disputes relating to incidents arising before 18 July, the Court will only have jurisdiction to hear a case arising after 18 July. This would be the case regardless of which state was the applicant—that is, if state B in spite of its reservation attempted to bring before the Court a dispute relating to an incident on 25 May, state A could rely on state B's reservation to prevent the Court being seised of the case. A reservation of this type is a reservation *ratione temporis*. In the case of *Military and Paramilitary Activities in and against Nicaragua*,[69] the Court held that Nicaragua (whose declaration has no reservation) was entitled to invoke against the US the six-month time *proviso*, contained in the latter's 1946 declaration, stating that the declaration could be terminated, but that termination would only be effective six months after notice of such intention had been intimated. The undertaking to give six months' notice formed an integral part of the declaration, and, accordingly, the 1984 notification providing for immediate effect could not "override the obligation of the United States to submit to the compulsory jurisdiction of the Court vis-à-vis Nicaragua."[70] In this context, the Court held that the most important question was whether the US

> "was free to disregard the clause of six months' notice which, freely and by its own choice, it had appended to its 1946 Declaration. In doing so the United States entered into an obligation which is binding upon it *vis-à-vis* other States parties to the Optional-Clause system."[71]

The Court refuted the argument, advanced by the US, that Nicaragua had not accepted the same obligation for the purposes of art.36(2)[72] and stated that the notion of reciprocity is one "concerned with the scope and substance of the commitments entered into, including reservations". Furthermore the Court stated that "reciprocity cannot be invoked to excuse departure from the terms of a state's own declaration, whatever its scope, limitations or conditions." The Court then reiterated the position it had

---

between Spain and Canada, because the said dispute came within the terms of the reservation contained in para.2(d) of the Canadian Declaration of 10 May 1994—*Fisheries Jurisdiction (Spain v Canada)* I.C.J. Rep. 1998 p.432.

[69] Above, fn.65.
[70] Above, at 421.
[71] Above, at 419.
[72] The US argument was based on the undefined duration of the Nicaraguan Declaration.

adopted with respect to the effect of reciprocity in the *Interhandel* case[73]

> "Reciprocity enables the State which has made the wider acceptance of the jurisdiction of the Court to rely upon the reservations to the acceptance laid down by the other party. There the effect of reciprocity ends."[74]

What this means in effect is that a state may invoke a reservation to an acceptance which it has not expressed in its own declaration, but which the other party has expressed in its own declaration.[75]

Reservations most frequently exclude disputes for which another means of peaceful settlement is provided; which arose before a specific date or which relate to a situation prior to that date, normally the date of the state's initial declaration; which arose during or because of hostilities; which arise between certain states, e.g. as between Commonwealth countries[76]; which relate to matters falling within the domestic jurisdiction of the declaratory state, as determined by international law[77] or by the declaratory state itself as, e.g. expressed in the United States' 1946 declaration.[78] Such automatic or self-judging reservations particularly undermine the idea of compulsory jurisdiction. It is possible for a government, relying upon such a reservation, to declare that a question in relation to the subject matter of the proceedings initiated against it falls within its national jurisdiction, and thereby seek to deprive the ICJ of jurisdiction. Such a reservation was successfully invoked in the *Certain Norwegian Loans* case,[79] when the ICJ discussed the French claim and allowed Norway to invoke, on the basis of reciprocity, the automatic/self-judging reservation contained in the French declaration.[80] Although the Court itself has not pronounced on the validity of such reservations, judges in both the *Norwegian Loans* case (Lauterpacht and Guerrero JJ) and

---

[73] I.C.J. Rep 1959 p.6.

[74] Above, at 23, quoted in the *Nicaragua* case, above fn.65, at 419.

[75] See decision in *Norwegian Loans*, I.C.J. Rep. 1957 p.9; and judgment in *Interhandel* case, above, fn.73.

[76] See the UK Declaration deposited 31 December 2014.

[77] See the Canadian Declaration deposited 10 May 1994.

[78] US Declaration, 26 August 1946, 61 Stat.1218; 1 U.N.T.S. 9.

[79] Above, fn.75.

[80] It was also invoked in the *Interhandel* case, but was not dealt with by the Court, as the case was dismissed on grounds of the non-exhaustion of local remedies; see also *Aerial Incident* of 27 July 1955, I.C.J. Rep. 1960 p.146. Note the American statement in the *Nicaragua* case that the US did not intend to invoke such a reservation before the Court but that this did not prejudice its right to do so in any subsequent pleadings, proceedings or cases before the Court, above, fn.65, at 422.

the *Interhandel* case (Lauterpacht, Spender and Klaestad JJ) have questioned their validity. The principal objection being that they are contrary to art.36(6) of the Court's Statute, which provides "in the event of a dispute as to whether the Court has jurisdiction, the matter shall be settled by the decision of the Court." The Court is also prohibited, as an organ of the United Nations, from intervening in matters "which are essentially within the jurisdiction of any State".[81]

Declarations are generally made for a specific period, normally five years, with tacit renewal. Declarations can generally be terminated on notice, taking effect after a specified time or immediately and may also be subject to modification. Ideally, at least from the Court's standpoint, declarations should be for a definite period. A declaration which can be unilaterally terminated at any time provides a state, anticipating a dispute, with the opportunity of denying the Court jurisdiction.[82] Thus in 1954, Australia withdrew its existing declaration and issued a new one, excluding from the Court's jurisdiction any disputes relating to pearl fishing off the Australian coast. The possibility of Japan raising a dispute on such a matter under art.36(2) prompted this move. The UK narrowed the scope of its declaration so as to exclude an application to the Court in its dispute with Saudi Arabia over the Buraimi Oasis (after the breakdown of the attempted arbitration).[83]

A temporal reservation relating to the termination of acceptance cannot operate retroactively so as to de-seise the Court's jurisdiction by reserving to themselves the right to remove on notice certain classes of disputes from the Court's competence. For example on 6 April 1984, the US withdrew from the Court's jurisdiction "disputes with any Central American State or any dispute arising out of or related to events in Central America over a period of two years." The ICJ found it had jurisdiction, as, inter alia, the US could not validly derogate from the time-limit proviso included in its 1946 declaration. Namely "this declaration shall remain in force for a period of five years and thereafter until the expiration of six months after notice may be given to terminate this declaration."[84] The UK Government, in its acceptance, reserves

---

[81] art.2(7) of the UN Charter.
[82] See Separate Opinion of Jennings J in the *Nicaragua* case, above fn.65, at 551 in which he considered the "most striking examples".
[83] Above, on effect of Reservation 1(b) contained in UK's declaration excluding a dispute which has already been submitted to arbitration by agreement with any states which had not at the time of submission accepted the compulsory jurisdiction of the ICJ.
[84] The US on 7 October 1985 terminated its acceptance of the Court's jurisdiction under art.36(2), 24 I.L.M. 1742 (1985).

"the right at any time, by means of notification addressed to the Secretary-General of the United Nations, and with effect as from the moment of such notification, either to add to, amend or withdraw any of the foregoing reservations, or any that may hereafter be added."

There also exists what is known as a multilateral treaty reservation, the effect of which is to exclude disputes "arising under a multilateral treaty", and require that "all parties to the treaty affected by the decision "be parties to the case before the Court." The US 1946 Declaration accepting art.36(2) contained such a reservation which the US invoked before the Court in an attempt to exclude the Court's jurisdiction in the *Nicaragua* case. The US accordingly maintained that the Court would only enjoy jurisdiction if all treaty parties (that is, to those treaties being submitted to the Court by Nicaragua—including, inter alia, the UN Charter) affected by a prospective decision of the Court were also parties to the case.[85] The Court observed that all the "affected" treaty parties were not only free to invoke art.36(2) (all having made a declaration) but could avail themselves of the incidental procedures offered by the Court's Statute. The affected states were not left defenceless against any consequences that may have arisen out of adjudication by the Court, or their needing the protection of the multilateral reservation of the US.[86] As to the question of which states could be affected by the decision, the Court concluded that this itself was not a jurisdictional problem and that this US objection did not constitute an obstacle to the Court's exercise of jurisdiction.

Declarations must be valid at the time of application for proceedings to be initiated. However, the modification or expiry of a declaration once the Court has been validly seised of a case will not deny the Court jurisdiction.[87]

Article 36(5) of the Statute of the ICJ provides that declarations made under the optional clause of the Statute of the Permanent Court of International Justice, and still in force, are "deemed, as between the parties to the present Statute, to be acceptances of the compulsory jurisdiction of the ICJ for the period which they still have to run and in accordance with their terms." This provision's applicability was discussed at considerable length in the *Nicaragua* case,[88] as a consequence[89] of the US' allegation that the ICJ was

---

[85] The affected parties in this instance were El Salvador, Honduras and Costa Rica.

[86] Above, fn.65 at 425.

[87] *Nottebohm (Preliminary Objection)*, I.C.J. Rep. 1953 p.111 at 122.

[88] Above, fn.65 at 392.

[89] And considered here in some length because, in the Court's words, of the "novelty" of the problem.

not competent to hear the case brought by Nicaragua. The latter had never become a party to the Statute of the Permanent Court of International Justice and, although Nicaragua had made a declaration in 1929 accepting the Court's jurisdiction, no instrument of ratification was received by the League of Nations in Geneva. Accordingly, the American argument was that Nicaragua could not and did not make an effective acceptance of the compulsory jurisdiction of the Permanent Court of Justice, and that the 1929 acceptance could not be said to be "still in force" for the purposes of art.36(2).[90] The Court responded by acknowledging that although Nicaragua's Declaration "had not acquired binding force prior to such effect as art.36(5), of the Statute of the ICJ might produce", the Declaration "could have done so." The Court continued by articulating the nature of the Nicaraguan Declaration as having a "potential effect which could be maintained indefinitely" because of the fact that it had been made "unconditionally" and was valid for an unlimited period.[91]

The Court, on the basis of the potential effect argument, was able to conclude:

> "Nicaragua's 1929 Declaration was valid at the moment when Nicaragua became a party to the Statute of the new Court".[92]

Reservations apply only to the Court's jurisdiction under art.36(2). The Court may have jurisdiction over the subject matter in question by some other means, for example a treaty. Some states have made declarations recognising the jurisdiction under the Court as compulsory ipso facto without special convention, on condition of reciprocity. Notwithstanding this, the majority of cases come before the Court by means other than art.36(2). Cases in which art.36(2) formed the basis of jurisdiction include the *Temple*

---

[90] Above, fn.65 at 400.

[91] The Court illustrated this point by stating that if the declaration had contained a time limitation provision of five years then the potential effect would have disappeared in 1934.

[92] Above, fn.65 at 404. Nicaragua ratified the ICJ Statute in 1945 and the Court cited in favour of its conclusion official publications of the Court identifying Nicaragua as having made a declaration under art.36(2) by virtue of art.36(5), and the non-registration of any objection by any state to this being the position (pp.411–415). Cf. the *Aerial Incident (Israel v Bulgaria)* I.C.J. Rep. 1959 p.127 where the issue was whether a declaration that was binding under the Permanent Court of International Justice could be transposed to the ICJ when the state making the declaration was neither present at the San Francisco Conference nor had become a party to the ICJ Statute until long after the extinction of the PCIJ. The Court concluded that in these circumstances the Bulgarian declaration was not valid.

case (1962),[93] *Military and Paramilitary Activities in and against Nicaragua*,[94] the arrest warrant of 11 April 2000 (*DRC v Belgium*).[95] The importance of art.36(2) lies in it being the only provision which seeks to establish universal compulsory jurisdiction by an international legal body over disputes, which arise between states. The Court has highlighted a "fundamental distinction between the existence of the Court's jurisdiction over a dispute, and the compatibility with international law of the particular acts which are the subject of the dispute."[96] This has been held to be the position even with respect to obligations *erga omnes* or *jus cogens* norms. Jurisdiction remains dependent upon the agreement of the disputing states.[97]

Incidental jurisdiction

The Court may be called upon to exercise an incidental jurisdiction, that is, independently of the main proceedings: of preliminary objections; an application to intervene; and interim measures.

Preliminary objections

A party may challenge the Court's jurisdiction. The most common instance is that of preliminary objections raised by the respondent state in an attempt to prevent the Court from delivering a judgment on the merits. The filing of objections suspends the proceedings on the merits (and obviously delays any decision on the merits) and gives rise to independent proceedings pursuant to which the Court will either uphold or dismiss each objection. Preliminary objections must be raised and made within three months after the delivery of the memorial of the applicant state.

Intervention

A state which is not a party to the main proceedings but is party to a convention which is before the Court, has the right to intervene.[98] Under art.62 of the Court's Statute, a state which considers that it has an interest of a legal nature which may be affected by the decision in the case may submit a request to the Court for permission to intervene. It is for the Court to decide upon such a request to intervene, e.g. in 1981 Malta's request to intervene in

---

[93] I.C.J. Rep. 1961 17—Judgment on Preliminary Objections.
[94] Above, fn.65.
[95] I.C.J. Rep. 2002 p.3.
[96] *Serbia and Montenegro v United Kingdom*, I.C.J. Rep., 2004, p.1307 at 1351.
[97] *Democratic Republic of the Congo v Rwanda*, I.C.J. Rep., 2006, p.632 and p.652.
[98] art.63 of the ICJ Statute.

the case between Tunisia and Libya was rejected by the Court. The Court considered that the interest invoked by Malta would not be affected by the decision in the case.[99] However, in 1990, Nicaragua was granted permission to intervene with respect to the *Land, Island and Maritime Frontier Dispute* between El Salvador and Honduras,[100] establishing new principles of intervention by third parties. In that case the purpose of intervention was identified as being that of protecting a state's "interest of a legal nature" that might be affected by a decision in an existing case already established between other states, the parties to the case, and not to enable a third state to "tack on a new case". "Interest of a legal nature" and its meaning was considered by the Court in *Sovereignty over Pulau Ligitan and Pulau Sipadan (Indonesia v Malaysia) (Philippines intervening).*[101] The Court in that case stated that an "interest of a legal nature" included the reasons constituting the necessary steps to the judgment as well as the dispositif or the operative paragraphs of the judgment itself. The state claiming it has an "interest of a legal nature" warranting intervention has to demonstrate that such is the case[102] and it is that state that has to discharge the burden of proof. That state has to show with a particular clarity the existence of the interest of a legal nature which is being claimed.[103]

Third parties are in any event protected by art.59 of the Court's Statute, which states "the decision of the Court has no binding force except between the parties and in respect of that particular case." Provided the immediate dispute before the Court does not form the "very subject-matter" of a dispute involving an unrepresented state, the interests of a third state which is not a party to the case are protected by art.59. This was applied in the *Certain Phosphate Lands in Nauru (Nauru v Australia, Preliminary Objections)* case.[104]

Interim measures

Article 41 of the Court's statute provides that the Court "has the power to indicate, if it considers that circumstances so require, any provisional measures which ought to be taken to preserve the respective rights of either party." The Court can, on the basis

[99] I.C.J. Rep. 1981 p.3.
[100] *Case Concerning Land, Island and Maritime Frontier Dispute (El Salvador v Honduras)* (Nicaragua Intervention), I.C.J. Rep. 1990 p.92.
[101] I.C.J. Rep. 2002 p.625, at para.82.
[102] Above, fn.100, at pp.117–118.
[103] See the Court's order of 4 July 2011 granting Greece permission to intervene in the *Jurisdictional Immunities of the State (Germany v Italy)*, Judgment of 3 February 2012.
[104] 1993, 32 I.L.M. 46.

of art.41, indicate interim measures of protection for the purpose of protecting "rights which are the subject of dispute in judicial proceedings."[105] If appropriate, the Court may then call upon the parties to refrain from any acts that might jeopardise the effectiveness of any decision, which the Court may make on the request. A request for interim protection is given priority so a quick decision can be reached. Not all requests are granted. The Court will indicate provisional measures if "there is urgency in the sense that action prejudicial to the rights of either party is likely to be taken before a final decision is given."[106] Interim orders may request parties not to take any action that may aggravate the tension between the parties or increase the difficulty of resolving the dispute, e.g. the *Case Concerning United States Diplomatic and Consular Staff in Tehran*.[107] Interim measures may be indicated to prevent "irreparable prejudice" to the rights which are in dispute, as in the *Nuclear Tests* cases[108] where the possible effect on Australian and New Zealand territory of radioactive fall-out as a consequence of the French tests, was considered irreparable.[109] The principal difficulty confronting the Court in respect of interim measures has been that of identifying the conditions in which measures should be indicated before the Court's jurisdiction has been established. Accordingly, the Court must be satisfied that there is, at least prima facie, a good basis for jurisdiction. Interim measures will only be indicated if the Court is of the opinion that it does not, manifestly,

---

[105] *Aegean Sea Continental Shelf* I.C.J. Rep. 1976 3 at 9; *Diplomatic and Consular Staff in Tehran* I.C.J. Rep. 1980, p.3 at 19. cf. *Passage Through the Great Belt (Finland v Denmark)* Provisional Measures, in which the Court was asked by Denmark to adjudicate not on whether there was a basis of jurisdiction but whether or not Finland possessed any rights which required protection.

[106] *Passage through the Great Belt (Finland v Denmark)* (Provisional Measures) I.C.J. Rep. 1991 12 at 17. Although the Court refused to indicate provisional measures the refusal was issued with an assurance to reach a decision on the merits with all possible expedition, above, at 20.

[107] Above, fn.105.

[108] I.C.J. Rep. 1973 99, 135.

[109] Libya on 3 March 1992 requested that the Court indicate provisional measures in order "to preserve the rights of Libya." The Court found by 11 votes to 5 on 14 April 1992 that the circumstances of the case(s) did not warrant indicating provisional measures. In the *Application of the International Convention on the Elimination of All Forms of Racial Discrimination (Georgia v Russian Federation)* 15 October 2008 General List No.140, the Court found interim measures were appropriate the Court was of the view such interim measures should be addressed to both parties to the dispute. The request for interim measures had initially come from Georgia. The Court noted in *Request for Interpretation of the Judgment of 31 March 2004 in the case concerning Avena and Other Mexican Nationals (Mexico v United States of America)*, Judgment, I.C.J. Rep. 2009, p.3, that the United States had breached the Order indicating provisional measures of 16 July 2008 in the case of Mr Jose Ernesto Medellin Rojas who was executed 5 August 2008.

lack jurisdiction. However, such measures are only "indicated" and are not required or ordered. For instance, the Court declined to exercise certain aspects of its jurisdiction in the case of *Libya v UK* (the "*Lockerbie*" case) as the Security Council was seised of the dispute at that time and had adopted substantive measures under Ch.VII of the UN Charter.[110] Interim measures were, however, indicated in the *Prevention of Genocide* case, due to the gravity of the case.[111] Requests for interim measures have to date come only from an applicant state, though they may be requested by the respondent state or by a motion of the Court itself. The granting of interim measures is not a guarantee that the respondent state will comply, e.g. as in the Tehran Hostages Incident. The International Court of Justice has made it unequivocally clear that "orders on provisional measure under Article 41 have binding effect."[112] The Court continued that the Order issued on 3 March 1999 "was not a mere exhortation. It had been adopted pursuant to Article 41 of the Statute. This Order was consequently binding in character and created a legal obligation for the United States."[113] The Court in *LaGrand* interpreted art.41 of the ICJ Statute in the light of the Statute's object and purpose and noted the "preparatory work of the Statute does not preclude the conclusion that orders under Article 41 have binding force." Importantly, from the object and purpose of the Statute, the Court concluded

> "the power to indicate provisional measures entails that such measures should be binding, in as much as the power in question is based on the necessity, when the circumstances call for it, to safeguard, and to avoid prejudice too, the rights of the parties as determined by the final judgment of the Court. The contention that provisional measures indicated under Article 41 might not be binding would be contrary to the object and purpose of that Article."[114]

The law applied by the Court

The function of the International Court of Justice is "to decide in accordance with international law such disputes as are

---

[110] The Court specifically declined to indicate interim measures of protection. See I.C.J. Rep. 1992 p.3. It also refused to order interim measures in the *Guinea-Bissau v Senegal* case in I.C.J. Rep. 1990 64.

[111] *Case Concerning the Application of the Convention on the Prevention and Punishment of Genocide (Bosnia and Herzegovina v Yugoslavia Serbia and Montenegro)* (Indication of Provisional Measures) 1993, above, fn.44.

[112] *LaGrand (Germany v United States)* 27 June 2001 (2001) 40 I.L.M. 1069 at para.109.

[113] Above, at para.110.

[114] Above, para.102.

submitted to it"[115] and in furtherance of its task, the Court applies

> "(a) international conventions, whether general or particular, establishing rules expressly recognized by the contesting States;
>
> (b) international custom, as evidence of a general practice accepted as law;
>
> (c) the general principles of law recognized by civilized nations;
>
> (d) subject to the provisions of art.59, judicial decisions and the teachings of the most highly qualified publicists of the various nations, as subsidiary means for the determination of rules of law."[116]

The Court may also decide a case *ex aequo et bono*—according to the principles of equity—should the parties agree thereto.[117]

The decision

A case may be brought to a conclusion in one of three ways:

> (a) at any stage in the proceedings the parties concerned may inform the Court that they have reached a settlement. On receipt of this information, the Court will issue an Order for the removal of the case from its list—e.g. the *Border and Transborder Armed Actions (Nicaragua v Honduras)* case, 11 May 1992;
>
> (b) the applicant state may decide to withdraw and not proceed any further with the case. An Order for the case to be removed from the Court's list will then be made. If the Court is not sitting, the President will issue the Order;
>
> (c) the Court delivers a judgment.

Effect of judgment

"The decision of the Court has no binding force except between the parties and in respect of that particular case."[118] In spite of the absence of the doctrine of precedent (stare decisis) the Court does give regard to previous decisions to substantiate its reasoning for

---

[115] art.38(1) of the ICJ Statute.
[116] See Ch.2 in which art.38 is fully discussed.
[117] This provision has never been applied.
[118] art.69 of the ICJ Statute.

arriving at a judgment. There would have to be good reason for the Court to depart from an earlier decision if confronted with a case based on similar facts, e.g. the subsequent development of international law.

The Court's decision is binding, final and cannot be appealed.[119] The Court will, however, interpret at the request of either party a judgment where there is uncertainty or disagreement as to the meaning and ambit of the Court's judgment.[120] A revision of the Court's judgment may be requested if material of a decisive nature previously unknown to both the Court and the party requesting a revised judgment comes to light.[121] A revision of the judgment must be requested within six months of the new fact(s) emerging and within 10 years of the delivery of the judgment.[122]

In 1985, the Tunisian Government requested a revision and interpretation of the judgment of 24 February 1982 in the *Continental Shelf (Tunisia v Libya)* case. This was the first time the International Court had received a request to revise one of its judgments and only the second time it had been requested to interpret a judgment.[123] The Tunisian request was also the first combined request for a revision and an interpretation.

Compliance with the Court's decision

The majority of the Court's judgments have been complied with by the parties. There have been exceptions, for example Albania did not adhere to the Court's order to pay compensation to the

---

[119] A number of treaties provide that appeal may be made to the Court following a decision, e.g. from an organ of an international organisation—art.84 of the Convention on International Civil Aviation (the Chicago Convention) Cmd.8742 provides for appeal to the ICJ from decisions of the Council of the International Civil Aviation Association.

[120] Requests for interpretation of judgments may be denied, e.g. the ICJ on 19 January 2009 held that matters claimed by the United Mexican States to be in issue between the Parties, requiring an interpretation under art.60 of the Statute were not matters that had been decided by the Court in its Judgment of 31 March 2004 in the case concerning *Avena and Other Mexican Nationals (Mexico v United States of America)* and as such could not give rise to the interpretation requested by the United Mexican States.

[121] art.61 of the ICJ Statute.

[122] For the Court's interpretation of art.61 see *Application for Revision of the Judgment of 11th July 1996 Concerning Application of the Genocide Convention (Preliminary Objections)*, I.C.J. Rep., 2003, p.7 and the *Application for Revision of the Judgment of 11th September 1992 Concerning the El Salvador/Honduras (Nicaragua Intervening)* case, I.C.J. Rep., 2003, p.392.

[123] The first application for an interpretation was in respect of the judgment given by the Court in the *Asylum* case, November 1950. The Court ruled unanimously on 10 December 1985 that the request for a revision of the 1982 judgment was inadmissible and that although the request for an interpretation was admissible the 1982 judgment should be implemented.

UK for the damage inflicted on the latter's warships while passing through the Corfu Channel in 1946.[124] Iran also failed to comply with the Court's decision in the *Case Concerning United States Diplomatic and Consular Staff in Tehran*.[125] The issue of compliance is not one which is of concern to the Court. In the *Nuclear Test* case the court made its position clear and expressed the view "once the Court has found that a state has entered into a commitment concerning its future conduct it is not the Court's function to contemplate that it will not comply with it."[126]

Non-appearance however, presents a problem. There have been a number of cases particularly in which the respondent state has failed to appear, absenting itself from either certain parts of the proceedings or from the entire case—as did the US in the *Nicaragua* case.[127] The Court will proceed with the case if it is satisfied that it has jurisdiction and will eventually issue judgment, even though it is likely to be disregarded by the respondent state, as in the *Fisheries Jurisdiction* case.[128]

Advisory Opinions

In addition to its jurisdiction in contentious cases, the ICJ is also competent to give an Advisory Opinion[129] on any legal question at the request of the General Assembly of the United Nations, the Security Council[130] and other bodies so authorised. States are excluded from seeking an Advisory Opinion, but they may participate in proceedings before the Court.[131] Advisory Opinions are not legally binding on the requesting body, though an international organisation may undertake to recognise such an Opinion as binding. As such, an Advisory Opinion is, in theory, a weaker statement of law than a judgment. In practice, Advisory Opinions have largely been accepted by the requesting body and any other party so affected.[132] Certain Advisory Opinions have

---

[124] *Corfu Channel* (Assessment of Compensation) I.C.J. Rep. 1949 p.244. Compensation was fully paid in 1996.

[125] I.C.J. Rep. 1980 p.3.

[126] I.C.J. Rep. 1974 p.477.

[127] *Nicaragua (Merits)* case, I.C.J. Rep. 1986 14. Note Security Resol. (UN Docs S/18250 (1986); 25 I.L.M. 1352–65 (1986) and GA Res. calling for "full and immediate compliance" with the Court's judgment. See also case *Concerning the Maritime Delimitation and Territorial Questions (Qatar v Bahrain)* I.C.J. Rep. 1995 p.6, in which Bahrain failed to appear, although it did indicate this in advance and submitted written pleadings.

[128] I.C.J. Rep. 1974 p.3.

[129] art.65 of the ICJ Statute.

[130] art.96 of the UN Charter.

[131] art.66 of the ICJ Statute.

[132] Note art.30 of the 1946 General Convention on the Privileges, Immunities of the United Nations, which provides if a difference arises between the UN and

undoubtedly contributed to the development of international law, e.g. the *Advisory Opinion on Reparation for Injuries Suffered in the Service of the United Nations 1949*[133] (legal personality of United Nations); *Advisory Opinion on Certain Expenses of the United Nations*[134] (legitimate expenses of the organisation); *Advisory Opinion on Western Sahara*[135] (decolonisation); the *Advisory Opinion on the Legality of the Threat or Use of Nuclear Weapons*[136] (which specifically dealt with the issue raised in UN General Assembly Resolution 49/75 K as to whether the threat or use of nuclear weapons is, in any circumstance, permitted under international law)[137]; and the *Advisory Opinion on the Legal Consequences of the Construction of a Wall in the Occupied Palestinian Territory* (the right to self-determination and a number of issues of humanitarian and human rights law). Other Advisory Opinions have been concerned with more specific issues raised by the requesting body: *Applicability of Art.VI, Section 22, of the Convention on the Privileges and Immunities of the United Nations*[138] (first request by the Economic and Social Council of the United Nations); *Application for Review of Judgment No. 333 of the U.N. Administrative Tribunal* (international administrative law/the law of the international civil service)[139]; *Difference Relating to Immunity from Legal Process of a Special Rapporteur of the Commission on Human Rights* (again, a request by the Economic and Social Council, of which the Commission on Human Rights was a subsidiary body)[140]; and the *Accordance with International Law of the Unilateral Declaration of Independence in respect of Kosovo.*[141]

Role and impact of the Court

The impact of the ICJ has been somewhat limited. This is understandable given the Court has to wait until it is seised of a case or requested to give an opinion. The UN Secretary-General's Trust Fund was established in 1989 to encourage states, in particular developing states, to seek a solution to their legal disputes through the Court. The Trust Fund makes available limited

a member a request should be made for an Advisory Opinion by an organ of the UN and the Opinion rendered by the Court is to be accepted as decisive by the parties.
[133] I.C.J. Rep. 1949 p.174.
[134] I.C.J. Rep. 1962 p.151.
[135] I.C.J. Rep. 1975 p.12.
[136] 35 I.L.M. 809 (1996).
[137] I.C.J. Rep 2004 p.136.
[138] I.C.J. Rep. 1989 p.177.
[139] I.C.J. Rep. 1987 p.18.
[140] I.C.J. Rep. 1999 p.62.
[141] I.C.J. Rep. 2010 p.403.

financial assistance to help defray the cost involved in employing the Court procedures.

The Court's jurisdiction is restricted to legal disputes and art.36(2) specifically limits the jurisdiction of the Court to "legal disputes", but art.38(1) of the ICJ's Statute instructs the Court to "decide in accordance with international law such disputes as are submitted to it." The Court has acknowledged that there are limitations on the exercise of its judicial function,[142] and yet no dispute has ever been rejected because it involved non-legal issues. The Court has maintained that to dismiss a case because the legal aspect is only one element of a political dispute would be to impose a "far-reaching and unwarranted restriction upon the role of the Court in the peaceful settlement of international disputes."[143] The Court's decision in finding jurisdiction in the *Nicaragua* case precipitated the termination of the US' acceptance of art.36(2) as, according to the US, that decision represented "an over-reaching of the Court's limits, a departure from its tradition of judicial restraint, and a risky venture into treacherous political waters."[144]

In international relations political and legal issues are intertwined, and the decision to seek judicial settlement is itself often a political one. The PCIJ refused to deliver an opinion in the *Eastern Carelia* case,[145] as the Court felt to do so would be tantamount to giving a decision in a dispute. The only occasion when the ICJ has refused to provide an Advisory Opinion when requested was in the *WHO Nuclear Weapons case*, in which the Court found that the question did not fall within WHO's competence because it concerned the legality of the use of nuclear weapons rather than the effect of their use on human health.

One question which has not yet been fully addressed but has certainly appeared in a dissenting opinion is the relationship between the Court and the Security Council, and the extent to which the Court may have competence to review the legality of Security Council resolutions.[146] The ICJ does not have the com-

---

[142] *Northern Cameroons* case I.C.J. Rep. 1963 p.15 at 29.

[143] *Case Concerning United States Diplomatic and Consular Staff in Tehran* I.C.J. Rep. 1980 p.3 at 19 endorsed in the *Nicaragua (Jurisdiction)* case at 439–440.

[144] Department of State File No.P85, 0009–2151, reproduced in 79 A.J.I.L. 441 (1985).

[145] P.C.I.J. Rep. ser.B, No.5 (1923).

[146] Dissenting opinion of Judge Weeramantry in case *Concerning Questions of Interpretation and Application of the Montreal Convention arising out of the Aerial incident at Lockerbie (Provisional Measures Libya v United Kingdom)* I.C.J. Rep. 1992 p.3. See also the case of *Kadi and Al Berakaat v Council of the EU and EC Commission*, Judgment of the Grand Chamber of the European Court, 3 September 2008, in which the European Court held that a community measure designed to give effect to a Security Council Resolution infringed the

petence of judicial review or appeal with regards to the Security Council's actions. The extent of the ICJ's competence to make pronouncements on the extent or legality of Security Council actions remains, as yet, undecided.

CONCLUSION

The ICJ, as a permanent institution, has served as a constant reminder to states that judicial channels do exist through which the peaceful settlement of international disputes may be sought. The Court's procedures and jurisdiction are known to the international community; however, the ICJ is no longer the only player in the field. There has been a marked growth in the number of bodies established to deal with disputes in specific subject matter, which are frequently limited geographically and temporally. Notwithstanding the number of mechanisms available, the future role of international judicial settlement still lies with states. States must be willing to submit their disputes to independent adjudication and demonstrate a willingness to comply with judicial decisions.

Appellant's fundamental rights, their right to an effective legal remedy and a right to property. On 18 July 2013, the ECJ upheld the September 2010 decision of the General Court annulling the European Regulation relisting Mr Kadi in 2008, and dismissed the appeals against that decision brought by the European Commission, the Council of the European Union and the UK. The ECJ held that none of the reasons for listing Mr Kadi set out in the UN Narrative Summary was substantiated by the evidence (C-584/10 P, *Commission and Others v Kadi*).

13. CONCLUSION

Law students and lawyers may find international law disconcerting if they approach it with the prejudices of a lawyer trained to deal with a mature domestic legal system. Of course this is not surprising as law is most commonly associated with, and encountered via, authoritative domestic institutions. Such institutions possess the competence to prescribe the necessary legal rights and duties for the community within which they operate or to proscribe certain conduct. International law does not fit into such a mould. This, to many, and particularly the legally trained, can make international law confusing in character and disappointing in outcome if it fails to meet their expectations. International law faces two contrasting criticisms with some perceiving it as intrusive, interfering in state sovereignty, whereas others regard it as seeking to protect and preserve state sovereignty rather than setting a common global standard, which is shared, respected and mutually supported. This tension is reflected in the mechanisms which have evolved and are now in place ensuring, e.g. that individuals can be held responsible under international law for actions perpetrated within a national context. However, these laws are not consistently abided by or enforced, depending on states' willingness and political expediency.

The international legal system is to a large extent voluntary in character. International law is not imposed on states, as demonstrated by the ability of states to make reservations to international treaties. International law has evolved as states have come into greater contact with each other and have been confronted by problems of common concern, including that of establishing the boundaries of state action. International law is an expression of the need for states to co-exist. The problems confronting the international community are complex, and the search for solutions demands not only co-operation, but an acknowledgement of the inter-dependency of all participants within the global community. Such an acknowledgement is pre-requisite if effective solutions are to be realised.

International legal personality is not a static concept, and any definition must be sufficiently flexible and able to deal with non-state actors which may appear on the international plane. Law does not operate in a vacuum, and other factors, such as politics, play a role in interstate relations. Lawyers can however be guilty of over-emphasising rules of law. There can be a failure to appreciate that states are influenced and motivated by politics, and that in international relations there is, as a norm, more than one course of action available. It is important to be aware of the ways in which politicians may utilise and indeed manipulate international law, e.g. to identify and accomplish goals. Indeed, international law has been described as the politicians' "box of tools".[1]

The absence of mandatory sanctions distinguishes international law from municipal law. This however is a consequence of the intrinsically different character of international law, rather than a fault or weakness in the international legal system. The primary aim of international law is the achievement of international peace and security, not through the characterisation of an alleged offending state as "guilty", but through the promotion of conciliation. Hence, negotiations among states are the principal channels initially utilised in efforts to settle international disputes.

All states are in theory equally sovereign, however not all states share common ideologies nor do they have the same weight in international relations. The number of independent states increased markedly in the latter half of the 20th century, and a noticeable effect of this was a questioning and challenging of some of the traditional established rules of international law. International law is not confined to regulating the relations of a homogeneous grouping of states, but rather is confronted with bringing within its ambit states which differ politically, economically, ideologically and socially from each other, that is, a very

---

[1] R. Fisher, "International Law: A Toolbox for the Statesman" (1979) 9 C.W.I.C.J. 3.

heterogeneous group. The challenge facing contemporary international law is to regulate the behaviour of states and other entities such as international organisations, non-governmental organisations and civil society groups, multi-national corporations, armed and terrorist groups and even individuals.

The subject matter of international law is not exhaustively defined. Its boundaries are not firmly established, and it now embraces areas that were traditionally considered exclusively the preserve of domestic jurisdiction.

Why are the expectations of international law higher than the expectations of municipal law? There seems to be a belief that international law should be able to prevent all breaches when, for example, domestic criminal law does not prevent all crimes and the existence of contract law does not prevent contracts from being broken. It seems to be forgotten that municipal law is disregarded regularly and yet criticism and scepticism of international law is partly based on the fact that international law may be, and indeed is, breached. Such a stance forgets that international law in itself cannot exert influence independently, but only primarily through the organs of the state. The most vocal critics of international law overlook that international law functions very efficiently over a wide range of activities every day and that violations of international law occur predominantly in politically sensitive areas. That is what makes them newsworthy and is responsible for them receiving extensive, high-profile media coverage. Violations of international law must be seen in perspective, as a legal system rooted in the rule of law can accommodate a breach of law.

What international law can do is mould behaviour and encourage compliance with international norms. It can do this by being dynamic, adapting to, accommodating and responding to different conditions and sets of circumstances. International law is a system, but it may also be conceived of as a language—a language which will not necessarily provide the answers to all international problems but which will facilitate the resolution of the issues which confront and concern the contemporary global community. For the participating members of this community to speak to each other, there must be a medium of communication—a common language—the vocabulary of which includes respect for the rule of law, democracy, justice, and above all the dignity of all human beings, without distinction. In a multilingual international community there is one language which is readily translated—international law. An increasing fluency in international law is required so it may be employed to educate and inform the conduct of those responsible for the policies of states, and those other actors which now feature on the international stage. What must be fostered is the development within the international forum of a political culture which possesses a respect for the international rule of law and reflects the truism "that united, there is little we cannot do in a host of cooperative ventures. Divided, there is little we can do—for we dare not meet a powerful challenge at odds and split asunder".[2]

This vision has not yet been universally accomplished and remains elusive, given the effects of increasing globalisation; environmental degradation; the threat of international terrorism and organised crime; and the prevalence of conflicts which often lead to the mass displacement of civilian populations. However, none of the events or structural changes which have occurred in the years since this aspiration was expressed have negated the goals, nor the role which international law can have in its eventual realisation. As the President of the International Court of Justice, Hisashi Owada, highlighted to the UN General Assembly in October 2009:

> "The importance of the rule of law is crucial against the backdrop of the deepening process of globalization. Law does not replace politics or economics, but without it we cannot construct anything that will last in the international community."[3]

---

[2] John F. Kennedy, Inaugural Address, 20 January 1961.
[3] The President of the International Court of Justice, addressing the General Assembly, welcomes the growing trust and respect of the international community for the Court, International Court of Justice Press Release, No.2009/31, 2 November 2009.

BIBLIOGRAPHY

General texts

I. Brownlie, *Basic Documents in International Law*, 6th edn (Oxford: Clarendon Press, 2008).

A. Cassese, *International Law*, 2nd edn (Oxford: Oxford University Press, 2004).

J. Crawford, *Brownlie's Principles of Public International Law*, 8th edn (Oxford: Oxford University Press, 2012).

M. Evans, *International Law Documents*, 12th edn (Oxford: Blackstone Press, 2015).

M. Evans, *International Law*, 4th edn (Oxford: Oxford University Press, 2014).

D.J. Harris, *Cases and Materials on International Law*, 8th edn (London: Sweet & Maxwell, 2015).

R. McCorquodale, M. Dixon and S. Williams, *Cases and Materials on International Law*, 5th edn (Oxford: Oxford University Press, 2011).

J.G. Merrils, *International Dispute Settlement*, 5th edn (Cambridge: Cambridge University Press, 2011).

J. O'Brien, *International Law* (London: Cavendish Publishing, 2001).

M.N. Shaw, *International Law*, 7th edn (Cambridge: Cambridge University Press, 2014).

Specialised texts

The list of texts identified below should not be treated as exhaustive

P. Alston and R. Goodman, *International Human Rights: The Successor to International Human Rights in Context*, 3rd edn (Oxford: Oxford University Press, 2012).

A. Aust, *Modern Treaty Law in Practice*, 3rd edn (Cambridge: Cambridge University Press, 2013).

P.W. Birnie, A. Boyle and C. Redgwell, *International Law and the Environment*, 3rd edn (Oxford: Oxford University Press, 2009).

R.R. Churchill and A.V. Lowe, *The Law of the Sea*, 3rd edn (Manchester: Manchester University Press, 1999).

J. Crawford, *The International Law Commission's Articles on State Responsibility* (Cambridge: Cambridge University Press, 2002).

I. Detter, *The Law of War*, 3rd edn (Farnham: Ashgate Publishing Limited, 2013).

T.M. Franck, *Recourse to Force; State Action Against Threats and Armed Attacks*, Hersch Lauterpacht Memorial Lectures, (Cambridge: Cambridge University Press, 2009).

G. Goodwin-Gill and J. McAdam, *The Refugee in International Law*, 3rd edn (Oxford: Clarendon Press, 2007).

C. Gray, *International Law and the Use of Force*, 3rd edn (Oxford: Oxford University Press, 2008).

R. Higgins, *Problems and Process: International Law and How to Use It*, (Oxford: Clarendon Press, 1994).

R.M.M. Wallace, *International Human Rights, Text and Materials*, 2nd edn (London: Sweet & Maxwell, 2001).

T. Weiss and S. Daws, *The Oxford Handbook on the United Nations* (Oxford: Oxford University Press, 2008).

Journals

Journals featuring articles on general issues of contemporary international law

American Journal of International Law
Australian Yearbook of International Law
British Yearbook of International Law
Canadian Yearbook of International Law
Cornell International Law Journal
European Journal of International Law
Georgia Journal of International Comparative Law
German Yearbook of International Law
Harvard International Law Journal
International Comparative Law Quarterly

Melbourne Journal of International Law
Netherlands International Law Review
Recueil des Coeurs
Stanford Journal of International Law
Virginia Journal of International Law
Yale Journal of International Law

There are an increasing number of law journals which focus on specialised topics of international law in addition to those which provide a more general coverage. The following examples are particularly recommended:

Human rights

Human Rights Law Journal
Human Rights Quarterly
International Journal of Refugee Law

Use of force

International Affairs
International Peacekeeping
Journal of Armed Conflict

Environmental Law

International Environmental Law
Colorado Journal of International Environmental Law and Policy
Harvard Environmental Law Review
Yearbook of International Environmental Law

USING THE INTERNET

International law is particularly well served by the internet. There are an increasing number of websites which a student of international law would be well advised to consult in order to keep abreast of developments in contemporary international society. The relevant international organisations contain the treaties and other international law sources related to their activity. Most international treaties can be found through the United Nations website. There is also an increasing number of blogs where academics and international law practitioners comment on recent developments in the field.

The sites identified below are merely starting points for further research, and because of this the list has been kept to a minimum, rather than extended.

WORLD WEBSITES (N.B. SITE LOCATIONS ARE SUBJECT TO CHANGE

United Nations

www.un.org
http://untreaty.un.org/

Sources

http://untreaty.un.org/
International Court of Justice
www.icj-cij.org
European Court of Human Rights
www.echr.coe.int

Human Rights

www.umn.edu/humanrts/index.html
www.ohchr.org
United Nations High Commissioner for Refugees
www.unhcr.org
International Red Cross
www.icrc.org/eng

Law of the Sea

http://www.un.org/depts/los/index.htm

U.K. Foreign and Commonwealth Office

www.gov.uk/government/organisations/foreign-common
wealth-office

US Supreme Court

supct.law.cornell.edu/supct

General international law

www.asil.org
http://www.esil-sedi.eu/
http://www.kent.ac.uk/lawlinks/
http://www.llrx.com/
http://worldlii.org
http://amnesty.org/

Electronic Journals

European Journal of International Law: www.ejil.org
American Journal of International Law: http://www.asil.org/
resources/american-journal-international-law

Comprehensive list of international law journals

http://stu.findlaw.com/journals/international.html

INDEX

LEGAL TAXONOMY
FROM SWEET & MAXWELL

This index has been prepared using Sweet and Maxwell's Legal Taxonomy. Main index entries conform to keywords provided by the Legal Taxonomy except where references to specific documents or non-standard terms (denoted by quotation marks) have been included. These keywords provide a means of identifying similar concepts in other Sweet & Maxwell publications and online services to which keywords from the Legal Taxonomy have been applied. Readers may find some minor differences between terms used in the text and those which appear in the index. Suggestions to *sweetandmaxwell.taxonomy@thomson.com*.

Accession
  treaties, 276
Accidents at work
  state responsibility for environment,
    235–236
Accretion
  acquisition of territory, 112
Act of State
  incorporation of international law,
    59–62
Acts of aggression
  See **Use of force**
"Adhesion"
  treaties, 276
Adoption of treaties
  See **Accession**
Advisory opinions
  International Court of Justice,
    358–359
African Union
  See also **Organisation of African
    Unity**
  sources of law, 34
"Age of Discovery"
  development of international law, 5
  territory, 104

Aggression
  See **Use of force**
Air accidents
  jurisdiction, 129
Air pollution
  state responsibility for environment,
    233–234
Airspace
  aircraft in distress, 118–119
  entry, 116
  generally, 116–117
  International Civil Aviation
    Organisation
    establishment, 120
    use of weapons against civilian
      aircraft, 119
  Five Freedoms Agreement, 117–118
  right of entry, 116
  shooting down civilian aircraft,
    119–120
  Two Freedoms Agreements, 116, 117
Aliens
  state responsibility
    breach of contract, 222–223
    Calvo Clause, 223
    companies, 226–228

compensation, 220–221
discrimination, 220
dispute resolution, 221–222
exhaustion of domestic remedies, 228–229
expropriation of property of non-nationals, 218–219
international minimum standard, 214–216
introduction, 212–213
national treatment standard, 214
nationality of claims, 223–226
nationals, 216
public purpose, 219
refugees, 216–218
scope of liability, 212–213
shareholders, 226–228
standard of treatment, 213–216
Amendments
treaties, 285
Annexation
acquisition of territory, 109–111
state recognition, 70
Antarctica
territory
claims, 115
conservation, 115–116
dispute resolution, 116
minerals, 116
Apartheid
human rights, 260
universality principle, 131
Applicable law
International Court of Justice, 355–356
Appropriation
outer space, 121
Arbitration
agreement to arbitrate, 337–338
generally, 336–339
Permanent Court of Arbitration, 337
procedure, 337–338
UN Compensation Commission, 338
use, 336–337
Archipelagic states
territorial waters, 167–168
Arctic
environmental protection, 114–115
territorial claims, 113–114
Armed attack
use of force
anticipation, 306
generally, 304–307

Armed conflict
customs and laws of war, 323–326
Attribution
state responsibility, 205–208
Authors
sources of law, 30–31
Avulsion
territory, 112

Bangladesh
state recognition, 70
Banjul Charter on Human and Peoples Rights 1986
environment, 230
generally, 263
Baselines
archipelagic states, 167–168
Arctic, 113
bays, 164
contiguous zone, 173
continental shelf
delimitations, 191
generally, 189–190
delimitation of territorial seas, 167
exclusive economic zones, 184–185
islands, 166
judicial decisions, 28
measurement of territorial sea, 162–164
Bays
territorial waters, 164–166
Bill of Rights
United Nations, 250
Biodiversity
environmental protection, 235
Bosnia and Herzegovina
state recognition
capacity, 68
criteria, 78
Boundaries
defined territory, 66, 104
judicial decision-making, 30
jurisdiction
passive personality principle, 135
territorial principle, 127
treaty succession, 293
Breach
termination of treaties, 289–290
Breach of contract
treatment of aliens, 222–223
Breach of the peace
collective measures through the UN, 311

Broadcasting
high seas, 180

"Calvo Clause"
treatment of aliens, 223
Cambodia
human rights tribunals, 266
Canada
Arctic, 113–115
baselines, 168
continental shelf, 193
international law in national courts,
58
Quebec, 73
responsibility to protect, 321
self-defence, 303
state immunity, 144
state recognition, 80
state responsibility, 203, 230
Capacity
individuals, 94–98
states, 68–70
Case law
sources of law
national courts, 30
precedent, 28–30
Central American Court of Justice
procedural capacity of individuals,
95
Cession
acquisition of territory, 111–112
Chambers
International Court of Justice,
341–342
Change of circumstances
termination of treaties,
290–291
Child sex offences
human rights, 260
jurisdiction, 128
Children
human rights, 260
Civil war
state recognition, 67
Climate change
state responsibility for environment,
234–235
Codification
meaning, 34
Coercion
validity of treaties, 287
Commencement
treaties, 281

**Commission on the Limits of the
    Continental Shelf**
establishment, 195
Commissions of inquiry
dispute resolution procedures, 335
**"Committee on Enforced
    Disappearance"**
procedural capacity of individuals,
98
Companies
treatment of aliens, 226–228
Compensation
state responsibility
expropriation of property of non-
nationals, 218–219
generally, 210–212
treatment of aliens, 220–221
Conciliation
use of in international disputes, 335
**"Congressional executive
    agreements"**
incorporation of international law,
57
Consent
treaties, 276
Constitutions
state recognition, 76–77
Consuls
immunity from jurisdiction, 156–157
Contiguous zones
territorial waters, 173
Continental shelf
baselines
delimitations, 191
generally, 189–190
coastal state's rights, 190
Convention definitions, 189
delimitation between states with
opposite or adjacent coasts,
191–195
exploitation, 190
exploration, 190
extent, 189
generally, 188–190
meaning, 188
Conventions
See **Treaties**
Corruption
validity of treaties, 287
Council of Europe
closed organisations, 89
sources of law, 34
state recognition, 89

Court of First Instance
procedural capacity of individuals, 98
Covenant on Civil and Political Rights 1966
implementation, 252
individual communications to HRC, 255–256
inter-state complaint, 254–255
introduction, 248–250
reporting system, 253–254
rights protected by, 251–252
Covenant on Economic, Social and Cultural Rights 1966
implementation, 252
individual communications to HRC, 257
introduction, 248–250
reporting system, 253–254
rights protected by, 252
Crimes against humanity
universality principle, 131
Croatia
state recognition
capacity, 68
criteria, 78
Custom
definition, 11–12
duration, 12–13
evidence of state practice, 17–18
extent of state practice, 13–17
instant custom, 20–21
introduction, 11
material element, 12–18
meaning
generally, 11–12
material element, 12–18
instant custom, 20–21
international law
characteristics, 4
environmental protection, 230
sources, 9–21
opinio juris, 18–20
psychological element, 18–20
self-defence, 303–304
state practice, 12–18
Customary law
incorporation of international law
United Kingdom, 43–46
United States, 50
Customs and laws of war
See also **Use of force; War crimes**
armed conflict, 323–326
generally, 322–323

De facto recognition
See **Recognition**
De jure recognition
See **Recognition**
Declarations
International Court of Justice
jurisdiction, 346–352
sovereignty, 106
state recognition
Alma Ata Declaration, 74
generally, 77
Delimitation
continental shelf, 191–195
exclusive economic zones, 187–188
territorial waters, 167
Desertification
state responsibility, 232
Detention
jurisdiction
Guantanamo Bay, 129
Diplomats
diplomatic privileges
existence, 146
state recognition in UK, 83
diplomatic relations
existence, 146
severance, 291–292
state recognition in UK, 83
free movement and travel, 150
immunity from jurisdiction
administrative staff, 152–153
diplomatic agents, 151–152
diplomatic bags, 150–151
diplomatic missions, 146–148
diplomatic premises, 148–150
free movement and travel, 150
generally, 146–153
implementation of Convention, 153
objective, 147
persona non grata, 153
respect for local laws, 153
service staff, 152
state recognition in UK, 83
tax, 153
technical staff, 152–153
persona non grata, 153
respect for local laws, 153
special missions, 157–158
state immunity, 142–145
tax, 153
Disabled persons
human rights, 260

Discrimination
  human rights, 260–263
  treatment of aliens, 220
Dispute resolution
  See also **International Court of Justice**
  aliens, 221–222
  arbitration, 336–339
  commissions of inquiry, 335
  conciliation, 335
  good offices, 334
  introduction, 333–334
  mediation, 334–335
  treatment of aliens, 221–222
Double jeopardy
  jurisdiction, 142
Dualism
  incorporation of international law, 40–41

East Timor
  human rights tribunals, 266–267
Economic development
  continental shelf, 188
  seabed, 195–196
Enabling Acts
  incorporation of international law, 47
Environment
  state responsibility
    biological diversity, 235
    climate change, 234–235
    customary international law, 230
    desertification, 232
    hazardous waste, 235
    industrial accidents, 235–236
    injurious consequences of permitted acts, 238–239
    international co-operation, 230–231
    introduction, 229
    nuclear weapons, 236–238
    ozone depleting substances, 234
    regulatory developments, 229–229
    Rio Declaration, 231–232
    trans-boundary air pollution, 233–234
    watercourses, 236
Environmental protection
  Antarctica, 115
  Arctic, 114–115
Equity
  sources of law, 26–28

"Erga omnes"
  state responsibility, 208–210
European Convention on Human Rights
  generally, 263
European Union
  sources of law, 34
Exclusive economic zones
  delimitation between states with opposite or adjacent coasts, 187–188
  establishment, 20
  fisheries, 184–185
  introduction, 184
  rights of coastal states, 185–187
  rights of other states, 187
  territorial waters, 162
"Executive agreements"
  incorporation of international law
    congressional executive agreements, 56–57
    generally, 55–56
Executive certificates
  See also **Suggestions**
  incorporation of international law, 50
  state recognition, 87
Exemplary damages
  state responsibility, 212
Exhaustion of domestic remedies
  treatment of aliens, 228–229
Explanatory memorandums
  treaty incorporation, 47
Exploration
  continental shelf, 190
  outer space, 120–121
Expropriation
  treatment of aliens, 218–219
Extradition
  jurisdiction, 140–141

Federalism
  incorporation of international law, 57–59
Finland
  state recognition, 67
Fisheries
  exclusive economic zones, 184–185
  high seas, 180
  territorial waters, 162–162
"Fitzmaurice compromise"
  dualism, and, 40–41

Foreign nationals
jurisdiction, 128–129
Foreign Office
executive certificates, 50
Fraud
validity of treaties, 287

Genocide
human rights, 260
individual responsibility, 97
international war crimes tribunals,
264–267
universality principle, 131
Germany
non- recognition, 85
"Good offices"
international dispute resolution, 334
Governments
government recognition
distinction from state recognition,
75–76
generally, 79–80
state recognition, 67–68
Guantanamo Bay
jurisdiction, 129

Hazardous waste
state responsibility, 235
Heads of state
immunity from jurisdiction, 154–156
High seas
fishing, 181
freedom, 173–174
hot pursuit, 181
human trafficking, 180–181
introduction, 173
jurisdiction
generally, 177
people trafficking, 180–181
piracy, 177–178
powers of seizure, 177–180
unlicensed broadcasting, 180
marine environments
International Maritime
Organisation, 183–184
international measures, 183–184
oil pollution, 181–182
pollution from land sources,
182–183
pollution from ships, 181–182
radioactive waste, 182
meaning, 173
nationality of ships, 175–176

nuclear tests, 174–175
people trafficking, 180–181
piracy, 177–178
seizure powers, 177–180
trafficking, 180–181
unlicensed broadcasting, 180
Holy See
international personality, 99–100
Hot pursuit
high seas, 181
Human rights
conclusion, 269
Covenant on Civil and Political
Rights
implementation, 252
individual communications to
HRC, 255–256
inter-state complaint, 254–255
introduction, 248–250
reporting system, 253–254
rights protected by, 251–252
Covenant on Economic, Social and
Cultural Rights
implementation, 252
individual communications to
HRC, 257
introduction, 248–250
reporting system, 253–254
rights protected by, 252
discrimination, 260–263
European Convention on Human
Rights, 263
Human Rights Council
complaints procedure, 258–259
country procedure, 258
generally, 257–258
thematic procedure, 258
universal periodic review, 259
indigenous peoples, 261
international criminal law
hybrid tribunals, 266–267
International Criminal Court,
267–269
international war crimes
tribunals, 263–267
UN special courts, 265–266
introduction, 241
meaning, 242
nature
classification, 242–245
jurisdiction, 243–246
meaning, 242
protection, 245–246

relativist theory, 242
rights of individuals in
    international law, 246–247
Organisation of African Unity, 263
right of individual application, 95
special procedures
    complaints, 258–259
    country, 258
    generally, 258
    thematic, 258
    universal periodic review, 259
state recognition, 74
treaty incorporation, 47–49
UN Commissioner on Human
    Rights, 259–260
UN Conventions, 260–263
United Nations
    Action Programme, 250
    Commissioner on Human Rights,
        259–260
    Covenant on Civil and Political
        Rights, 248–256
    Covenant on Economic, Social
        and Cultural Rights, 248–257
    Human Rights Council, 257–259
    implementation machinery, 252
    International Bill of Rights, 250
    introduction, 247
    Universal Declaration on Human
        Rights, 247–248
    Vienna Conference, 250
Human trafficking
high seas, 180–181
jurisdiction, 128
Humanitarian intervention
generally, 319–321
Humanitarian law
See **International humanitarian law**

Immunities
conclusion, 158
consuls, 156–157
diplomatic immunity
    administrative staff, 152–153
    diplomatic agents, 151–152
    diplomatic bags, 150–151
    diplomatic missions, 146–148
    diplomatic premises, 148–150
    free movement and travel, 150
    generally, 146–153
    implementation of Convention,
        153
    objective, 147

persona non grata, 153
respect for local laws, 153
service staff, 152
state recognition in UK, 83
tax, 153
technical staff, 152–153
heads of state, 154–156
international organisations, 158
introduction, 142
jurisdiction, from
    consular relations, 156–157
    diplomatic immunity, 146–153
    heads of state, 154–156
    introduction, 142
    special missions, 157–158
    state immunity, 142–145
special missions, 157–158
state immunity, 142–145
Immunity from suit
state recognition in UK, 81–82
Impossibility
termination of treaties, 290
Incorporation
United Kingdom
    customary international law, 43–46
    executive certificates, 50
    treaties, 47–50
United States
    Act of State doctrine, 59–62
    congressional executive
        agreements, 56–57
    customary international law,
        50–50
    executive agreements, 55–56
    federalism, 57–59
    suggestion, 59
    treaties, 50–55
Indigenous peoples
human rights, 261
Individuals
See **Persons**
Industrial accidents
See **Accidents at work**
**Inhuman or degrading treatment or
    punishment**
human rights, 260–261
Innocent passage
territorial waters
    compliance with national laws,
        169
    dangers to navigation, 169
    jurisdiction, 171
    meaning, 168–169

national security, 169–170
shipping lanes, 170
warships, 171
Insurgents
See **Rebel groups**
Interim measures
International Court of Justice,
353–355
**International Civil Aviation
Organisation**
establishment, 120
use of weapons against civilian
aircraft, 119
International co-operation
state responsibility for environment,
230–231
International Court of Justice
advisory opinions, 358–359
applicable law, 355–356
composition, 340–342
conclusion, 361
declarations, 346–352
establishment, 339–340
forum prorogatum, 344–345
future, 359–361
incidental jurisdiction, 352
interim measures, 353–355
international personality
individuals, 96, 98
United Nations, 91–93
intervention, 352–353
introduction, 339–340
judgments and orders
advisory opinions, 358–359
compliance with, 357–358
effect, 356–357
jurisdiction
agreement of parties, 343–344
declarations, 346–352
incidental jurisdiction, 352
locus standi, 342–343
prorogated jurisdiction, 344–345
reservations, 346–350
locus standi, 342–343
preliminary objections, 352
prorogated jurisdiction, 344–345
provisional measures, 353–355
reservations, 346–350
role, 359–361
settlement, 356
territorial claims
Antarctica, 116
withdrawal of case, 356

International crimes
jurisdiction
apartheid, 131
crimes against humanity, 131
generally, 130–133
genocide, 131
quasi-universal jurisdiction,
133–135
piracy, 131
slavery, 131
war crimes, 131
International Criminal Court
human rights, 267–269
jurisdiction, 135–136
International criminal law
human rights
hybrid tribunals, 266–267
International Criminal Court,
267–269
international war crimes
tribunals, 263–267
UN special courts, 265–266
International humanitarian law
generally, 328–330
Red Cross, 330
International investment disputes
procedural capacity of individuals,
98
International law
Act of State doctrine, 59–62
characteristics, 4–5
conclusion, 363–366
customary international law, 50–50
definition, 2
executive agreements
congressional, 56–57
general, 55–56
executive certificates, 50
federalism, 57–59
historical development, 5–7
incorporation by United Kingdom
customary international law,
43–46
executive certificates, 50
treaties, 47–50
incorporation by United States
Act of State doctrine, 59–62
congressional executive
agreements, 56–57
customary international law,
50–50
executive agreements, 55–56
federalism, 57–59

suggestion, 59
treaties, 50–55
meaning, 2
national courts in the UK, before
  customary international law,
    43–46
  executive certificates, 50
  treaties, 47–50
national courts in the US, before
  Act of State doctrine, 59–62
  congressional executive
    agreements, 56–57
  customary international law,
    50–50
  executive agreements, 55–56
  federalism, 57–59
  suggestion, 59
  treaties, 50–55
nature, 2–3
non-recognition of states, 84
peremptory norms, 36–37
public policy, 36–37
sources of law
  authors, 30–31
  case law, 28–30
  conclusion, 37
  custom, 11–21
  equity, 26–28
  generally, 9–11
  International Law Commission,
    34–36
  international organisations,
    32–34
  jus cogens, 36–37
  principles, 25–26
  regional organisations, 34
  soft law, 31–32
  treaties, 21–24
treaties
  competence to make, 275
  generally, 4
  incorporation by UK, 46–50
  incorporation by US, 50–55
  sources of law, 21–24
International Law Commission
codification, 34
establishment, 34
generally, 34–36
membership, 35
responsibilities, 35
state immunity, 145
International Maritime Organisation
role, 183–184

International organisations
immunities, 158
international personality
  closed organisations, 89
  determination, 89
  generally, 88–89
  open organisations, 89
  United Nations, 90–94
sources of law 32–34
International personality
conclusion, 102
Holy See, 99–100
individuals, 94–98
insurgents, 98
international organisations
  closed organisations, 89
  determination, 89
  generally, 88–89
  open organisations, 89
  United Nations, 90–94
introduction, 63–64
multinational companies,
  100–101
national liberation movements,
  98–99
non-governmental organisations,
  100
rebel groups, 98
recognition of states and
  governments
  constitutive theory, 76
  criteria, 78–79
  de facto recognition, 80–81
  de jure recognition, 80–81
  declaratory theory, 76–77
  distinction between states and
    governments, 75–76
  duty to recognise, 77–78
  generally, 74–75
  governments, of, 79–80
  modes of according, 87–88
  non-recognition, 84–87
  UK practice, 81–84
states
  capacity to enter agreements,
    68–70
  governments, 67–68
  human rights, 74
  introduction, 64–65
  meaning, 65
  population, 65
  self-determination, 70–74
  territory, 66–67

violations of international law, 70
transnational corporations, 100–101

International Seabed Authority
role, 196–197

International Telecommunications Union
role, 122

International Tribunal for the Law of the Sea
role, 197–199

International war crimes tribunals
human rights
Cambodia, 266
East Timor, 266–267
introduction, 263–264
Rwanda, 264–265
Sierra Leone, 265–266
Yugoslavia, 264–265

Intervention
International Court of Justice, 352–353

Iraq
use of force
authorised by competent organ of UN, 322
breach of the peace, 311
collective-self-defence, 307
economic sanctions, 312
peacekeeping, 316
self-defence, 305

Islands
territorial waters, 166

Judges
International Court of Justice, 340–341

Jurisdiction
bases
generally, 126
nationality principle, 129–130
passive personality principle, 135
protective principle, 130
security principle, 130
territorial principle, 127–129
universality principle, 130–135
conclusion, 158
double jeopardy, 142
extradition, 140–141
high seas
generally, 177
people trafficking, 180–181
piracy, 177–178
powers of seizure, 177–180
unlicensed broadcasting, 180
human rights, 243–246
immunity from jurisdiction
consular relations, 156–157
diplomatic immunity, 146–153
heads of state, 154–156
international organisations, 158
introduction, 142
special missions, 157–158
state immunity, 142–145
innocent passage, 171
International Court of Justice
agreement of parties, 343–344
declarations, 346–352
incidental jurisdiction, 352
locus standi, 342–343
prorogated jurisdiction, 344–345
reservations, 346–350
international crimes
apartheid, 131
crimes against humanity, 131
generally, 130–133
genocide, 131
quasi-universal jurisdiction, 133–135
piracy, 131
slavery, 131
war crimes, 131
introduction, 125–126
national security, 130
nationality principle, 129–130
passive personality principle, 135
protective principle, 130
security principle, 130
territorial principle, 127–129
universality principle
apartheid, 131
crimes against humanity, 131
generally, 130–133
genocide, 131
quasi-universal jurisdiction, 133–135
piracy, 131
slavery, 131
war crimes, 131
unlawful arrest, 141

Jure gestionis
state immunity, 143

Jure imperii
state immunity, 143

Jus cogens
  sources of law, 36–37
  validity of treaties, 287–288
Jus in bello
  See **Customs and laws of war**

Kosovo
  human rights tribunals, 267
  state recognition
    capacity, 68
    duty, 79

Law of the sea
  conclusion, 199–200
  continental shelf
    baselines, 189–190
    coastal state's rights, 190
    Convention definitions, 189
    delimitation between states with
        opposite or adjacent coasts,
        191–195
    exploitation, 190
    exploration, 190
    extent, 189
    generally, 188–190
    meaning, 188
  development, 159–161
  exclusive economic zones
    delimitation between states with
        opposite or adjacent coasts,
        187–188
    fisheries, 184–185
    introduction, 184
    rights of coastal states, 185–187
    rights of other states, 187
    territorial waters, 162
  fisheries, 184–185
  fishing, 180
  generally, 159–161
  high seas
    fishing, 180
    freedom, 173–174
    hot pursuit, 180–181
    human trafficking, 180–181
    introduction, 173
    jurisdiction, 176–180
    marine environments, 181–184
    meaning, 173
    nationality of ships, 175–176
    nuclear tests, 174–175
    people trafficking, 180–181
    piracy, 177–178
    seizure powers, 177–180

    trafficking, 180–181
    unlicensed broadcasting, 180
  hot pursuit, 180–181
  human trafficking, 180–181
  International Seabed Authority,
      196–197
  International Tribunal for the Law
      of the Sea, 197–199
  introduction, 159–161
  nationality of ships, 175–176
  nuclear tests, 174–175
  people trafficking, 180–181
  piracy, 177–178
  seabed
    exploitation, 195–196
    International Seabed Authority,
        196–197
  seizure powers, 177–180
  territorial waters
    archipelagic states, 167–168
    bays, 164–166
    contiguous zones, 173
    delimitation between opposite or
        adjacent states, 167
    exclusive economic zones, 162
    fisheries, 162–162
    generally, 161–162
    innocent passage, 168–171
    islands, 166
    meaning, 161
    measurement, 162–164
    passage through straits, 171–173
    territorial limits, 162
  trafficking, 180–181
  unlicensed broadcasting, 180
Legal sources
  See **Sources of law**
Legislative competence
  treaties
    accession, 276
    adoption and confirmation of
        text, 275
    consent, 276
    international law, 275
    national law, 275
    reservations, 276–279
Legitimate expectation
  incorporation of international law,
      49–50
Liechtenstein
  state recognition, 69
Limited Test Ban Treaty 1963
  nuclear weapons, 326–327

"Litvinoff Agreement"
  incorporation of international law, 55
"Lockerbie bombing"
  jurisdiction, 129
Locus standi
  International Court of Justice, 342–343
  state recognition in UK, 81

Marine environments
  protection
    International Maritime Organisation, 183–184
    international measures, 183–184
    oil pollution, 181–182
    pollution from land sources, 182–183
    pollution from ships, 181–182
    radioactive waste, 182
Marine pollution
  land sources, 182–183
  oil pollution, 181–182
  radioactive waste, 182
  ships, 181–182
Mediation
  use of in international disputes, 334–335
Migrant workers
  human rights, 260
Military occupation
  state recognition, 68
Minerals
  Antarctica, 116
Missing persons
  human rights, 260
Mistake
  validity of treaties, 286–287
Modification
  treaties, 286
Monaco
  state recognition, 69
Monism
  incorporation of international law, 40
Moon Agreement 1979
  territory, 121
Multinational companies
  international personality, 100–101
Municipal courts
  See National courts
Municipal law
  incorporation of international law by UK

customary international law, 43–46
  executive certificates, 50
  treaties, 47–50
incorporation of international law by US
  Act of State doctrine, 59–62
  congressional executive agreements, 56–57
  customary international law, 50–50
  executive agreements, 55–56
  federalism, 57–59
  suggestion, 59
  treaties, 50–55
international law and
  dualism, 40–41
  incorporation, 39–40
  monism, 40
  supremacy, 41–43
non-recognition of states
  United Kingdom, 84–87
  United States, 87
treaty-making powers, 275

NAFTA
  incorporation of international law, 57
Namibia
  self-determination, 71–73
National courts
  international crimes, 137–140
"National liberation movements"
  international personality, 98–99
National security
  innocent passage, 169–170
  jurisdiction, 130
Nationality
  treatment of aliens, 223–226
National law
  See Municipal law
Nationality principle
  jurisdiction, 129–130
Natural resources
  coastal states within EEZ, 185–187
  continental shelf
    delimitation, 191
    generally, 188–190
  outer space, 121
  seabed, 195
  state responsibility, 223, 230
  treatment of aliens, 218

Negotiations
international dispute resolution, 334
Nicaragua
International Court of Justice
declarations of jurisdiction,
350–352
Non-compliance
validity of treaties, 286
Non-governmental organisations
international personality, 100
Non-Proliferation Treaty 1968
nuclear weapons, 327
Nuclear tests
high seas, 174–175
Nuclear weapons
state responsibility for environment,
236–238
use of force, 326–328

Occupation
characteristics, 107–108
critical date, 108
discovery, 105
effective occupation
characteristics, 107–108
generally, 105–106
intention, 106
state symbols, 106
generally, 104–105
intention, 106
state symbols, 106
terra nullius, 104–105
Oil pollution
marine environments, 181–182
Opinio juris
custom, 18–20
Organisation of African Unity
See also **African Union**
human rights, 263
refugees, 217
Organisation of American States
jurisdiction, 129
sources of law, 34
state recognition
closed organisations, 89
Outer space
appropriation, 121
exploration, 120–121
International Telecommunications
Union, 122
Moon Agreement, 121
registration of objects launched, 122
Rescue and Return Agreement, 122

Ozone depleting substances
state responsibility for environment,
234

Passive personality principle
jurisdiction for international crimes,
135
Peacekeeping
collective measures through the UN,
316–319
Permanent Court of Arbitration
generally, 339–340
role, 337
**Permanent Court of International
Justice**
See **International Court of Justice**
Persons
international personality, 94
international responsibility
genocide, 97
war crimes, 94–97
procedural capacity, 94–98
Piracy
high seas jurisdiction, 177–178
international personality, 96
universality principle, 131
Poland
state recognition in UK, 83–84
Polar Regions
See **Antarctica; Arctic**
"Political question doctrine"
Act of State, and, 61
Population
state recognition, 65
Powers of seizure
See **Seizure**
Precedent
sources of law, 28–30
Preliminary objections
International Court of Justice,
352
Prescription
acquisition of territory, 108–109
Provisional measures
International Court of Justice,
353–355
Public benefit
treatment of aliens, 219
Public policy
sources of law, 36–37

Quebec
self-determination, 73

Race discrimination
human rights, 260–261
Radioactive waste
marine pollution, 182
Rebel groups
international personality, 98
Reciprocity
characteristics of international law, 5
Recognition
annexation
acquisition of territory, 109–111
state recognition, 70
constitutive theory, 76–77
criteria, 78–79
de facto recognition
annexation, 110
generally, 80–81
de jure recognition
annexation, 110
generally, 80–81
declaratory theory, 77
distinction between states and
governments, 75–76
duty to recognise, 77–78
generally, of, 74–75
governments, of, 79–80
modes of according, 87–88
non-recognition, 84–87
UK practice, 81–84
Red Cross
human rights, 263
humanitarian protection, 330
measures not involving use of force,
312
Refugees
treatment of aliens, 216–218
Reparations
state responsibility
expropriation of property of non-
nationals, 218–219
generally, 210–212
treatment of aliens, 220–221
Reprisals
use of force, 300–301
Reservations
jurisdiction of ICJ, 346–350
treaties
acceptance, 279
competence, 275–279
legal effect, 280–281
objections to, 279–281
Rescues
outer space, 122

Retorsions
use of force, 301
Retrospective effect
state recognition in UK, 82
Rhodesia
See **Zimbabwe**
Right of individual application
procedural capacity of individuals,
95
Right to self-defence
See also **Use of force**
anticipation of armed attack, 306
armed attack, 304–307
collective, 307–308
customary international law,
303–304
inherent right under Art.50 UN
Charter, 304–307
introduction, 303–304
intervention in civil wars, 307–308
**Rio Declaration on the Environment
and Development 1992**
state responsibility for environment,
231–232
Rwanda
international war crimes tribunals
crimes against humanity, 137–138
establishment, 264–265
individual personality, 97
jurisdiction, 132

SALT 1969–1972
nuclear weapons, 327
San Marino
state recognition, 69
Sanctions
characteristics of international law, 4
implementation in UK, 50
Satellites
See also **Outer space**
registration, 122
rescue and return, 122
Seabed
exploitation, 195–196
International Seabed Authority,
196–197
International Tribunal of the Laws
of the Sea, 199
Secretary-General
See **United Nations**
Security Council
International Court of Justice
composition, 340

recommendations to refer to
court, 342
use of force
collective measures through the
UN, 310–311
Self-defence
See **Right to self-defence**
Self-determination
acquisition of territory, 112–113
state recognition
generally, 70–71
Namibia, 71–73
Quebec, 73
Soviet Union, 74
Yugoslavia, 73–74
Senegal
human rights tribunals, 267
Settlement
International Court of Justice, 356
Sex discrimination
human rights, 260–261
Shareholders
treatment of aliens, 226–228
Shipping lanes
archipelagic states, 168
innocent passage, 170
passage through straits, 172
Ships
innocent passage
shipping lanes, 170
warships, 171
marine pollution, 181–182
nationality, 175–176
state-owned vessels
state immunity, 144
Sierra Leone
human rights tribunals, 265–266
Slavery
universality principle, 131
Slovenia
state recognition
criteria, 78
Somalia
state recognition, 67
use of force
collective measures through the
UN, 311
peacekeeping, 318
Sources of law
authors, 30–31
case law
generally, 28–30
national courts, 30

conclusion, 37
custom
definition, 11–12
duration, 12–13
evidence of state practice, 17–18
extent of state practice, 13–17
introduction, 11
material element, 12–18
meaning, 11–12
instant custom, 20–21
opinio juris, 18–20
psychological element, 18–20
state practice, 12–18
equity, 26–28
generally, 9–11
International Law Commission
codification, 34
establishment, 34
generally, 34–36
membership, 35
responsibilities, 35
international organisations, 32–34
jus cogens, 36–37
principles of law, 25–26
regional organisations, 34
soft law, 31–32
treaties, 21–24
writers, 30–31
South Africa
state recognition, 69
South West Africa
See **Namibia**
Sovereign debt
state recognition in UK, 83
Sovereignty
aggression, 301
airspace, 116, 119
arbitration, 338
Arctic, 113
cession, 111
declarations, 106
domestic jurisdiction, 322
jurisdiction
diplomatic immunity, 149
extradition, 141
generally, 125
Namibia, 72–73
natural resources, 218
outer space, 120
protection of national abroad, 310
responsibility to protect, 319–320
state recognition, 80
territorial sovereignty

airspace, 116
Arctic, 113
cession, 111
introduction, 103–104
occupation, 105–108
prescription, 108
territorial waters, 161–162, 168
Soviet Union
state recognition, 74
Special missions
immunity from jurisdiction, 157–158
State responsibility
aliens
breach of contract, 222–223
Calvo Clause, 223
companies, 226–228
compensation, 220–221
discrimination, 220
dispute resolution, 221–222
exhaustion of domestic remedies, 228–229
expropriation of property of non-nationals, 218–219
international minimum standard, 214–216
introduction, 212–213
national treatment standard, 214
nationality of claims, 223–226
nationals, 216
public purpose, 219
refugees, 216–218
scope of liability, 212–213
shareholders, 226–228
standard of treatment, 213–216
compensation
expropriation of property of non-nationals, 218–219
generally, 210–212
treatment of aliens, 220–221
conclusion, 239
Draft Articles, 202–203
environment
biological diversity, 235
climate change, 234–235
customary international law, 230
desertification, 232
hazardous waste, 235
industrial accidents, 235–236
injurious consequences of permitted acts, 238–239
international co-operation, 230–231
introduction, 229

nuclear weapons, 236–238
ozone depleting substances, 234
regulatory developments, 229–229
Rio Declaration, 231–232
trans-boundary air pollution, 233–234
watercourses, 236
introduction, 202–203
meaning, 202
nature
attribution, 205–208
erga omnes, 208–210
generally, 203–205
imputability, 205–208
reparations
expropriation of property of non-nationals, 218–219
generally, 210–212
treatment of aliens, 220–221
States
See also **State responsibility**
capacity to enter agreements, 68–70
defined territory, 66–67
governments, 67–68
human rights, 74
immunity from jurisdiction
consular relations, 156–157
diplomatic immunity, 146–153
heads of state, 154–156
international organisations, 158
introduction, 142
special missions, 157–158
state immunity, 142–145
introduction, 64–65
meaning, 65
population, 65
recognition
constitutive theory, 76–77
criteria, 78–79
de facto recognition, 80–81
de jure recognition, 80–81
declaratory theory, 77
distinction from state recognition, 75–76
duty to recognise, 77–78
generally, 74–75
modes of according, 87–88
non-recognition, 84–87
UK practice, 81–84
self-determination, 70–74
succession to treaties, 293–295
symbols of occupation, 106

territory
    defined, 66–67
    generally, 103
violations of international law, 70
Straits
    passage through, 171–173
**Strategic Arms Limitation Talks
    1969–1972**
    nuclear weapons, 327
Succession
    treaties, 293–295
"Suggestions"
    See also **Executive certificates**
    Act of State, 61
    generally, 59
    state recognition, 87
Suspension
    treaties, 292–293

"Tate-letter"
    state immunity, 143
Tax
    diplomatic immunity, 153
Termination
    treaties
        change of circumstances, 290–291
        consequences, 292–293
        generally, 288
        impossibility, 290
        material breach, 289–290
        severance of diplomatic relations,
            291–292
        supervening impossibility of
            performance, 290
        treaty provision, 288–289
Territorial waters
    archipelagic states, 167–168
    bays, 164–166
    contiguous zones, 173
    delimitation between opposite or
        adjacent states, 167
    exclusive economic zones, 162
    fisheries, 162–162
    generally, 161–162
    innocent passage
        compliance with national laws,
            169
        dangers to navigation, 169
        jurisdiction, 171
        meaning, 168–169
        national security, 169–170
        shipping lanes, 170
        warships, 171

islands, 166
meaning, 161
measurement, 162–164
passage through straits, 171–173
sea-lanes
    archipelagic states, 168
    innocent passage, 170
    passage through straits, 172
territorial limits, 162
Territory
accretion, 112
acquisition
    accretion, 112
    annexation, 109–111
    avulsion, 112
    cession, 111–112
    introduction, 103–104
    occupation, 104–108
    prescription, 108–109
    self-determination, 112–113
airspace
    aircraft in distress, 118–119
    entry, 116
    International Civil Aviation
        Organisation, 119, 120
    Five Freedoms Agreement,
        117–118
    generally, 116–117
    right of entry, 116
    shooting down civilian aircraft,
        119–120
    Two Freedoms Agreements, 116,
        117
annexation, 109–111
Antarctica
    claims, 115
    conservation, 115–116
    dispute resolution, 116
    minerals, 116
Arctic
    environmental protection, 114–115
    territorial claims, 113–114
avulsion, 112
cession, 111–112
conclusion, 122–123
conquest, 109–111
jurisdiction, 127–129
occupation
    characteristics, 107–108
    date, 108
    discovery, 105
    effective occupation, 105–107
    generally, 104–105

intention, 106
state symbols, 106
terra nullius, 104–105
outer space
appropriation, 121
exploration, 120–121
International Telecommunications
Union, 122
Moon Agreement, 121
registration of objects launched,
122
Rescue and Return Agreement,
122
prescription, 108–109
self-determination, 112–113
state recognition
defined, 66–67
generally, 103
title
accretion, 112
annexation, 109–111
avulsion, 112
cession, 111–112
introduction, 103–104
occupation, 104–108
prescription, 108–109
self-determination, 112–113
Third countries
application of treaties, 284–285
Trafficking in human beings
See **Human trafficking**
Treaties
amendments, 285
application, 281–282
authentication in two or more
languages, 284
competence to make
accession, 276
adoption and confirmation of
text, 275
consent, 276
international law, 275
municipal law, 275
reservations, 276–279
conclusion, 295
definition, 272–274
diplomatic relations, 291–292
entry into force, 281
generally, 271–272
incorporation
United Kingdom, 46–50
United States, 50–55
international law

characteristics, 4
sources, 21–24
interpretation
authentication in two or more
languages, 284
generally, 282–284
invalidity, 292–293
jurisdiction
extradition, 140–141
international crimes, 136–137
meaning, 272–274
modifying agreements, 286
nuclear weapons, 326–328
observance, 281–282
registration, 274
reservations
acceptance, 279
competence, 275–279
legal effect, 280–281
objections to, 279–281
self-executing treaties, 53–54
severance of diplomatic relations,
291–292
state recognition, 87–88
state succession, 293–295
suspension, 292–293
termination
change of circumstances,
290–291
consequences, 292–293
generally, 288
impossibility, 290
material breach, 289–290
severance of diplomatic relations,
291–292
supervening impossibility of
performance, 290
treaty provision, 288–289
third countries, 284–285
validity
coercion, 287
corruption, 287
error, 286–287
fraud, 287
introduction, 286
invalidity, 292–293
jus cogens, 287–288
non-compliance, 286
Vienna Convention, and, 271–274
Treaty interpretation
authentication in two or more
languages, 284
generally, 282–284

Treaty of Versailles 1919
cession, 111
human rights, 264
procedural capacity of individuals, 95
sources of law, 23
war crimes, 264

United Kingdom
incorporation of international law
customary international law, 43–46
executive certificates, 50
treaties, 47–50
state recognition
generally, 81–84
non-recognition, 84–87
UN Human Rights Council
complaints procedure, 258–259
country procedure, 258
generally, 257–258
thematic procedure, 258
universal periodic review, 259
Universal Declaration on Human Rights
generally, 247–248
United Nations
Compensation Commission, 338
human rights
Action Programme, 250
Commissioner on Human Rights, 259–260
Covenant on Civil and Political Rights, 248–256
Covenant on Economic, Social and Cultural Rights, 248–257
Human Rights Council, 257–259
implementation machinery, 252
International Bill of Rights, 250
introduction, 247
Universal Declaration on Human Rights, 247–248
Vienna Conference, 250
international personality
headquarters agreements, 90–91
International Court of Justice, 91–93
treaty-making powers, 94
UN Charter, 90
Secretary-General
collective measures through the UN, 315–316
Security Council

International Court of Justice, 340, 342
use of force, 310–311
state recognition
membership, 87–88
open organisations, 89
veto, 313
United Nations Commission on Human Rights
generally, 259–260
individual communications to
Covenant on Civil and Political Rights, 255–256
Covenant on Economic, Social and Cultural Rights, 257
United States
incorporation of international law
Act of State doctrine, 59–62
congressional executive agreements, 57
customary international law, 50–52
executive agreements, 55–56
federalism, 57–59
suggestion, 59
treaties, 50–55
state recognition, 87
Universal Declaration on Human Rights
generally, 247–248
Universality principle
apartheid, 131
crimes against humanity, 131
generally, 130–133
genocide, 131
quasi-universal jurisdiction, 133–135
piracy, 131
slavery, 131
war crimes, 131
Unlawful arrest
jurisdiction, 141
Unlicensed broadcasting
high seas, 180
Upper Silesian Convention 1922–1937
procedural capacity of individuals, 95
Use of force
aggression, 301–302
anticipation of armed attack, 306
armed attack, 304–307
authorisation by UN, 322
collective measures through the UN
aggression, 311

armed force, 313
Article 41, under, 311–312
Article 42, under, 313
authorisation by competent organ, 322
breach of the peace, 311
domestic jurisdiction, 321–322
General Assembly, 313–315
humanitarian intervention, 319–321
measures not involving use of force, 311–312
peacekeeping, 316–319
Security Council's role, 310–311
UN Secretary-General, 315–316
threat to the peace, 311
types, 311
veto, 313
collective self-defence, 307–308
conclusions, 330–331
countermeasures, 300–301
customs and laws of war
armed conflict, 323–326
generally, 322–323
domestic jurisdiction, 321–322
economic pressure, 302–303
exceptions to general prohibition
collective self-defence, 307–308
introduction, 303
regional arrangements, 308–309
self-defence, 303–307
generally, 297
humanitarian intervention, 319–321
humanitarian law
generally, 328–330
Red Cross, 330
intervention in civil wars, 307–308
introduction, 297
jurisdiction, 321–322
jus in bello
armed conflict, 323–326
generally, 322–323
meaning of 'force'
aggression, 301–302
countermeasures, 300–301
economic pressure, 302–303
political pressure, 302–303
reprisals, 300–301
retorsions, 301
nuclear weapons, 326–328
political pressure, 302–303
pre-1945 law, 297–298

prohibition under Art.2(4) UN Charter
exceptions, 303–309
extent, 299–300
generally, 298–299
scope, 300–303
protection of nationals abroad, 309–310
regional arrangements, 308–309
reprisals, 300–301
retorsions, 301
self-defence
anticipation of armed attack, 306
armed attack, 304–307
collective, 307–308
customary international law, 303–304
inherent right under Art.51 UN Charter, 304–307
introduction, 303–304
intervention in civil wars, 307–308

Validity
treaties
coercion, 287
corruption, 287
error, 286–287
fraud, 287
introduction, 286
invalidity, 292–293
jus cogens, 287–288
non-compliance, 286
Vatican
See **Holy See**
Veto
collective measures through the UN, 313
Vienna Conference on Human Rights 1993
generally, 250
Vienna Convention on Consular Relations 1963
immunity from jurisdiction, 156–157
Vienna Convention on Diplomatic Relations 1961
diplomatic immunity, 146–147
diplomatic premises, 148
International Law Commission, 36
special missions, 157
staff immunities, 152–153

Vienna Convention on the Law of Treaties 1969
customary international law, 22
erga omnes obligations, 209
International Law Commission, 36
introduction, 271
municipal law, 42
peremptory norms of international law, 37
reservations, 276–278
Vienna Declaration and Programme of Action 1993
generally, 242
refugees, 217
review, 250
Volcanoes
acquisition of territory, 112

War crimes
Act of State doctrine, 61
individual responsibility, 94–97
international war crimes tribunals
Cambodia, 266
East Timor, 266–267
introduction, 263–264
Rwanda, 264–265
Sierra Leone, 265–266
Yugoslavia, 264–265
universality principle, 131
Warships
See **Ships**

Watercourses
state responsibility for environment, 236
Women
human rights, 260–261
World Health Organisation
capacity, 93
World Trade Organisation
incorporation of international law, 57
Writers
See **Authors**

Yugoslavia
international war crimes tribunals
crimes against humanity, 137
establishment, 264–265
individual personality, 96
mediation, 334
state recognition
criteria, 78–79
self-determination, 73–74
use of force
authorised by competent organ of UN, 322
measures not involving use of force, 312
peacekeeping, 317

Zimbabwe
state recognition, 69